ANTHONY HOPKINS

ANTHONY HOPKINS

The Biography

by Quentin Falk

For my father

This paperback edition first published in Great Britain in 2005
by Virgin Books Ltd
Thames Wharf Studios
Rainville Road
London W6 9HA

This updated edition first published in hardback in 2004

First published in Great Britain in 1989 by Columbus Books Ltd
and Virgin Books

Reprinted and updated 1993, 1995, 2000

A catalogue record for this book is available from the
British Library

ISBN 0 7535 0999 7

Typeset by
Phoenix Photosetting, Chatham, Kent

Printed and bound in Great Britain by
Mackays of Chatham, Chatham, Kent

CONTENTS

List of Illustrations   vii
Introduction and Acknowledgements   ix
Preface   xiii
1. Workaholic: Part I   1
2. Philip Anthony   9
3. Lionhearted   40
4. Beef and Thunder   66
5. California Dreaming   97
6. Drying Out   120
7. Monsters   148
8. Chasing Shadows   182
9. National Hero   200
10. Workaholic: Part II   223
11. Gone Hollywood   269
12. Too Good to Waste   302
13. Hannibal (Re)Calling   316
14. Change of Life   348
The Credits: Theatre, Television, Films   363
Index   381

LIST OF ILLUSTRATIONS

Hopkins as a 3-year-old
With his mother on holiday
As a 15-year-old at Cowbridge Grammar School
As Audrey in the National Theatre's all-male *As You Like It*
   (Zoe Dominic)
As Richard the Lionhearted in *The Lion in Winter* (National
   Film Archive)
As Pierre Bezukhov in the BBC's *War and Peace* (BBC)
In the 1972–3 Old Vic *Macbeth* (Zoe Dominic)
First wife Petronella Barker
As Bruno Hauptmann in *The Lindbergh Kidnapping Case*
   (Columbia)
With Sir Laurence Olivier on the set of *A Bridge Too Far* in 1976
   (United Artists)
In Los Angeles for the 1977 production of *Equus*
In *Magic (Twentieth Century-Fox)*
In Jonathan Miller's BBC production of *Othello* (BBC)
As Dr Frederick Treves in *The Elephant Man* (Brooksfilms)
As Hitler in *The Bunker* (CBS)

In the 1983 remake of *The Bounty*, as Captain Bligh (Orion)
As Quasimodo in *The Hunchback of Notre-Dame*, off-set with
   wife Jenni
As Lambert Le Roux in the National Theatre's *Pravda (Nobby
   Clark)*
At the National Theatre as King Lear in 1986
In the BBC's *Across the Lake* as Donald Campbell (BBC)
With daughter Abigail at the premiere of *The Dawning* (PIC)
With Prince Charles at the University of Wales in 1988 (Western
   Mail and Echo)
As René Gallimard in *M. Butterfly* (Nobby Clark)
As Henry Wilcox in *Howards End* (Merchant-Ivory Productions)
As Van Helsing in *Bram Stoker's Dracula* (Ralph Nelson/
   Columbia TriStar Films)
As Stevens in *The Remains of the Day* (Merchant-Ivory
   Productions)

With Richard Attenborough on the set of *Shadowlands (Keith Hamshere/UIP)*

As Colonel William Ludlow in *Legends of the Fall (Kerry Hayes/TriStar Productions)*

The moment of triumph: with the Best Actor Oscar, March 1992 *(Academy of Motion Picture Arts and Sciences)*

As Chianti-loving cannibal Dr Lecter in *The Silence of the Lambs (Orion)*

With Jenni outside Buckingham Palace after collecting his knighthood in the 1993 New Year's Honours List *(Michael Fresco/Evening Standard)*

As Dr John Harvey Kellogg in *The Road to Wellville (J&M Entertainment)*

As President Nixon in *Nixon (Entertainment)*

As Pablo Picasso in *Surviving Picasso (Warner Bros)*

Hopkins versus Bart the Bear in *The Edge (Twentieth Century-Fox)*

In action as a sword-wielding masked avenger in *The Mask of Zorro (TriStar Pictures)*

As John Quincy Adams in *Amistad*, with director Steven Spielberg *(Andrew Cooper/UIP)*

Reprising his role as Dr Lecter in *Hannibal*, with Julianne Moore *(UIP)*

As Dr Lecter once again in the *Lambs* prequel, *Red Dragon*, with Edward Norton *(UIP)*

As a psychic on the run in the Stephen King short story, *Hearts in Atlantis*, with Mika Boorem *(Warner Bros)*

As Coleman Silk in *The Human Stain*, with Nicole Kidman *(Miramax Films)*

As Ptolemy in *Alexander (Warner Bros)*

With Jodie Foster receiving his star on the Hollywood Walk of Fame *(Rex Features)*

With new wife, Stella, at their St David's Day wedding *(Rex Features)*

INTRODUCTION AND
ACKNOWLEDGEMENTS

WHEN this biography was first published back in 1989, Anthony Hopkins had almost resigned himself to being, in his own words, 'a respectable actor poncing around the West End and doing respectable BBC work for the rest of my life'. And, yes, perhaps the odd movie from time to time. As for Hollywood, after a concerted if generally unrewarding tilt at Tinseltown through the mid-70s and early 80s, that was now, he reflected somewhat ruefully, 'a chapter closed'.

Certainly when I originally wrote a chapter entitled 'Monsters', who could ever have expected – perhaps Hopkins least of all – that less than three years later he would be responsible for helping to create one of the screen's most memorably monstrous characters, Dr Hannibal 'The Cannibal' Lecter in *The Silence of The Lambs* . . . in Hollywood? At 55 Hopkins won his first Hollywood Oscar at his first attempt and a year after that he received a knighthood in the New Year's Honours List.

Since his 1991 Academy Award for Best Actor as Dr Lecter, he has, at the time of writing, received a further three Oscar nominations and firmly established his credentials as a bona fide international movie star in films by Francis Ford Coppola, Michael Cimino, Alan Parker, James Ivory, Oliver Stone, Martin Campbell, Steven Spielberg, Julie Taymor and Robert Benton. He has also returned twice more – in a sequel and prequel to *Lambs* – to the character of Lecter who, in two separate post millennial polls conducted either side of the Atlantic, was named Greatest Screen Villain. Another huge public vote placed Hopkins at seven (the highest placed Brit, just ahead of Sean Connery and Ewan McGregor) in a list of the Greatest 100 Film Stars. His latest films include a key co-starring/narrator role in Oliver Stone's pre-Christian epic *Alexander*, and opposite Gwyneth Paltrow in an adaptation of the stage hit *Proof*.

At 67 Hopkins, now boasting American citizenship, a Malibu home and a third wife, has reached a new level both in his career and in his private life which, frankly, seemed almost inconceivable when we both first embarked on this biography.

After being approached in 1987 to write the book ('No, not the Antony Hopkins who talks about music,' explained my commissioning editor helpfully), I quickly accepted the assignment because, although I didn't at the time know him personally, I'd admired much of his work from afar and had also been intrigued by the countless interviews he'd given, both in his so-called 'hell-raising' days and during, at that time, twelve years of studied sobriety. In view of the yawning weight of library material in existence, I decided to see if I could get the subject's co-operation in the venture, if only to try and find a fresh way through.

Hopkins, who had just turned fifty, agreed to talk long and openly (and continued to do so for the purposes of several subsequent updated editions) as did family, friends, and many producers, directors, actors and executives who know (or knew) him or have worked with him.

However, eagle-eyed observers of this collaboration may notice that the book's subtitle has now subtly been changed from 'The Authorised Biography' to, simply, 'The Biography'. After I invited Hopkins to contribute his usual incisive, often witty and frequently self-deprecating thoughts for a fifth edition, he politely but very firmly declined – predictably, perhaps, in view of his new West Coast life and desire to put most of the past (including me) completely behind him. He wrote back: 'I don't have anything to add really; also I'm "talked out" on the boring subject of myself and acting and all the rest of it. Apart from all of that I am well and living quietly in Malibu . . .'

Incidentally, the chapter titled 'Too Good To Waste' (which was also the title of the original hardback version of this book) comes from an award-winning American documentary on teenage alcoholism by one of Hopkins' closest friends, Bob Palmer, who kindly gave me permission to borrow it.

My grateful thanks as ever to the very many people who have helped me with this book through all its various editions: to Stephanie Billen (also for library research) and Barbra Paskin for conducting some interviews; Marney Wilson and Chris Brown for transcribing tapes; my mother-in-law Val Sillery for the original index; the British Film Institute Information Department, BBC Written Archive Centre, the National Film Archive, and Theatre Museum (especially Amanda Fielding and Jo Laurie); Anwar Brett, Ceri Thomas, Russell Forgham, Scott Fannen, Paul Brown-Constable and Ben Falk; Anne Gayford and Emma Davie; Peter Pryer and NE Palmer; Jonathan Rutter; my agent Jane Judd; Kirstie Addis of Virgin Books; and Gill Rowley, who first suggested the subject.

For their generous recall: Sheila Allen, Lindsay Anderson, Lord Attenborough, Chrissie Beveridge, Michael Blakemore, Mel Brooks, Martin Campbell, Terence Clegg, Jackie Collins, Professor Philip Collins, Jeremy Conway, John Davies, Dame Judi Dench, Bo Derek, John Dexter, James Doolittle, Andy Dougan, Lesley-Anne Down, Brian Doyle, Mary Doyle, Dr Raymond Edwards, Robert Ellis Miller, Julian Fellowes, Bryan Forbes, David Foster, Freddie Francis, Patrick Garland, Patric Gilchrist/Ann Williams, Jack Gold, Cuba Gooding Jr, Gawn Grainger, Patrick Hannan, David Hare, Anthony Harvey, Katharine Hepburn, David Jones, Freddie Jones, Janet Key, Richard Lester, Innes Lloyd, George Martin, Marsha Mason, Tony Maylam, Mike Medavoy, Ismail Merchant, Jane Merrow, Professor Brian Morris, Mike Newell, Bob and Nancy Palmer, Alan Parker, Christopher Plummer, Clive Perry, Rebecca Pidgeon, Tony Pierce-Roberts, Stefanie Powers, Lynn Redgrave, Adrian Reynolds, Marion Rosenberg, David Ryall, David Scase, George Schaefer, James Scott, Judith Searle, Marian Seldes, Ann Skinner, Ian Soutar, Oliver Stone, David and Paula Swift, Siobhan Synnot, Lee Tamahori, Julie Taymor, Alun Thomas, Felix Trott, Michael Tuchner, Adrian Turner, Jon Turteltaub, Mrs Jon Turtle, Colin Vaines, Robin Vidgeon, Simon Ward, Bernard Williams, Tracey Williams, Michael Winner, Robert Wise and Marjorie Yates. And, most valuably, Anthony Hopkins and Jenni Hopkins. Also a very special belated thanks to Muriel Hopkins – who died in 2003 just short of her ninetieth birthday – for first taking me on a fascinating guided tour of her son's early years in South Wales.

Many of the photographs in this book are from the Hopkins family collection and, where requested, credit has been given to the photographer. I should like to thank, for the use of photographs: J & M Entertainment, Clear Blue Sky Productions, Majestic Films, Merchant-Ivory Productions (Paul Bradley), UIP, the Academy of Motion Picture Arts and Sciences, the BBC, Zoe Dominic, NBC, CBS, Columbia TriStar Films, Entertainment Film Distributors, Buena Vista International, Brooksfilms, Lambeth Productions, Twentieth Century-Fox, Camera Press, PIC Photos, Malcolm Parker, David James, Carolco Pictures Inc, Warner Bros, Nobby Clark, Miramax Films and Rex Features. Extracts from the following television programmes: *One-to-One* with Michael Parkinson (Yorkshire TV, 1988); *Revelations* with Eric Robson (Border TV, 1988).

Grateful acknowledgement to the following books and their authors: *The Bright Lights: A Theatre Life* by Marian Seldes (Houghton Mifflin); *Curtain Times: The New York Theater 1967–1987* by Otis L. Guernsey Jr (Applause); *Pravda* by Howard Brenton and David Hare (Methuen); *Subsequent Performances* by Jonathan Miller (Faber & Faber); *5001 Nights at the Movies* by Pauline Kael (Elm Tree); *The Actors' Director: Richard Attenborough Behind the Camera* by Andy Dougan (Mainstream); *Richard Attenborough* by David Robinson (BFI); *Nixon: An Oliver Stone Film* edited by Eric Hamburg (Bloomsbury); *Ismail Merchant's Paris* by Ismail Merchant (Abrams); *Steven Spielberg* by Joseph McBride (Faber); *Playing With Fire* by Julie Taymor (Abrams); *Lynch On Lynch* edited by Chris Rodley (Faber); *Reflections on Success* by Martyn Lewis (Lennard Publishing); *The Human Stain* by Philip Roth (Vintage).

Little Marlow/London/Los Angeles 2004

PREFACE

*I*T'S *Christmas Day, a cold, bright, frosty morning. I'm lying in my cot. A little blue donkey is hanging over the side. I can hear my mother's voice from downstairs, cups and saucers being placed for breakfast, my grandfather's voice too. Suddenly I hear my father laughing; then I hear a clicking sound coming from the end of my cot and there's a face in the woollen blankets, a man's face reminding me of Mr Hodges who was the postmaster from Tolgeen Road. The face was sinister. Not frightening, but sinister. And I recognised it as something that was wicked, even evil. Not so much diabolically evil but somehow the spirit of wickedness. He introduced himself to me as somebody I might have known from another time; now he was just reminding me he was there. A very knowing, wicked smile. Large teeth with all the gums showing and bright yellow eyes. I can remember the frostiness of the morning, the smell of distemper, an unmade bed in another corner of the room. I stared back at the clicking teeth. Then I could hear more voices from below and my father was coming upstairs, and the face at the end of the cot gradually faded into the blankets as if to say, 'We'll meet again one day . . .'*

All these years I have had the memory of that devil's face alive in me. He has been my companion but I've made friends with him. It's almost as if we struck a bargain that bright morning years ago. It became more or less clear to me when I was living in Los Angeles. The bargain was that if I were smart enough to find my way out of the maze, I would be finally spared all the ravages of Hell. What I have done all my life is keep moving, keep ahead of the game. I have never let anyone in close, just kept dodging and weaving. That's what I've done; I've presented a front of warmth and friendliness, but inside I have always felt empty; no compassion, just carelessness all my life; the booze and the drunkenness for fifteen years. It was, on that winter's day in 1975, as if God came along and picked me up, dusted me down and said, 'Stop analysing, stop drinking, because you cannot do that any more and get on with your life and live it and have some fun with it.'

That was the turning point.

1. WORKAHOLIC: PART I

Just after 11.30 on the morning of Wednesday, 24 September, Anthony Hopkins posed for photos outside the Kodak Theatre on Hollywood Boulevard. With him were Stella, his wife of six months, Jodie Foster, sometime co-star from *The Silence of the Lambs*, and Gary Sinise, who appeared alongside Hopkins in his latest film, *The Human Stain*.

The occasion was the official 'unveiling' of Hopkins' bronze star plaque – the 2,237th – now embedded in pink and charcoal terrazzo squares on the legendary Hollywood Walk of Fame. While everyone from singing cowboy Gene Autry and *Sesame Street*'s Big Bird to canine stars Lassie and Rin Tin Tin – and now Hopkins – already seemed to be underfoot on this favourite tourist attraction, there were still some notable absentees including local 'royalty' like Robert Redford, Jane Fonda, Mel Gibson and Clint Eastwood.

Foster and Sinise were invited to say a few words about the actor before Hopkins, looking distinctly unHollywoodlike in a sober suit and tie, and clearly awed by the sense of this particular occasion, stood at a temporary lectern to offer his reaction to this latest 'honour'. With the kind of PR tact which must have thrilled the Hollywood Chamber of Commerce who assign the stars, Hopkins compared receiving the accolade to that of winning an Oscar and even his knighthood. 'It's everything, you know. I'm not blasé. I think it's wonderful,' he gushed.

Hopkins had driven with Stella to the ceremony in Hollywood from his beautiful cliff-top home at Point Dume, Malibu which is perched between the Santa Monica Mountains on one side and the bay on the other.

It's probably less than 35 miles as the road winds inland, but that journey, in another sense, represented the enormous, once seemingly unattainable, distance between teenage dreams in South Wales of fame and fortune and the reality, half a century later, of authentic stardom in Hollywood.

'When I was an actor living in England,' he told the small but enthusiastic pavement crowd, which also included other celebrities like Salma Hayek and Josh Lucas, 'I wanted to come out to here, to Hollywood, more than anything. So this really is a symbol of what I always wanted to achieve . . .'

The coincidence of birthplace, profession, reputation and talent has, like it or not, forever bracketed Anthony Hopkins with his fellow Welshman, the late Richard Burton. It is quite surprising to discover that they only ever met twice. The first time was when Hopkins, as a young, movie-mad teenager, went in search of an autograph at Cissie Jenkins' house, just up the hill from the Hopkins' bakery in Tai Bach. The memory remains vivid. Burton, a dozen years Hopkins' senior, was standing in the kitchen in his vest, shaving and talking Welsh to his sister. More than 25 years on they met again for half an hour in the star dressing room at the Plymouth Theatre in New York after Burton had taken over the role of the psychiatrist in *Equus* from Anthony Perkins, who had, in turn, succeeded Hopkins in the role on Broadway. 'Like everyone else,' Hopkins recalls, 'I was charmed by him.'

Burton was, of course, the archetypal professional Welshman – miner's son, noisy, extrovert, poetry-spouting, beer-drinking, rugger-loving, Welsh language-speaking. Hopkins was to acquire, to his cost, some of the more anti-social of these characteristics in his drinking days (though never the rugby-loving nor the indigenous tongue), and admits, moreover, to sizeable chunks of Welsh temperament, with a tendency to melancholy, wistfulness and red-hot anger.

Burton would have been in his element early that January, soon after Hopkins' 50th birthday, when what must have been the largest gathering of professional Welsh outside of Cardiff Arms Park on match day turned up at the Air Studios in Oxford Street, London, to take part in a lavish new recording of Dylan Thomas's *Under Milk Wood*, under the enthusiastic direction of the producer George Martin.

It was wall-to-wall Celt: Sir Geraint Evans, Bonnie Tyler, Jonathan Pryce, Gemma Jones, Mary Hopkin, Nerys Hughes, Freddie Jones, Sian Phillips, Angharad Rees, Windsor Davies, Molly Parkin, Ruth Madoc ... and many more. 'The whole bloody Taffia,' noted the actor Ray Smith. If Burton could not actually be there in the flesh he most certainly hovered in spirit, for the whole enterprise was in a sense deeply imbued with his memory: this was the first complete recording of the work since his own as First Voice in the BBC trailblazer of 1954. Less than a week after his 50th birthday, and still with a month to go of an increasingly tiring *Antony and Cleopatra* run at the National Theatre, marking the end of almost three solid years on the South Bank, Hopkins, sporting his grizzled old soldier's beard, arrived in the general throng. Exuding bonhomie, though not looking entirely comfortable amid this scrum of 'boyos', Hopkins was to create a new First Voice – in other words, to run off those parallel lines and directly into Burton's track.

Sir Geraint, who had recorded the same piece with Burton as part of a fund-raiser about five years earlier, was impressed: 'Anthony has a different style but I think it's complementary and in some ways even better than Burton's interpretation ... They both speak it beautifully but whereas Burton had a bit of a cynical tone because he felt that was right, Anthony brings a slightly drier edge to the part.' Looking back on the event, George Martin says: 'I think Tony had a greater insight into the meaning, but then he had more time to study; Burton was rather pitchforked into that original recording and, as such, did a remarkable job.'

'It is a cold, moonless Christmas Eve in the Waterloo Road . . .' Hopkins, exaggeratedly Burton-esque, with the distinctive rhythmic resonances of *Under Milk Wood*, guides the listener down 'the dark, labyrinthine corridors' of the Old Vic – 'now a mental institution for retired actors'. All the greats are there, 'in varying degrees of dotage' – Richardson, Olivier, Gielgud, O'Toole – reliving past performances as Nicol Williamson arrives with a sackful of presents.

This narration is not, however, for public consumption. It is a privately recorded (if widely circulated) tape, scripted and entirely voiced by Hopkins, whose extraordinary gift for mimicry is perhaps most instantly acknowledged by his peers. The tape is a jape, but it is also a way of exorcising the demons that pursued him during his Old Vic days and into his more recent stint of subsidised theatre. So, as he and Judi Dench took their final bows at the end of *Antony and Cleopatra*, he could hardly wait to rush away and dash north to the Lake District to begin work on a new project, *Across the Lake*, the BBC film about the last days of Donald Campbell.

The following day, the press were arriving at Lake Coniston for the first day's shooting of Campbell's ill-fated attempt, in January 1967, to break his own water speed record. The director, Tony Maylam, was awed at Hopkins' preparation for the role: 'He kept going through all the videos, the old interviews, the accident itself. He even talked to me about having a nose job because he felt his was a bit bulbous for the part, and about cutting off "just a bit more hair?". He's not vain as an actor. It wasn't "I want to look good". It was always "Is it Donald?" '

Clad in blue overalls, hair dyed and swept back from a widow's peak, cigarillo clamped between his teeth, a carefully clipped public school accent (deliberately not a slavish imitation after being told by the director that his more accurate reproduction made him sound 'pissed'), Hopkins stood framed for pictures against a remarkable £35,000 replica of *Bluebird*.

The pressmen left, delighted not only with good lookalike shots but also a juicy little story about death threats against Hopkins at the National Theatre by 'a crazed rival', which eventually reached a head when a fire was found to have been started under his parked car. Away from that madness, Hopkins relished the role and, perhaps just as much, the restorative powers of this corner of Cumbria where he could run up and down mountains, join the congregation of the local church and read voraciously – all kinds of books, including volumes on the function of the brain and enhancement of memory. 'Keep-your-head-on-straight' books, he and his friends call them. They reflect his penchant for endless self-analysis, a need to dissect his own character, which he describes, with disarming candour, as 'immature, neurotic and self-obsessed'.

The script, which lay open on his caravan table, was a colourful collection of jottings and doodles: 'During *Antony and Cleopatra* I sat in my dressing room one night and thought, "This is madness. I'll never learn it all." It was like being in an Alcatraz of words. There were days when I wanted to get on a train and go to the Outer Hebrides . . . anywhere but the theatre. I'd sit in the room at night, turn another page and think, "God, there's more." Suddenly I thought, "I know what I'll do", and started writing out the speeches on the opposite page. Twice each. Looked at them, fell asleep, woke up . . . and I knew them. It was like being let out of prison. Then there are the drawings. They act as mnemonics, buzzwords for things in the script. For instance, a little picture of me with plaster over my mouth because I haven't told someone something. Or Desperate Dan, to remind me I'm desperate.'

Campbell's desperation was chillingly portrayed by Hopkins in the resulting film. Andrew Hislop wrote in *The Times*: 'The Campbell of the film, seen only in his last 60 days, was in great need of support. This was no assured national hero, but a troubled, desperate man, in pain, drinking too much, with financial difficulties and marital problems. Anthony Hopkins was superb, delicately nuancing the emotions of the man so vulnerable behind his ill-fitting Bulldog Drummond patriotic shell that it was a wonder that he could go on, let alone drive himself at 320 mph to the point where he need drive no more.'

Meanwhile Hopkins talks, not for the first time, about his disillusion with the stage – and of how films suit him so much better: 'You do the scene, it's in the camera and then you can move on to something else. As a lifestyle I find that much more suitable for my personality and temperament.'

There is no sign here, it seems, of his legendary prickliness with directors . . . until the last day: 'I was doing a scene with Angela Richards [playing Campbell's third wife, Tonia Bern] and I sensed an atmosphere. The producers were there looking ashen-faced, glancing at their watches, waiting to pounce. Tony Maylam was getting uptight and on my nerves because he was rushing the scene. "Don't keep prompting all the time," I said to him. "You're hassling me, always hassling me. . ." So I counted to ten and walked away.'

Behind the hail-fellow-well-met mellowness lies solid steel.

'Anthony . . . dear!' Michael Winner calls firmly from the stage. Memories of the debonair Campbell are excised as a hunched figure pads up the centre aisle. Short-cropped grey hair, shabby grey trousers, green cardigan, carpet slippers, glasses on string suspended round his neck, biros stacked in a stained shirt-pocket, preoccupied, rather pathetic. The setting is the lovely little Opera House in Scarborough where Winner is filming Alan Ayckbourn's 1985 National Theatre hit, *A Chorus of Disapproval*, about the on- and offstage antics of an amateur dramatics group in a small seaside town. Hopkins is playing the manic director, Dafydd ap Llewellyn, a rare Welshman among his gallery of performances, and he has even had special lessons to learn the words of 'Ar Hyd y Nos' ('All Through the Night').

Winner tells me: 'Alan suggested Anthony as Dafydd

even before I started making lists. I'd always been a great admirer but I've never seen him have the expansiveness of this role and the high comedy, at which he's totally brilliant.

'The character in the play has always been portrayed as a rumpled, crumpled person – as you now see him playing it.

'So, at first, I get a message from the wardrobe department: "Tony doesn't want us to mess up the clothes. He has decided to play it very neat and tight. He has taken the view that this man is held together by the neatness of his clothes." This, of course, is totally wrong.

'I rang Alan and said, "You'll laugh, but you'd better give me some dialogue to tell him." Alan said: "By day he's a solicitor, very tight and together. At night he goes right the other way, pretends he's a Bohemian and lives like a mess. So you've got to have messy clothes." I told Anthony this and we did a shot of him early in the day that was quite neat and I was getting a bit worried. Then he had a few days off. By the time he came back he was such a mess, you wouldn't believe it. He'd put ink stains all over his clothes, torn buttons off. . . He was a different man. I said to him: "Thank God you didn't have two weeks off, or you'd have come back on crutches with blood pouring from you." '

Considering Winner's reputation for being less than gentle with cast and crew, it might be expected that he and Hopkins were on a permanent collision course. Not a bit of it. Hopkins happily mimicked Winner; the cigar-chomping director beamed about his star, 'the nicest, most professional, positive, kind actor I've *ever* worked with.'

Not even an unfortunate little episode during a rather physical scene could scupper the mutual admiration society. Hopkins, as Dafydd, is bellowing on stage at a long-haired young man, Crispin (played by Pete Lee-Wilson); unable to take any more, Crispin knees the director in the groin. Lee-Wilson is understandably nervous about quite how he should weigh the blow.

'You're not a bloody ballet dancer,' Winner screams at him after a few takes.

Hopkins bridles: 'Don't get after him, Michael. He's doing the best he can.'

Winner giggles nervously and quickly draws back. On the next take, Lee-Wilson goes for it, leaving Hopkins in some distress curled foetally on the floor.

Hopkins has pieced together his Dafydd character from parts of people he has known, including his late father:

'My father was a very forceful, vigorous, energetic personality who used to go off in all sorts of directions, and used to get flustered very quickly. He smoked very heavily, so I put that in. When I went shopping for clothes, I asked for a grey coat which came just above the knee. My father used to wear a coat like that. Always did all the buttons up – looked like he was bursting out of it. I put it on and did the first scene. Then I thought, "This is beginning to feel all right."'

2. PHILIP ANTHONY

Some of Hopkins' earliest memories still remain crystal clear, like one of lying in his pram on a bright, sunny afternoon and staring up balefully into the face of a neighbour, Mrs Griffiths, as she leans down making 'goo-goo' noises at him. Her face is pink, hair fluffy and blonde, eyes piercing blue and there's a flesh-coloured mole on her cheek. Behind her there looms a large poplar tree. Mrs Griffiths lived across the street from the Hopkinses in Wern Road, Margam, outside Port Talbot. Hopkins' parents, Dick and Muriel Hopkins, had moved into number 77 – a solidly built, three-bedroomed semi-detached – when they were married. Dick, christened Richard Arthur, was one of three children, a boy and two girls, born to Arthur Richard Hopkins and his wife Enna. Richard senior, originally from Neath, was a master baker and confectioner who had learned much about his craft, first in London, where he worked for Peek Frean (he created their little star biscuits), and later back in his native Wales under the tutelage of an uncle.

By all accounts Richard, who died when he was 82, was a rather remarkable man. A late Victorian, he was a self-educated disciple of Bernard Shaw and Darwin, a Fabian, a devotee of cold baths, a vegetarian, a non-smoker and, unlike his father, who had been an alcoholic, a non-drinker. A small man physically, he had, Hopkins remembers, 'this huge fist which he'd roll up saying, "Look at this, give it a punch" and you'd almost break your arm trying.' It was however the master confectioner's personality that dominated: strong, dogmatic, he was even, occasionally, tyrannical.

At the turn of the thirties he opened his own bakery business, A. R. Hopkins and Son, at 151 Tanygroes Street in Tai Bach ('little houses', or 'lavatories', according to some disgruntled exiles), just a couple of miles outside Port Talbot. The family lived there too.

Muriel, now in her mid-eighties, was one of two daughters (her sister died aged twelve) born in Port Talbot to Thomas Frederick – known as Fred – Yeats, a Wiltshire exile who was employed as a foreman in a local steel company, and his Welsh-speaking wife Sophia. Muriel and Dick, who by now was working for his father, were married on 2 August 1936 at the Church of the Holy Cross just across the road from the bakery.

Sixteen months later, on New Year's Eve, 1937, Philip Anthony Hopkins, 7¾ pounds in weight and not much hair, was delivered by Dr Donald Isaac at Wern Road. It was not an easy birth and the Hopkinses decided against any more children. The name 'Philip', which came from Muriel's mother, whose maiden name was Phillips, was very quickly ignored, and the 'Anthony' was eventually shortened by request to 'Tony'. Even Muriel has learned to call him 'Tony' now.

The Margam and Tai Bach of then and now are separated not only by time but also by the dramatic incursion of a swirl of tarmac and concrete, better known as the M4 motorway, which ripped unceremoniously through the otherwise unspoiled countryside of the Vale of Glamorgan in the late sixties and early seventies. Before the M4, Mynydd Margam, peaking at over 1100 feet, fell away spectacularly, and unhindered, to the town below; there were acres of uncluttered parkland and easier access to ancient workings as well as to the ruins of a Cistercian abbey, said to have been more splendid even than Tintern in the Wye Valley, far to the east on the Wales–England border.

As the M4 snaked west through Tai Bach, it left the inevitable detritus of demolition in its path. The stilted monster now lurks as a kind of dead end at the top of Tanygroes Street. All the houses further up were felled; 151 was the final victim. A number of shops in the vicinity now stand empty or boarded up.

Dick, Muriel and the baby stayed at Wern Road throughout the war. In addition to his daytime work, Dick was in the Observer Corps; from those parts you could observe quite a lot, for across the bay from Port Talbot the night sky would light up over Swansea with the explosion of German bombs. Part of old Swansea was completely flattened and Port Talbot itself, as a coal-exporting docks and steel town, was not immune from the onslaught. With the approach of D-Day, Hopkins remembers his parents inviting home for tea a couple of American soldiers who were waiting for a bus to Swansea. It was his first contact with the United States, which increased greatly when old Richard retired and Dick took over the business. The family moved, first, to Tanygroes Street and then, in a fit of expansion, down on to the Commercial Road in Tai Bach. Opposite number 19 was the Regent Cinema where, in the late forties, Hopkins fell in love with the movies, particularly Hollywood movies, and especially those starring Cagney or Bogart.

Until this move A. R. Hopkins and Son had been purely a manufacturing and delivery business, with distinctive little green vans dispensing the bakery's wares. Now, at 19 Commercial Road, it comprised a bakery and bread shop, a delicatessen and a family home. The staff expanded too. In the bakery were two bakers, a confectioner and four girls; in the delicatessen Muriel had five girls working for her.

Hopkins was a very slow learner and a very solitary child. At the village school in Groes (now buried under the motorway), a couple of miles by bus from Margam, he had the first inkling that he could not easily grasp the essentials: 'I was absolutely hopeless. I didn't know what they were talking about most of the time. "Two and two makes four" came like a revelation during Miss Thomas's Bible class, when I suddenly blurted out the answer. I could read, but I didn't really read very much.' So how did he spend his time? According to Muriel, 'drawing, sketching and playing our shabby old piano. He spent a great deal of time on his own.' She arranged for him to have piano lessons, first with a Miss Llewellyn in Port Talbot, who was thin and very strict and whom he disliked intensely. Much later on, after he studied with Iris Thomas and Winifred Richards, a Neath teacher, Hopkins showed such an aptitude and appetite for the piano that for a brief moment a concert career suggested itself.

By the time he was about twelve, Dick and Muriel were becoming distinctly concerned not only about Hopkins' indifferent academic performance but also about his solitariness. After much discussion they decided he should leave the Central School in Port Talbot, to which he had moved after Groes, and go instead to boarding school, which, they concluded, would be likely to make him mix more, be good for discipline and perk up his marks. So for the Christmas term of 1949 he was dispatched to West Monmouth School at Pontypool, north of Newport and a long, long way from home. After five miserable terms at West Mon (as the school was known), Hopkins was transferred much closer to home, to Cowbridge Grammar, halfway between Bridgend and Cardiff. There he was to spend the next four years in, if you believe him, a complete daze.

Abutting the walls of the small market town, Cowbridge Grammar had been set up in Henry VIII's reign and was an uneven mixture of direct grant and fee-paying pupils; it was predominantly a state school with just a genteel hint of public school. Out of a total of 350-or-so boys, 11- to 17-year-olds, there were about fifty boarders. Roughly seven in each year were drawn from all over South Wales as well as a handful of sons of parents who were abroad in the Forces. In the middle of the school was a beautiful garden which boasted the biggest copper beech in Wales and a plaque, set into one of the walls, bearing the motto *Virgiliis et Virtute* – Watchfulness and Virtue. The guardian of this rallying cry was the headmaster, Idwal Rees, a gaunt, beak-nosed man who would swoop across the quad with his black gown flowing behind him. A renowned classicist, he was even better, and forever, known as a brilliant centre three-quarter (moving to the wing later in the game) in the Welsh rugby team that had beaten the rampant New Zealand All-Blacks 13-12 in 1935.

One of Hopkins' fellow boarders, the journalist and broadcaster Patrick Hannan, recalls their dreary, spartan existence: 'It was strange that as a boarding school it seemed to have so little to offer in the way of facilities. The doors were locked by 6.15 p.m. and that was your lot. There was this large room called "the schoolroom" which was used for things like assembly and we sort of lived in there at night. They did have a piano in there and Hopkins was often to be found sitting at it playing what sounded most terrible dirges. He made it clear that he hated school very much indeed. He was an odd boy in that lots of people don't fit in totally, but he just didn't seem to fit in at all. The school was very keen on academic ability and even more so on sporting prowess, neither of which were his line.

'I don't think it was ever a case of his being victimised or bullied. He was a loner, an outsider. He just didn't wish to fit in. Nobody would have picked him out in any way to achieve anything at all. You certainly wouldn't have said: "There's a boy with a tremendous talent tucked away." ' Was he actively rebellious? 'Well, he smoked in the shrubbery as we all did. But no. He had what you would call a sullen air. He suffered it, put up with it and avoided the worst of it the best he could; but you could always sense the gloom and desperation, especially in those piano-playing times. Because of that he had a nickname, Mad Hopkins, to distinguish him from the four or five other Hopkins in the school, but also in the sense of a mad, piano-playing professor. The nickname probably tells you more about him than I ever could.'

Hopkins quit piano lessons – and any faint hope of a concert career – when he felt that his teacher, Miss Richards, over-complicated the tuition and tried to progress him, in his view, too quickly. Lacking self-confidence too, he simply gave up, perhaps a little feebly, on the notion.

Nevertheless the piano has continued, informally, to be an important part of Hopkins' life. On his precious Steinway he plays Scriabin, Bach, Rachmaninov, Beethoven, Bach and Chopin purely for relaxation. 'To a layman,' he laughs, 'I might occasionally even sound like a concert pianist.'

The sounds of the piano emanating from the schoolroom served to pinpoint Hopkins – other boys would be running about in the playing fields while he dashed up and down the keyboard indoors – when Dick and Muriel arrived at the school to replenish his tuck-box and take him out for a Saturday or Sunday afternoon treat, usually to nearby Cowbridge Common. Muriel recalls: 'They had a little tea-hut there where everything was homemade, like bread and apple tart. He seemed to enjoy those Sunday afternoon treats, devouring platesful of bread and butter.' Family holidays, on which they were accompanied by Muriel's parents, were invariably spent in Cotswold villages such as Broadway and Willersey.

Hopkins has talked long and often about the doom and gloom of those days at Cowbridge but his unhappiness there seems to have been much more to do with his own personal, if imagined, inadequacies than with the school itself, which actually tried to do the best it could for a boy who was, it seems, totally unresponsive.

Hopkins admits: 'The school itself wasn't awful. There were boys there who really got on with and enjoyed it and fully participated. It was simply that I was inadequate.'

The master he still most regularly recalls – with a mixture of fear, loathing and genuine admiration – was the history man, Jim 'Pinky' White, an ex-prisoner of war who, according to Hannan, 'could behave very oddly and had an explosive temper'. 'He was a very demanding teacher,' Hopkins remembers, 'and quite a hard man, but they *were* harder in those days. They didn't mess about with psychology on kids. But, nevertheless, he took an interest in me and because I was so slow told me not to get downhearted and to try and follow my instincts. Although I've said since how I used to imitate him and used elements of him for various roles like Lambert Le Roux in *Pravda*, I still have a tremendous respect for him and he had a very deep influence on me.'

Hopkins emerged from Cowbridge at the age of seventeen with just one O-level, for English: 'I actually believed I was somehow genetically maladjusted. This has stayed with me, although to a lesser extent, all my life. The feeling that there is something wrong with me, that I've got a missing gene that hasn't allowed me to learn another language or to finish anything. I just wanted to be off this bloody planet. I had this notion that there was some special book they passed out at birth and I'd been missed. On the piano I never completed a piece. In the end I never took the grades. I think that my last teacher Miss Richards did actually ruin it for me by complicating things, by trying to make me go ahead too fast. So I just gave up. The only time I started completing things was when I began acting and could do a play from A to Z.

'Naturally I've done a lot of self-analysis and obviously realise I'm not genetically at fault. What I did was fill my mind with anxieties, probably inherited anxieties, because my father was a very anxious man, a compulsive worrier, and I sort of imitated him.

' "I don't know what the hell's going to happen to you," my father would say to me. My mother was much more philosophical: what will be will be. Then my grandfather Fred used to say, "Oh, let him go, Dick. For God's sake, let the boy have his way; let him take it easy. You'll worry him to death." Whenever I played the piano, my father would say, "Can't you play something a bit lighter, like Charlie Kunz, or something?" Because I believed I couldn't ever finish anything, I also believed I would never achieve anything. That's the role I played for years.'

Hopkins remembers being chased out of the bakery as a little boy by his grandfather after stealing some currants off the cakes. 'What age can you retire?' Hopkins once asked the old man. 'You haven't even started yet, boy!' old Richard replied. Hopkins gradually began to realise how hard all his family worked; it may have been harsher down the mines, but this was still hard work. Years later, when Dick and Muriel came out of a brief retirement to run a pub, The Ship, in Caerleon, near Newport, Hopkins agreed to take it over for a week so they could have a break: 'I was on my knees by the end of the week, it was such hard work. My father said, "You're soft; don't know you're born." He was rather like Lee J. Cobb in *Twelve Angry Men*, an honest-to-goodness sort of man.'

There was no suggestion that he would, or should, ever follow his father into the family business. So Hopkins mooched around the house, playing the piano, drawing, going to the cinema, talking long walks to Margam Abbey, into the woods and down to the beach, and working for a few months in the stores of a steel works. He had no sense of direction.

One day Dick said in desperation: 'For goodness' sake, get out of the house and make some friends,' recommending quite forcefully that he should go to the YMCA with a young neighbour, Brian Evans, and learn to play snooker. At the 'Y', an acting group under the direction of one Cyril Jenkins was preparing an Easter play called *Emmanuel*. Evans joined in and, almost against his better judgement, Hopkins decided to do so too: 'The memory is so clear. The lights all arranged, straw-coloured stuff on the lamps, *Lohengrin* music on an old, scratchy record, Mary Magdalene... The thrill of that night, Easter 1955. With a sheet over my head, I opened my mouth and spoke my first, and only, line: "Blessed are the meek, for they shall inherit the Earth." And I thought, "At last, I've found somewhere I can belong."'

A couple of weeks later Hopkins spotted an advertisement in the local paper announcing the Prince Littler Scholarships, worth £100, to the Cardiff College of Music and Drama. He applied and, to his great surprise, was summoned for an audition by the head of the drama department, Dr Raymond Edwards. A few days after that he heard he had been accepted. The College, in the precincts of Cardiff Castle, had been instituted purely as a music establishment in 1951. A year later Dr Edwards (who eventually became Principal in 1959 and remained so for 25 years) started a much smaller drama section, to which he and his wife devoted much loving care.

'Restless, fidgety, never still for a minute,' is how Dr Edwards affectionately remembers the rising 18-year-old. 'Bags of energy, a bit like a boxer in his prime. He had a particular talent for mimicry, a voice to match that body and a well-chiselled head. He was explosive too. Backs of chairs tended to come off when he was around.'

During his two years at the College, in which he boarded at the home of the castle custodian, Eddie Donne, and his wife, Hopkins seemed to find a direction at last. Dr Edwards particularly recalls two of his roles, in Lorca's *Blood Wedding* and Wilder's *The Skin of Our Teeth*, as well as Hopkins' participation in tours of South Wales. Coachloads of students would go to such towns as Neath, Llanelli, Pwhelli and Festiniog to perform in local schools. The route invariably took the bus past the Hopkins' shop in Tai Bach, where it would stop while Hopkins popped out to collect buns and scones for his fellow thespians.

Hopkins became eligible for National Service at the end of 1956 but as he was still at the College he was granted a deferment. After graduating, he managed again to keep the Forces at bay when he got a job with the Arts Council working as an assistant stage manager – with a few small parts thrown in – on a 'back-breaking' sixteen-week UK tour of *She Stoops to Conquer* and *Look Back in Anger*.

Hopkins could not put off National Service any longer, and after a medical in Swansea, at which he pretended, unsuccessfully, to be deaf, he was dispatched to Oswestry in Shropshire where, in February 1958, he joined the Royal Artillery: 23449720 Gunner Hopkins.

'There was,' he recalls, 'a sense of Abandon Hope All Ye Who Enter Here. On the first day we were introduced to Sergeant Major Hackett. He looked as though he'd had his face bashed in. He was just one big mouth, no teeth and he smoked Woodbines. You'd never heard a voice like it. You learned things like how to get out of PT clothes and into full gear within what seemed to be seconds. You were terrified not to. I don't know how we managed to do it, but we did.'

In the April of that year Hopkins was posted to Clerks' School in Woolwich, South-East London, after which he rather hoped he might get a chance to go to Cyprus: such a stint would at least earn him some embarkation leave. No such luck. On a damp day in May, Hopkins arrived at Bulford Camp, on Salisbury Plain, where he was to spend the remainder of his two years pen-pushing, or, to be more accurate, typewriter-hammering. Four young soldiers arrived together that day, and after getting off the train at Salisbury, Hopkins and Gunner Ken Simmonds from Wigan were ordered to the Chief Clerk's office. Staff Sergeant Little asked them their names and their marks from Clerks' School.

Hopkins takes up the story: 'I gave him the number and for some reason I got the edge on this guy Simmonds, who in fact seemed much brighter than me. Little said, "Right, Simmonds, I want you to work at 30 Battery – that's Roger's Company. Hopkins, you'll work under me here at this office." It was a dreadful day, pouring with rain. We went off to our billets, unpacked and then got started.'

Bulford was – indeed, still is – a military training camp for the Light Artillery Company. Hopkins was in 16 Light AcAc Regiment RA under the command of Colonel Willoughby Cubitt and admits, 'I couldn't understand a word he said. I used to dread typing letters he'd drafted because his writing was rather like his speech: no consonants. It was also very spidery. The Chief Clerk could read it but I couldn't. Our adjutant was a fellow called Captain Mike Witt and he didn't seem to use consonants either.

'On one occasion I was detailed to type out a regimental report – a Board of Enquiry – and I knew it had to be typed perfectly, sixteen pages of it. I spent all night in the office doing it and was meticulous. Afterwards I checked it right through and couldn't believe it. It was absolutely correct, all sixteen pages on these skins. "Right," I thought, "no one can get me for this." I had a bit of sleep and then was up early to open the office. Ernie Little came in and said, "Have you finished it?" I told him I had. He then checked through all of it himself; it took him about half an hour. He was a very bright man, a trained accountant. And then he told me to run them off. I went over to the Stores, got out this box of beautiful white paper, put it in the machine, ran the first skin off, did two dozen copies, tore the skin up and did the remainder likewise. When I'd finished I took everything to Sergeant Little, who told me to take them through to Captain Witt to be signed. Mike Witt said, "Has Staff Sergeant Little checked these?" I said yes. He wrote his signature and then he asked me, "When do you go on leave?" I said, "Next week, Sir." "Thank God for that," he replied. "Could you send the Chief Clerk in? You've rolled all these off on blotting paper!"

'They had to be signed in ink, couldn't be done in just biro, so the whole lot had to be typed again. It was a wonder I wasn't court-martialled or even executed. I felt a prize idiot then – and most of the time, to be honest. We were pretty isolated at Bulford. Most of the Regiment had just come back from Cyprus where there had been some sort of Middle East Crisis [the continuing EOKA-inspired unrest], so it was all work. I think we, the National Servicemen, were regarded as a pain-in-the-neck by the regular soldiers. We seemed to be more in the way than anything else. Cheap labour, of course. I was on 30 bob a week all found. You didn't have to buy clothes, you were fed, you had some money for the pub and the NAAFI. Character-forming? It was, actually, and looking back I have strangely fond memories of it all. One of the ways I survived was by being a good babysitter. When Sergeant Little and his wife Cynthia both wanted to go to the Sergeants' Mess, he'd ask me if I'd babysit for their three children. In return, they'd give me sausages, which I loved. He was a marvellous man and also had a great sense of humour. I could see him looking at me while I was in the office typing – I was supposed to be an ace typist – and he'd say, with a twinkle in his eye, "I mean, how did you get into this office?" I have a feeling I was all the time regarded as a bit of a joke because everyone knew I wanted to be an actor.'

By the time of his demob Hopkins had, despite his own feelings of complete inadequacy, risen to the dizzy heights of Bombardier, equivalent to the more familiar NCO rank of Corporal. After two years out of life he was suddenly back in the swim, living at his parents' new home at Laleston outside Bridgend, Mid Glamorgan, where they had moved in 1958 after selling out the bakery business to Lovell's, the toffee manufacturers.

Gymerwch chi Sigaret? has a kind of mysterious Welsh lilt about it which somehow gets a little lost in translation (*Have a Cigarette?*). First produced in 1956, it is one of more than fifteen plays by the distinguished Welsh writer and dramatist Saunders Lewis. *Have a Cigarette?* was chosen as the launch-pad of a newly formed (if short-lived) national touring company called the Theatre of Wales, organised by Richard Rhys, later Lord Dynevor. Thomas Taig, one of the visiting lecturers at Cardiff College, also professor of drama at Bristol University, was to produce the play. He called Hopkins to ask him to join the group and play the lead role in it.

Hopkins recalls: 'The play is set in East Berlin and is about a young man called Mark. He has to make contact with a Western diplomat and then shoot him with his cigarette case. It was, I believe, based on a true-life incident. I mustn't make fun of the play because I gather it's rather highly regarded. What happens is that as Mark is about to pull out his cigarette case, a crucifix (which his wife has left in it) falls out on to the floor and he's suddenly converted from Communism. Very Graham Greene. I can tell you it was very hard to act that. I'm glad

I did it because it at last gave me the feeling I could do something in the theatre, even though I was lacking woefully in experience and had no real technique at all. My real hero then, as he had been in my Cardiff days too, was James Dean. So I thought acting was just about looking miserable and scuffling around.'

They toured the play all over South Wales. Muriel saw it at the old Empire Theatre in Swansea and was, not unnaturally, impressed with her son's theatrical début.

Audiences were, however, variable. On one night in Carmarthen there were probably more people on the stage than in the auditorium.

That summer Hopkins wrote to David Scase, who was running the Library company in Manchester, to see if he had any vacancies. The reply informed him that an open audition was to be held at the Arts Theatre in London. Armed with two audition pieces – the bed-chamber scene from *Othello* and a section from *Monna Vanna*, an obscure play by Maeterlinck set during the Hundred Years War – Hopkins took a train to London and met Scase, who seemed impressed by Hopkins' choice of the Maeterlinck (probably because he'd never heard of it before). Back at Laleston, Hopkins had to wait anxiously for a week or so before hearing that he had been invited to join the company as an assistant stage manager and play small roles, including Mickser in Behan's *The Quare Fellow*. Since only two to three were accepted from the 150 or so who auditioned each year, it was a singular honour. But the honeymoon did not last long. After a little over three months at Manchester, Hopkins was sacked.

Scase, a long-time theatre man who had been a founder member of the Theatre Workshop with Joan Littlewood, believed that Hopkins had great presence but that he was too raw at the time and that he 'lacked the basic vocabulary of theatre'. He suggested strongly to Hopkins that he should go to drama school. At Manchester, where work was intense (twelve to thirteen plays a season), there simply was not time during rehearsal periods to take someone aside and work privately.

'Although I resented it at the time,' says Hopkins, 'the truth was I was hopeless. I didn't know what I was doing. I was a complete mess.'

Undaunted, Hopkins then hitch-hiked from Wales to Nottingham, to the old Playhouse, where they were looking for members for the repertory touring company run by Roy Battersby. He got a job playing the older brother in *The Winslow Boy*. Armed with £5, Hopkins set off to find digs and found an address by looking in a nearby tobacconist's shop window, trudged up the hill and secured a room for 3 shillings a week. His room-mate was a fellow actor, Roy Marsden, three years Hopkins' junior, who found his new colleague's mercurial approach to his art bewildering. Ignoring all suggestions about drama school, Hopkins was determined his acting training was going to be a do-it-yourself job. He bought Clifford Turner's influential tome *Voice and Speech Training in the Theatre* and ploughed through it night after night, much to the consternation of Marsden who, from his corner of the room, gently made his own drama-school plea. 'Look,' he said, 'you're good. I tell you what, I'll even send away for the forms myself.' He did so, too, and seems to have brought about Hopkins' change of heart over formal dramatic training.

It was a brief but happy time at Nottingham. Apart from Marsden, other actors from the lovely old theatre who would pack the local coffee shop included Robert Lang, James Cossins and Michael Williams, who, Hopkins remembers, sat at the table wearing a cap and eating his meals in the manner of Albert Finney.

In the summer of 1961 Hopkins was invited to audition in the little theatre at the Royal Academy of Dramatic Art (RADA), where he performed two pieces, an Iago speech from *Othello* and part of Chekhov's one-act comedy *The Bear*. Hopkins could not actually see anyone in the auditorium while he was performing. He merely heard a number of voices somewhere in the darkened middle distance, thanking him politely when he had finished.

He and fellow hopefuls including Alex (Victor) Henry, Simon Ward and Geoffrey Hutchings had a drink together afterwards, little expecting that they would all be part of the coming September's RADA intake.

The night before he was due to start at RADA, Hopkins went to the pictures in North Finchley, where he was staying with friends of friends: 'It was *The Naked Edge* with Gary Cooper, Deborah Kerr and Eric Portman. I remember going back to the house after that thinking, "My God, I'm going to become an actor; I'm really going to be an actor." I'd just been excited by all this piano music and Eric Portman rushing about. "God, that's acting!" I'd had no experience. I'd never had any lifelines as a child. A lot of people know they want to be an actor by the time they're three. Yet now I knew I really wanted to be a film actor.'

In those days RADA accepted new entrants every term rather than every year and the Academy prided itself on producing stars. Sarah Miles had only just left; David Warner and John Hurt were in their final year and during that ensuing period Terry Hands, Nicola Pagett, Hildegarde Neil, Susan Clark, Ronald Pickup, Gabrielle Drake, Susan Fleetwood, Isla Blair and Angela Richards went about their learning at different stages of the two-year course. The new students were broken up into two groups – A and B – but told to make nothing of the distinction. In Hopkins' B group were, among others, Bryan Marshall, Anton (Tony) Vogel and Adrian Reynolds. Reynolds first spotted Hopkins in the canteen: 'His initial impact on me was one of a dynamic Celtic individual, multi-talented, chaotic, dangerously good, a man hungry for success.

'He would sit in a faded cream raincoat and while some of us, still in our adolescence, fumbled away fighting our nerves, he held court like a cavalier, drawing his contemporaries to him like honey to bees. He looked upon me, dare one say, fondly. I was inclined to be gullible. I remember once he came out of the secretary's office and looked at me sadly, shaking his head. "I've just seen your progress report. It was on top of the pile. Oh dear! It has been so nice knowing you." So subtle was his performance that I was totally taken in and spent the day in torment. Imagine the jubilation and relief, indeed the gratitude, when he nudged me at the end of the day and said, "Fooled you!"

'I was slightly better off financially than he was [Hopkins had to exist on a £7-a-week grant from Glamorgan County Council] and so he used to come round to my Marylebone digs for the occasional free bath. In return for such minor favours, he would teach me more than most of my tutors. In ten minutes one night at a party, he made clear a whole year's slightly over-intellectualised rendering by somewhat sadistic lecturers of an invaluable approach to performance which I've used both as an actor and as a director ever since.'

Hopkins now had to move out of the room in North Finchley and after spotting a promising-sounding berth in East Finchley was on his way to check it out when he bumped into Alex Henry at the station. A Miss Hetterick, who had placed the advertisement, had a large Victorian villa, but when Hopkins and Alex arrived she pointed to the greenhouse: 30 bob to share, bunk beds, use of the kitchen. The young men decided they would give it a go together, and they stuck it out in the greenhouse for a couple of terms.

Although he eventually became a silver medallist, Hopkins recalls his RADA days as 'a troubled time. Since I used to go to the pub [every evening], I would have to work all night to learn my lines.

'I never knew how to apply myself to work, so I'd go at it hammer and tongs then come in the next day absolutely exhausted. I used to take caffeine tablets to keep me awake. I would have terrible outbursts of temper because I was so tired.'

Reynolds' recollection of Hopkins' work is rather more positive: 'He was not only awesome in our rehearsals – what a Chebutykin he was in *The Three Sisters* in our second term – but could also play the piano from memory, composed his own music and could mimic casts of thousands. Once he clambered up on the stage at RADA minutes before the Principal was due to address the Academy and took him off with dazzling accuracy to a huge response from the students and staff. Yet he was never vicious; he went for affection in his parodies. There was also a refreshing generosity towards his colleagues. In our fourth term we performed Peter Shaffer's *Five Finger Exercise*. Tony turned in a fabulous display as the German student. I was cast as the father, about 30 years too young. Yet, when a student went up afterwards to praise him, Tony replied, "No, it's Adrian's performance that really deserves your accolades. Look at the obstacles he overcomes." '

Simon Ward remembers Hopkins as 'the first person who spoke in our class, who actually recited anything or did anything. There is no group of people more paranoid or neurotic than a group of drama students on their first day and when he did his bit I recall thinking that if they were all going to be as good as that then I might as well go home. Later we shared a room together in Kilburn for about a year. He was extremely hard-working and would sometimes be up till five in the morning working on the text. That used to be bloody annoying and we once had a terrible row about it.

'It was annoying for two reasons: that the light would stay on and the fact he was making me feel bad that I wanted to go to sleep; and that made me feel even more inadequate and lazy. I'd run out of heroes by then. With Tony, I had a sort of talent worship. I wanted to possess the qualities he had, particularly what seemed to be his maturity of outlook [Hopkins was four years Ward's senior]. I also wanted that quality of "magic" he seemed to have. There was something deeply strange and mysterious about him. Perhaps it was to do with the Welshness. In one sense, it was rather frightening. He had, you see, this ability to foresee things. One evening we were sitting in Bertorelli's eating spaghetti and he suddenly knew something awful had happened back at RADA. One of the students had actually fallen off the stage and broken both his legs. Tony "saw" this happen. He could also do hypnotism; there was a man in our class who probably wasn't the strongest-willed person I've ever come across, but Tony was able to put him in a deep hypnotic sleep by sort of pulling his ear lobe. Bang, he'd go down. And he did it a couple of times to him, often at the most embarrassing moments.'

Hopkins graduated from RADA in July 1963. That same month he was having a drink in the Marlborough pub off Goodge Street, killing time while he waited for a date with Clive Perry, artistic director of the new Phoenix Theatre at Leicester. It was a lovely, hot day, just the excuse for a few beers. He told his drinking companion, Hywel Bennett, that he had to be at an audition in Westminster that afternoon at 2.30 p.m. 'What time is it now?' Bennett asked. Hopkins recalls: 'I looked at my watch and it was 2.15.

'I had to run all the way down Tottenham Court Road, across the streets, through the traffic and just managed to get there in time. I rushed into the hall. Clive Perry was already there. "Right," he said, "would you like to play Undershaft in *Major Barbara*?" I asked him if he'd like me to audition. "Not really," he replied, but nevertheless heard a speech from *Waltz of the Toreadors* [in which Hopkins had played the General in an uproarious RADA production].' Perry particularly remembers a second audition piece: 'He did Charles Condomine from *Blithe Spirit*. Tony was, I suppose, in his mid-twenties then, but I recall it was a Condomine of extraordinary subtlety for someone so young.'

Hopkins learned the Shaw that summer and then moved up to Leicester in September. The Phoenix arose, figuratively, from the ashes of the old Theatre Royal in the city. In the seven years since the Theatre Royal had been first threatened (it later succumbed) with closure and demolition, various interested parties had rallied around feverishly to try to retain strong drama for the city. The Phoenix was built on a site originally earmarked for a bus station and the inaugural company, under Perry, opened for business on 8 October 1963 with Thornton Wilder's comedy *The Matchmaker*, starring Thelma Ruby as the irrepressible Dolly Levi.

David Swift, who was playing Malachi Stack in the production, was sitting in the theatre watching a rehearsal when Hopkins, wearing a three-piece suit and smoking a pipe, came in and sat down beside him. David, a very un-actorish sort of actor who had been in business before going on the stage, immediately struck up a rapport with the newcomer and they were, together with David's actress wife Paula, to become firm friends. Hopkins had the tiny role of Rudolph, a waiter, in *The Matchmaker*.

In the next production, Robert Storey's *Life Worth Living*, Hopkins admits he was 'totally miscast', as an 'upper-class twit. I was called Neville Bookings, a sort of county toff, and I was so embarrassed I could hardly speak my lines. It was a strange play, with John Sharp, Ken Farrington, Richard Kay and Patricia Burke, who wanted me fired – quite rightly, I think, because I couldn't get the hang of it at all. Clive, who wasn't the nicest director I've ever worked with, stood by me on this occasion, for which I'm most grateful because in the next play, *Major Barbara*, I had some success. At the time he must have wondered about the wisdom of casting me in the Shaw. In fact, I had a wonderful time playing Undershaft and based a lot of it on my father's father, who'd been a very dynamic man and was such an influence that, in a way, I've based everything I've done on him. They say that ignorance is bliss; well, I don't think I knew really what I was doing so I tackled Undershaft with sheer bravado. I was far too young for the role but it seemed to work.'

Paula first saw Hopkins in *Major Barbara*. 'Yes, you were marvellous,' she told Swift afterwards, 'but what about that man with the blue eyes?' She was overwhelmed by his performance and could hardly believe that Hopkins was only 26.

Shortly before the end of the two-week run –

rehearsals had also begun for *The Hostage* – between the afternoon and evening performance on 22 November, news came through of President Kennedy's assassination. The cast was shattered. Swift says Hopkins immediately sat down in the communal dressing room, picked up a pen and some paper and started writing a letter of condolence to Mrs Kennedy – 'I'm sure he posted it, too.'

As he wrote, some cynical lines he had to speak as Undershaft, the armaments manufacturer, darted back into his mind: 'Your pious mob fills up ballot papers and imagines it is governing its masters; but the ballot paper that really governs is the ballot paper that has a bullet wrapped up in it.'

At Leicester, Hopkins met up with David Ryall and Victor (he dropped the Alex) Henry, two of his wilder friends from RADA, and they became a notorious roistering trio. Ryall recalls: 'We had some mad escapades in Leicester. We shared a flat. Actually, you could hardly call it a flat – just a couple of large, cold rooms in a terraced block opposite the prison. I seem to remember that Victor and I found it, then Tony joined us. We were all paid next to nothing so a fair amount of imbibing went on just to keep warm. We'd often stay in bed until play time, go off to the theatre then it was back to bed again. We used to have late-night discussions about philosophy and stoicism. I suppose we were all coping with various problems in our own sorts of ways. For me, being an actor seemed then a bit like living on the edge of the law. Which we weren't, of course, so it was all a bit pathetic really.

'One night I remember coming back to the flat with Victor and Tony was hiding. We crept up the stairs and suddenly he leapt out of a cupboard with an incredible roar; it frightened the hell out of us. His idea of shopping was a bit odd too. He'd go out to get something for us to eat and come back with pots of jam and pickle, perhaps a pound of sausages – which he liked cooked to a cinder – and a funny cake.'

In January 1964 Nick Barton directed a highly successful production of Wesker's *Chips with Everything* (an apt description too of the way of life at Leicester for impoverished actors, says Ryall).

David Swift played the aggressive parade-ground NCO, Corporal Hill, Hopkins was Archie and Ryall played Smiler. Swift says that Hopkins and he had some considerable fun improvising with their roles: 'I was untrained as an actor and so was a bit mad. There's a marvellous drill scene in the play and each night I'd improvise a bit more, get more and more aggressive and unpleasant in the part. Tony and I seemed to get an exciting chemistry going and the environment existed in which we felt we could try to do something different. On this occasion, I started ad-libbing quite a bit and was getting particularly aggressive and he was getting bolshie, which was the nature of his character. I then put in some old army adage like "Am I hurting you . . .?" Something pretty simple. And Tony got so angry he just stormed off stage in the middle of a scene. I'll never forget it; it was very funny and was entirely in character. He *would* have walked off the parade ground at that point.'

Hopkins went from strength to strength with the company, playing Bolingbroke in *Richard II* and Judge Brack in *Hedda Gabler*. He was also in a production of Marlowe's *Edward II*, with Richard Kay, Ken Farrington and John Quentin, that was brought down to the Arts Theatre in London. His Brack is most vividly remembered by Clive Perry: 'He gave a most extraordinary performance as Brack – like an enchanting devil, with this enormously dangerous sexual presence. It was a middle-aged part and he was still very young, but it was this projection of an older man coming from someone so young that was such a major factor in his performance.'

These latter roles had also forced a radical reappraisal by Professor Philip Collins, another of the leading administrative lights at Leicester, who, after Hopkins' first month or so, had confided to Clive Perry: 'Tony's a lovely boy, but he'll never make it.'

After *Edward II*, Hopkins left the Phoenix company and tried, unsuccessfully, to get first radio work then something in television. In fact, he had made his television début while still at Cardiff in 1956 as a schoolboy in a BBC production of *The Corn is Green*, with Flora Robson. It was a tiny, non-speaking role for which he was paid threepence. They rehearsed at Cardiff, then travelled up to London to perform the play live at Lime Grove. Four years later, on his second (and last until *The Men in Room 17* in the mid-sixties) TV assignment, Hopkins also acquired his first small-screen lines. He appeared in a party scene in a play called *A Matter of Degree*, with Hugh David, Colin Jeavons, Peter Gill (with whom he had been at college) and Pat Ward (one of his co-stars in *Have a Cigarette?*).

As Hopkins explains, 'It wasn't live television as such but on Ampex, which was very expensive to cut, and the tape was going out on the air the following night. It was in the days of the six-shot, which meant we all had to huddle together on camera – very old-fashioned and nerve-wracking. I was meant to be standing with a girl looking at this guy who's miserable. She had to say to me, "What's his problem?" and I reply, "He's in love with a Czech from St Hilda's and she treats him like dirt." Except that line actually came out as "He's in love with Hilda's cheques and she treats him like dirt!" And I think it was transmitted like that.'

Back home in Wales, Hopkins wrote to David Scase, who had, by this time, moved from Manchester to the Liverpool Playhouse; having reminded him of his sacking, Hopkins described his subsequent stints at drama school and Leicester. As a result, he was invited to audition at the Cambridge Theatre in London. Scase first asked him how he was and whether he had improved; after the audition, he expressed his delight at Hopkins' obvious transformation.

While still at the Library, Scase regularly used to visit the Liverpool Playhouse. He much admired the set-up there: 'They always did things well. If you wanted to see how the West End looked, say, ten years ago, that's where you went. They had a leading lady and character actors – things we'd abandoned at the Library. When I joined the Playhouse, I made this sort of macho statement about how I wanted the place to be and about the sort of plays they should be doing – like those of Alun Owen, which they'd never done. Tony absolutely fitted in with my thoughts. He epitomised the masculine image I wanted. He had a marvellous sense of humour and was unafraid of making a fool of himself. Although he had the image of being strong and masculine, he also had – still has – a lovely feminine delicacy which makes him a really complete actor.

'At the Library, I think Tony was very pent-up emotionally and didn't seem able to release that into his work. When he came back to me he was able to do that. Even so, I do remember he'd sometimes take it out on inanimate objects. After one rehearsal that hadn't seemed to work, he put his fist through a lavatory door. The Liverpool period brought him out and extended him. I've heard him say it was the happiest period of his theatrical life and certainly there was a wonderful run of plays.'

In *Sparrows Can't Sing*, Hopkins played Fred. His wife was played by Maggie Jones. Scase reveals: 'For all his training, he could no more do a Cockney accent than I could a Welsh one, so he played it as Welsh. At one point, Maggie ad-libbed: "Get back to Cardiff, you Welsh ****," and it was so good, we retained it in the play. After that he was Donnelly, the sympathetic warder in *The Quare Fellow* [Hopkins had wanted to be Regan, but Scase thought him too young], and he really put his stamp on the play. He was one of the few in the cast who didn't double up on prisoner and warder.

'He also did *The Caucasian Chalk Circle* [Brecht], Bill Naughton's *All in Good Time*, Priestley's *Kettle and Moon, Dial M for Murder* [Frederick Knott] and *The Beaux' Stratagem* [Farquhar]. In *The Playboy of the Western World* [Synge] he was Christy Mahon, the playboy, to Marjorie Yates' Pegeen Mike. They made a striking couple' (even if, he might have added, their Irish accents ranged from pure Welsh – Hopkins – to broad Birmingham – Yates). The *Liverpool Post*, however, noted

Irish accents so thick that you could hardly understand them.

Liverpool was Yates' first repertory job and she retains vivid memories of Hopkins.

'I particularly remember all this black, curly hair. He'd tell us that he wanted to be a famous film star – not just a film star, but famous, too. And his eyes would burn as he told us. "Wow, imagine that!" we thought. He was so passionate; he'd rush into rehearsals with sweat pouring from him, hot from some great romantic affair. He was madly attractive but a lot of people couldn't cope with his Welshness. He was still very raw then – like I was – and this passion for life was, in those days, all over the place. He was a wonderful pianist. He'd come up to our digs in Faulkner Street and play the piano – all the old pub songs as well as classical – and my mother would be in floods of tears. With his acting he was totally unselfish. To get a good performance, he knows that you can't do it on your own so he'd find ways of contacting you on stage, like putting his hand on your shoulder, and it made it much more real.'

Says Scase: 'When Tony came back to me at the Play-house he had the quality of knowing where he was going as actor, although I think he was always convinced he had an actor inside him.

'Now he wanted to become a bloody good actor. Discipline was what he brought back from drama school, though I doubt I'd have advised him to go to RADA.'

During his stint at Liverpool Hopkins was approached by Lindsay Anderson to audition for the English Stage Company's production of *Julius Caesar* at the Royal Court. 'It's a bloody pain in the neck,' said Scase, 'but you can go.' Hopkins said, hopefully, 'I'd love to come back.' Scase told him, 'Consider yourself very lucky. I'll let you go until January. How long does the play last?' 'Till December,' Hopkins answered.

After a couple of months of Shakespeare in London, Hopkins was only too delighted to get back to Liverpool.

Nicol Williamson had originally been due to play Brutus but quit the cast to be replaced by Ian Bannen (known as Ian D. Bannen in those days). Paul Curran was Caesar, T. P. McKenna Cassius, Daniel Massey Mark Antony, and Graham Crowden Casca. Hopkins and Ronald Pickup played, respectively, Metellus Cimber and Octavius Caesar as well as understudying Brutus and Cassius. 'We rehearsed,' says Hopkins, 'in a dirty old place in Hammersmith. Once I actually saw a rat walking across the floor and then under the chairs in the hall there.'

The critics didn't like it much either. 'Disappointing'; 'Too many shreds and patches'; 'Verges on banality'. Hopkins wasn't mentioned, which was probably just as well. Lindsay Anderson was, however, quite impressed with the 27-year-old making his proper London début. 'It wasn't a big part but he did it extremely well. He had a sort of presence and youthful enthusiasm as well as a feeling for style which was very marked. I remember being struck by the fact that he revealed great ambition. It made one think he would indeed go somewhere.'

The following year Hopkins was about to join the National when he and Anderson worked together again. Anderson wanted him for a day's work in Salford singing a Brecht song in the community centre for his superb satirical short, *The White Bus*, written by Shelagh Delaney. Hopkins recalls: 'I think I must have had Movie Star in my mind because I asked if I could be flown up to Manchester. Actually, the reason was I had to be up there and back again quickly so I could start at the Old Vic. I learned German phonetically and sang the song. While I was waiting for the car to take me to Manchester Airport, I saw newspaper headlines about an air disaster at London Airport and thought, "God Almighty, I'm flying there."' A BEA Vanguard from Edinburgh had crashed in fog at Heathrow with the loss of more than 30 lives. When Hopkins flew in later, you could still see the wreckage near the runway.

The White Bus was not quite Hopkins' first film. A couple of years earlier, just out of RADA, he and a fellow alumnus, Jacqueline Pearce, were invited by a young film-maker, James Scott (son of the painter William Scott), to play husband and wife in a short drama called *Changes* which he had written and was going to produce with another actor, Drewe Henley, directing. Scott (who has since gone on to direct the Oscar-winning short *A Shocking Accident*) had scraped together £500, which just about paid for the black-and-white film stock. Scott explains: 'It was a little contemporary romantic story about a man who takes no notice of his wife. She goes off and then he gets jealous. I'd sort of based it on Jocelyn Stevens, the man who ran *Queen* magazine. I couldn't pay the actors anything and I remember Tony asking me if I could *lend* him the money to pay for his train fare to Wales.

'We didn't even have enough money for sound so we had to post-synch it all afterwards. I showed the finished film to the BBC, who were very snooty about it. Cardboard characters, they said. The only thing that happened to the film was that it was eventually bought by German television. Why did I ask Tony to be in it? I suppose he must have begun to have had some sort of reputation.'

At just 24 hours' notice Hopkins was called down to London from Liverpool to audition at the National. They were looking for walk-on actors for John Arden's *Armstrong's Last Goodnight* – tall ones, preferably. Unsuccessful, he returned north and then decided it was probably about time he moved on anyway. But the decision was not easy: 'David Scase wrote to me saying that he was sorry I was leaving but, he said, "You know what you have to do." I was touched by that because I knew he really wanted me to stay. I'd actually become the blue-eyed boy, working like a demon, tearing up the stage, demonstrating colossal energy. He liked that and I enjoyed it very much too.'

There followed some ten depressing weeks out of work. Then a friend of Hopkins' from RADA days called him up to ask if he would like to be recommended for a job with the Queen's Theatre at Hornchurch in Essex. The result was a happy couple of months of Shaw and Shakespeare. His first juicy part was Dick Dudgeon in *The Devil's Disciple*. The *Essex Gazette* wrote: 'The play centres round Dick Dudgeon, who is an unexpected arrival at the reading of one of the family wills. He stomps flamboyantly round the room wearing clothes sharply in contrast to the rest of the grey figures. Hopkins plays the part well and seems to improve as the play progresses . . .'

Prompter, in the *Hornchurch Echo*, was perhaps signalling things to come when he noted: 'Dick Dudgeon was played in the grand manner by Anthony Hopkins, a cross between Richard Burton and Dickie Henderson – pausing a fraction too long at times as though waiting for a TV lens to loom up in readiness for a close-up. A likeable actor with the right approach to the part.'

The producer, Tony Carrick, who was also making his début at the Queen's, then went on to stage *A Winter's Tale* with Hopkins as Leontes and, down among the credits, Martin Shaw as Cleomenes. During the run of the Shakespeare Hopkins was called up for another audition at the National.

Panic-stricken because he felt he had no good audition pieces, Hopkins felt especially nervous about doing his Othello turn because Sir Laurence Olivier was currently having a notable success in that very role. However, it was too late to learn anything else.

'What's he like?' Hopkins asked one candidate, who emerged from his audition before Olivier looking rather pale. 'He's nothing like you think he is. Very nice,' said the other hopeful, promisingly.

Hopkins was not entirely reassured: 'I couldn't believe I was meeting Olivier. I suppose I was expecting to see someone dressed in black, sitting on a throne or something. In fact, he looked a bit like Harry Worth. He had glasses, a three-piece suit and was a bit thin on top. Anyway I went in and he said, "Hello, dear boy. How are you? What are you going to do for us?" There was a group of other people there – Bill Gaskill, a couple of other directors and casting directors – sitting at a table. Olivier got out a silver pen and said, "What are you going to do for your first audition?"'

Hopkins: 'Well, I'll do a bit of Chekhov – Tusenbach in *Three Sisters*.'

Olivier: '*Three Sisters*. What else?'

Hopkins: 'Shaw – *Major Barbara*.'

Olivier (noting with the silver pen): '*Major Barbara*. What are you going to do for the Shakespeare?'

Hopkins: 'Othello.'

Olivier: 'Othello? You've got a bloody nerve.'

Hopkins: 'It's the only Shakespeare I know.'

Olivier: 'Well, good for you!'

Hopkins: 'I did the first two auditions. I was so nervous. I had my hands in my pockets for the first scene just to try and relax myself. As I made a gesture, a comb and some handkerchiefs came flying out. Anyway, I managed to get through all that then Olivier said, "What are you going to do for dear old Othello?" I told him I'd do the bedchamber scene, and just as I was about to start, he leaned over to one of his people and said, "Billy, do you have a cigarette?" Then he said to me, "I'm terribly sorry. I'm so nervous in case you're better than me," which was his charming way, I think, of trying to relax me. I did the piece and afterwards he came up to me and said, "Well done. I don't think I'll lose any sleep tonight but I think you're awfully good. Would you like to join the company?"'

Hopkins needed no second bidding.

On 21 October 1965, under the headline 'Another Key Man Leaves the Hornchurch Theatre', the *Hornchurch News* reported: 'Anthony Hopkins, who has delighted us with his fantastic performances in two recent productions at the Queen's, is leaving the theatre. For on Wednesday he is to join the National Theatre and go on tour with them for their productions of *Othello* and *Love for Love*. The company will tour Belfast, Liverpool and Edinburgh and play for the remainder of the season at the Old Vic. "I have been very happy at the Queen's," said Tony on Tuesday. "The theatre has a pleasant atmosphere and I shall, in a way, be sorry to leave. But I may return one day." Producer Anthony Carrick commented, "Although I'm very pleased for Tony, I shall be sorry to lose him." Indeed we shall all be sorry to see Tony go. He is one of the cleverest actors to be seen at the Queen's for a long time. But everyone, to be sure, wishes him the best of luck for this great opportunity before him.'

Not long after he had forsaken Hornchurch for The Cut, Hopkins was wishing he was back in Essex playing leading roles. He might in theory have taken a step up on the theatrical ladder, but his principal prop remained a spear. His first night with the Company was far from auspicious. He was the Cyprus Messenger in *Othello* and made a mess of it when he went down on one knee and started mouthing Iago's lines instead of his own. When they returned to the wings, Frank Finlay, the production's Iago, said: 'Would you like to go on and do the *rest* of my part as well?'

Olivier said to Hopkins: 'Oh, dear heart, my ears were flapping. I thought we were going to start the whole fucking play all over again.'

After about a month, when they had returned from the tour, Hopkins marched into the theatre one morning and demanded: 'Haven't you got any parts? Who do you have to sleep with to get any work round here? I don't want to stand around in wrinkled tights carrying a spear for the rest of my life.' He was told that Olivier was preparing *Juno and the Paycock*. Wasn't there a decent part in that for him? he asked. Hopkins was understudying Colin Blakeley and Olivier unexpectedly dropped by understudy rehearsal one day. 'Why don't you imitate Colin? I hear you're a very good mimic,' Olivier said to Hopkins.

'Imitate?' said Hopkins.

Olivier: 'He's a very good actor.'

Hopkins: 'Yes, I know. But imitate?'

Olivier: 'Don't be so bloody pure about it.'

Suddenly Hopkins found himself cast as An Irregular Mobiliser in Olivier's boisterous staging of the O'Casey. This at least persuaded him to abandon immediate plans to rush back to Liverpool or Hornchurch.

In that first year or so he appeared – briefly – in Congreve's *Love for Love* (as a sailor), John Dexter's production of Peter Shaffer's *The Royal Hunt of the Sun* (as Inca general Challcuchima), Borachio in *Much Ado About Nothing*, in Ostrovsky's *The Storm* (as a citizen), and in Feydeau's farce *A Flea in Her Ear* (replacing Robert Lang as Etienne Plucheaux when Lang took over from Albert Finney in the dual roles of Victor Emmanuel Chandebise and Poche).

In February 1967 Olivier returned to the stage for his first major new role for two years as Captain Edgar in Glen Byam Shaw's remarkable new production of Strindberg's harrowing tale of marital misery, *The Dance of Death*, co-starring with Geraldine McEwan, Robert Stephens and Janina Faye in three hours of domestic strife set on an island fortress towards the end of the nineteenth century. Even by Olivier's yardstick the latest plaudits for the then 59-year-old actor were awesome.

As Olivier's understudy (also playing a sentry), Hopkins watched, fascinated, as his mentor 'spread destruction all around him', oscillating, noted Ronald Hayman in *Queen*, 'between strength and weakness, lying down to die with his collar askew and his boots on, so as to be ready for the enemy, and rallying to dance vigorously to the music of the Boyars' Entry, only to flop down in a sudden collapse,' flinging himself 'athletically but quite convincingly into each fit and into the final stroke'. The performance was as exhausting as it was compelling.

When Olivier suddenly collapsed for real and was taken to hospital suffering from acute appendicitis (which led to pneumonia), Hopkins thought the performance would be cancelled, but on 21 June the stage manager rang him to tell him to report for rehearsals.

'I went in and I was so nervous I was speaking like an

express train. Robert Stephens, God bless him, stopped the rehearsal and took it over. He just told me, "Slow down!" That night I remember the curtain going up and I was sitting on stage thinking, "This is madness. These people didn't come to see me, they came to see Olivier. What am I doing here?" Geraldine McEwan, who was playing my wife, was white as a ghost, she was so frightened for me. I had to get up, cross the stage, pour a drink and light a cigar, and I thought, "I can't! This is crazy." And all the time the dialogue was coming out of the mouth. After five minutes I returned to sanity. It's amazing what the brain will do, the way our defence mechanisms take us over.'

Hopkins went on four times for the great man, during which one of his main concerns, as a fine mimic, was to avoid simply imitating him. But it was, he admits, a losing battle: 'You fall into his style. You have to fit his rhythms or you upset everyone else in the play.'

Olivier reflected later in his memoir *Confessions of an Actor*: 'A new young actor in the company of exceptional promise named Anthony Hopkins was understudying me and walked away with the part of Edgar like a cat with a mouse between its teeth.'

Both critics and audiences had noticed that too.

3. LIONHEARTED

Hopkins' success in 1967 as Andrei in Olivier's production of *The Three Sisters* gave him not only enhanced status at the National but also a new visibility. Now he could get his teeth into what was to be his first really meaty and sustained role with the company in Chekhov's tragicomedy of provincial life. With settings by Josef Svoboda and using a new translation by the Russian baroness Moura Budberg, Olivier created what one critic described as 'an exceptionally swift and flowing production that made me often feel I was seeing this play for the first time'.

Many felt that Olivier's *Uncle Vanya* four years before had proved to be the finest British Chekhov production since the war, so this *soi-distant* sequel was bound to prompt comparisons not only, in fact, with the *Vanya* but also with a Royal Court *Three Sisters* (featuring the pop singer Marianne Faithfull) revived as recently as April; this was July. In *The Times* Irving Wardle, dismissing the Court's staging as 'cold-blooded', noted 'vivacious realism' and 'superlative performances' at the National, citing in particular Louise Purnell (Irina) and Hopkins, whose 'impassioned outcries against provincial life' provoked 'the enraged convulsions that one associates with being buried alive'.

Peter Lewis in the *Daily Mail* suggested that Andrei, usually presented as a wash-out of a brother, had been made 'far less despicable than usual – he is an intelligent man disillusioned by the blinding power of love'. Philip Hope-Wallace, in the *Guardian*, claimed to be 'much struck' by Hopkins' despairing brother.

Referring back to *Vanya*, he felt this Chekhov was less good than the same company's earlier piece because it was 'less strong on humour'. Where, added Wardle, *Uncle Vanya* was 'a show for stars, *Three Sisters* is a company production. But it is one that largely vindicates Olivier's programme note: "In Chekhov we are all stars." '

It was 'star quality' much more than any sort of track record they were looking for when the producers of the film *The Lion in Winter* began their trawl to find a supporting cast deemed worthy of Peter O'Toole and Katharine Hepburn, the two top-billed artists already signed up for the multi-million-dollar film. Martin Poll and Jane Nusbaum had bought the screen rights to James Goldman's play soon after it opened on Broadway. A semi-historical, semi-dramatic, extremely colloquial comedy about the succession to the throne of England in the twelfth century, the movie is set in a fictional Christmas court at Chinon, to which in 1183 Henry II summons his estranged wife Eleanor of Aquitaine and three sons – Richard (later the Lionheart), Geoffrey and John – for a prolonged bout of festive bitchery, scheming and double-cross in the days before primogeniture determined the succession.

The play had received extensive reviews: the *New York Times* ravaged it (probably fatally) while the *New York Herald Tribune* praised Rosemary Harris' Eleanor as one of a dozen or so of the best performances anyone was likely to see in a lifetime of theatre-going. A disastrously (and to many inexplicably) short run ensued.

Goldman was, nevertheless, signed up to write a screenplay and with finance promised from the flamboyant entrepreneur Joe Levine, head of Avco Embassy Pictures, the project moved ahead swiftly.

O'Toole, who had played Henry II before on screen in *Becket* (1964), committed to the film first and was prime mover in persuading Hepburn to come out of semi-retirement (she had gone into a sort of purdah after the death of Spencer Tracy six months earlier) to portray Eleanor. Anthony Harvey, a fine young British editor who had recently made his directorial début with *Dutchman*, a thoroughly contemporary urban racial drama in monochrome set on the New York subway, might have seemed, at first glance, an unlikely choice for this wide-screen, medieval romp in glorious Eastmancolor, but his technical skill was beyond question.

O'Toole was convinced and he pushed hard for him. But who exactly, Hepburn enquired, from an ocean and a continent away, was this Harvey? O'Toole took it upon himself to fly a secret mission to California, even going so far as to disguise himself and adopt another name. Under cover, as it were, the actor escorted Hepburn to a seedy Los Angeles theatre where *Dutchman* was showing. As the final credits rolled, she turned to her co-star and exclaimed: 'But of *course* he's our director.'

Hepburn was determined to have some hand in choosing the cast. Scrutinising an early list, she was dismissive, reportedly telling O'Toole, 'The trouble with most actors today is that they're either skeletons or eccentrics.'

Back in London, with the *Three Sisters* notices still reverberating, Hopkins' agent rang to tell him he had fixed a meeting with O'Toole.

Now a fixture at the National, Hopkins had acquired a London agent in the person of Richard Page of Personal Management. It was a far cry from Hopkins' first representation. That was fellow Welshman Morgan Rees-Williams, younger son of the first Baron Ogmore, who had taken on the actor soon after drama school. Hopkins, signposting his later way with some agents, dumped him after just a year – 'showing my ruthlessness early,' he reflects. Page's partner, Jeremy Conway, who subsequently bought out his associate, also took on Hopkins and, as they say, handled him until the actor left for the United States. When he returned to Britain's shores more than a decade later, it was only a matter of time before he once again joined up with Conway. Meanwhile, Richard Page was doing the hustling for Hopkins.

Hopkins recalls: '*Lion in Winter* was my first crack at

a film and, of course, I had always wanted to do films more than anything, so I went along to see O'Toole. I think it was in Eaton Square that he had an office. I went in and met him and I can remember he was sitting there with a green jacket and green cap, looking like a sort of leprechaun with a beard.

'I so admired him because I'd seen his Jimmy Porter at the Bristol Old Vic in 1957 and he was the most extraordinary actor I'd ever seen. But I didn't tell him any of this because I was so in awe of meeting him. He gave me the once-over and said, "I want you to read Richard the Lionheart. Now take the script, go away, read it and then I'd like you to do a test." All I could say was "Great!"'

A couple of days later Hopkins' agent rang again to tell him to learn one of Richard's scenes.

'Which scene?' Hopkins asked.

'I don't know; any scene you can, I suppose,' came the reply.

The only scene Hopkins could find that had any substance, any lines at all (he had no speeches as such), were in some exchanges with Eleanor (being played by 'dat owld bat Hepburn', O'Toole had told him), so he committed them to memory for his next meeting, this time with O'Toole *and* Harvey elsewhere in Chelsea.

'There at the same time was Peter Egan, who was up for the role of Philip of France. There was a bottle of Scotch to relax us and with O'Toole sitting beside the camera we started the scene with him reading Hepburn's lines. Then he said, "Ted Hardwicke told me you do a marvellous improvisation." This was a little scenario about a rat catcher I once developed for an audition with John Dexter.

'So I did this rather horrendous little piece, after which O'Toole jumped up, came over to me and sat down again saying "Let's do another one", this time improvising with me. We did a number of improvisations together, at the end of which he suddenly said, "You've got the part."'

Exhilarating as this piece of news must have been at the time, it was still subject to rubber-stamping by Hepburn. After completing the tests, all personally supervised by O'Toole, the would-be cast was summoned to the private upper room of a restaurant in Charlotte Street to meet Hepburn.

Hopkins describes what happened: 'We could hear her coming up the stairs and I particularly remember Peter being very nervous in a boyish, excited sort of way because it was in a sense his "team" he was having to present to her. I suppose I expected someone like Joan Crawford. In came this woman wearing a khaki jungle outfit and forage cap, as if she'd just come off *The African Queen*. Much smaller than I imagined. "What's your name?" she asked me. "Tony Hopkins." "I've just seen your test. I guess you'll do." Moving on round the room she said, "You're Timothy Dalton? Yeah, you look good, I think you're going to be OK," and so on. Eventually we sat down to lunch and were all dumbstruck – apart from Peter, who was fairly boisterous – by this extraordinary presence.'

A shorter, sharper, funnier (and probably apocryphal) casting story has also been handed down over the years. O'Toole called Hopkins in and said, 'Tony, love, I'm Henry II, that c*** Hepburn is playing my wife. I've got three children: John, son of a bitch, Geoffrey, the bastard, and Richard, who's queer. Have a read of each.' Hopkins read them, and O'Toole said, 'You're the queer. See you Monday!'

By this time a potentially major problem had arisen for Hopkins which had been only partly solved: the question of his contract with the National. After casting him, O'Toole wanted him straight out of the contract, but it was not that easy.

Olivier was away in Canada on tour with the company and Hopkins was already cast as Audrey in an all-male version of *As You Like It* due to begin its repertory run at the Old Vic a full six weeks or so before shooting was due to start on *The Lion in Winter*, at the end of November.

With sideline pressure being exerted by O'Toole, Olivier eventually agreed to let Hopkins do the film. But there was one condition: Hopkins must stick with his theatrical commitment until the end of the year. There would therefore be a month's overlap of the play and the filming, which could only add to the pressure already beginning to pile up on him.

The play was perhaps the least of his problems, although it had worried him enough after early rehearsals for him to ask the director, Clifford Williams, if he could bow out, because, he told him, 'There's a huge wall and I don't think I can make the sexual leap.'

The notion of an all-male *As You Like It* had originated in the early sixties with the Polish poet and critic Jan Kott, who in an essay entitled 'Bitter Arcadia' had pointed up the ambiguity in Shakespeare's sonnets about the true nature of love between fair youth and the Dark Lady. Then, referring directly to *As You Like It*, Kott had noted, 'Rosalind plays Ganymede playing Rosalind. She plays her own self marrying Orlando ... The outstanding poetry of these scenes has never yet been fully revealed. As if the contemporary theatre did not possess an appropriate instrument.'

Olivier read the essay and set his sights on fashioning just such an 'instrument'. He was nearly scuppered at the outset when John Dexter, the original choice of director, refused to go through with an all-male version.

It took a frenzied call from Olivier to Clifford Williams, who was teaching at Yale while on leave from the Royal Shakespeare Company, to persuade him to return and take over the reins. It was early September when Hopkins, who had recently married, confessed his fears to Williams.

In a fascinating *Sunday Times* article by Kenneth Pearson tracing the progress of the project from Kott's essay to opening night, he writes that the director was 'sympathetic. "Relax over the weekend and when you come back and do it again, something will come through."

'Hopkins returns to the company. At the next rehearsal

he wears a rough shift and it dictates the way he walks. He then adds a wig of long hair and the natural gestures to keep it out of his eyes help to ease his problem. He keeps his voice in its normal low register. "It's what I want," agrees Williams. "Moo-cowish." '

A couple of days later Pearson noted that Ronald Pickup and Charles Kay, as Rosalind and Celia, were now complaining: ' "We're not feeling relaxed like girls are when they're together. Perhaps we need more physical contact." And, as women do, they began to confirm their friendship with small touches and sudden embraces. Hopkins at least is happier. In his long skirt, revealing a pair of stout hairy legs, he is doing "Knees Up, Mother Brown" in the corner.'

Towards the end of the month, and with just days to go before its opening, the cast assembled for a run-through of Act One: 'Taking its cue from its leading man/lady, the company gallops through the act. Hopkins, with a flaxen pigtailed wig, resembling nothing less than a bucolic Brunnhilde, evokes spontaneous laughter from a scattered audience of blasé National Theatre staff. Only once does Olivier interrupt the play to suggest a move to Celia.

' "Don't forget," he says ambiguously, "they're all paying fifty bob in the front rows to see this." '

A week later, the critics may not have been paying fifty bob but, except in a few cases, they *were* paying compliments to the trail-blazing production. Hopkins' Audrey was singled out by Irving Wardle as 'the funniest of all the performances . . . that seems to have grown out of embarrassment; and the result is a bass-voiced Brunnhilde who sits expressionless through Touchstone's advances and then grasps him in a bear-hug.' He was also described, variously, as 'Kensingtonianly dashing', 'a pantomime dame in embryo', 'lumpy', 'a hefty goat girl', and, in Ronald Bryden's *Observer* challenge to the fundamental wisdom of the whole enterprise, 'basic ENSA knockabout'.

It was actually the same weekend when Hopkins was

re-evaluating his 'sexual leap' as Audrey in *As You Like It* that he got married to his first wife, the actress Petronella Barker. Though the couple had become something of an 'item', the marriage itself came as quite a bolt from the blue to many of their friends. Four years his junior, Petronella, known as Peta, was the daughter – an only child, too – of the popular comic performers Eric Barker and Pearl Hackney. Hopkins and Peta had first met when she was in the 'crowd' at the Royal Court during the production of *Julius Caesar* and she, like him, had then gone on to become part of the National Theatre company at the Old Vic. A rather intense woman, with strong features, she was, by all accounts, a fine character actress. David Swift, Hopkins' old friend from Leicester Rep days, was best man at the wedding, held near Peta's parents' lovely old thatched home in Kent in early September 1967. With both partners of this ambitious duo carving out their separate careers, the relationship must have been under some strain from the very start.

Joining Hopkins in the cast of *The Lion in Winter* were John Castle, as Geoffrey, Nigel Terry (John) and Timothy Dalton, who had beaten out Peter Egan for the role of Philip. As Alais, the King's mistress and likely candidate for Richard's hand, was Jane Merrow, who had played the title role in a BBC television serial of *Lorna Doone*.

Harvey rehearsed his actors for two weeks at the Haymarket Theatre so that the seven members of the 'royal family' could get fully acquainted with each other before shooting began, with interiors, at Ardmore Studios outside Dublin on 27 November.

'The rehearsals,' said Harvey, 'helped the younger actors break down the barriers that one usually comes up against in a first film. By the time we arrived at the studios [with sets primarily doubling for the parlour, bedrooms and outer courtyard of Chinon Castle] we felt we were a family.' At the National Hopkins had been earning £16 a week plus 30 shillings for each performance; for the film he received £3000 for three months' work.

Before filming began, O'Toole told Hopkins he must

grow a beard. 'How can I when I'm also having to play Audrey?' he asked. 'Grow a beard, and add mortician's wax,' commanded O'Toole.

Hopkins tried to comply: 'I started growing a beard and I went on stage with this big blonde wig and mortician's wax sticking on. I looked like a hag. Charlie Kay and Derek Jacobi [Touchstone] took one look at me and had to walk away. In the interval, I had to go and shave it all off. It was terrible, a nightmare. So the film people had to resort to sticking on a beard, which annoyed them. They had a good make-up man, though, and every morning I'd go to the make-up chair and he'd do all this curling the beard on. Sometimes he was hung over and had the shakes; I'd be going one way, he'd be going the other. We had a few laughs together.'

Having films and TV already to her credit, Jane Merrow was easily the best-known of the young cast to date: 'I had never heard of Tony at that time but they were very excited about him – heir apparent to Olivier and Burton, and all that.

'Very early on I got the feeling that he was the one who was special although, interestingly enough, when we actually started filming, the only one who had a long-term contract discussed with him was Tim Dalton, because Tim had much more the film-star image. Tim, however, at that time, was terribly young and terribly aware of how gorgeous he was and the other guys – Tony in particular – used to tease him unmercifully. When we began, the thing Tony was very concerned about was keeping his performance on a film level and not being too much, too big. Hepburn and O'Toole were very helpful to him and the result was that he was quite remarkable. I think what I remember most was observing a man who was driven and who was also undergoing a tremendous amount of stress at that time.'

The truth was that only a couple of months into his marriage to Peta, things already seemed to be going awry. His emotional turmoil was compounded when she told Hopkins a little later that she was pregnant. Peta was quite volatile, and Hopkins was beginning to drink heavily.

Jane Merrow has never forgotten the nightly scene: 'I always recall seeing Tony in the bar after shooting at the studios, hunched over a beer and the telephone, his face full of anguish, trying to deal with a person who was obviously his wife. He was in what appeared to be a not tremendously successful marriage and she was demanding attention, which seemed unfair because he couldn't really give it to her at that time. On top of that he was having to fly back to London maybe twice a week to fulfil his stage commitment – and that was additional stress because he didn't care for flying that much. Tony was a man under strain, but he used it in the film. He was like a bottle of soda that was about to explode all the time. Of course, it only added to the dramatic tension.'

On Hopkins' first day of filming with Katharine Hepburn – a scene where they are alone together in a room unwrapping presents – they rehearsed, then she said: 'I'm going to give you some advice. Why did you play the whole of that scene with the back of your head to the camera? The camera's yours – use it.'

Hopkins was somewhat fazed: 'How?'

'Favour yourself,' she replied. 'Don't be so modest. Don't act. You've got a good voice, a strong voice. Don't force it, just let it fall out of you. You don't need to act in a film. Look at Spencer Tracy.'

Hopkins had, in some respects, the movie's most complex role. 'Constant soldier, sometime poet, I will be king,' he spits, as oldest of the three scheming princes. He was a homosexual, too, if Goldman's version of history is to be believed, who had indulged in an affair with the younger Philip of France much to his macho father's subsequent chagrin.

Although his was a much less showy role than those of the roistering principals, it was given an intricacy and complexity by Hopkins which, for Jane Merrow, adds up to one of his best-ever, if perhaps less trumpeted, perform-ances on film.

Towards the end of January 1968, the cast – with Hopkins now clear of his National contract (John Stride had taken over Audrey's plaited wig just after Christmas) – and crew moved to the first of a number of locations, at Montmajour Abbey, a restored twelfth-century monument near Arles in the south of France. Situated on a hill overlooking a vast plain below the French city, the abbey was used as the setting for the entrance of Henry and Eleanor into the Great Hall of Chinon Castle, while a herb garden became the backdrop for a key scene between Eleanor and Richard and an inner courtyard doubled as a vast and bustling kitchen and the castle vaults (for the climactic dungeon scenes). The chapel and outward aspect of Chinon was represented by, respectively, La Chapelle de St Gabriel and the Château du Roy René, both at Tarascon.

The walled city of Carcassonne and the Tour Philippe Le Bel at Avignon lent further medieval authenticity to the exteriors.

In the French portion of the schedule, the inevitable strains of filming a long, expensive chamber epic started to surface in a variety of ways. The most spectacular confrontation was at dinner in a restaurant at Les Baux one evening towards the end of the shoot, and involved O'Toole and Nigel Stock, who was playing his confidant William Marshall in the film. While everyone drank Calvados, Stock was fondly recalling his wartime service with Wingate's Chindits in Burma when O'Toole happened to describe the outfit as 'tin soldiers'. This triggered a violent argument between the two, with Stock having to be physically restrained from attacking O'Toole before the episode was finally brought to a close, in great bitterness.

Hopkins admits that by this time the situation had begun to sour all round: 'There were flare-ups in various quarters, probably to do with the production – who was actually in control and so on. Suddenly people got very bitter and bleak. I decided to take myself off and keep out of the way and was on my own one night in a restaurant when O'Toole's minder came in and, for no particular reason, started a savage attack on a couple of us who were there. I was just glad to get off the film although, looking back, it had been a new, interesting and often happy experience working with those extraordinary actors.'

This was not quite the end of the story, however, for on the last day of filming in France, at Carcassonne (Hepburn had left the company a week earlier after presenting everyone with a beautiful glass containing a tear and the inscription 'From Eleanor of Aquitaine'), Hopkins had to take part in a horseback joust for a sequence that in fact comes right at the beginning of the movie.

He was not an experienced horseman, as Jane Merrow reveals: 'When we started the film none of the boys knew how to ride and we'd go out practising in Ireland. Tony never seemed to look that comfortable on a horse but he did it anyway. Came the time to do the scene, the horse he was on got frightened and reared, dumping Tony, who was wearing a full suit of armour, unceremoniously on the ground.'

Hopkins broke his right arm quite badly and while the rest of the company left for England he was left behind in a French hospital. Showing yet another side of his complex character, Nigel Stock generously elected to stay behind and keep Hopkins company until he could leave hospital. Meanwhile, on the way home Anthony Harvey had landed himself in a Paris hospital with hepatitis, a continuing ill-effect from some bad oysters.

A couple of weeks on, Hopkins was asked if he would remove the plaster from his arm so that he could shoot a final scene at Pembroke Castle in Wales. It was a painful end to his first experience of filming – one which had also begun to establish what would become a recurring feature of later assignments: confrontations with the director.

Hopkins found Harvey 'a very prickly little man who wanted to do everything himself. I didn't get on too well with him. I suppose I was flexing my muscles and I used really to let go at directors if they got in my way. On one occasion he asked me to do a line a certain way and I said, "I can't." He said, "I insist you do it that way" and I replied, "You can do what the hell you like. I'm not going to do it that way." At which point Hepburn intervened, saying to Harvey, "Let him do it *his* way – he's the actor!" '

Hepburn, who later won the third of her four Hollywood Oscars for Eleanor (one of the film's three Academy Awards, the others being for James Goldman's screenplay and John Barry's score), fondly recalls Hopkins as 'a damn good actor – bright, unusual, diffident and very well cast as Richard.'

But as for dealing with 'prickly directors', Hopkins admits that 'that part of my personality always worried me, because I thought there must be a more efficient way of dealing with other egos. I knew I'd one day have to find a balance because it's a dead end just shouting and screaming. But, yes, I used to go for them and it was effective; it shut them up.'

Poised on the edge of film stardom, drinking heavily and with his marriage in disarray, Hopkins inevitably invited comparisons with Burton at this stage of his career. It was just that sort of irresistible equation which Jane Merrow felt had made Olivier so apparently hard-nosed when he was dealing with Hopkins' contract at the National: 'I believe Olivier was gravely disappointed that Burton hadn't stuck around in the theatre to fulfil his promise, and had, in effect, dissipated a lot of his great talent in films. I gather Olivier saw a potential in Tony that he hadn't seen since Burton and he wanted to be sure he didn't slither away in the same situation. I got the feeling that Olivier was afraid Tony was going to do the same thing and so wanted to hang on to him.'

On cue, Hollywood did indeed beckon to Hopkins, almost immediately after he had finished *The Lion in Winter*, but the outcome of this particular encounter could hardly have been less glamorous or less promising.

Still nursing a broken arm, Hopkins, accompanied by Peta and his agent Richard Page, flew out to Los

Angeles at the behest of David Wolper Productions to test for a Second World War movie, *The Bridge at Remagen*.

Hopkins describes his role: 'They wanted me to play this German officer as a sort of Marlon Brando *Young Lions* type. They'd seen photographs of me but by the time I stepped off the plane I had become very overweight. I looked like a big version of Oliver Reed – like a balloon. We were taken to the Intercontinental and that night had to go to a party, at the director John Guillermin's house, which was horrendous. Strangely, the house was on Benedict Canyon where I'd be living some years on. I was exhausted, got very smashed and the next day I did the test, which was a disaster. I had to do a couple of scenes, not helped by Guillermin shouting and screaming at everyone in sight.

'On the other hand, the people couldn't have been more hospitable. When I failed the test [the role eventually went to Robert Vaughn] they paid me off by giving me a trip to Disneyland and San Francisco on the way home. It was the first time I had ever been to the States and so I also stopped off in New York. One of my dreams had always been to see the Statue of Liberty. We stayed opposite the Algonquin, at the Royalton, and on that first night in the city I went out to buy a paper and, through the mist, saw the Empire State Building. It was all very exciting.'

Hopkins and Ralph Richardson, puffing away on his pipe, were sitting in the rear of a mock-up car at Shepperton Studios while a back projection sped them away from London Airport. Richardson was back on film duty after a couple of weeks away. Hopkins looked extremely preoccupied, and as they waited for the shot to be prepared Richardson started chatting.

Richardson: 'How're you getting on, old bean – not too happy?'

Hopkins: 'It's all a bit frantic down here.'

Richardson: 'I hear that. Why?'

Hopkins: 'I don't know.'

Richardson: 'Oh come on, be a sport. Tell me. I love a bit of gossip.'

Hopkins: 'Well, I don't really know. Unnecessary tensions. The producers are at loggerheads with the director. Things like that.'

Richardson: 'How's our Yankee chap, Christopher? Nice bloke, isn't he? Not very forthcoming or communicative, but a nice bloke.'

Hopkins: 'He's all right.'

Richardson: 'Don't like him?'

Hopkins: 'Oh, he's all right.'

Richardson: 'Look, I'm determined to drag it out of you. You look awfully bereft.'

Hopkins: 'OK, I'll tell you. He's been trying to get people fired. He wants the sound man fired, he wants the cameraman fired, he wants . . .'

Richardson: 'Good Lord, does he want to have *you* fired?'

Hopkins: 'I don't know.'

Richardson: 'Silly fucker.'

The 'silly fucker' in question was Christopher Jones, a rather pale young American actor – facially a little reminiscent of James Dean – who would achieve some transient stardom later in *Ryan's Daughter* before vanishing from the film scene almost as quickly as he arrived. He was top-billed in *The Looking Glass War*, the third and last, not to mention bleakest and least successful, of a trio of John le Carré's fashionably downbeat spy novels to be adapted for the big screen during the sixties, before it was belatedly realised that the novels worked better in TV's more leisurely arena.

Hopkins, in a kind of artistic limbo between the end of his National contract and the première of *The Lion in Winter* the following New Year, was playing an ex-public school spy, John Avery. An unremarkable role, confined to the studio, it denied him the opportunity to travel to Spain, which was doubling for the East German scenes. Hopkins had to brief Jones, as a Polish refugee chosen by cynical spymasters Ralph Richardson and Paul Rogers, on his inevitably doomed mission to retrieve vital filmed evidence of secret Russian missile sites in East Germany.

On the first day of shooting the film's executive producer, 'Big' Mike Frankovich, commanded everyone to lunch together in Shepperton's best restaurant. Jones, not only looking like James Dean but also doing what Hopkins recalls as a 'heavy number' worthy of his role model, seemed to puzzle Ralph Richardson, who, nevertheless, tried to get some conversation going.

Richardson: 'Where do you come from?'

Jones: 'California.'

Richardson: 'Oh, I love California, though I haven't been there for some time. Particularly love the climate. I hear you like motorcycles?'

Jones: 'Yes.'

Richardson: 'I have a Harley Davidson myself.'

Jones: 'Yes.'

Richardson: 'Do you know what a Harley Davidson is?'

No reply at all. At this, Richardson confided, 'Not awfully communicative, is he?' to the rest of a bemused gathering.

Hopkins sums up: 'It was a very strange film, not helped for me because it was a deeply unhappy period of my life with everything at home really going to pieces. My daughter Abigail was born in the August and that was the only thing, I think, that kept me sane; the thought of a baby at home. Poor Christopher Jones. He was a nice fellow and a beautiful-looking man but he had a manager who has since died of a drug overdose, and who used to feed him on the stuff. I enjoyed working with Richardson, though, and he made me laugh a great deal.'

While still filming *The Looking Glass War* Hopkins received a phone call at Shepperton from Tony Richardson, who asked him to play Claudius in his forthcoming production of *Hamlet*, with Nicol Williamson in the title role. Hopkins met Williamson, with whom he had worked briefly at the Royal Court, soon after

Richardson's call and told him he had received the summons. Williamson seemed pleased and assumed Hopkins was going to play 'boring Horatio'.

With a cast that included the modish Marianne Faithfull as Ophelia, Judy Parfitt as Gertrude, Gordon Jackson as Horatio, Michael Pennington as Laertes and Mark Dignam as Polonius, the idea was to stage the Shakespeare first for a few weeks at the Roundhouse, the converted engine turntable shed in Camden Town, then, with the established ensemble fully 'rehearsed', as it were, film the show within the confines of the building for theatrical posterity.

What might have worked as an explosive staging, with Williamson characteristically dangerous as the moody Dane, translated to the screen with somewhat mixed results. The filming, in oppressive close-up, seemed only to aggravate the artifice and theatricality. For Pauline Kael, Williamson's acting was 'all pathos and vituperation, snarls and tantrums, and he stares so much that he's in danger of wearing out his eyeballs'. Richardson's interpretation was, she concluded, 'just cheap Jacobean-Mod, sexed up whenever possible'.

Her assessment of Hopkins' performance was more generous: 'He is an appealing though very young Claudius – one rather wishes he were left in peace to rule the country, since Hamlet is obviously unfit.' The excessive youth of the Prince's parents was further underlined by Ivan Butler: 'Hamlet's mother looks as if she must have given him birth when she was around the age of ten – indeed, before she was born herself.'

Almost half an hour shorter than Olivier's classic film of twenty years earlier, this *Hamlet* also shed, among other things, the final entrance of Fortinbras (nor even did the ghost appear here). Clearly this was Shakespeare on a shoestring.

Hopkins rather liked the production and the film: 'Richardson was very inventive and made, I thought, a good, if rather bizarre, film. For me, though, the play was a deadly experience because I think I was so bad in it. I was very erratic. I changed my performance every night. Sometimes I was slow, sometimes fast. It was all very undisciplined. After the film the plan was to take the play to Broadway and I wasn't in any shape to go anywhere. I was in such trouble at home that all I wanted to do was to go into a hole in the ground. I think it was assumed that we were all itching to go to the States so when I told Richardson I wouldn't he was beside himself. Poor old Patrick Wymark took over as Claudius and had only a week to prepare. It was his last job and I think it virtually killed him because he was dead within months.'

The lead role in a new Alistair MacLean adventure, *When Eight Bells Toll*, had been narrowed down to a shortlist of just two: Hopkins and Michael Jayston, a year his senior and well-known for his co-starring role in a popular recent television series, *The Power Game*. *The Lion in Winter* had not yet opened when producer Elliott Kastner and his assistant Marion Rosenberg arranged for a private viewing to assess Hopkins' big-screen presence.

Marion Rosenberg vividly remembers the occasion: 'What really did the trick was the scene when he talks to a bird. I still have a very clear recollection of that particular scene. One had the feeling it could almost have been an extemporised thing, as if it wasn't even scripted. Whatever it was, it was absolute magic and as far as we were concerned that was it.'

Hopkins was invited to meet Kastner at his Pinewood office. A former agent and an archetypally tough American who could be formidably rude, Kastner came straight to the point: 'You're overweight. OK, listen, we're very interested in you for our film but it's a kind of James Bond character.' Sitting in was the film's stunt man, Bob Simmons, who took one look at Hopkins and said: 'You've really got my work cut out for me, haven't you? We're going to get you in shape so first I want you to go to a fat farm.'

With Marion – 'I loved it because I took off some weight too' – as his minder, Hopkins was booked in at

Forest Mere where, agonisingly (he recalls), a stone was shed and he emerged ten days later altogether trimmer and somewhat fitter. Before starting on *When Eight Bells Toll,* and because he was desperate for 'anything to get out of the house, anything to keep working', Hopkins raced to Hastings to do three days on an historical short, *The Peasants' Revolt*, playing Wat Tyler. This stint completed, he joined fellow actor Maurice Roeves and together they flew north to Glasgow then drove to Oban. By the time they arrived on the Isle of Mull, the principal location, the pair were legless.

Even before filming started Marion was perfectly aware that Hopkins had a considerable drinking problem: 'He seemed at the time to be very confused about his identity. Did he want to be an actor or did he want to be just a movie star? We had made a couple of pictures with Richard Burton and Tony clearly was concerned about whether he was going to become another Burton and, as so many in the acting community felt about Richard, squander his talent. Tony was afraid of that happening to him and was drinking to try and figure out who he was and what he wanted to be when he grew up.'

In fact, Hopkins was confronted rather directly about his 'problem' as he and another veteran actor on the film were having lunch together at the Western Isles Hotel one wild and woolly day. Robert Morley, at an adjoining table, leaned across and said to Hopkins: 'Why do you drink so much? I think it's terrible. You're rather talented and still young. I don't think it's at all funny walking around the hotel drunk. I saw you drunk last night, and I think you're an idiot.'

'Don't you agree?' Morley asked Hopkins' companion, who replied: 'Oh well, maybe Tony needs to have a drink now and again.'

'Do *you* drink?' Morley asked him.

'No, I'm an alcoholic,' came the stark response, which stunned Hopkins. Some years later he came across the same old Scots actor while working at the BBC on *Corridors of Power*.

'I heard that you got sober and that you're all right. I'm so pleased about that,' he told Hopkins, who responded: 'I want to thank you because of what you once said. It just took years for the penny properly to drop.'

The memory of this man's openness had been stored up in Hopkins' subconscious along with other 'hints', such as the time Katharine Hepburn told him on *The Lion in Winter*, 'I think it's pathetic and you're going to die of it one day.'

But it was not time to quit just yet.

Hopkins explains: 'Like most actors who drink heavily, or most alcoholics, you just don't drink during the day. I was quite disciplined then. The occasional beer at lunchtime was enough. I was never falling-down-in-the-gutter drunk. Rather, I'd get boring, boorish, aggressive and stupid. I'd drive my car drunk, that kind of mad thing.'

When Eight Bells Toll, directed by a rather elegant Belgian called Etienne Perier whose family ran Sabena Airlines, was nothing much more than a routine thick-ear thriller, blessed with some spectacular Scottish locations, plenty of action and a few dry lines. Hopkins, top of the bill for the first time (with a fee of £8000 to match), played a naval secret agent, Commander Philip Calvert, endowed with the requisite 'questionable attitude to authority', who is detailed to investigate the pirating of gold bullion ships in the Irish Sea.

Some of Hopkins' more familiar mannerisms – shoulders-back walk, scratching eyebrows, rubbing top of head – got their first real airing here as he tangled with a dubious tycoon (Jack Hawkins), a duplicitous wife (Nathalie Delon) and his own bosses, led by 'Uncle Arthur', Robert Morley.

Morley's directness generally delighted Hopkins. They were filming at a place called Grassy Point on Mull when the bulky actor, wearing a green Robin Hood-style hat, arrived on the set for the first time. He introduced himself to everyone then came up to Hopkins and said: 'You're Welsh! Obviously no sense of humour, and I hear you're a Method actor. This is going to be terribly difficult. If acting were comparable to the art of brain surgery it would be worth taking seriously. Since it isn't, we must all have a jolly good time. I do *hope* you have a sense of humour, by the way.'

Hopkins nodded. 'I think I have.'

'Jolly good. Are you a Method actor?' Morley asked. Hopkins said no, and Morley seemed mightily relieved.

Towards the end of October 1969, cast and crew returned from Mull to begin studio shooting at Pinewood. It was a Saturday afternoon when Jennifer Lynton, the associate producer's secretary, received a call at home in Kew. Earlier in the day Jenni had organised cars to pick up all the principals from the airport and ferry them home for the weekend. Now the production manager, Ted Lloyd, was ringing to tell her that a couple of the actors – Hopkins and Leon Collins – had got stuck in a bar and missed the plane down. They were now arriving at 5.30 p.m.; would she be a dear and pop out to Heathrow to meet them?

Jenni, who had never seen or spoken to Hopkins, drove to the airport, thinking, 'All I know about Tony is that he's meant to be a little bit troublesome. I'd heard reports from Ted in Mull, who said: "Oh boy, we've got a live one here. He jumps into a bottle every night and pulls the cork in after him. His wife and babe-in-arms are up here and, Christ, it's just awful . . ." '

Jenni was thinking, 'Will I even recognise him?' as she waited. The flight came in, and 'these two men came off the plane, Tony in a leather coat they'd bought him for the film, and I thought, "Oh God, that's the man I'm going to marry." It was just like that: an absolutely immediate blinding flash of recognition – so strong in fact that I actually wrote to an old school-friend that night and told her this funny thing had happened, that the man was already married and the rest of it.'

Drunk and aggressively annoyed that he had been 'deserted' in Scotland – he demanded Lloyd's number so he could go and blast him from a public callbox – Hopkins did not quite seem to come from the same mould as suave, debonair Dirk Bogarde, with whom Jenni had fallen in love at the age of ten.

Even from that early age, Jenni had known she wanted to work in films. The nearest cinemas to her family home in Rustington, Sussex were at Littlehampton where, through her early teens, she would haunt the one-and-nines and devour the numerous film magazines that then proliferated. After boarding school in Kent followed by secretarial college, she joined the publicity department at the Rank Organisation where four years earlier she had walked in and asked for a Dirk Bogarde poster. Three years at Rank made her conclude she was at something of a dead end, so she quit, did some temping and then got a job at Park Royal working for the *Look at Life* documentary unit. Still determined to be active in the production side of film-making – continuity is what she really fancied – Jenni finally landed at Pinewood, in the travel department. Within six months she was working for Elliott Kastner's associate producer, Denis Holt, who was doing the groundwork for *Where Eagles Dare*, an earlier, and rather more successful, MacLean adventure starring, of course, Hopkins' constant spectre Richard Burton.

Meanwhile, back at Heathrow, Jenni bundled the still fuming, and still drunk, Hopkins into a car and took herself home. Within two minutes of arriving back at his house in Putney, Hopkins was through the door again for the last time – walking out on his marriage of two years and deserting both Peta and his 14-month-old daughter. That night he made his way to Leon Collins' home in North London and stayed there.

The hype had begun even before the film started shooting. 'The man who could be a bigger hero than 007' proclaimed the *Sunday Mirror* in a profile of Hopkins as he limbered up for duty at Forest Mere. Again the familiar comparison: 'At 31, he has the appearance and voice of a younger Richard Burton (coincidence – they used to live only five miles apart in Glamorgan)', after which it went on to elicit a few choice quotes about the role from Hopkins.

'Calvert is more real than Bond. For instance, Bond-style sex is out. Sex maniacs don't make good spies. I've always thought that if a spy spent as much time in bed with the broads as Bond does, he wouldn't have the strength even to pull a hair trigger. Nudity is out, too. Alistair MacLean proved with *Where Eagles Dare* that audiences nowadays prefer adventure stories without a sex angle. In a film like this it just clutters up the action. That suits me.'

Try telling that to the *Sun*, which, later, leered: 'OK, fellas, you've had your turn with the *Sun* dollybirds. Now, [we] present *The Sun* beefcake. Every day this week we are picturing some of the men who make our nerve ends tingle and our toes turn up. Number One is Welshman Anthony Hopkins, of the brooding eyes and sensuous mouth. One critic said, "He makes James Bond look like a tame tiger." We couldn't agree more. He has a powerful face and a penetrating, blue-eyed stare. This 32-year-old could leave 007 at the starting grid.'

As it happened, Bond would barely have had to move out of second gear to leave *When Eight Bells Toll* standing in commercial terms. Even *The Sun* eventually had to admit it was a 'big disappointment' and a 'real dog watch' for Hopkins, who, despite the build-up in the *Mirror* and a decent performance in the film, was not to become an overnight Connery Mark II.

Marion Rosenberg was vividly aware of Hopkins' true state of mind while he was making the film: 'Tony was going through a lot of personal problems at the time and it was a very, very difficult picture for him. His wife came out to the location with their child, which made things even harder. I'm not saying it affected his performance in any way – actually he gave a wonderful performance – but the fact he didn't capitalise on the film and the fact it was his first leading part in movies may have had a lot to do with what was going on in his private life.'

Aside from his various problems, Hopkins enjoyed much of the actual filming: 'Bob Simmons did all the big stunts, but I wanted to have a go at as much as possible. Ever since I had my accident on *The Lion in Winter* I had been – and still am – put off horses, but here I got to do a lot of running about, throwing myself around and, though I'm no great swimmer, I did quite a lot of the underwater stuff. I also started to take on board what Katharine Hepburn had told me about screen acting. Economise and economise. At the time of *When Eight Bells Toll*, I didn't tend to learn a script too well. Sheer laziness, I suppose. So I'd ad lib as I went along, hoping the director wouldn't notice. Etienne rather seemed to like that. I also tried to use the camera more, attempting on each take to make it seem like it was always the first, to try and achieve a sense of realism – just be real.'

After her less-than-promising first encounter with Hopkins, Jenni began to wander on to the set at Pinewood from time to time, much to the displeasure of her boss, who felt it was hardly the done thing for secretaries to talk to the actors. Hopkins had now moved in with Bob Simmons, who was extremely supportive and kind.

Marion thinks that Jenni had begun from afar to harbour 'a tiny crush' on Hopkins throughout this period; even Simmons joshed her about it, but as far as she was concerned Hopkins was virtually unaware of her existence except for the odd 'Good morning'. What she did not know was that Simmons was pitching on her behalf. He had been taking Hopkins out on the town but was fed up with his habit of turning down all the more flamboyant girlfriends flung at him. Now Simmons suggested that perhaps Jenni was just the sort of girl Hopkins should be going for.

The regulation end-of-picture party was arranged for the Thursday night before filming finished. It started in the Pinewood Bar and when the bar had to close while the festivities were still in full swing someone suggested carrying on elsewhere. Jenni volunteered her flat in Kew

Gardens, and as Hopkins had dismissed his driver she ferried him there. On the way, they talked together properly for the first time, although, as Jenni recalls, 'It all seemed a bit strained and odd.' The party-goers, including Hopkins, who had arranged for his driver to pick him up, eventually dispersed at about midnight. Friday was the final day of shooting.

On Saturday afternoon Jenni left the house to go to the hairdressers and almost bumped into Hopkins, who was walking up the path.

Jenni still finds it odd that he should have managed to find her flat that day: 'Tony is usually so vague about places and, to this day, I can't understand how he ever found his way back to one he had only been brought to and from. Anyway, there he was so I let him into my flat and he played the piano while I went to have my hair done. When I got back we went for a drive and ended up in Kingston at the pictures. It was a ridiculously awful film called *The Valley of Gwangi* but we decided to see it because we knew that the son of Alistair MacLean's ex-wife was in it.'

A week or two after this, in early December, Hopkins called Jenni up, told her he could not face going home to Wales for Christmas and asked if she would go away with him to Vienna for the holiday. After some hesitation, she agreed.

'In fact,' says Jenni, 'we ended up in Dublin and it was the pits. Why Dublin? O'Toole was over there doing something and it seems Tony had suddenly changed his mind about Vienna and decided to go to Ireland instead. He was already there when I joined him at the Royal Hibernian Hotel. It was a nice enough hotel but such a depressing time. Tony was very down: he'd just finished the film, there was nothing on the horizon, his marriage had broken up and he was desperately missing Abigail. We drank, ate and mooched about, but it was miserable.

'He didn't talk to me all the way home. A car picked us up at the airport, dumped me and my suitcase off at Kew Gardens and took Tony on to Islington, where he was now subletting a flat from a chum who'd gone away on location for a couple of months. It seemed to me then that was that. I suppose the fear had dawned on Tony that "Here I am, just two months out of a marriage – what on earth am I doing getting involved with another woman?" '

A couple of days later Hopkins rang up as if nothing had happened and, within a few weeks, had moved in with Jenni at Kew.

4. BEEF AND THUNDER

'Somewhere in transit from the thickset shadow of Richard Burton towards the leaping light of Laurence Olivier,' wrote Caryl Brahms in an extremely prescient 1970 *Times* profile of Hopkins, 'there simmers a volcano: Anthony Hopkins. I predict that his ascent will take place in a series of eruptions rather than a gracefully curving graph. He reminds me not a little of Charles Laughton. The same ample voice, the same ample face. The threat of the same ample physique kept in check by optimistic crash-course dieting. The same flaccid appearance in repose. The same lightning movement as inactivity is flung off and action takes over. But where Laughton's gaze was apt to be heavy-lidded, his eyes darting and withdrawing like a lizard's tongue, Tony Hopkins' eyes are open widely on the world; he is still learning about it. He is a player who hangs on to his cool to the last split second and then blazes, tellingly theatrical, stopped almost as it starts.'

Brahms and her regular collaborator Ned Sherrin had been working with Hopkins on a television centenary programme, *The Great Inimitable Mr Dickens*, in which they traced the writer's life through scenes in his novels. 'It gave me,' said Brahms, 'an opportunity to watch the volcano at the simmer and in eruption and to realise that Hopkins is a very concentrated actor for all the flaccid, fishslap hand, which galvanises into a jabbing finger to make a point ... What made me so entirely accept this medium-tall Welshman as that short, precise, choleric Londoner, Charles Dickens, between the ages of twenty and 58? His understanding of the passions and pain of Dickens' complicated nature and his pace in moments of fierce emotion.

'And then, oddly enough, his own round face, which

takes splendidly to make-up. A round face is no bad thing in an actor, who must subdue his features into a regiment of parts yet never disguise certain aspects of his own personality ... "He always," wrote Max Beerbohm of Herbert Campbell, "seemed to be the offspring of some mystic union between Beef and Thunder." Almost he might have been writing of the 33-year-old Anthony Hopkins.'

Hopkins had just finished working with Helen Cherry and Clive Francis recording a play in Leeds for Yorkshire Television called *Decision to Burn*, one of ten 50-minute contributions under the umbrella title *The Ten Commandments*. Not long after he got back through the door at Epsom, where he and Jenni were living, the phone rang.

'Is that Tony Hopkins? This is Ken Tynan.'

Hopkins: 'Who?'

Tynan: 'Do you remember who I am?'

Hopkins: 'Are you kidding? I recognise your voice. How are you?'

Tynan: 'Would you like to do a play for the National?'

Hopkins was flabbergasted. He had already blotted his copybook when he left to do *A Lion in Winter* and the rest. Olivier had said to him, 'You shouldn't be going off to do films,' even though Hopkins reminded him that Olivier himself had done exactly the same thing. And some months before this call from Tynan another 'mix-up' had occurred which might have permanently closed the National's doors to Hopkins. He had been invited to play Rogozhin in Simon Gray's adaptation of *The Idiot*, starring Derek Jacobi as Prince Myshkin, with Anthony Quayle directing. When he arrived for rehearsal, Hopkins noticed that everyone had different-looking scripts from his.

He asked about this and was told he had been sent the wrong script. The script he was then handed was altogether slimmer, with his role trimmed to about sixteen lines. He stayed for the reading, went to the pub and then phoned his agent. 'I'm not going in any more,' he told him. 'You agreed that it was a good part. It was a misrepresentation. It's sixteen lines. I'm leaving.' Hopkins received a pleasant letter from Olivier – 'Sorry, dear boy, maybe next time' – but neither Jacobi nor Quayle were too pleased.

Tynan continued: 'It's *The Architect and the Emperor of Assyria*. It's a wonderful play written by a genius called Fernando Arrabal. I'll send you the script, but could you come up straight away and meet Sir Laurence?'

Hopkins: 'Who else is in it?'

Tynan: 'Jim Dale. Do you know him? Just come up.'

Recalls Hopkins: 'So I got the train that afternoon. It was a wintry day, very foggy – actually it always seems to be winter for me in the British theatre. I went up to Tynan's office and after waiting for a bit was told to go in. "Hello, how are you?" I said to him and there behind the door was this man who looked like an upside-down lavatory brush. "This is Victor Garcia," Ken said. Garcia was wearing a matador's cape with what looked like bloodstains on it. I said, "Hello" and, trying to be polite, "Do you speak English?" '

Tynan: 'He's a genius.'

Hopkins: 'What's he going to do?'

Tynan: 'He's going to direct the play. He's going to bring fire into it. Fire and blood, because this man is a genius. Tomorrow I want you to see a film he made of Genet's *The Balcony*. Now go in and see Sir Laurence.'

Olivier: 'Hello, dear boy, how are you? Lovely to see you. Would you like a drink?'

Hopkins: 'Yes – whatever you've got.'

Olivier: 'You're a lucky chap. Have you met Señor Garcia? I'm told by dear Kenneth that he is a genius. I'm told that he is going to bring fire on to the stage; but the fire regulations won't permit that. Ha-ha.'

Hopkins: 'What's the play like?'

Olivier: 'I think it's a load of rubbish, but Ken is very keen on it and I'm sure you babies will have a good time.'

The next day they all gathered in a private viewing

theatre in Wardour Street to watch what turned out, says Hopkins, to be 'a remarkable and extraordinary film. It was set in a tubular theatre on a giant perspex stage. Naked bodies were writhing about to the strains of Monteverdi. I thought it was a knockout.'

The Chekhov and Shakespeare of his first National Theatre experience three years earlier must have seemed light years away when Hopkins returned to the Old Vic in the guise of leading actor. A strange, allegorical two-hander in two acts, *The Architect and the Emperor of Assyria* seemed, to all intents and purposes, a sort of re-working of *The Tempest* that focuses only on Prospero and Caliban, washed up together on a desert isle. The Emperor/Prospero character (Hopkins) lands there after a plane crash; the native Architect/Caliban (Jim Dale) starts out as a simpleton but begins to gain the upper hand in the pair's subsequent clashes. Both are gradually divested of their clothing until near-naked as they play out their scenario on a set that is empty save for parachute silks and a fork-lift truck; finally, and climactically, they succumb to cannibalism.

Rehearsals began in a cold, dank church hall periodically plunged into darkness owing to an electricity strike. The two actors were not allowed to read the script at this stage but were 'promised the Universe'. The key man in the proceedings was a student from the Lycée, Olivier Pierre (later to become a fine National Theatre player himself), who, being fluent in French and Spanish, acted as translator.

Hopkins: 'We weren't allowed to move. We had to sit as if in meditation with parachute silk over us. I thought to myself, "I'm a square, bourgeois actor; I've obviously missed out on the great years of the Royal Court. Here I am sitting in a dustbin liner. I must stick around and learn." It was a nightmare, though. We didn't know what we were supposed to be doing.'

Olivier phoned and asked to see Hopkins early the next morning.

Olivier: 'I can't fucking sleep. What is this little shit

doing? I hear that you've threatened him with physical violence. What's he doing?'

Hopkins: 'He's not rehearsing at all. We don't know what the hell we're supposed to be doing. He's a madman and I just want to kill him.'

Olivier: 'Wait until I get there and then you can kill him!'

They drove together to the rehearsal, where there was no sign of Garcia but they did hear the word 'Chinois'. Olivier said, 'He loves the Chinese.' 'What's that got to do with it?' asked Hopkins. Olivier said, 'He's going to have a Chinaman in the play driving a fork-lift truck.'

By this time Jim Dale's eyes were out on stalks and his voice was going too because he was allergic to Brazilian tree bark.

Says Hopkins: 'This was used to build an elephant on stage. The stage directions clearly stated: "We now proceed to make an elephant." We had this dress rehearsal on a Sunday and Joan Plowright said to me that she and Olivier were coming to see the play. They sat down fairly near the front. It was the first act, I was sitting on the fork-lift truck and I had this speech which lasted about four pages. At the same time I'm pulling apart all this tree bark. I was possessed with energy, like a titan. Glancing down into the audience, I saw Larry and Joan there looking at me – lost in admiration and horror. About two and a half hours later I went to my dressing room and Olivier came in. "Is that it?" he asked. "That's just the first act," I told him. He said, "I've had it up to here. Where is the little shit?" There was no sign of Garcia. "Where's Ken?" said Olivier. "I'll kill him." After the play, Olivier said to Jim and me: "Babies, you've got to cut it. I don't know how you've managed to do it; you're made of steel. But you've got to cut it. The audience will leave in droves. You'll be a laughing stock. You must cut it."'

Hopkins and Dale went into the theatre early the next morning. They threw out the tree bark, the elephant stuff and a deal besides. As a result the play was cut from 4 hours to 2 hours 10 minutes. Hopkins said to Olivier

Pierre, 'Please translate. Señor Garcia had been talking about giving us a gift. Well, this is our gift to him.'

Garcia sat in the audience as Hopkins and Jim Dale did their first preview, 'up and down in the fork-lift truck. Just over two hours. Afterwards he came backstage, said, "Merci" – and we never saw him again. The audience had stayed, I think mesmerised by it.

'It was about ten past nine and they told me there was a phone call for me. It was Olivier: "Dear boy, is that you? Have you finished the first act?" "We've finished the whole play," I told him. "Oh thank you, thank you," he said.'

'Nudity at the Old Vic in the balance,' proclaimed a headline in the *Daily Telegraph* on 1 February 1971 as it reported, with ill-disguised relish, 'The National Theatre company may introduce male nudity for the first time [in *The Architect and the Emperor of Assyria*] ... With other companies in other London theatres, this exposure has almost become commonplace ... The company and the actors stress that the nudity is only a possibility. Both actors appear in briefs. In one rehearsal, a week ago in a room in the Lambeth public library building, Mr Hopkins removed them. When I asked him if the public performances would include nudity, he replied that with this play and the way rehearsals were going, anything was possible. Each rehearsal was different from the one before and no doubt each performance in the theatre would be different. It was impossible to forecast what would happen on Wednesday. Neither he nor the director could be certain in advance.'

Irving Wardle was greeted that first night by at least loin-cloth restraint. He suggested it was unlikely that the audience would have been able to see Arrabal's work ('very private affairs; a settling of grievances with the past, and no more related to general experience than the average masturbation fantasy') if Garcia had not been available. J. C. Trewin demanded, 'Who was responsible, originally, for suggesting this crude nightmare of the *avant-garde*? ... And who could have decided that blasphemy was fun?'

Harold Hobson commented: 'Never have there been so many lights with so little illumination.' Amid general bafflement about the work itself was some grudging praise for its ingenuity and much praise for the 'brave and tireless', 'vital, darting' actors. It was not their fault, concluded Wardle, 'that you leave the theatre only admiring the emperor's new clothes.'

Hopkins had previously worked with John Dexter only in subsidiary roles, during his first season with the National. Dexter, with his formidable intellect and reputation for withering sarcasm, was perhaps the most respected – and feared – of all Old Vic directors during the Olivier era. After Hopkins' first spell with the company Dexter too had left, first to work in the States and then to make a couple of films, including *The Virgin Soldiers*. Their respective returns to the Cut happily coincided in Thomas Heywood's *A Woman Killed with Kindness*.

In this detailed portrait of late Elizabethan domestic life and strife set in a Northern country house, Hopkins was playing Master John Frankford – 'businessman, wool merchant, a North Country Methodist, solid and reliable,' in Dexter's estimation, 'and underneath there's a turbulent interior which I thought Tony would do very well, and indeed he did. We had the idea to do it with nothing at all – just a bare platform. He had the voice, and he had the imagination to be able to make invisible doors work by turning the key; all the technical things he could solve easily. When you do a play like that it's on one level terribly naturalistic and on another moves into a strange dramatic poetry. It is important to keep it centred in the acting of that particular role; it's really the motor of the play.

'It was a tough struggle to get him to do that, to get him to accept that responsibility. He had, you see, a tendency to make things difficult for himself. He'd give a brilliant reading and then, as is the wont of many actors, take it apart completely, lose it totally then get it back again. All part of the process. Tony would agonise a mite more than he needed. He wasn't at that time secure enough in his technique to do the whole of his job.

'But in this play one could see the emergence of a potential classical actor of some authority. It was the first time he was able to step on a stage as a leading man and be able to lead. One of his problems is that he shies from that position. I remember Olivier saying to him when he was later doing the Scots piece and appeared to be holding back in preview: "Look, my boy, we pay you enough money to be a leading man; will you please lead?" By the time we got to New York together on *Equus*, he really knew what was expected from him in the area of leading. There is something more required from a leading part than just acting; apart from acting, he must lead others, and, as it were, gather them to him. *A Woman Killed* was the most interesting thing I think I've done with him from all points of view. His performance was really extraordinary and the whole production matched up quite well with it.'

The critics concurred: 'A thrilling performance' (*The Times*); 'a performance powerfully suggestive of boiling passions just held back' (*Punch*); 'beautifully measured' (*Evening News*); 'rich in sympathy and truth' (the *Lady*). In a poll of London theatre critics by the American trade paper *Variety*, Hopkins was declared 'most promising new actor'. After the Latin pyrotechnics of Arrabal and Garcia at the beginning of the season, a controversial Brechtian interpretation of Shakespeare's *Coriolanus* ended it. Manfred Wekwerth and Joachim Tenschert, the distinguished East German producers who had supervised Brecht's posthumous version of the play for the Berliner Ensemble's 1965 London season, returned to the Vic with what seems, in rehearsal at least, to have been a somewhat fraught production.

After four days Christopher Plummer walked out on the title role.

He explains: 'It was Olivier's last season at the National as artistic director and there was a prevailing atmosphere of a camp divided. I thought I had come to do the Shakespeare play only to be told it was the Brecht version. "We've got to do something about this: we've got to get rid of these German fellows," I said to Ken Tynan, who was dumbfounded. To make a long story short, they couldn't fire the directors because they'd already bought the set, so I retired gracefully – or was fired.'

The phone rang at Hopkins' house on a Sunday morning. It was John Dexter: 'Now listen, dear, you're going to take over *Coriolanus*.'

Hopkins remembers his immediate reaction: 'I was so tunnel-visioned at the time, having finished *The Emperor* and started rehearsals for *A Woman*, that I didn't know what was going on in the rest of the company. "What *Coriolanus*?" I said. Dexter said that Plummer had walked out and I had to take over.'

Hopkins: 'But John, I'm in the middle of rehearsing your play. I can't walk out on that.'

Dexter: 'You can do both. Come on, it'll do you good. It's a tremendous challenge.'

Hopkins: 'Well, I've got a copy of the play here.'

Dexter: 'That's no good. If you come to the National this afternoon, someone will leave a copy of the play for you at the stage door, of their version.'

Hopkins: 'Whose version?'

Dexter: 'The Brecht Ensemble. Don't you know them? Pick up the play, take it home, read it and you start rehearsing tomorrow morning.'

Dexter recalls: 'There was a very heavy Brechtian-Marxist line and Chris couldn't take it, which was a pity because he could have been very good. Tony agreed to take on the part and I had to let him off rehearsals for *A Woman Killed*. Within the limits of that version – bearing in mind that some people don't like the Brecht view of *Coriolanus* as a political catastrophe – he was extraordinarily good and led the company solidly. There was a tremendous carry-on with Wekwerth and Tenschert at rehearsals; they were used to the Berlin way of working and we had to fall in with that, as did the company.'

Despite the extremely late notice, Hopkins found the

experience in many ways very stimulating: 'It was almost like a silent film, so stark but also very attractive and exciting. I wish I could have had longer because I did seem to get on their wavelength. I could see what they were getting at. But time was too short and I've never really been much good at short notice. Technically, though, it was matchless.'

Certainly the members of the company seemed united when, after Irving Wardle's review in which he suggested that the producers had run up against 'British resistance' leading to 'uneasy compromise', they wrote jointly to *The Times* stating that they wished to 'refute categorically' any such inference: 'On the contrary, we found their ideas stimulating and thought-provoking and we accepted them wholeheartedly. The rehearsals were conducted in an atmosphere of mutual respect and enjoyment and were wonderfully exciting. We all hope that we can have a further opportunity of working with them in the not too distant future.'

Hopkins had just a fortnight to adjust not only to an unusual interpretation but also to his first great Shakespeare role. Wardle, for all his apparently idle speculation about internecine tensions, welcomed Hopkins' work unreservedly: ' . . . caps his two superb other performances of the season by rising to authentically heroic scale. Ironically his is the most sympathetic Coriolanus I have seen. Modest and almost winsome, delivering his first insults to the crowd with offhand gentleness, and resolutely refusing to drop into infantility in the scenes with Constance Cummings' Volumnia. All the greater is the effect when he really releases his thunder, leaving you with the impression that Brecht still has some way to go to deflate the illusion of great men.'

Harold Hobson in *The Sunday Times* simply could not begin to reconcile the Brechtian line – that the play was about class warfare – with what he saw as the Shakespearean thread, 'human nature deformed by pressures of temperament and circumstance. Not at all the same thing.' At least, he wrote, 'our actors render ludicrous the interminable battle scenes invested with such stylised sadism by the Berliner Ensemble; but the maddening echt-Brechtian shower-bath curtain is back, whining flimsily to and fro between the briefest scenes, while the revolving stage creaks like a mill-wheel beneath fearful thuds and clashes.

'My heart bled for the players of known excellence cast down amid the chaos: most of all for the doomed integrity of Anthony Hopkins, latecomer in a line of candidates for Coriolanus [Paul Scofield predated even Plummer], dressed like a cross between a fisherman and an SS man, evoking doggedly a Welsh rugby-football captain at odds with his supporters' club.'

To add insult to insult, when Hopkins took over Coriolanus he had to relinquish the lead in Buchner's *Danton's Death*, which went to Plummer, who says: 'Tony would have been absolutely perfect for Danton as I was rather thin in those days. Yes, he would have made a splendid Danton. Well, obviously he was fit to be tied [furious]. The night I opened in *Danton*, he came backstage, clearly very pissed off with me and my performance and told me so. He stood at my dressing-room door in front of a lot of friends of mine who'd just arrived, made this wonderful drunken speech leaving me and my friends with egg on our faces. Years later, he apologised. "That was terrible the way I got pissed that night," he said to me. "I was just so fed up with the whole organisation too." I replied: "We all were."'

The combination of losing Danton to Plummer and having to pick up the pieces of Coriolanus drove Hopkins into a fury of bitterness and resentment. He demanded a meeting with Olivier.

'I hear you're very, very angry,' said Olivier.

'Yes,' said Hopkins. 'Punch me in the jaw,' suggested Olivier.

'Just give me a bloody explanation,' said Hopkins.

Joan Plowright was standing on the sidelines, laughing helplessly.

'Give me an answer. Why did you do it?' Olivier said.

'I'll tell you why. Because Chris is a big star and you're not.'

'I'm really *angry*,' insisted Hopkins.

Olivier said, with some finality: 'I know that. But that's the way it is.'

For a compulsive worrier about where the next job would be coming from – constant panics over tax, bills, the day when the phone might never ring again – employment was, happily, to prove almost as relentless as the compulsion to indulge in extra-mural drinking, for dotted between Hopkins' film and theatre engagements were a series of increasingly important television roles. In *Danton*, first of a new BBC2 series called *Biography*, Hopkins finally got to play the French Revolution leader who was sacrificed by Alan Dobie's Robespierre during the Terror. He was Astrov to Freddie Jones' Uncle Vanya in a BBC Play of the Month, and was a cross between Dylan Thomas and Brendan Behan – 'a drunken, wasteful slob whose marriage is breaking up' – in another BBC2 play, *Poet Game*, with Billie Whitelaw and Cyril Cusack. At quite the opposite end of the emotional gamut was his quiet, middle-class, homebody brother in Peter Nichols' *Hearts and Flowers* (beautifully directed by Christopher Morahan), a gently wry comedy about members of a family gathering for their father's funeral.

'It's the all-star Leo Tolstoy Show – with a cast and cost of thousands.' the *Sun*, with its usual exquisite vulgarity, was of course referring to *War and Peace*. At £600,000, 20 episodes and a total of 15 hours' drama, it was – perhaps still is (*Fortunes of War* notwithstanding) – the most ambitious series ever mounted by the BBC. For Hopkins, it was the first role to bring him before a really huge audience as the epic unwound over three months, first on BBC2, then BBC1 and, finally, around the world, notably on PBS in the USA (Time-Life had been an investor in the project).

Entailing a full year's production in the studios and on

location in Yugoslavia – where the local territorial army was recruited as extras – the series reunited Hopkins with his *Danton* director, John Davies, and co-star, Alan Dobie (here playing the dashing Count Andrei Bolkonsky). It was Davies who originally earmarked Hopkins for the part of Pierre Bezukhov: 'When you read the first chapters in *War and Peace*, he has all those qualities described by Tolstoy. The nervousness and the diffidence. He's even the right size and shape.'

Hopkins agreed it was a plum part: 'Pierre starts off as a well-meaning drunk. He tries marriage, dissipation, philanthropy, trying to find the truth about life. There's a lot of me in the role. We make the same mistakes. We both have a two-sided nature, part gentle, part very violent.'

With his tall hat, spectacles and early nineteenth-century togs (medium-portly), Hopkins often looked more like some well-meaning, owlish Mr Pickwick as he moved with disarming clumsiness from roisterer to reluctant hero. He survived a duel, the retreat from Moscow and even the threat of execution to marry the lovely Natasha (actress Morag Hood, selected, it was said, from '100 hopefuls after a flood of more than 4000 applications'). In the proverbial cast of thousands, it was his portrayal of Pierre that, more than anything else, seemed to capture the public imagination and, incidentally, later earned him a Best Actor award from the Society of Film and Television Arts.

John Davies found Hopkins 'hugely rewarding to work with – full of ideas and energy. That's marvellous for a director. He is also responsive to direction, much more so than many other actors. He doesn't walk into a rehearsal saying, "That's how I'm going to play it."

'He takes the beginning rather quietly, almost waiting for something to happen within himself. He tends to find read-throughs fairly unnerving, certainly no easier than most actors. Of all the things he's done for me, and he's done all told about 30 hours' worth [Davies, a decade later, produced *A Married Man*], Pierre was, I think, the most challenging. It's an extraordinarily complex character – for a start he must age from 20 to 50 – and you must take him through enormous crises, events and unhappiness. The role develops in such a wide range of ways, all of which Tony was able to handle consummately.'

Morag Hood recalls being very impressed with Hopkins' approach to the role: 'He always brought a lot of material with him; he was very well prepared, lots of ideas at an early stage of rehearsal [in the studio, a recording session would take place every fortnight following two weeks' rehearsal]. He had studied the whole thing, *knew* the text. I remember thinking that next time I did a serial I'd do the same; it was a great lesson to be learned, that when you were working at such speed it was good to be properly armed.'

The production had a full eight weeks in Yugoslavia, principally for the Borodino and Austerlitz battle scenes. For Hopkins, this long grind, with only cheap Yugoslav brandy for comfort and warmth, must have been considerably eased by having his old friend David Swift with him for part of the time.

Swift was playing Napoleon (he thinks that Hopkins may have had something to do with his being cast). He describes the location: 'The producer, David Conroy, had done a lot of research and discovered this place, Novi Sad [about 50 kilometres north of Belgrade], where snow had fallen at this time of year for the past twenty years ... except this year, the snow never turned up. We had to have snow because it was the sequence of the retreat across the Steppes. Tony had plenty to do anyway. I'd just gone out from England for a day or so to do a couple of lines – Napoleon retreating in his sleigh. But five weeks later (it wasn't actually *that* long, though it felt like it) I was still there. I started to get restless and began to make waves, threatening that I would fly home. The producer would take us out in his car and make sure we were occupied – Tony, I must say, behaved impeccably. Eventually they were forced to look for higher ground.'

During the long drive to and from a location near the

Austrian border, Davies felt he got the closest he ever would to Hopkins: 'By the end of the journey, during which we talked and talked, I think I knew him a lot better than I had done, even though I'd been working with him for months and months. We actually had a rather dramatic end to the journey, for coming into Belgrade we turned down a side street only to find that someone had opened a water main and it was very icy. I remember we slid down the hill sideways, spinning gently on the ice, with trams hurtling down around us. Tony just sat there quite quietly – almost resignedly – waiting for something awful to happen...'

Hopkins returned to the stage in Jonathan Miller's Chichester Festival Theatre production of *The Taming of the Shrew*, which was to run throughout the high summer of 1972. The advantage of directing a play of this sort, wrote Dr Miller in his book *Subsequent Performances*, 'is that it invites us to look at it on its own terms, and to see that the past is a foreign country with different customs and values from our own. The play at least offers us the opportunity to try and understand what is now the radically unvisitable past. Unlike Joseph Papp's approach to the play [Miller decries the American habit of making the piece suddenly become 'a test case for feminism'], my own enthusiastically recognises Tudor social ideas of the function of the woman in the household without agreeing with them. When I tried to modernise the play, it was not in the sense of putting it in the present but of looking much more carefully, through contemporary eyes, at what it was expressing in the past.'

Dr Miller's bible for his interpretation was Michael Waltzer's book *The Revolution of the Saints*, which among other things discussed the ideas prevalent among Puritans who had returned to England after exile under Mary Tudor. It was a very serious-minded society – by the time Shakespeare was writing, there was, says Dr Miller, a substantial Puritan squirearchy – so 'if you represented Petruchio as a serious man, you can take and develop the implications of lines such as "To me she's married, not unto my clothes" and " 'Tis the mind that makes the body rich" and see how consistent these are with a Puritan view. The alternative is to present Petruchio as a flamboyant bully.' Visualising the character as a Puritan squire, Dr Miller cast Hopkins 'because his personality as an actor seemed to conform to that image'.

In his *Times* review, and, in particular, his fascinating assessment of Hopkins' performance, Irving Wardle drew comparisons with the actor's Frankford in *A Woman Killed with Kindness* ('whose title Petruchio himself echoes') at the National a year earlier: 'Where, as Frankford, he showed the quiet stability of the Puritan home, here he shows its vitality and ruthlessness. But, in both cases, the life is austere and pious ... and one can imagine the couple [Joan Plowright, who had also been in *A Woman Killed*, was Kate in this production of *Shrew*] settling down to the same placid rhythm as the Frankfords.

'One might expect that this sober approach would knock out most of the fun: that it does not is due mainly to the sheer size and unpredictability of the temperaments involved. Mr Hopkins conveys a sense of freedom as strongly as any actor I have ever seen, and never more so than when he is working in confining styles. Within the general pattern of the play he has a life-line of his own, operating in resistance to external events; sometimes leading him to drop out and view the surrounding action with a puzzled stare, and sometimes to erupt into dance movements and volcanic spasms of fury that take possession of the whole stage.'

Wardle writes of the initial shock at seeing 'a close-cropped, grizzled Petruchio lumber on in coarse leather carrying Grumio (Harold Innocent) on his back ... It is clear from this moment that Anthony Hopkins's Petruchio is not the usual madcap. Rather he seems a mercenary soldier of the marriage bed ...'

During Hopkins' two months at Chichester he also caught up with Olivier, who was filming *Sleuth* nearby.

Sometimes he drove over and helped Olivier with his lines.

From summery Chichester Hopkins found himself moving on to autumnally bleak rehearsal rooms at the Old Vic. Macbeth, 'a God-Almighty part to play', was all set to be Hopkins' triumphant return to the National after a year's absence, the first in a series of demanding roles projected from the end of 1972 through '73, to be followed by Oronte in *The Misanthrope*, then *The Bacchae* and finally *The Cherry Orchard*. The director Michael Blakemore had asked Olivier if he could stage *Macbeth* and requested Hopkins for the title role.

Like Dr Miller, Blakemore had very specific ideas about 'modernising' a play that had too often, he felt, been confined to some timeless Dark Ages setting: 'I really did my homework and found that it was very contemporary in its references, many of them to Renaissance knowledge. It would have been performed in the reign of another Scottish king, James I, who was passionately interested in, for example, witchcraft, an obsession of the Jacobean era. I looked at contemporary pictures in the National Portrait Gallery and found how stiff and rigid – like magnificent butterflies – many of the people looked. I thought that if we could provide the same sort of costumes it would give a correct feeling of stiffness and confinement – almost of being unable to move.' This, he believed, would complement intriguingly the play's pent-up emotion.

It was not, admits Blakemore, a particularly happy rehearsal period for him or Hopkins: 'I think he was frightened of the role, that he was in Olivier's theatre and was also taking on a part that had been one of Olivier's greatest. When doing a play like this, a huge burden falls on the leading man. My concern was to offer him all the support I could.

'He did a great deal of preparation but like a lot of people without too much formal education he had, I think, an undue respect for academe. There's a time when you must cut yourself loose from others' insights. On one occasion, we were struggling with a scene. He'd read something about it and I took him aside and said that I was hoping to liberate him from what I saw as an uncalled-for respect for someone else's opinion. He was furious and stormed off to the pub. There was also trouble about the fight scenes. I had brought in Bill Hobbs to supervise them but Tony complained endlessly and so I had to let Bill go. He also hated the costumes.'

Hopkins used to let off steam about the National during late-night sessions at the home of Gawn Grainger, who was playing Macduff. Grainger's late wife, Janet Key, recalled: 'If you're married to a man at the National it's a bit like living with someone who has a couple of mistresses; they're out all day and when they do come home they're either half-cut or else buzzing with fury at something that has happened in the day or with enthusiasm for what's gone on. Gawn used to bring Tony back at about half eleven and they'd both be pissed *and* buzzing; we'd all stay up till two or three in the morning rabbitting about acting and the theatre. Then, first thing in the morning – I'd still be hungover and miserable – there'd be banging at our bedroom door and it was Tony saying: "Can we go and have breakfast now, Gawn?" They'd go off and when I got up I'd see Tony's socks still hanging out in the garden.'

Hopkins' great fondness was, and still is, for a good breakfast, so he and Grainger would traipse off at what seemed like crack of dawn to a workman's café in Smithfield for bacon and eggs – and the occasional pint of cider in a market pub – before walking on eventually to cross the river at Waterloo Bridge and thence reach the Old Vic. Grainger remembers one particular morning when they began chatting about Victor Henry, falling about laughing as they recollected his talent and his craziness. Later they heard that, that very same day, the young actor had been knocked down by a bus and gone into a long coma from which he was never to recover.

Grainger believes that Blakemore and Hopkins were not really compatible and matters were not particularly helped, he felt, by Olivier lurking like a spectre on the sidelines: 'On one occasion we had, I thought, an amazing run-through in rehearsal. Tony gave a fantastic performance, was quite electric. Then Larry came to see it. I think he might have been a bit tired or disenchanted and it seemed to communicate itself to Tony and from that moment on, aside from the costumes and the fights, something didn't quite work. Blakemore's a very detailed man, knew the play backwards, knew what he wanted. Tony's a fiery Welsh guy who wanted to go his own way, and at that time things weren't going too right for him.'

This undercurrent was not especially apparent when Hopkins was interviewed by the *Guardian* shortly before opening night. The only, guarded, reference to directors came when he said he quarrelled with 'the dehydrated Cambridge intellectual approach' to plays and with people 'who had never read a page of Stanislavsky yet tried to use his methods, learnt second-hand and probably garbled on the way'.

Hopkins was asked whether he acted from the gut rather than the head.

'Both,' he answered. 'Perhaps in fact I don't trust my instincts enough. I try to work it out rationally before I fire off my guns. And usually if you find the right objective within the text and the line of the play, you're in a better position to start acting from "the gut".'

Of the play itself Hopkins revealed that Olivier had sent Blakemore a note saying: 'The man knows everything. The woman knows nothing.' Hopkins explained his interpretation of this: 'She's silly. There she is saying, "You get the key to the executive lavatory, and we're away, baby." And he's saying, "No, baby, no. Look what we're doing. And look at this gas bill."

'Macbeth is a great soldier, a marvellous man in the field. She doesn't know what he's like in battle, any more than a suburban housewife knows what sort of hero or monster she sends off to the office. But she keeps urging him on, playing up the man of action in him . . . Macbeth is driven on, losing control over events. He has this thing that he wants to stop time, to concrete it in. But he can't. He gets to the point where he thinks the more murders he commits, the safer he will be. But it doesn't work.'

Hopkins also talked of the sheer challenge inherent in any new production of *Macbeth*: the 'lovely daring', as he described it, 'is to go on the first night. And every first night is a bloody miracle. Not a miracle in the mystic sense. But in the sense that it's a miracle the lights work, the set stands up and that you know your lines.'

Hopkins' inner feelings at this time were in fact more to do with misery than with miracles.

That misery was compounded when Hopkins focused on just a couple of poor notices among what were generally fine reviews of a production about which, for example, Wardle concluded: 'The atmosphere is dense with events, character and the mounting sense of evil more powerful than I have formerly experienced in any production.'

The credit side continued: 'Anthony Hopkins is from the first a shifty, uneasy figure, a man scared of his own shadow and betraying the latent evil when he wets his lips as he tells his wife of Duncan's proposed visit. One sweats with him as he degenerates into a frightened bully, he is so clearly a prey to the rooted sorrow of a mind diseased . . .' (*Daily Telegraph*).

'If she [Diana Rigg as Lady Macbeth] suggests an insect, Mr Hopkins increasingly comes over as a great golden toad, ingesting more and more poison with a devouring appetite as he increasingly loses contact with the world outside.

'It is a performance that begins by seeming calculated; particularly in its reversals of emphasis (a trick shared by numerous actors in the production), responding to evil news with a calm that erupts at the least expected moment. But by the end of the evening its spell is established . . . ' (*The Times*). 'The performance is full of excellent detail such as the gleam in his eye at the Witches' predictions which tell us they are merely affirming his own thoughts, and the look of blatant envy he casts at Duncan's crimson apparel. It is a well thought out performance one can imagine growing in scale and grandeur as the run proceeds . . .' (*Guardian*). There was praise not only for Hopkins but for, among others, Rigg, Denis Quilley (Banquo), Ronald Pickup (Malcolm), Gawn Grainger (Macduff) and Alan MacNaughton (Duncan).

However, the first editions of the following day's London evening papers brought far less cheer. Felix Barker's slaughter in the *Evening News*, made even more painful because it seemed he could not remember the leading actor's Christian name, suggested: 'Full of subtleties, this production piles up convincing details but dissipates the dramatic force. The general approach may well have been because John Hopkins is a good minia-turist, but without the inches or grandeur for a major tragic performance. He is a smiling Macbeth, tiptoeing about in a curiously buoyant way as if wearing pneumatic breeches inflated with helium. This cocky, genial fellow sometimes sweats apprehensively and occasionally bellows; but frequently he gives the impression that he is a Rotarian pork butcher about to tell the stalls a dirty story. As the equally accented scenes follow each other without any sense of progression, his Macbeth shows no development of character . . .' That final point was also underlined by Milton Shulman in the *Evening Standard*.

Hopkins' feelings when he chewed over these reviews can well be imagined, for they seemed only to compound what he describes as his own 'unhappiness with the play and myself' and, in particular, 'the awfulness of my own performance'. As the play, which ran 10–15 minutes longer on the second night (after which Hopkins went to a party and got very drunk), settled into its repertory run, he felt his working life was rapidly beginning to close in on him.

Coinciding with *Macbeth* were two other significant tranches of work – rehearsals followed by the filming of *A Doll's House*, and preparations for, and the taping of, a 50-minute portrait of Lloyd George as part of the BBC's series *The Edwardians*.

Three jobs at the same time. Up at seven in the

morning, in bed by two or three the next. Lines and yet more lines. Hopkins was reaching saturation point.

The Lloyd George play reunited him with John Davies, with whom he had made *War and Peace*, and although Davies sensed that Hopkins was personally finding the going tough this in no way impinged on his production. Focusing on a year and a half in the life of the politician (played just a year earlier as a cameo by Hopkins in Richard Attenborough's film *Young Winston*), the only trouble was generated by the play's material. Davies explains: 'The Lloyd George family decided it was scurrilous because we showed him in bed with some Polish countess; he was known to like the ladies and the writer had fictionalised this lover. Anyway, it was banned for repeats because the family threatened to sue the BBC.'

Hopkins had fallen in love with Claire Bloom as a teenager. When the Chaplin film *Limelight* arrived at the Regent in 1952 he went to see the movie no less than fifteen times. He was captivated by its music, its poignancy, and by its sheer sentimentality. But most of all he was captivated by Claire Bloom, then making her first major film at the age of twenty. Hopkins claims he decided at that moment to become an actor simply so that he might get a chance to meet Bloom: 'I don't think I wanted necessarily to become an actor as such but merely to do so as a way of becoming famous enough to meet her.'

Twenty years later he found himself walking on to the set at MGM-EMI studios in Borehamwood to play Torvald Helmer opposite Bloom, as his wife Nora, in a film version of Ibsen's *A Doll's House*. She had played the role in an acclaimed production of the work on Broadway the year before produced by her husband, Hillard Elkins, and directed by Patrick Garland using a Christopher Hampton adaptation. Made on a fairly hasty schedule running through the last three weeks of December 1972, this was effectively to be a filmed record of that particular staging under the same management.

The American stage revival of this neglected master-piece about a strong woman who begins to resist her husband's will coincided rather neatly with the emergence of the feminist movement. This probably accounted – fatally, from a box-office point of view – for the fact that an Anglo-French co-production of the same play, starring Jane Fonda, was shooting simultaneously in Norway. Directed by Joseph Losey, from a screenplay by David Mercer, the Nordic version substituted, principally, David Warner for Tony, Trevor Howard for Ralph Richardson (Dr Rank), Edward Fox for Denholm Elliott (Krogstad) and Delphine Seyrig for Anna Massey (Kristine). Women's Lib or not, it was still one *Doll's House* too many for a generally philistine cinema-going audience.

When he arrived at Elstree, Hopkins was a month into *Macbeth* and feeling both highly-strung and volatile.

Patrick Garland remembers: 'He told me he felt very silly wearing his doublet and hose. It was obviously an uncomfortable time for him and he was really rather restless. Torvald is an unattractive husband and butt for Nora but I felt it was crucial, and more in line with the production, if he were played by an attractive man. When he came to us he wasn't a big star yet, not that it was any surprise that he became one. Tony has a certain male quality about him that's lacking in most home-grown film stars – a passionate, explosive quality. We're very good at the Leslie Howard-type performance or the vulnerable undergraduate who doesn't quite know about going to bed. That's where he shines: in a certain sexuality.

'Tony also has a very special gift, which is his phrasing of a line. He uses a very eccentric, almost mannered way of breaking up a line. He'll put emphasis on odd words and put pauses in odd places – much more true to life and far from sounding as if he's reading out poetry or lines on a page. He has a spontaneity.

'As Torvald he was mercurial, explosive, as in the bit where he suddenly turns on his wife: he didn't do that in an intellectual, premeditated way. He used his instincts and he did that very well and truthfully. He was particularly touching in the last scene [begging her to stay as she prepares to leave him to seek a life of her own], swinging our sympathies round to his side. The character's such a stuffy prig yet Tony made you feel very sorry for him, which you don't in the other film. His was a much more profound and sensitive performance.

'When I saw our *Doll's House* again recently I found it stood up very well. As for Tony, it was all there: his acting style hasn't altered any more than his physical appearance.'

Hopkins seems to have been as explosive off screen as on during the filming, despite being matched with his childhood 'sweetheart'; 'Claire was very beautiful but I'd got well over my crush by that time. I wasn't in very good shape myself and she was a bit nervous because I was a little unreliable. She'd also be a bit moody from time to time and Hilly [Elkins] would stand on the set and glare at everyone. I remember lashing out at Patrick because I thought he was fussing me. I'd suddenly go berserk and tell him to fuck off. I must have been mad. I was suffering terrible paranoia in those days – I suppose I've still a bit of it now – that came when I felt I was being interfered with; when directors would tell me they knew me better than I knew myself.

'When anyone said that I'd go berserk. Whenever I heard a director say, "Trust me", I'd run a mile. But Patrick was lovely, such a nice fellow, and when I met him again I apologised for all those years ago. I told him I was sorry I'd been so touchy and he said, "But you weren't, you were charming." I know I wasn't exactly charming.'

The prospect of returning to *Macbeth* was beginning to weigh very heavily indeed. Over lunch at the studios one day Ralph Richardson said to Hopkins: 'You're playing the Scottish gentleman, I hear. My God, that's the worst part I've played. I've played it once and it takes twelve men to play it. I would willingly have blacked the boots of the entire company rather than go on stage at night in that.'

The play was dropped from the repertory while Hopkins was away filming *A Doll's House*. He returned to the run and the beginning of rehearsals with John Dexter for *The Misanthrope* with what was, for him, a sense of 'terrible oppressiveness; everything was closing in'. Dexter, he felt, was hammering him and 'I had neither the wit, humour nor resilience to cope. I tried taking Valium but it had no effect. I was, I suppose, deeply unbalanced.'

Came the final straw. One of the key elements of Blakemore's production was the use on stage of great portraits of the principals. In his, Hopkins appeared bearded. After *Doll's House*, in which he kept a beard, he had become clean-shaven (but using a false moustache) for Lloyd George. So when he came back to the Old Vic, he had to be fitted out with a false beard. He tried it out at rehearsal, pronounced it impossible to act with and went out that night on stage beardless. Blakemore was extremely annoyed and after the performance went round to see Hopkins to convey his displeasure and frustration that the actor seemed to reject all attempts at help. The next day, Blakemore and the National received a doctor's certificate (a 'cover-up', admits Hopkins) saying that Hopkins could not continue to work. John Shrapnel, who was playing the Sergeant, had to step in as understudy, while Denis Quilley was swiftly groomed to take over the role for the remainder of the run.

Blakemore today looks back on the period with sadness and some irritation at the way those events seem to have become distorted with retelling in various accounts down the years. He was particularly astonished to read at least twice in interviews with Hopkins how, on one occasion during rehearsal, the director had stormed out when the cast laughed after an ambulance had roared by outside the theatre during a murder scene.

What actually happened, says Blakemore, was that during one none-too-well-attended matinée, Hopkins was in mid-flow when the audience heard an ambulance and laughed. He threw down his dagger and stormed off stage.

Gawn Grainger offers a still more accurate account: 'The murders having taken place, I, as Macduff, had to come on stage – on this extraordinary set – and say "Horror, horror, horror!" At which point an ambulance from the station just beside the Old Vic shot by making a terrible noise and that brought the house down. Tony was obviously on stage at the time but the laugh came on my line.'

Blakemore would have been no happier with interviews in which Hopkins allegedly described him as 'a stubborn middle of the road director'.

Reflecting now on the actor, whom he still holds in the highest regard, Blakemore says: 'He's a romantic actor, in the style of Kean. He doesn't like directors and is, or certainly was then, hostile towards guidance. He rejects the technical requirements you need to tackle a great verse part, trying instead just for intuition and feeling. If you are doing a great formal part, you have to structure it; it can't really be done on spontaneous impulses as if waiting for lightning to strike suddenly in the middle of a scene. If you do Shakespeare that way, you're making it so difficult for yourself. However, Tony is, for example, a marvellous Chekhovian actor, where the words and text are an outward expression of concealed feelings. I also think of his breathtaking cartoon silhouette in *Pravda*; he has that centre-forward physical energy. I have to say too that he could be the most delightful companion.'

At a desperate stroke, and perhaps on the brink of his donning the mantle of Britain's greatest stage actor, Hopkins had effectively walked out of the production, out of a planned role in *The Misanthrope* (which Dexter gave to Grainger) and out of the National altogether. He would not return for more than ten years.

The following day, 13 January 1973, he married Jenni at Barnes Methodist Church. David Swift was best man again, and among the guests at the wedding were both Michael Blakemore and John Dexter. According to Dexter this was a gesture somehow signifying, 'Fine – we'll see you later.'

Hopkins and Jenni had by this time been living together for almost three years, first in Kew, then Epsom and, at the time of their marriage, at a flat in Castelnau, Barnes. Hopkins' divorce from Peta, after the requisite two years' separation, was originally going to be sought on the grounds of 'complete breakdown of marriage'. By the time the decree nisi came to be granted in court on 14 March 1972, adultery had been thrown into the hearing too, and Hopkins did not contest the allegation. Neither he nor Jenni were in court to defend the suit or hear Judge McIntyre award custody of Abigail to her mother and order Hopkins to pay the costs of the case.

Some months before that Hopkins had been quoted in the *Sun* as saying: 'As I get older myself, I prefer a woman of my own age. I'm very square. I'm absurdly shy of most women, so I pretend I don't like them and people then think I'm arrogant.

'I would never marry an actress. I know I'm impossible to live with. I can think of a thousand things that would drive a woman away from me. The moment when we would loathe each other I can take. But once we started to irritate each other, I know it would be time to leave. I have no intention of getting married for a very long time. But I have a lovely girl at the moment and when I do marry I hope my wife will be just like her.'

What Jenni must have made at the time of this sort of chauvinistic drivel (whether it was true or merely embellished) was less important than the fact that theirs was a mutually supportive and rewarding relationship. With Hopkins' drinking, hers was a chaperoning role too. 'Those,' says Jenni, 'were the days when I really felt he needed and wanted me to be there, from Day One, and I felt it was important too.

'I had never been around anyone who drank like that, though, looking back on it, it never was as bad as I sometimes think Tony fears it was. We'd go out to dinner, particularly in the romantic first months we were together, and he'd order a bottle of wine. Before we got halfway through, he'd order another. I suppose I used to think, "Oh, he just wants to prolong the chat ..."

'Drink always seemed to make him more open and talkative. What I didn't notice was that everything was sort of springloaded to a drink. He didn't like to come away from a pub before he absolutely had to. But he didn't fall down or appear to make an ass of himself. The way it took him was that after we went out to a party, he'd never want to come home. It would be getting to half one or two o'clock in the morning and there Tony would be, eyes slightly closed, droning on and on, getting more self-centred, opinionated and argumentative.

'I'd be sitting there thinking, "I'm the one who's got to drive us home. I want to go home. Please, can we go home?" No, one more drink, can't be boring, one more drink.

'I never, except on one occasion, felt, "Oh, blow this, I'm going home," because I suppose I felt you can't leave someone sleeping on someone else's floor. He'd get a bit aggressive on the way home, saying, "Why did we have to leave?" Then, in the morning, he'd say: "Oh God, was I awful last night? ... What did I say? ... I'm so sorry." His drinking was boring more than anything else; the same old thing over and over again.'

Jenni took Hopkins home to meet her parents quite early in the relationship. As well as noticing that he made a fair old dent in the Scotch, they were apprehensive at first about their daughter being involved with an actor because actors were foreign bodies to them. Nevertheless, Hopkins was polite and gracious, Jenni was clearly happy, so they seemed pleased about that.

At first marriage seemed to be right out of court. Hopkins had been shattered by his short, unhappy marriage to Peta and the subsequent split, particularly as he adored Abigail. But to see the baby would mean having to see his ex-wife again, and that he felt he simply could not do. So he was constantly having to steel himself not to see his child – perhaps ever again.

Jenni does not remember any formal proposal from

Hopkins. Their subsequent union seemed rather to evolve. She had been taken to Wales to meet Hopkins' parents, and got on well with them. When marriage did eventually loom, her relief was as much to do with such mundane considerations as the fact that at last they could be 'Mr and Mrs Anthony Hopkins' rather than people wondering, 'What do we call them? Hopkins and friend?' They could have gone on just living together; Jenni says she would probably have been as happy either way. But marriage appeared to make sense and Hopkins liked the feeling of protection it offered.

Having children, however, seemed to be completely ruled out, certainly as far as Hopkins was concerned. Jenni raised the matter and Hopkins, while not categorical about it, was clearly not keen.

'It was completely out of the question until we got married,' Jenni explains, 'and then it didn't seem the right idea for a number of reasons, among them economics. Also, Tony was single-minded about his career at the time; he was fiercely ambitious and I think he really wanted to concentrate, and have everyone else around him concentrate, on that. It wasn't as if he didn't trust our relationship but he must still have had the fear that having left one baby behind he couldn't go through even the possibility of all that again.

'There was a moment when I would quite like to have had a baby. Anyway, I'm a great believer in the idea that if it's meant to happen, it will happen. Nothing did happen and with that went along the realisation that it wasn't particularly the end of the world for me. In fact, it became pretty obvious that it would be better if we didn't have children because, with the way Tony's career was going, ours would in a way have amounted to a single-parent family.'

When Hopkins walked out of the National he was, he says, walking out into nothing – apart from a refreshing honeymoon in the Lake District with Jenni and a visit home to Wales: 'My way out had been to move fast before they could get you.' Naturally, he need not have worried – although he doubtless was – about where the next offer of work was coming from, for less than two months after throwing off the shackles of the Scottish play Hopkins was becoming immersed in 6 a.m. calls and dawn drives to Pinewood at the beginning of yet another major, though rather better-paid, three-month commitment. Apart from being the longest, costliest and, arguably, most ambitious film yet made for television, *QB VII* was also distinguished (though not creatively, according to many subsequent critics) as the medium's first-ever mini-series.

Adapted from Leon Uris' novel of the same name (the title refers to Number Seven court of the Queen's Bench Division in the Strand), it was a thinly disguised account of a real-life libel action that had taken place a decade earlier when a Polish doctor, Wladislaw Dering, sued the author after the publication of *Exodus*. In *Exodus*, Dering had been fleetingly mentioned as a perpetrator of hideous medical experiments on his fellow inmates in the death camp at Auschwitz during the Second World War. In the court case the jury had awarded Dering derisory damages of a halfpenny. He died a broken man not long after.

For *QB VII*, an intriguing little civil action was stoked up into a five-hour (technically six hours in terms of the advertisement-packed US transmission) epic as the case was used as merely the catalyst for a classy flashback melodrama about, among other things, Jewish guilt, Gentile culpability and a two-family saga spanning 30 years.

Dering became Sir Adam Kelno and Uris turned into a bad-tempered American writer called Ben Cady (Ben Gazzara).

'The universal catastrophe of ideological genocide,' wrote Clive James in the *Observer*, 'was reduced to a specious conflict in the mind of a Hollywood mediocrity. The few powerful scenes could only emphasise this central inadequacy, although they did lift the show a notch above *Judgement at Nuremberg*, which left a generation of young cinemagoers with the impression that the Nazi regime did

ANTHONY HOPKINS

bad things to Judy Garland ... The casting was adequate in
the leading roles – Ben Gazzara and Anthony Hopkins are
both good actors, although Hopkins increasingly took
refuge in mannerism as the script left him high and dry – but
the conceptions of character which the players were asked to
embody were hopelessly cliché-ridden, despite everything
the director, producer and writers could do to make them
profound. *Because* of everything they could do.'

Hopkins' 'witness-box mannerisms' were also in the
mind of Philip Purser in the *Sunday Telegraph*, who
reminded readers that the actor had been on trial only two
weeks earlier on BBC2 in the 'much better' *Lindbergh
Kidnapping Case*. 'Hopkins,' declared Shaun Usher in the
Daily Mail, 'has solidity allied with sensitivity so that even
mediocre drama gains importance from his presence.'
Variety had reservations about the drama but none about
Hopkins: 'Hopkins was outstanding even when his
motivations were no longer identifiable. His tormented
doctor, almost obsessively dedicated to medical
knowledge and practice, was the production's most
memorable and haunting character.'

No amount of carping could, however, prevent the
show from achieving gigantic viewing figures on ABC in
the States, and thus long-form television was well and
truly hatched. It was, of course, Hopkins' first taste too of
this sort of relentless picture-making, in which
achievement is strictly measured in minutes-committed-to-
the-can-per-day. He enjoyed the treadmill and rather
admired his tough director, the late Tom Gries, who, he
admitted, could be 'rough on people. He didn't give a
damn. For the court scenes, he had four cameras going; as
one finished, he'd cut to the other. Not the lighting
cameraman's dream – you get flat light. But we did that in
two weeks. Very exciting. Like really being on trial. You
learned your lines and spoke them until you ran out of
memory. "That's it," I said after one ten-minute take, "I
didn't learn any more for today."'

5. CALIFORNIA DREAMING

It was early in the New Year of 1974 when Hopkins walked from Brentano's bookshop in Hollywood and stood on the corner of the street opposite the Beverly Wilshire Hotel waiting for Jenni to come out of the shop and join him. He could have had no idea that about eighteen months later Los Angeles would be his home base, but he swears that at that precise moment he had the strongest feeling, almost a vision, that he would soon be back again to stay.

Hopkins was about to finish the filming on his first movie in Hollywood (and to do some looping on *QB VII*, including the dubbing of Jack Hawkins' voice) and return home – not that he should ever have been there in the first place, for Hollywood was only a belated substitute when the original plan to shoot *The Girl from Petrovka* entirely on location in Belgrade fell through at the last moment. The setting for this romantic comedy drama, about the relationship between a free-spirited Russian girl and a world-weary American foreign correspondent, was in fact meant to be Moscow.

The producers, David Brown and Richard Zanuck, and the director Robert Ellis Miller had done their homework with the Yugoslavian authorities very thoroughly, they thought.

Ellis Miller explains: 'I'd spent eight weeks in Belgrade with Vilmos Zsigmond, our cameraman, and we'd found the most phenomenal locations. In the old part of the city there was, for instance, a whole Russian section which had all kinds of shops with Cyrillic lettering over the doors.

'They read the script and I told them I was treating it as a love story and that I certainly wasn't out to make any huge, political statement. Curiously enough that also seemed to be a period of considerable *glasnost*.'

Just before Ellis Miller left Belgrade to return to London, where the principal actors were beginning to gather for a few days of rehearsal, he had checked the sets, chosen fabric for chairs, picked a hundred extras and even watched them being fitted for Russian costumes. As he flew west, the Iron Curtain slowly came down behind him, for when he arrived in London he found his wife, Zanuck and Brown standing on the kerbside as his taxi drew up, looking ashen-faced. 'The picture's closed down,' they told him.

There was never any official explanation, although Ellis Miller suspects the heavy pressure suddenly came from Moscow, where officials had apparently hated the original George Feifer book on which the screenplay, by Allan Scott and Chris Bryant, was based. Feifer had married a Russian girl and, after a long fight, managed to get her out of the Soviet Union. Universal Studios, who were backing the film, and had spent upwards of $500,000 on wardrobe, set construction and general preparation in Belgrade, sued the company in Yugoslavia – and won.

For Goldie Hawn and Hal Holbrook in the lead roles and Hopkins, playing Kostya, a cheery local black marketeer, there was a month's delay as the film-makers feverishly sought other suitable exteriors. Finland, Portugal, Spain and Belgium were all scouted.

Ellis Miller: 'We ended up using Vienna – and the funny thing is, Russia looked much worse as a result. Belgrade was elegant, newly built and still had a power and majesty which would have been good for the film and very positive for Russia.

'What we had to do in Vienna was use those old wintered buildings with cracked façades and ageing stone – because that's all they had. At that time Vienna was a very poor city – much more than it is today – and it showed. We only did a fortnight in Austria and then had to do the rest of the film on the back lot at Universal. The picture never overcame the loss of not being made in Eastern Europe.'

The writers, in London, cabled Hollywood: 'TAKE HEART, YOU'LL MAKE A WONDERFUL FILM. REMEMBER THAT BELGRADE IS ONLY BELGRADE, BUT THE BACK LOT IS UNIVERSAL.'

This turned out to be wittier than almost anything in the film itself, a drearily dated piece that tended to reinforce all the old prejudices. *Variety* commented: 'What 25 years of Cold War "comedy" clichés and the latterday Nixon détente haven't done to make irrelevant, *The Girl from Petrovka*, artless writing and direction have.'

What of the Girl herself, the wacky Miss Hawn for whom this was an unashamed vehicle? Although she tried desperately to subdue her usual, very American, *Laugh-In* zaniness to play a foreigner it was a problem, Ellis admits, as much for her as, finally, for the audience, who simply could not accept her in the characterisation. They wanted the fluffy Goldie they knew and loved.

Working with this scale, and generation, of star was an education for Hopkins: 'I was always baffled that people could be an hour late on set and no one would dare ask questions. You'd be there and notice much hurrying and scurrying, people looking at their watches, awful silences, then a hushed "Where's Goldie?" followed by whispering. I never knew what was going on but it was all very time-wasting. I supposed it had to do with the power games they play in Hollywood.'

When Hopkins first heard he'd been cast, there was just one problem: he was keen to find a copy of Feifer's original novel but scoured London's Charing Cross Road bookshops in vain. Dejected, he returned to Leicester Square station to catch the tube home. To his amazement, he found a copy of the book lying on a bench in the station. A year or so later when he was on location in Vienna, the production was visited by Feifer, who complained that he had lost his only copy of the book after lending it to a friend in London.

It had had particular sentimental value, he explained, because it was an advance copy which he had marked in preparation for publishing an Americanised version of the English edition, with words such as 'labour' changed to 'labor' and so on. 'Is this the one, with the notes scribbled in the margins?' Hopkins asked, who had been puzzled by the red corrections throughout. It was indeed the very copy, which had gone missing from Feifer's friend's car in Bayswater and had never shown up despite frantic searching and offers of rewards.

The first day of shooting at the studio happened to coincide with Goldie's birthday. Someone baked a fancy cake and various members of the top brass from the film stood around to be photographed with her. The photographer complained that the shot was too crowded and, pointing at Hopkins, asked 'Who's that guy?' urging him to keep out of the way.

Ellis Miller, who was working a great deal in London around the turn of the seventies, had conceived the idea of Hopkins playing a Russian after seeing much of his theatre work.

'I thought this Hopkins lad was phenomenal. For the role he fell into the accent so easily, not that he didn't have to work hard to find it first. Once he had it in his grip, it was wonderful and he gave the Russian quality a most wonderful English sound. I loved him in the picture. Goldie depended on him too and I think they were very good together, providing perhaps the best moments in the film.

'I can remember feeling his temperament – never animosity or anger, though years later he apologised [shades of Patrick Garland] for being "rough" on me – but that seemed to be part of his working hard at a character part. Leading roles are, in some respects, easier to play; they're closer to yourself. Once you're in a supporting mode, you are probably further away from yourself. I thought some of his obstreperousness was being in character.'

A month later, on a chill February morning, Hollywood could hardly have seemed further away (though Russia still had a resonance) as Hopkins stood on the quayside at Southampton and waved farewell to the transatlantic liner *Britannic*, about to embark – with band playing and streamers flying – on its first spring crossing.

'There's Daddy!' cried Caroline Mortimer to two small children as they helped pack the rail on the upper deck and waved back. The ship moved slowly away; Hopkins turned, walked from the crowd and climbed into the back of a police car parked nearby.

It was a fine, atmospheric opening to the vastly under-rated thriller *Juggernaut*, directed by Richard Lester, about a mad bomber (of the title) who holds a liner to ransom for £500,000. Hopkins was playing Superintendent John McLeod, who helps co-ordinate the against-the-clock search for eye-rolling Freddie Jones (whom the audience does not see – it merely hears his rasping instructions – until the very end), who conducts the terror from his suburban semi. At sea – the Irish Sea during a swell in a Russian cruise ship dressed up to be *Britannic* – Richard Harris, in one of his best-ever performances, leads the bomb disposal team with just 22 hours to defuse seven steel drums, each containing half-ton charges of amatol.

Hopkins' role was land-locked, though he was allowed briefly on board on one occasion to have lunch with Omar Sharif (playing the skipper) and Shirley Knight Hopkins (the skipper's lover) before anchor was weighed for a sequence that was, understandably, a one-take job. That night, he flew to Manchester to star in a play for Granada called *Possessions* about a drunken rag-and-bone man buying a pony from a poor widow and her family. He never actually managed to meet his screen wife, Caroline Mortimer.

After the sea-going sequences in *Juggernaut* were completed, Lester returned to Twickenham studios where the remainder of the shoot, including scenes with Hopkins, Ian Holm, Julian Glover, John Stride and, of course, Freddie Jones, was to be based.

Hopkins had never before worked with such a swift director as Lester: 'Smash-bang. Four cameras and you're finished in about a week. The actors would meet on the set. "Stand by, action." He'd do one take, then say to us, "Right, do you want to do another?" No, we'd say. "OK, on we go."

'He was an incredibly fast worker, and very pleasant too. I don't know whether it necessarily produces good results but it certainly pleases the producers.'

Amid all this constructive haste, Lester retains an enduring memory of working with Hopkins: 'We were shooting in Chelsea Town Hall, which we'd made the police operations room, and had gone to lunch in our caravans. As I came back I could hear a Beethoven sonata being played quite beautifully. I thought to myself, "Isn't this lovely, not having to think about the day's work but just hear this wonderful music?" and assumed it was someone preparing for a concert.

'There was this empty room next to the largest assembly room, where we were filming, and there I found Tony playing Beethoven on a concert grand. I remember thinking, "This is terrible. Not only is he extremely nice, a good actor, good-looking and attractive to women, but he can also play the piano." I'm a piano-player too, and this was good. I really wanted to kill him; I wanted to smash the piano lid down on his fingers. Seriously, though, the film was a pleasure to make and we had only six weeks to do it, so there was no time to get bored.'

Before James Herriot's popular semi-autobiographical stories about a Yorkshire country vet began their long, and as yet unfinished, run on BBC television a decade or so ago, Reader's Digest helped to sponsor two full-length cinema films chronicling the gentle pre-war yarns of an anxious-to-please young animal doctor working in harness with a more seasoned practitioner. The first of these, *All Creatures Great and Small*, reunited Hopkins with his old RADA flatmate Simon Ward. They had worked together only once, briefly, three years earlier when Hopkins did a cameo of Lloyd George opposite Ward's Young Winston. In *All Creatures* Ward was the callow Herriot with Hopkins as the crusty but benign senior partner, Siegfried Farnon.

Ward, who had unashamedly talent-worshipped Hopkins in their student days, regards those few pleasantly summery weeks in and around the North Yorkshire moors near Pickering as having been a continuing education: 'It was such a joy to work with someone who looks into your eyes and listens to what you say. Not a lot of people do because they've already worked out what they're going to do and you might as well not even be there. Tony always responds to who you are, what you're saying and how you're saying it; it's as if there's a genuine conversation going on.

'There were some memorable moments during the filming. On one occasion we had this scene where Tony was going to have to operate on a dog. Unfortunately they hadn't told the owners they shouldn't feed the dog before it came on to the set because it was going to be given an injection of Valium. We were in this very tiny room, about twelve of us in all including the dog, which had been out for about five minutes and was asleep on the operating table.

'As they said "Action", the dog evacuated its bowels. Within a short time, the room filled up with this terrible miasma. I told everyone I was sorry but that I was going to have to stop, the continuity girl fainted and Tony could hardly get a word out – he's not exactly mad about dog shit – but they said we must go on because they couldn't give the dog another injection. We had to do the scene three times. Then the stills man came in and said, "Can I do a picture?" Tony said, "Not on your bloody life", ran outside and threw up.

'Tony was also involved in a scene which, of all the things I've done, I've enjoyed watching the most. He had to drive into this farm (the wrong farm, as it turns out), be very bossy and suddenly announce he's come to dissect a pig or chop up some horse. So he asks for a knife. As a piece of comic acting it was just brilliant. I remember standing behind the camera when they were doing the close-ups and just thinking, "That's the way to do it. True, a bit dangerous and deeply comic." You actually got the feeling he was going to go in and chop up everyone in the house. It made me laugh a lot.'

As Hopkins' extra-mural drinking continued unabated so, with exquisite timing, art asked him to mirror life in a couple of memorable roles created by David Mercer. In *Find Me*, an *Omnibus* special for the BBC, he played Marek, a drunken Polish novelist haunted by memories of the Resistance. In *The Arcata Promise*, for Yorkshire Television's *Sunday Night Theatre* (his last job in Britain before his long exile in the States), he was the alcoholic actor Theo Gunge, living in a basement and finally resolving his problems by blowing his brains out.

On *Find Me*, Sheila Allen, who had barely registered Hopkins when they worked together in the Royal Court *Julius Caesar* (in which she was cast as Calpurnia and was moreover preoccupied with her impending marriage), was by now quite aware of her fellow actor's gathering reputation on and off screen. 'He had,' she recalls, 'enormous discipline – incidentally, he never used to drink during working hours as far as I knew – and great spontaneity. But he was like someone without a shell, no carapace at all. He just *was*. I remember being quite concerned about him. I knew he used to walk all the way from his home in Barnes to the BBC and I'd worry that one day he'd just walk under a bus or taxi.'

As they tried to keep cans of beer away from him, Hopkins says he particularly relished the role of Gunge: 'I had this line "I am a dipsomaniac" and I thought, "What a marvellous word!", not realising I was one myself.' When the programme was transmitted to great acclaim in the States in 1977 as one of a 'Great Performances' season on public television, one critic wrote: 'Theo, whose real name is John, is "nothing more than a marginally animated corpse", bitterly contemptuous of his own self-pity. He is a festering hulk with memories running through his head "like a bleeding film". He is infuriating and disgusting but, in a dazzling performance by Anthony

Hopkins, he is perversely mesmerising. Swilling beer or Scotch, frantically puffing on cigarettes, the battered, humiliated, impotent Theo becomes a creature of almost unbearable humanity in the hands of Mr Hopkins.'

Says Hopkins: 'I found that script years later [and adapted it himself into a play which he also staged and starred in for a couple of weeks in California] after I'd stopped drinking and thought, "Maybe that was it. Maybe a message had got somewhere into my thick brain."'

Within months of *Equus*' triumphant opening at the National in July 1973 plans were already being drawn up to take Peter Shaffer's play to Broadway. That autumn Jenni had a call at Elmbank Gardens from John Dexter asking to know Hopkins' whereabouts. She told him he was in Vienna filming locations for *The Girl from Petrovka*, so Dexter contacted Hopkins and said he wanted to fly out for a meeting. Knowing Alec McCowen did not want to continue playing Dr Dysart in any American run (Dexter would happily have settled for McCowen since 'it was a risky enterprise anyway, knowing Broadway, and would have saved me a lot of time'), Hopkins was, for Dexter, 'the automatic choice'. They met and dined together in Vienna, earlier misdemeanours at the National apparently well and truly forgotten, and Hopkins agreed.

The following September Jenni and Hopkins rented out the house and flew to the States 'thinking,' says Jenni, 'it would be just the nine months in New York then we'd be home again – and that was always presuming the play would go all right on Broadway.' After a week at the Algonquin, Hopkins said to Jenni, 'To hell with this – let's trust to luck and find an apartment.' Through one of the *Equus* producers, Doris Cole Abrahams, they were introduced to an ageing actress who lived in the penthouse of a fairly modern building on East 54th Street, between Park and Lexington, and owned another apartment in the same block. It had been offered first to Peter Firth (the only member of the original London cast who was going to reprise his role in New York) but he had turned it down. The Hopkinses met her and swiftly agreed terms. Jenni recalls: 'It was fully furnished and actually felt rather like being inside a gift box: one bedroom, bathroom, living room and weeny kitchen; silver wallpaper – rather camp, actually – and quite tiny. It was only three floors up and opposite the entrance of a huge office building. What we didn't realise, in the haste of taking it, was that there'd be garbage trucks going endlessly back and forth, so it was a bit noisy.'

Still faintly surprised to have been taken back into the fold so painlessly by Dexter and, by inference, the National, not to mention cheered that he clearly had not completely screwed up his theatrical future, Tony dived enthusiastically into rehearsals. However, before too long some old, familiar demons began to materialise.

'Come on, Miriam [Dexter's quaint nickname for Hopkins], these are the only decent fucking lines that Ruby Shaffer has written in many a decade, so let's have the bloody things right! None of this back-street Richard Burton acting!' he would yell. Hopkins regularly complained to Jenni that Dexter was impossible. Then, one Friday night, about three weeks into rehearsal, Hopkins returned to the apartment in a particular fury after Dexter had gone on at him about not knowing his lines. Having threatened at first to catch the first plane back to England – 'and you know what Dexter can do with the play' – Hopkins calmed down and, says Jenni, 'worked his socks off over the weekend – even more than he normally does, which is saying something.' On the Monday morning, after he had sat up with the Scotch until the stilly watches, he left for rehearsals saying, 'If there's just one word – that's it!' Dexter greeted him with a gentle, 'Hello, dear, how are you?' All sweetness and light. 'Why are you such a bastard?' Hopkins asked. 'Well, dear, it made you learn your lines,' Dexter replied.

Marian Seldes, who was playing the magistrate Hester

Salomon, notes in her perceptive autobiography, *The Bright Lights*, how, after several weeks of rehearsal, 'the temperature changed. Discontent. Looks. Avoidance of looks. Directions given with a cruel edge in Dexter's voice. Nervous laughter from the others. He was joking, wasn't he? They're old friends by now, aren't they? Selfishly I took pride in the knowledge that although Dexter could go after Hopkins, it would not happen to me. I was secure. I knew he had the right actress in the right part. How many days passed before *I* heard that edged voice? When did I change from a graceful, confident magistrate to an incompetent amateur actress? What went wrong? ... I had been warned by Tony that the warmth and brilliance John Dexter was lavishing on the company might change without warning.'

On the day the play was due to open, Dexter ordered a final run-through of the play – but with a slight difference. He asked Hopkins to do each scene using different famous impersonations. Hopkins reeled them off effortlessly: Olivier, Richardson, Burton, Brando, Cagney. Says Seldes: 'It was so funny and brilliant and it broke the nervousness of opening night.' After that first show, Hopkins gave each member of the company a silver key-ring with a horseshoe pendant, inscribed with his initials and theirs.

Equus is one of those rare theatrical experiences the abiding strength of which is its very theatricality, achieved through a perfect symbiosis of script and direction. Out of that initial fusion arose startling performances, brilliant use of light, outstanding design and also, in this particular case, innovative mime.

Shaffer's play (based loosely on a true story) is about the psychiatric investigation of a young man who has, somewhere in southern England, blinded six horses with a metal spike; the case of the stable boy whose misdirected passion has led him to commit the dreadful deed opens the doctor's eyes to the appalling lack of passion in his own staid life. In New York, as in London, the physical production was an arena of wooden benches occupied both by the actors (who step in and out of the arena, in and out of their roles) and by a segment of the audience. The horses are actors wearing cage-like suggestions of equine heads and they move across the stage in slow, jointed rhythms. By any standards, this was yardstick drama. It was not without its critics, of course; Jonathan Miller has publicly condemned the piece as 'malignant'.

Equus opened at the Plymouth Theatre on 24 October 1974. After the performance, and in true theatrical tradition, cast and friends repaired to an upstairs room at Sardi's to try to make merry while waiting for critical reaction in the first editions of the following morning's papers. Muriel and Dick were there with their friends Vivian and Cynthia Jones; Richard Burton's first wife Sybil, an old friend from Port Talbot days, was there too, as were Rachel Roberts, Lauren Bacall and Peter Firth's parents. Much of the initial merriment, to Hopkins' embarrassment (recalls Paula Swift, who was also at the party with David), centred on 'How on earth did they stop Peter's willy from wobbling about?' in his nude scene.

Then the papers arrived. The verdict? In the New York *Post*, Martin Gottfried wrote: 'In London, *Equus* was a trite social drama ... disguised as an artistic work. Last night at the Plymouth ... it was a simply devastating experience.'

Gottfried went on to praise Hopkins' 'staggering inner power' and declared him 'largely responsible for the difference in production effectiveness'. Clive Barnes, in the *New York Times*, referred to *Equus* as a 'very important play'. Miss Roberts needed no second bidding to climb on the table and begin singing Welsh songs. Double tequilas flowed. It was, as they say, a palpable hit.

Despite Gottfried's comments, Dexter believes the productions hardly varied, 'certainly not in the critical details nor in the emotional pattern. Perhaps the New York one was actually better, but I still prefer the London one. Was I ever tempted to make changes for the States? Absolutely not. When you're faced with a play like *Equus*, you simply aim to make it as theatrical as possible and hope that at the end of it everyone will find it impossible to turn it into a film [however, it *was* filmed, a couple of years later, with Richard Burton as Dysart]. In Hopkins' case *Equus* was a quite deliberate introduction to America, to films and all that. It was also the first time he'd ever had to sustain a leading role for a run, which is in itself a problem for an actor. He did it remarkably well; that was where he really learned to take the lead and control the stage.

'In rehearsal, since the play was physically already all worked out all I had to do with Tony was place him, explain it, make sure he was comfortable and then go straight into the text. I sent Peter away for a couple of weeks because after the first few days I knew that Tony was feeling that since Peter knew it already, this was pressuring him to go too fast. I had the understudy – Tom Hulce – on instead and this gave Tony the freedom to make the mistakes and forget lines. And he never got to agonise about it because, as with *A Woman Killed*, there's a firm physical structure to the production to fall back on.

'It was, I think, a comparatively easy time and it was obvious even from the first preview that Broadway had accepted Tony.'

In a buoyant season on Broadway – box-office rose by 25 per cent – *Equus* topped a trio of foreign works in the New York Drama Critics' Circle voting (Athol Fugard's *The Island* and Peter Nichols' *The National Health* were, respectively, two and three). The New York Drama Desk named Hopkins best actor, to which were later added an Outer Critics' Circle award and a special citation from the American Authors and Celebrities' Forum.

During the run, Marian Seldes recalls, 'we were having a benefit and a bus with seventy people was late. They came trooping down the aisles after the play had been on about ten minutes. Tony stopped the play, asked the latecomers to find their seats quickly, suggested that we start with my entrance into the Doctor's office and we began again, to a round of appreciative applause. Another time we had to stop the play because he suddenly became ill [it was phlebitis].

The colour of his face just changed and I thought he was going to faint or fall. I got up from my seat and led him off the stage. The stage manager came on and explained that Tony had been taken ill and that his standby, Alan Mixon, would be ready in about 20 minutes [he was having to race to the theatre]. "Do you want to wait?" he asked. Nobody left. Alan arrived and finished the play.

'We were told Tony would be back with us on a certain Monday and did not expect to see him before that. On a Saturday afternoon as we gathered for coffee between the acts not one of us expected the visitor who seemed to be occupying Tony's usual place. The man sitting there with one leg up on a chair in front of him was Richard Nixon!

'Without my glasses his features looked softer than they did in photographs but it was a sickening likeness. A split second later we were all screaming with laughter as Tony pulled off the lifelike rubber mask, rose to his feet and let us welcome him home.'

Mary Doyle, who was playing the nurse, recalls another of Hopkins' little wheezes: 'As Dr Dysart, he had a clipboard which he carried all the time. Well, he used to write little notes and then flash them at me during the performances; it would completely break me up. Things like, when the boy is going on and on near the end, "I think that boy is crazy!" I'd get into terrible trouble but he never lost it. He was also very generous. When I was going to take over the role of the mother on Christmas Eve he told me that if I wanted to rehearse with him he'd be only too happy.'

Hopkins was contracted until July 1975 and as the hottest new face in town slotted acres of publicity in between six nights (and two matinées) a week of work. Jenni stayed put in New York throughout the duration of the contract, settling into a sort of routine which consisted of getting up late in the morning, working out two or three times a week at a health club, and usually meeting Hopkins after the show.

An occasional break in that pattern came at weekends with new friends they met through Sybil, for which Jenni was particularly grateful: 'These two wonderful past-middle-age gay guys had a rather beautiful house out on, of all places, Staten Island. They used to go out there every weekend and we had almost an open invitation to go there whenever we wanted to. For me it was an absolute lifeline, a complete break. We'd go out on the last ferry on a Saturday night and come back to the city with them in the car on Monday morning.

'They were very good because if they knew we were coming they didn't pile the house up with other guests, as they knew Tony was faintly anti-social. I could happily have gone out there every other weekend but Tony wasn't so keen. He was quite happy to stay put in town, so I suppose we actually ended up only going out there about half a dozen times. Anyway, I loved it.'

Then there was the drinking – never before he went on stage, or at lunchtime or even between a matinée and an evening performance. But after the show Hopkins would go across the road to Charlie's, throwing down white wine spritzers. A fellow member of the cast remarked on one occasion that he seemed to be drinking rather heavily and, as she had had that problem herself, knew what to do about it and would be happy to help if he wanted to talk about it. He brushed the idea aside.

A number of old friends from home popped in to catch up with him during the run, including Simon Ward and then, ironically, some of the cast from *The Misanthrope*, which had transferred to New York. According to Gawn Grainger: 'We decided to meet up in Sardi's. Tony, me, Peter Firth, Nicky Clay. I think John [Dexter] was there too and also Diana Rigg. It was a very merry evening. Tony and I inevitably ended up at my hotel where I had this wonderful great big bottle of vodka, and the two of us got stuck in. The next day, I remember Dexter saying: "If you two meet again during the run of either show – that's it!" '

Hopkins says that when he started *Equus* he had already made the decision, without telling Jenni at that stage, that whatever happened he wanted to stay put in the States and further his career there, preferably in films.

When *Equus* was established in its run, they had applied for Green Cards and Hopkins had new representation, the William Morris Agency. By May of 1975, with his contract due to end in July – though the producers would have been only too happy to extend it – the agency had negotiated two interesting Hollywood offers, to play the George Brent role in a telemovie remake of the 1939 weepie *Dark Victory*, and to portray Bruno Hauptmann in an ambitious TV film of the Lindbergh kidnapping case. And there was also Richard Attenborough's film of *A Bridge Too Far* somewhere on the horizon.

Obviously much in demand, Hopkins might have been expected to feel more secure than at any time in his career to date. However, he comments: 'Any money I made in *Equus* vanished because I was paying British tax. I remember that we set off for Los Angeles with just $1200, our life savings. It was rather like starting all over again.'

Crack two or three ice cubes and place in a cocktail shaker. Add one measure of tequila to two and a half measures of orange juice and shake to mix. Put another couple of cubes into a narrow tumbler and strain the tequila over. Slowly pour in two teaspoons of grenadine and allow to settle. Just before serving, stir once. Out in California, and as his drinking became steadily worse, Hopkins discovered Tequila Sunrise. He was filming *Dark Victory*, with Elizabeth Montgomery and Michele Lee, and, after eating and drinking with people from the film when shooting finished, would regularly not return home until the early hours; often he was unable even to remember *how* he got home.

After *Equus*, Hopkins and Jenni had arrived from New York and were able to move straight into an apartment on Wilshire Boulevard at Westwood, near UCLA, found for them even before they had left the East by their good friends Shel and Arlen Stuart. Within days of arriving, they realised that you simply could not exist in that hotchpotch of sprawling conurbations without a car. Hopkins had no driver's licence, so he borrowed Arlen's old car and took a test which was scarcely worth the paper it was written on. The combination of drinking and driving particularly worried Jenni: 'It was getting very bad. One night, at about four in the morning, he came back not being able to remember how he'd returned or where he'd left the car. It eventually came back to him the next day and he was able to pick up the car.'

Jenni clearly felt she could not, even at that stage, confront Hopkins too forcefully with what was obviously a deteriorating situation. They did not row about it; instead she would try to suggest, gently, that it might be time to cut down.

Aside from the drinking, it was an exciting time for them both. The sun was shining, Hopkins was working, the house in England was rented out and they had, with Hopkins earning $80,000 for *Dark Victory* (his best-ever money to date), more than enough to live on.

One minor cloud was the continuing delay in the issuance of their Green Cards. Application is a sort of Catch-22. You have to stay put in the States until your case comes up for consideration; if you leave the country before that, it can negate all the work that has gone on until then.

By the late autumn of 1975, Jenni felt she needed to get away, in particular to see her family back in England. But how could she go home without blowing the Green Card situation? The solution was an elaborate charade whereby she got her brother to send a telegram saying that their father was not well and asking Jenni to come home. She was then able to take the telegram to Immigration and get a sort of compassionate parole (Hopkins had had suddenly to return to Wales when Muriel, genuinely, became dangerously ill and was rushed to Gwent Hospital). Jenni told Hopkins that she had decided to go home for Christmas. He said he would be fine; there had been invitations from, for instance, Shel and Arlen. He told her that he would probably go away on his own – 'just take off in the car'.

It was just after Christmas when Hopkins phoned

Jenni. He was in Phoenix, Arizona, and he had, he told her, truly frightened the life out of himself because he was unable to remember anything about the journey. Recalls Jenni: 'He then properly realised, and was able to acknowledge, that his drinking was out of control.

'He said that he had made the decision then and there that he wasn't ever going to drink again. "Tomorrow I'm going to drive back to Los Angeles and do something about it. This is it, I'm not going to drink any more, I promise you. It's over. It's finished." I probably thought to myself, "That all sounds jolly nice but I'll believe it when I see it." '

Jenni had only ever known Hopkins as a drinker: 'It wasn't as if he was ever a nine-to-five drinker. There were bouts of it; a week here, three days there. Then he'd be pretty impossible, mainly because you couldn't rely on him; he would have made all these plans about what *he* wanted to do and where *he* wanted to go. He'd be thoughtless about not coming home and not phoning. If you tried to talk about it, he'd only become aggressive. There were no "lost weekends" as such. From my point of view, it was the dreadful uncertainty all the time. He might say, "I'm going out for half an hour" and you'd never know whether it would be just thirty minutes or, more likely, have your own dinner, watch TV, go to bed and just expect him when you see him.'

The Phoenix episode had coincided with another jolting scare for Hopkins. After they had finished shooting *Dark Victory*, Michele Lee threw a party for everyone on the picture. Hopkins drank very heavily at the gathering and had to be taken home, where he blacked out. Michele's agent, the late Ed Bondi, volunteered to chauffeur Hopkins back to the Westwood apartment. On the way he told him he should do something about his drinking and that he was too fine a talent to be jeopardising it with alcohol abuse. He gave Hopkins the telephone number of Alcoholics Anonymous.

Hopkins describes what then happened: 'I phoned up the organisation and they said, "Do you want somebody to come over and see you?" I said, "No, I'll come over and see you", arrogant to the last. I went in to their Westwood office and there was just one person in there, an elderly woman called Dorothy. It was about 11 o'clock on a sunny Monday morning, December 29, 1975. I told her that I'd talked to her a quarter of an hour before. She said, "Do you have a problem with drink?" I said, "Yes, I do, and I don't know what to do." And we sat and talked for a little while and I knew it was over and that a part of my life was about to change. As I got up to go I said, "What do I do?" She said, "Give me your phone number and I'll get somebody to contact you and we'll help you."

'I said, "Thank you", and I knew the next thing she was going to say before she said it. It was like a premonition. I knew she was going to mention the dreaded word "God", and yet I wanted her to say something. I wanted her to mention it; I was yearning for someone to push the door open for me – to be given permission, as it were – because I was too arrogant or rather, too stupid, to make the decision for myself. I was blind and confused. She said, "Why don't you just trust in God?" And it was the most extraordinary experience. I knew my battle was over. I gave her a big embrace and I felt very weepy. I walked out on to the street, on to Westwood Boulevard, that beautiful, sunny morning, and the street lit up even more. I felt as if I was charged with some tremendous energy, as if I could feel every muscle in my body. There was this extraordinarily powerful voice inside my head and it said, "It's all over. Now you can start living, but remember it all because it has been for a purpose."

'And instantly I knew what it was. It was God. So much flooded back from those early school days, like a tremendous revelation. It seemed to last for about five seconds, and after it I knew the battle was over.'

That night Hopkins went to one of the group's regular meetings in a Catholic church in Pacific Palisades. He sat down and listened to various people telling their stories. The people in the room looked to Hopkins like anything but what alcoholics are somehow meant to look like.

Attractive people, for the most part, a mixture of old and young. The time came for the regular ritual, to present a birthday cake to one of the assembly with candles to mark each year of sobriety. The recipient this particular evening was a robust-looking man in his late seventies and his cake marked 40 years of not drinking. It turned out that he had quit drinking at the age of 38 – which just happened to be Hopkins' age at the time.

Sitting elsewhere in the same gathering was a neat, pleasant-looking man, a writer-publicist named Bob Palmer. He was extremely tired because he had just flown back to California from New York after sorting out some family problems. A friend of his came up to him and said that there was a new man in that night: would he come over and say 'Hello'? By an extraordinary coincidence, Bob had met Hopkins briefly the year before when Hopkins was in the States finishing off *The Girl from Petrovka* and doing some dubbing and publicity for *QB VII*, on which Bob had also been working.

Recalls Bob: 'I said, "Hello, Tony," and he looked at me and replied, quite surprised, "What are you doing here?" I said, "Well, I'm here for the same reason you're here" [Bob had been 'dry' for four years at that point]. So he asked where I was sitting and I asked him to come over and sit with me. And we have been close friends since.

'The following day we met for lunch and agreed to meet again in the evening. At that particular time of sobriety you are hanging on a day at a time. After the meeting in the evening I took him back to his apartment and we sat and talked for quite a while as he drank can after can of soft drink. The third night we came back to my house after the meeting – he really didn't feel like being alone at that stage – and Tony started asking me about my background and experiences. I sort of tried to make light of it, told him what a fool I had made of myself. I told him about the sixties, the hippie era, when I just wanted to be one myself and I would wear a sweat-band and carry my son's guitar about, which I couldn't even play. Tony said that I looked such a serious, responsible sort of person and this image of me as a hippie struck him as very funny and he began to laugh.

'My son, Chris, was home at the time and the next day he asked whether "that man was laughing or crying". I told Chris he was laughing, that he was a new person I was working with. Tony had just kept saying how good it was to laugh – a sort of catharsis.'

A few days later, just into the New Year, Jenni returned to Los Angeles, where Hopkins quickly introduced her to Bob and his wife Nancy, a diminutive New Yorker with a dry sense of humour. According to Nancy, she and Jenni 'met and clicked right away. Jenni talked about Tony and how she'd gone back to England because she was really upset about the way he was drinking and to spend Christmas with her parents. I was having to fly out to New York the next day because my parents were very ill but I told her I'd be back in a couple of weeks. And we became close friends, just as Bob and Tony had. The four of us just seemed to click.'

'From then on,' says Jenni, 'everything started to fall into place. We got our Green Cards through, *A Bridge Too Far* was coming up and life seemed absolutely fine.'

Hopkins embraced sobriety with the same kind of energy, enthusiasm and passion he had consumed booze in increasing amounts for fifteen years. Though it was often painful and traumatic – and 'one day at a time', to coin a phrase – there was no backsliding. He had drunk to counter his insecurities and somehow to increase an admittedly spurious 'sense of belonging'. Hopkins has talked about how, in the last months before quitting, the effect of increasing amounts of tequila became hallucinogenic: 'I was really on a sort of prolonged acid trip. I saw things – hallucinated – and I had peculiar quasi-religious experiences. One moment I thought I was John the Baptist and I would actually talk to the sea when I was at Malibu filming and the sea would talk back to me. It was weird. For many artists, actors and musicians, alcohol becomes their rocket-fuel. And it eventually can burn them up. It didn't get me because I suppose I suddenly became frightened of where I was going – down to Hell in a wheel-barrow.'

Temperance can become almost as addictive as drinking. Hopkins devoted, and continues to devote, much time to Alcoholics Anonymous. Ironically he and Jenni became, according to her, 'more social than we'd ever been at any time since I'd known Tony. He was out most nights of the week at meetings and people were always having parties. Coffee and Perrier. They were good fun, surprisingly, considering there was no drink involved. For the first six months or so we didn't have a drink in the house and for quite a while didn't even mix with people who did drink. The relief of Tony not drinking made up for a lot. He took it very seriously and worked extremely hard at it.'

Dark Victory, a not inappropriate title in the light of what had been achieved in Hopkins' private life, received its NBC première on 5 February 1976. This story of a woman with a brain tumour who has a few months of romance with her neurologist was pure schmaltz when first filmed in 1939 and scarcely less treacly when reworked as *Stolen Hours* in 1963. For the new version the story was updated and Bette Davis' thirties social gadfly was trans-muted into a no-nonsense television producer.

Whatever reservations they had about the telemovie, the trade papers were unanimous about Hopkins: 'As the doctor, Hopkins brings extraordinary nuance and depth of feeling to the character. His scene on the beach, in which he weeps alone because he can no longer keep up a brave front, is heartbreaking and makes one realise that the survivor is really the more deeply wounded' (*Hollywood Reporter*). 'Hopkins' warmth and strength carries the picture' (*Variety*).

Three weeks later, Hopkins' second television film since arriving in the States was launched on the same network: an extremely well-made, two-and-a-half-hour account of the kidnapping and murder of Colonel Charles Lindbergh's baby son, followed by the subsequent arrest, trial and execution of a German immigrant, Bruno Hauptmann, for the crime that, as they say, rocked a nation. 'Big, fidgety and bear-baited ... impressive enough to make most of the others look like trees walking,' wrote Nancy Banks-Smith when the marathon was shown in Britain, on BBC2, less than two months after its American screening.

That May, Hopkins won his first Emmy for best actor in a special drama. An old colleague of his, Gordon Jackson, also earned a trophy that night for his work in *Upstairs, Downstairs*, in particular an episode entitled *The Beastly Hun*.

With the work plentiful and cashflow therefore reasonably assured, to say nothing of Green Cards having now been secured, there seemed little point in continuing to pay rent. Hopkins and Jenni had agreed they were 'going to give it a jolly good go in California and there was really nothing to stop us now buying our own place and putting down some roots'.

They did not as yet have enough money to put down a deposit on a property but, says Jenni, 'as the contract for *A Bridge Too Far* was coming up in the fast lane, there wasn't likely to be too much of a problem with that. The idea was that we'd go to Holland and do *A Bridge* while the mechanics of buying a house went through. After the film I could go to England, do all the clearing up there and put our house on the market. We'd be back in California around July time, the house would be ours and we could start moving in properly.' All depended on the right house coming up. Hopkins' business manager, Lee Winkler, put them in touch with a realtor, who suggested a number of likely properties, including 1672 Clearview Drive, off Benedict Canyon Road. They began a swift bout of house-hunting and after viewing probably no more than six decided to plump for Clearview Drive. Having seen it, Hopkins exclaimed, 'That's it!'

6. DRYING OUT

THE purchase of the new house in Clearview Drive was still to be completed when Hopkins flew to Holland to begin his nine-week stint on *A Bridge Too Far* during the long, hot summer of 1976. Richard Attenborough, with whom Hopkins had worked once before in 1971 when he played the cameo role of Lloyd George in *Young Winston*, had first approached Hopkins about his Second World War epic of the Arnhem disaster during the Broadway run of *Equus*.

The reason Attenborough asked him to do the film was, he thinks, not entirely unconnected with the fact that the director was also keen that Hopkins should play Gandhi in a long-cherished, much-awaited but endlessly postponed project that Attenborough had been working on ever since 1962: a sprat to catch a mackerel (Attenborough recalls it differently – that he did not think of Hopkins for Gandhi until after *Bridge*, 'though Joe Levine [the producer] may have said something: that's a possibility').

When Attenborough called him in New York, told him he was going to see the play, and asked if Hopkins would have dinner afterwards with him and Joe Levine because he had something to offer him, Hopkins thought it must be connected with Gandhi and felt apprehensive. In fact, the offer was to play Lt-Col John Frost, in many ways the real hero of Arnhem, in *A Bridge Too Far*. Cornelius Ryan's inspirational book of the same name, minutely detailing the heroism and tragedy of Operation Market Garden, was sent on to him – William Goldman's script had not even been started yet – when Hopkins returned to California. He was very impressed.

The following January, with Hopkins, Dirk Bogarde (General Browning) and Laurence Olivier (Dr Spaader) committed to the film, along with a $25 million budget and, astonishingly, a cinema *opening* date of 15 June 1977, Attenborough and Levine arrived in Los Angeles for the most expensive, and swiftest, talent raid in film history.

Steve McQueen declared himself out, then wanted in – for a salary of $3 million for three weeks' work – but was too late; there was no part left. Michael Caine, Sean Connery, Gene Hackman, Ryan O'Neal and James Caan all joined up, followed by Robert Redford (in the McQueen role), who hesitated only briefly before accepting a hefty $2 million for his star cameo.

With Attenborough's 'private army' – a group of young actors who were to be the backbone of the fighting soldiers – Hopkins endured some square-bashing under the guidance of a regimental sergeant major in order, he believed, to carry some conviction as Frost. He told the director: 'When I march into that town at the head of my chaps, every man – whether you get real soldiers or not – must believe in me.'

Attenborough, who thought that Hopkins had been 'electric' as Lloyd George, cast him in *Bridge* as a direct result of the 'indelible impression' he had made in the earlier film: 'He has that element in his actual persona and that charisma which I thought could suggest people would follow him. Tony was the first person I cast in the film, long before any of the bigger names.'

Attenborough was also perfectly aware that Hopkins had by now quit drinking: 'If he was an inebriate, you could still cast him in, say, *Magic*, because all there is is his dummy and Ann-Margret. If he wasn't fit or knocked off after lunch for three days, you would give him hell and he could then get on with it.

'In *Bridge*, we were going to have 1800 men parachuting in, so there was no way this guy could be pissed. Unless I'd been absolutely certain that he'd licked his problem, I couldn't have cast him for the film, no matter how wonderful he *might* have been.'

Attenborough is also convinced that without the post-drinking confidence Hopkins gained playing in *Bridge*, he could not have achieved the acting heights to which he soared later in *Magic*.

'Without his performance as Johnny Frost, I don't believe he would have reached that degree of confidence required for Corky. I don't know what alcoholism does in terms of its actual impact but it must, in some ways, release elemental forces when you're pissed. Some marvellous drunks I've known have done the most incredible things that they would never contemplate doing when they're sober. Tony first had to deal with that element within his personality in getting rid of the requirement of the bottle which permitted him to do that. He then had to reach out and find that particular freedom without benefit of alcohol. I think the chances of him doing that prior to the confidence he gained in *Bridge* would have made it unlikely.'

Frost was tall, about 6 feet 4 inches, and gangling; physically, Hopkins – at only medium height and solidly built – could hardly have resembled him less. On the day they started filming the march by Frost's platoon from the parachute drop-zone to a house in beleaguered Arnhem (actually nearby Deventer), the old soldier himself (by now a general) was standing on the set.

Frost: 'Their boots are dirty.'

Attenborough: 'But General, they've just marched in.'

Frost: 'I don't give a bugger. I always made them clean their equipment straight away. Discipline, you see. Morale. Had them all shave, too. First thing we did.'

Hopkins, who found it a little disconcerting to have his role model lurking in the vicinity, did however politely listen to whatever advice was on offer. Frost noticed that, under gunfire, Hopkins ran from one house to another. He had never run.

Hopkins retorted: 'Well, *I* bloody well do.'

Frost: 'I never ran. I walked. If you run you can easily fall and then you're dead. So I used to walk and I never carried a rifle because it got in the bloody way. But never run, because that would panic the chaps.'

Hopkins (stunned): 'You just walked?'

Frost: 'Bugger it; if you get hit, you get hit. Usually you were so padded up with the stuff they issued that you'd only be grazed – unless you got it in the head. Then you'd had it anyway.'

Hopkins thoroughly enjoyed his stay in Holland, even though he was acting in isolation from the film's more publicised stars, who drifted in and out of the country for the duration of the six-month schedule. When Connery turned up he suggested dinner with Hopkins, and over the meal asked how it was all going. Fine, Hopkins told him. Connery was relieved because he feared it might be 'a Mickey Mouse outfit' which could interfere with his plans to get home soon to Spain and play golf.

Hopkins' favourite story of the shooting is, he admits, second-hand. Redford arrived on set and was gently instructed by Attenborough to get his hair cut. Redford refused. So the pair went into a caravan for a huddle.

When Attenborough emerged a couple of hours later, some electricians were hovering about and one asked him: 'Well, Dickie, is he going to get his hair cut?'

'No, darling, he won't and it's dreadful,' he replied.

'How much are you paying him for this then?' the electrician asked.

'Two million dollars.'

'Oh yes,' said the technician. 'For that I'd have my balls cut off – well, one of them, anyway!'

Outside America, the film was well received and performed very respectably. Indeed, it is arguably one of the most successful ever of its genre. But, bearing in mind the mighty budget, the film was going to have to do huge business in America to make it a commercial blockbuster.

William Goldman was certain the film would wow the critics; he had enjoyed the experience so much, the pre-opening word-of-mouth was so positive, and the film itself was, he considered, so good that he could not even conceive of anybody 'spoiling our party'.

'But,' as he wrote in his book *Adventures in the Screen Trade*, 'we didn't make it with most of the important American critics. And I was stunned. Not that the critics were wrong. But the main thrust of the negative comments seemed to be amazing. They didn't believe us. The reason that amazed me was that it was one line of attack we never in this world expected – because *nothing* dealing with the spectacularity of the film is invented. All those incredible heroics were true. *Bridge* is at least as authentic as *All the President's Men* [also scripted by Goldman] and everyone took that film as sooth . . . We were too real to be real.'

Those reviews in fact ranged from plain wounding – 'one finds oneself angered and harrowed by a film that can make something like *A Night of a Thousand Stars* at the London Palladium of such an unforgettable military tragedy' (Penelope Gilliatt in *The New Yorker*) and 'a three-hour war bore' (Rona Barrett) – to ecstatic, 'the most humane and intelligent anti-war movie since *Paths of Glory*' and 'artistry, power and sincerity and also something of the pity and terror that belong to classic tragedy' (*Film & Broadcasting Review*, which also noted Hopkins' 'subtle, understated portrayal').

Jack Kroll's review in *Newsweek* was a mixture of generosity, 'well-crafted, honourable', and carefully argued criticism: 'The big-name cast has no time to develop characters in depth. What you get is a kind of moving mural of personalities. The film's sensibility is British and Attenborough is more successful with his British (and German) characters than with the Americans . . . [Edward] Fox (as Horrocks) becomes a modern Henry V urging his men into the breach with a patriotic euphoria that seems heartbreakingly out of date in these cynical times. Such cynicism has forgotten that there is a tragic and even absurd side to heroic conduct – as in the performance of Anthony Hopkins as Colonel Frost, the gentleman soldier who brings his hunting horn and dinner-jacket into battle and holds out at Arnhem until he's smashed by overwhelming odds . . .'

The film was, in the final analysis, too downbeat and, probably, too British (even with the Hollywood Squares-style cameo line-up) at a time when the international film currency was comic-strip and/or intergalactic.

Go west on Sunset and just after the pink-shaded Beverly Hills Hotel, take a half right into Benedict Canyon Road; six minutes' drive along the winding Canyon and you must fork quite suddenly right on to steeply rising Clearview Drive, which snakes ever higher up and over the hills. 1672 Clearview, tucked into the right on about the second long leg of that incline, greets you first with a somewhat daunting message attached to a tree at the entrance to the drive: 'Warning: Armed Patrol.' It is the brashest thing about what is, by Hollywood standards, one of the community's more modest dwellings: a small garden with a cactus, humming birds, a sun deck but no swimming pool.

With some furniture from the apartment in the back of the car, Hopkins was driving up the hill towards the new house. He stopped at the side of the road, got out of the car and looked out over Los Angeles: 'There suddenly came into my mind this image, a flash if you like, of a time – it must have been more than twenty years earlier – when I was standing on a hill overlooking a city. I had had no idea of what Hollywood looked like then; it was just the movies. But now that same image came back. It was exactly as I'd seen it then.'

Hopkins paid a psychiatrist called Gillis $50,000 (Jenni does not recall it being quite so inexpensive) for the house. 'It was very reasonably priced,' said Hopkins. 'It was just before all the prices went up, so we were lucky. Later, it actually quadrupled in value.'

Before returning to the Coast after *A Bridge Too Far*, Jenni had packed up the house in Barnes and sorted out what she wanted shipped out to California. The new house had been just about stripped bare – apart from the odd washing-machine – by the previous owners, so the first things to organise were the basics, such as carpets, curtains, bed, linen and towels.

Sofa, coffee tables and similar items were hired, because naturally the Hopkinses were not keen to start buying until they could see how their own furniture from England fitted in. Their first few months in Clearview Drive were almost like camping out.

Mrs Turtle, whose producer husband Jon bought the house from the Hopkinses when they finally left California in 1984, has very clear memories of what the home was like when they purchased it: 'It was very dark – heavy English, I'd call it. A gold carpet, baby grand piano, heavy wood bookshelves. They had cats too [Winston and Clemmie, a couple of adopted strays], and I could see I was going to have to clean the carpet. For me, it was rather depressing.'

Bob and Nancy Palmer's impression was somewhat different: 'From the outside it was very Californian, but inside it was so cosy. It was very much Jenni's taste – very English, brown and autumny colours, warm-looking. Thickly carpeted, drapes, flowers, lots of bookshelves, piano and a lovely little secretary desk. Jenni's a fantastic housekeeper and so the house was always kept beautifully.'

Hopkins admits that one of his main reasons for staying put in the States was simply that 'I wanted to be famous; I didn't particularly care what the quality of work was like, I just wanted to be famous. I knew the chances of being so were fairly remote, but ever since I'd been a kid I loved the idea of America and wanted to be part of it.'

Now, as he sat in his Cadillac, the lights of Sunset casting shadows of palm trees, surrounded by famous neighbours such as Orson Welles, Glenn Ford, Stefanie Powers and Jack Palance, Hopkins almost had to pinch himself – just to make sure this realisation of a youthful aspiration was not merely a dream.

* * *

'I used to be an agnostic, but I believe in some force of God. I can't believe I'm sitting here. If someone had said ten years ago I'd be on a Hollywood soundstage I would have said, "You belong on a funny farm." Los Angeles has given me a tremendous peace of mind, making me untight instead of striving and worrying. I feel more at home here, like I've been here before. If we accept we have eternity before us it makes our problems small indeed.'

Hopkins was at MGM Studios in Culver City talking to Ray Loynd, entertainment editor of the *Los Angeles Herald Examiner* and issuing one of the sorts of quotes that, however sincere and well-meaning, the publicist himself would have been proud to have manufactured during the making of a film like *Audrey Rose*.

The story goes that Frank De Felitta one day suddenly heard his 6-year-old son, who had never played the piano or studied a note of music, hammering out an inspired hybrid of ragtime and Fats Waller. An 'incarnation leak', it is called. De Felitta was so stunned by the experience that he began studying mysticism, reincarnation and Hindu scriptures – not to mention the case of Bridey Murphy, a real-life housewife who had vividly recalled a past existence under hypnosis. The result was the best-selling novel *Audrey Rose*.

More specifically it is the story, New York-based, of the parents of a well-adjusted 12-year-old daughter, Ivy, who are suddenly confronted by a mysterious stranger with a bizarre tale to tell. He claims that Ivy was born just minutes after his wife and young daughter were killed in a car crash and is a reincarnation of the incinerated offspring, Audrey Rose.

They are naturally sceptical, particularly when Hopkins, as the bereaved father, Elliot Hoover, intones such lines as 'Your daughter is in mortal danger ... My daughter's soul returned too soon.' Scepticism turns to anguish and an uncomprehending sense that what Hoover says might just be true when Ivy starts having fits, myste-riously burning her hands in the process.

The director, Robert Wise, whose Oscar-winning

career had spanned musicals (*The Sound of Music, West Side Story*) and the supernatural (*The Haunting*), recalls that both Hopkins and his co-star Marsha Mason (as Ivy's mother) were 'very much into other-world thinking. Marsha had been to India a time or two and had gotten into the whole Indian spiritual thing there. So when we first had them meet together, before we pinned everything down and actually got started, they surprised each other with their love and knowledge of "the other world".'

Hopkins says of Mason: 'She's a much more fervent seeker of truth than I am or was. I accept anything now and don't search as much as I used to. Then I was very caught up with all that stuff, such as the manifestation and spiritualisation of individual particles of God.'

Owing to the 'nature of the piece, the difficulty and challenge of it', Wise was very anxious to have a rehearsal period, however brief, and United Artists gave him a week on sets already constructed at MGM to resemble the New York apartment where much of the action takes place: 'We rehearsed all the key scenes in the apartment thoroughly,' he reveals, 'so the actors were up on their lines, and we had the cameraman there too and worked with a sketch artist to provide storyboards.'

For a key confrontation – the first meeting, in a restaurant, between the parents and Hoover, in which he outlines the shock scenario – they used Valentino's on Pico, filming on a day when the popular eatery was closed. The exterior of Ivy's school and a zoo scene were both shot in New York while the original car crash (a curiously unconvincing and unatmospheric sequence) was filmed out in New Jersey on a new stretch of freeway that had not yet been opened.

At the court case which forms the climax of the film – Hoover has been brought to trial for kidnapping Ivy – a hypnosis experiment on the child leads to Audrey Rose's soul being freed (hurrah) but Ivy's death (groan).

Wise's best intentions were unable to disguise the fact that the film was somehow old-hat at a time when supernatural dramas were as thick on the ground as the vomit spewed about like pea soup in more graphic screen encounters. Heads were swivelling (*The Exorcist*) or being decapitated (*The Omen*). The mood was either ultimately upbeat (when Goodness triumphed against all odds) or relentlessly grim, thereby paving the way for diabolical sequels. *Audrey Rose* fell between all possible stools.

Looking back, Hopkins reflects: 'Wise was nice and usually well-prepared but they simply didn't know how to end the film. De Felitta was producer as well as writer and he started re-writing it towards the end. Actually he'd had to do some re-writing anyway because there were scenes where I added stuff and he didn't buy that at all. I'm not sure those kinds of movies tend to work anyway. *Don't Look Now* was an exception.'

Sporting, at first, a patently false beard before emerging for the bulk of the film clean-shaven, Hopkins gave his first wholly Hollywood movie a real go – leading Charles Champlin of the *Los Angeles Times* to comment, 'His desperate conviction as he tells his story comes close to overweighing its coincidences and making it credible' – with a conscientiousness that dazzled Wise.

'He digs and delves, thinks and works over his character, investigating all levels and possibilities within it. I've certainly never had an actor who had so many little notes on the left-hand side of his script.'

Hopkins' cerebral quality perhaps tended, if anything, to unbalance the piece slightly. What it certainly did was to make seem extremely superficial the contribution of his male co-star (both Marsha Mason and 12-year-old new-comer Susan Swift, as Ivy, are excellent) John Beck, a tall, pleasant-looking actor with an exaggeratedly square jaw. Beck, whom technicians round the set would chide as coming from the 'Polish School of Acting', was, recalls Hopkins, 'Mr Cool, like a lot of those men, but also had a great sense of humour.'

After *Audrey Rose* and *Victory at Entebbe* (the most star-studded and easily most inept of all the catchpenny attempts to reconstruct the Air France Israeli hostage drama, in which Hopkins, as Prime Minister Rabin, fought a losing battle with a dreadful script and screaming co-stars – Kirk Douglas and Elizabeth Taylor), Hopkins had plenty of time to contemplate his new Californian lifestyle: from the end of 1976 right through to the summer of 1977 he was out of work. He was fit, well and 'dry', but tempting job offers were signally missing.

Towards the end of that eight-month bout of 'resting' – Hopkins was, by now, becoming extremely rest*less* – his agents put in a call to James Doolittle of the Huntingdon Hartford Theatre to tell him that their client was 'very interested' in doing a play. Doolittle was rather intrigued because this approach came from what was primarily a motion-picture agency; usually film actors were wary of doing 'legitimate' work in Los Angeles because it could so easily expose them in a town that lived by film and television. For the little they might get out of it the risk of damaging whatever reputation they enjoyed might not be worth the candle.

Doolittle knew Hopkins' name from the Broadway production of *Equus* (which he had greatly admired) and, although he had not particularly followed his progress since, readily agreed to a meeting. Doolittle had, incidentally, staged Dexter's production the year before at the Hartford with Brian Bedford and Dai Bradley and it had proved one of the theatre's most successful runs ever.

They lunched together and Hopkins revealed that he would like to do his own adaptation of *Hamlet* – shortened text, whittled-down cast-list.

Doolittle was less than enthusiastic, for in his long experience, apart from the occasional, starry British 'import', Shakespeare has always been a difficult 'sell' in Los Angeles (ironically, Nicol Williamson's *Hamlet* had been the only nod in the direction of the Bard in more than twenty years of the Hartford). Doolittle was, however, very impressed with what he perceived as his lunch-guest's dedication to legitimate theatre and his obvious sincerity, so he made a suggestion: why didn't Hopkins re-do *Equus*?

▲ Tony as a 3-year-old with his father on the beach at Aberavon.

▲ As a 15-year-old at Cowbridge Grammar School.

◄ With his mother on holiday in Devon.

▲ As Audrey in the National Theatre's 1967 all-male
As You Like It, with Derek Jacobi as Touchstone.

▲ As Richard the Lionhearted confronting Katharine Hepburn in 1968's *The Lion in Winter*.

▼ As Pierre Bezukhov in a scene from the BBC's *War and Peace*, with Morag Hood as Natasha.

▲ A troubled 1972-73 Old Vic production of *Macbeth*, with Diana Rigg as his Lady.

◄ First wife Petronella Barker soon after the divorce in 1972.

▲ Preparing for execution: an award-winning
performance as Bruno Hauptmann in *The
Lindbergh Kidnapping Case*.

▼ Reunited with his old mentor Sir Laurence
Olivier on the set of *A Bridge Too Far* in 1976.

▲ Discussing a scene with co-star Tom Hulce in the 1977 Los Angeles stage production of *Equus*.

▼ With the dummy Fats in *Magic*.

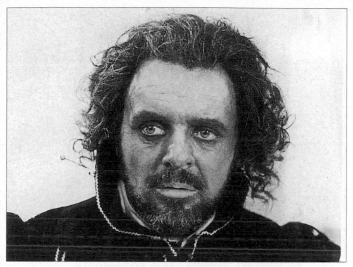

▲ As a 'Mediterranean magnifico' in Jonathan Miller's 1981 production of *Othello* for the BBC.

▼ As Dr Frederick Treves with his mysterious patient in *The Elephant Man*.

▲ In full rant for his Emmy award-winning
performance as Hitler in *The Bunker*.

The idea stunned Hopkins. Was this, he queried, a particularly practical notion? After all, the Hartford had only recently, in theatre timescales, mounted the play, to great acclaim in terms of both box-office and awards. Doolittle explained his reasoning: Brian Bedford's approach to the role had been precise and clinical; Hopkins' was emotional and had a seething potential which Bedford had not tapped. With the sort of playing that he had seen in Hopkins' performance in New York, Doolittle (also sensing that Hopkins was desperate to get working again and would apparently be prepared to participate for the minimum fee) said he would be willing to risk staging the play again.

Hopkins began, slowly, to warm to the idea. He felt that he could actually give the part even more power and emotion than he had previously within the limitations of Dexter's direction. So, suggested Doolittle, why should Hopkins not also *direct* the piece this time round? No one knew the play better than he and the way Hopkins was talking it might possibly even attain a different dimension from the earlier production. Doolittle, in his 30 years in the business (he was, effectively, Mr West Coast Theatre), had never repeated a show, certainly not in the same city and in the same theatre, least of all so soon.

It was a calculated gamble, particularly as Hopkins was committed to the film of *International Velvet* from the second week of September and it was now the back end of July; there were just three weeks to go before Doolittle planned to open *Equus* on 12 August. In that time the show had to be set up, cast, promoted and advertised, not to mention auditioned and rehearsed.

Judith Searle, a busy and successful Los Angeles-based writer and actress, had remembered first seeing, and being impressed by, Hopkins in *The Architect and the Emperor of Assyria* at the Old Vic, noting him again in *War and Peace* and finally being hooked by *Equus* in New York: 'I thought this was a really amazing actor. He was someone whose eyes reached out to the very last row of the audience and took hold of you. The only other actor I could remember this happening with was Olivier when I saw him play Henry II in *Becket* during a US tour in 1961. Tony similarly generated a kind of electricity, a physical energy. I had gone to the play with a girlfriend of mine and afterwards, while we were having coffee, I said, "I would do anything to work with that man . . ." '

Out in California Judith, who had worked a number of times for Doolittle, mentioned *Equus* to him and how she had seen 'one of the great performances'. If, she said, he ever decided to bring Hopkins to the Hartford, 'I want to audition for the part of Hester' (the magistrate). She continues: 'When it turned out that they were indeed going to do the play, James arranged for me to go in and audition for Tony. I must admit I was really quite intimidated at the thought of meeting someone I had so admired from afar. I memorised the whole scene I was to read because I wanted the role so much.

'Tony turned out to be very gracious and kind, put me fully at my ease, and when I'd finished the audition he told me straight away that the part was mine. Naturally I was thrilled.'

As he set about the task of directing for the first time, Hopkins was able to reflect on his eight months as a performer in *Equus*, time that would provide much of the groundwork for his thoughts now as he gathered together an ensemble. The role of Dysart had, he told the journalist Kay Gardella, provided some of those rare moments for an actor: 'The play was going well and I could feel I was on top of it. It's like an elevation out of the body, or another force taking it over. It's an extraordinary experience. You go on stage and voom! You say, "My God, it's like being on a trip." Especially if you prepared well for your job, that's when the inspiration comes. When you feel secure that the foundation is there, that's when you can take off. But you must do it with tremendous passion and love.'

More practically Hopkins had, during that entire run, jotted notes on a clipboard as in the course of the action he interrogated the boy, his father, mother and nurse at the clinic: 'My responses to the other characters were basically the same, but they did vary a bit every time. The writing kept me fresh.' He had retained all the notes and it helped him to refer back to these jottings as he planned his approach. The speed of pulling together this production had all the exhilarating elements, recalls Doolittle, of one of those old Garland-Rooney 'Let's put the show on in the barn' musicals; it also, inevitably, meant that some too-quick casting decisions were just as quickly regretted.

There were no regrets however about the casting of Alan (after an initial brouhaha), for although Hopkins had originally had another young actor in mind for the troubled stable boy, he fell in with Doolittle's suggestion of Tom Hulce, who had first understudied, then played, the part successfully on Broadway.

The nuts and bolts of the staging were essentially the same as in New York (with Joe Daccato, who had been stage manager throughout the Broadway run, on board at the Hartford to supervise the technical cues). It was, according to Searle, 'the same set and the same arrangement whereby the actors sat around in this sort of amphitheatre, rather like medical students looking down on an operation. So Tony followed the general outlines but whereas Dexter had insisted all the actors speak their lines out front and never relate to each other on stage – declaim, as it were – Tony went for much more connection between the actors which, I thought, worked much better. In rehearsal I don't recall his giving any speeches. I just remember his working with each person to sort of find the through-line of the character and to make it work technically. I had the feeling he was always tactful [even though there were some tensions with one particular actress], and would always attempt to tap the other actors' strengths, trying to find what would work best in the interchanges. One never had the feeling he was ever trying to impose some great directorial concept.'

Doolittle had not anticipated a heavy advance for the show, and he was not disappointed. However, neither had he been prepared for the veritable explosion of excitement and interest immediately after the critics had had their say.

'New *Equus* Towers Over Past Version', declaimed the headline in the *San Fernando Valley News*. Writing in the *Los Angeles Times*, Sylvie Drake, after noting that the revival was essentially the same as the one created by Dexter, went on to say, 'Wisely, Hopkins has made no changes; he has merely articulated Dexter's concepts and, if anything, intensified the drama.' In the *Los Angeles Free Press*, Charles Faber said, 'While actor Hopkins builds his performance as the good doctor to demonic intensity, director Hopkins is shrewd enough not to allow him to dominate the play. Even though it stresses Dysart's story as much as Alan's, this interpretation allows the boy, played by Thomas Hulce with a chilling blend of sensitivity and animalistic fierceness, to raise his performance to an overwhelming pitch that would scarcely be permissible without Hopkins' powerful complementary one' (which won him the LA Drama Critics' Award). *Variety* merely added its nod to the overall wave of congratulation.

If there had been some initial hesitation in beating a path to 1615 Vine Street, this quickly evaporated as word-of-mouth spread. The sudden intensification of business was, Doolittle says, 'very remarkable. The first week we played, in total, to a third of the house, the second week to two-thirds and then, finally, to capacity – about the fastest increase we have ever had on a show.'

Judith Searle explained how the theatre itself – now renamed the James A. Doolittle Theatre in honour of the veteran entrepreneur after he sold it in the mid-eighties – played its part in the play's success: 'It's a wonderful theatre to act in because of its size and because it doesn't have all that awful electronic stuff. You don't have to be miked and so there's this contact with the audience you only really get when the natural voice is projected.

'Sitting watching the whole play every night from my place on stage, I was very aware of an energy interchange taking place. There really is a sense in which an actor puts out energy to the audience and connects; it comes back to you and feeds you on stage before going out again. That's why actors aren't tired after a performance; they are high. Tony used to be terrified every single night of going on stage. Frightened to death. More so than any actor I have ever known. But once this energy cycle got established, it was magical. I have never seen it so markedly there with any other production. Every night, after the final curtain, there was absolute stunned silence – then all hell would break loose and people would get to their feet for a standing ovation.'

The pre-publicity for *Equus* also coincided with the announcement of plans for a grander scheme whereby the Hartford would become home to an annual season of locally produced plays 'of high quality'. Doolittle says: 'We had serious discussions about forming a resident company with Tony as artistic director. By that time he had complications on film commitments so I came back to him very quickly asking whether he'd be interested in doing either *Pygmalion* or *A Man for All Seasons*. He thought about them for a while, decided against both but once again suggested *Hamlet*. I'm afraid I still wasn't interested. He was determined to do some Shakespeare and, about eighteen months later, did *The Tempest* at the Music Center here. It wasn't a success and I know he wasn't at all pleased with it. I'm sorry we haven't worked together again since *Equus*. I have often thought that if Tony and I had stayed together perhaps we could have filled the creative void that still plagues the Los Angeles Theatre.'

Hopkins finished his three-week run in *Equus* on 4 September and flew back to Britain to start work on *International Velvet* the following week. Bryan Forbes had offered him a choice of roles – as John Seaton, writer and live-in lover of Aunt Velvet, guardian to aspiring Olympic horsewoman Sarah (Tatum O'Neal), or Captain Johnson, crusty trainer to the British team.

Hopkins reflects: 'The riding instructor was, I thought, the best-written part in the film. I think it was Bryan actually. It was his personality in a way. Anyway, I needed the cash then so I did the film. The trouble was that since *The Lion in Winter* I'd loathed horses and I wouldn't go near them. It was like looking at a double-decker bus. Those show-jumpers are nightmares on four legs. So I was very, very wary of them and I certainly wasn't going to get on one of the things.

'I never worked with Bryan before and we did have a couple of arguments. He seemed to get very uptight about things and would sometimes say to me, "Come on – act!" Actually I think I might have got under his skin a bit because I wasn't very sociable. I didn't, for example, spend much time talking to Tatum because, to be honest, I had nothing in common with her. In between shots, I'd just go back and sit in my trailer reading a book.'

What many critics felt was a misguided, woefully old-fashioned venture from the outset came about when, according to Forbes, 'Richard Shepherd, who was then head of production at MGM, rang to ask if I would direct a remake of the original Enid Bagnold story *National Velvet*. I declined, since to remake a classic is a one-way ticket to oblivion. They then came back to me and asked if I'd be interested in writing an original sequel, and I agreed to this.

'I carefully re-read the Bagnold novel and then attempted to dramatise what possibly could have happened to the original young Velvet. Like Tony, I am not enamoured of horses, and even less so having made the film. I think I can quote John Oram, who was my equestrian technical adviser and one-time manager of the British Olympic team, who once said to me that horses possess minimally less brains than those who ride them. Certainly they were more difficult than prima ballerinas, I found.

'I don't ever recall offering Tony the choice of the two main male leads, but possibly this is true and my memory is at fault. Equally, I don't recall any hesitation on Tony's part in accepting the role and, of course, I was delighted to have him in the film since I'd long been an admirer of his talents and we had never worked together before.

'Far from Tony getting under my skin, I fear that on one occasion I got under his, though it was all a storm in a teacup. This concerned a very difficult sequence in the film, based on a true-life experience, whereby a horse went mad while flying the Atlantic and on the orders of the aircraft captain had to be destroyed in flight. We built a mock-up of the jet in the studio which was large enough to take the Olympic team and four horses.

'The stall housing the condemned horse was built of balsa wood and the bolts securing it were sawn through to weaken them. The whole set was up on rostrums to simulate an aircraft in flight and I, as much as anybody else, was ignorant of what would happen. Naturally we didn't want the horse to suffer in any way and therefore the fearless John Oram actually lay down out of sight in the stall with a compressed air-line.

'When I said "Action", he gave the horse a quick blast of cold air on a very sensitive region and naturally the horse reacted and started to kick.

'Seeing that he met with no resistance, he went on kicking and proceeded to demolish the entire plane. Everybody on the rostrums, except myself and the cameraman, scattered and jumped for their lives. Tony scattered somewhat wider than the rest and, in fact, left the studio vowing never to return and muttering that he was working for a madman.

'Later that evening I persuaded him to return, and, despite the rumour to the contrary, the horse was not damaged in any way and appeared to enjoy the experience. This was the only occasion when Tony and I had any differences of opinion, and I found working with him a complete delight because he has unique qualities as an actor and brought to that particular role something beyond the evidence.'

Forbes' wife Nanette Newman says she only accepted her role as the mature Velvet because of Hopkins: 'They tried to get Elizabeth Taylor [who had played little Velvet as an 11-year-old in the 1944 film]. Then MGM offered it to me and I was wary about doing it because of Bryan writing it; I thought it would look as if I were in it only because of him. I went out to dinner with Tony and Jenni and we discussed it. He just said, "Why do you think all these other things? Just do it and what the hell!" He put it in perspective for me: that you have to dare to do these things.'

If the reviews are to be believed, Hopkins made an extremely wise choice of roles (Christopher Plummer played Seaton) when he plumped for the Captain.

'With the exception of Anthony Hopkins', all the performances are flat' (*Time*); 'in splendid tweedy form' (*Evening News*); 'gives the film a much-needed electric charge' (*Financial Times*); 'brings an authority that is really impressive' (*Sunday Express*); 'takes my silver medal as the British team's trainer, a gruff dictator with a heart of gold' (*Sun*). Agreeing that Hopkins added a 'special touch of class' to the proceedings, Philip French in the *Observer* drolly suggested that in casting him 'the computer clearly turned up both his irascible senior vet in *All Creatures Great and Small* and his psychiatrist in the Broadway production of another horsy piece, *Equus*'.

Richard Attenborough claims that only Olivier – and Olivier at his very best – could have played Corky Withers, the schizo ventriloquist, in *Magic* anywhere near as well as Hopkins. Hopkins, who thought he was being offered the role only as part of some longer-term *Gandhi* deal, initially believed himself quite wrong for the demanding portrayal of a troubled New York entertainer who was not only going to have to be proficient in ventriloquism but also in legerdemain. Surely, he hazarded, what the part really needed was a Dustin Hoffman or Robert De Niro (who were both, along with Jack Nicholson, considered for Corky).

Attenborough, in some ways a curious choice himself to direct this very American, claustrophobic chiller, first persuaded Hopkins then had to persuade Joe Levine, who had bought the rights to William Goldman's novel, which the author was adapting to screenplay. Levine (who had, briefly, wanted Hopkins fired from *A Bridge Too Far* because he thought him no good) was sold on Hopkins, so much so that by the end of shooting on *Magic* Joe, who by then also owned the rights to *Gandhi*, wanted Hopkins to play the Mahatma as well.

'What do you need?' Attenborough asked Hopkins in reference to the Corky Withers role, when filming was due to begin in the States just six weeks later, at the end of January 1978. 'I'd like to work with a magician,' Hopkins told him.

While still occupied with *International Velvet* he was put in touch with a magician called Michael Bailey, who drove from his home in Kingston to meet Hopkins at his temporary flat in Redcliffe Gardens, Earls Court. Bailey handed him a pack and asked if he could play cards. Hopkins said he knew nothing about cards. Could he try to shuffle them? Bailey suggested. Hopkins tried and they fell all over the floor.

Hopkins (desperate): 'I don't know how I'm going to do this.'

Bailey: 'No problem – you're going to be all right. I'll give you several packs of cards and I'm going to teach you a couple of one-hand cuts. They look impossible but you do it slowly. Just carry them around with you and practise all day until you're sick of the sight of them. Keep practising. Your hands will ache, but just have confidence and you'll be able to do it.'

Every Saturday Hopkins would go down to Kingston to be shown more and to provide an update on his own developing skill. He learned to cut a pack of cards with one hand, then fan and spread whole packs. He would practise in his dressing room, restaurants and at home, 'driving everyone barmy'.

Bailey then moved on to coin tricks: the 'French Drop', which Hopkins' father had shown him, and the 'Knuckle Roll', whereby you thread a coin in and out with the fingers of one hand, from little finger to thumb and back – 'you just let your hand go with the gravity'.

Hopkins: 'I sank myself into it, did meditation –

closed my eyes and saw myself doing it. "Positive visu-alisation", they call it. One morning I left Michael's house at 11.30 after doing a session of tricks and got down to the station when suddenly I thought, "By George, I've got it!" '

Basic sleight of hand was one thing, ventriloquism quite another. In Los Angeles Hopkins was introduced to Dennis Alwood, who had a dummy also called Dennis. One day Alwood came up to the house carrying a stiff brown box, rather like a big make-up box. They went into the kitchen and Hopkins asked him if he would like a cup of coffee. As he turned round with the cup, Hopkins noticed Alwood now had the dummy on his knee.

'Hi,' said Hopkins to no one in particular.

'This is Dennis,' came the reply. 'Say "Hi" to him.'

'Hello, Dennis.'

'Hi. Are you shy?' the dummy asked Hopkins. This is really weird, Hopkins thought.

In the film Corky starts out as a shy young magician who is a dismal failure when he attempts his first try-out doing card tricks on an amateur show. There follows a cut to ten years on, when Corky is a roaring success in the clubs executing an extraordinary routine in which he does card tricks on stage while a foul-mouthed dummy called Fats, planted in the audience, shouts abuse at him. Corky's agent and a TV executive are planning a network break-through for the artist which will first necessitate a routine medical.

The prospect of this and the anticipated pressure drives Corky to flee for the hills – or rather, a deserted Catskill resort where he seeks out his childhood sweetheart, played by Ann-Margret, who is now married to a brutish husband (Ed Lauter). Corky is, of course, cracking up; his personality and the more assertive dummy's are becoming scarily intermingled as the scenario turns first to sex then violence.

Fats is Corky's other self. While Corky is ordinary, humble and intense, Fats is sinister, possessive and demanding. Fats instructs Corky to kill, but Corky has to recoil, with ever less effectiveness, against the power of his dummy.

Probably Hopkins' most difficult moment in the film comes in a scene towards the end of the movie in which Corky and Fats argue in a room. Hopkins had to do both voices, use three or four different expressions and somehow convince everyone they were listening to two people, not one. In the end, they shot the scene in short takes and after Attenborough finally called 'Cut', Hopkins was shattered.

Hopkins based Fats' voice on that of the acerbic American comic Don Rickles, with his distinctive high-pitched squeal: 'What I did, I listened to Rickles over and over. I was trying to get a rhythm. I don't know technically what rhythms are – my ear's not tuned that way – but I can *hear* a rhythm. I wanted to get that kind of raspy, tough *schtik*.

'It's funny. Dickie asked me before I started the film whether I'd like to sit down and discuss the role so we could analyse it fully. I said no, let's just do it. I felt that I knew what I had to do.' Hopkins also claims that Corky was a personified version of an alienation and insecurity he felt when he was younger: 'Corky is destroyed by his own inadequacies to cope with other people. He's too egotistical to talk to anyone. He's such a perfectionist that he mistakenly believes he's unique, just as I did in my youth until one day I realised that I was just emotionally growing up. So I do identify with Corky.'

He also became quite attached to the 16-pound dummy whose facial dimensions were exactly his own: 'I endowed him with human characteristics and even started thinking of him as a human. But I'm told that this happens to all ventriloquists. In fact, I'm told that Edgar Bergen used to demand a separate hotel for his dummy, Charlie McCarthy.'

According to Attenborough, Hopkins had Fats sleep with him at night, and the dummy was treated with particular respect on the set. On one occasion, Fats shouted 'Cut!' when Hopkins had fluffed a scene. 'We all laughed,' Attenborough said, 'thought it was terribly witty on Tony's part. But Tony was totally unaware he'd done it.'

Early on during shooting Hopkins had some qualms about his American accent.

'I was so un-American, so un-New York, that it was daunting. I'll never forget the first day I had to speak in the accent. I had a dialogue coach, Patrick Watkins from Brooklyn, and he had been very, very helpful. I asked him how I was doing and he said fine, great. I thought it sounded awful.

'There was a scene when I'm going around my old childhood haunts. I had to speak but I could barely get the words out. So I decided I must have a proper go. Nobody laughed, fell over or spat their coffee out so I suppose it must have been OK.'

Attenborough decided to try to give Hopkins as much freedom as he could within the complicated shooting process: 'During some of the bravura moments in *Magic* I would say to the camera operator: "He may not make it" [referring to planned movements], or to the focus puller, "He may miss his mark or go on to a different position." Tony would take off, as it were, and there are few actors – Olivier was one, Kim Stanley another – with the courage to do that. Now it can be a bugger in a rather sombre scene because very often a split focus can be wrecked if you haven't got Tony where he was, the result being the person you're splitting with is in a mess. But if you've got the dummy and it's just him holding the dummy then you're in reasonably good nick.

'With *Magic*, the whole decision to shoot or not to shoot, to rehearse or not to rehearse, could be at Tony's behest. Often he'd just mark a move that I wanted to do, wouldn't even play it, and we would shoot first time. It's very rare that you can do that.'

Their only major difference of opinion arose over a nude bed scene Hopkins had to share with Ann-Margret soon after their belated reunion.

'For some reason,' said Attenborough, 'he was

suddenly terribly embarrassed about the whole idea and behaved in the most extra-ordinary way. I was absolutely bowled over as he walked off the set and we had to stop filming. At this point of his career he'd achieved a freedom which now permitted him in his acting to arrive at a point without reservation of any kind.

'Lying stark naked in bed with Ann-Margret, he may have felt that this lack of reservation could have landed him in something of an embarrassment. Anyway I eventually managed to persuade him back.'

Hopkins' version is rather different. He says he was perfectly happy to do the scene but that Ann-Margret was hesitant: 'Dickie said to me, "Can you relax a bit more?" I told him that I was but that she didn't want to do the scene. I said to her: "Come on, we've been paid a lot of money, let's do it." And then when it didn't seem to be working – she was very stiff and I think she was having a bad time then – I said, "Fuck it" and walked off.'

The steamy scene eventually went ahead with Hopkins under the sheets – but, allegedly, keeping his trousers on.

There was, incidentally, to be a bizarre sequel to this screen encounter. An American magazine called *High Society Celebrity Skin* published a photograph, taken from a still of the film, which showed the couple grappling and, to Ann-Margret's great dismay, one of her breasts clearly visible. The actress claimed that the magazine had violated her privacy. Under the headline 'Beauty Loses Saucy Snaps Battle' one newspaper reported that a New York judge found against Ann-Margret because it had been her decision to appear unclothed in the widely distributed film. She was, said Judge Gerard Goettel, 'a woman who has occupied the fantasies of many film fans over the years and who chose to perform unclad'.

For the pre-opening hoop-la Attenborough, Hopkins *and* Fats did a global publicity jaunt from Toronto to Tokyo, via London and Dallas, telling anyone who was interested about everything from what they had eaten for breakfast that morning to their individual lifestyles.

'He [Hopkins] looks out of place here in Dallas,' proclaimed the *Weekend Journal*, 'in his very-British tweed jacket, Marks and Spencer's Shetland sweater and unfashionably correct haircut. But he has now moved to Los Angeles and describes himself as having gone completely California. He drives a Cadillac Seville, stays at good hotels and drinks coffee instead of tea ...'

There appeared to be a mutual admiration society between actor and director. The 'most compassionate director I've ever worked with', said Hopkins of Attenborough. 'If he isn't nominated for best actor this year, I think I'll be even more disappointed than him. He deserves to win hands down,' enthused Attenborough of Hopkins.

Far from winning anything, when the Academy Award nominations were announced Hopkins was absent even from the shortlist, which included Jon Voight (the eventual winner, for *Coming Home*), Gary Busey (*The Buddy Holly Story*), Warren Beatty (*Heaven Can Wait*), Robert De Niro (*The Deer Hunter*) and, irony of ironies, Hopkins' old mentor Olivier, in one of his least interesting roles, in *The Boys from Brazil*. A Golden Globe nomination from the Hollywood Foreign Press Association was scant compensation for a performance which, like the film itself, divided the critics.

The reviews were, for the most part, predicated on a wrongful assumption that the film was merely a straight lift from *Dead of Night*, a classic Ealing portmanteau comedy-chiller of 1945, the most memorable segment of which featured Michael Redgrave as a ventriloquist becoming possessed by his dummy. The critics might just as well have summoned comparisons with *The Great Gabbo* (1929) or *The Devil Doll* (1963), further variations on the same theme. The premise was undeniably old-hat; but somehow to tinker with Ealing was regarded by some as tantamount to sacrilege. Anyone who has any doubts about the chilling possibilities of the subject should harken to the words of Edgar Bergen's widow who, after the ventriloquist's death, allegedly said to their daughter Candice: 'You know, your father and Charlie were the *same* person.'

While Ann-Margret enjoyed perhaps her best-ever reviews (again, all to no avail as far as awards were concerned), reaction to Hopkins was altogether more mixed. Pauline Kael considered him 'bewilderingly miscast', while Philip French wrote: 'Anthony Hopkins, a fine actor in danger of becoming an irritatingly mannered one, is crazy too soon and too obviously.' French also went on to scoff: 'In a recent Twitch report on British screen acting, he came out just behind Dirk Bogarde for quantity and marginally ahead for quality.'

Felix Barker (*Evening News*), Alexander Walker (*Evening Standard*) and Richard Barkley (*Sunday Express*) were unconditionally enthusiastic but there was almost an apologetic note in Margaret Hinxman's review: 'He gives a sweaty, anxious performance I'd never have believed he was able to manage' (*Daily Mail*).

Hopkins' performance in *Magic*, benefiting from atmospheric photography by Victor Kemper and a haunting score by Jerry Goldsmith, remains one of his best ever, certainly up there with his performances as Frank Doel in *84 Charing Cross Road*, Dr Lecter in *The Silence of the Lambs* and Stevens in *The Remains of the Day*. It is subtle without being too cerebral, moody without being mannered, mercurial without resorting to obvious fireworks, and almost unbearably poignant while avoiding bathos. The scene where Burgess Meredith, as his agent, challenges Corky to be himself for five minutes, without resorting to protection from within the dummy's persona, is a chilling classic. Corky cannot make it and Meredith knows it, but the suspense is almost unbearable.

The film, made for $3 million (peanuts even by the standards of the late seventies, and about equivalent to a week's work on Hopkins-Levine-Attenborough's previous collaboration, *A Bridge Too Far*), was a modest commercial success. Moreover, it truly convinced the director he had found his ideal Gandhi.

Attenborough publicly announced his casting coup

even before *Magic* was released. 'The long quest,' revealed the *Daily Mail* (under the inspired headline 'A Pound or Two Too Far'), to 'find an actor for the title role of *Gandhi* is over – and, astonishingly, a Welshman has the part ... "With careful make-up and by losing a little weight, he would be superb as Gandhi," said Sir Dickie.'

Looking back now, Attenborough admits: 'You wouldn't cast Tony in a million years as Gandhi. And yet in *Magic* he ventured in a direction, produced such moments and convinced not only himself but us that he could achieve almost anything, that I got excited about the possibility of his playing the role.

'The mistake was, of course, that there are funda-mental indigenous attributes within an oriental which a Caucasian European can't really manage. Whereas we were prepared, say twenty or thirty years ago, to watch Burt Lancaster browned up, we're not any more.'

Such thoughts did not impinge when, the following spring, Attenborough flew out to Los Angeles to talk to Hopkins further about his tackling the role. Hopkins was playing Prospero at the Mark Taper Forum.

Attenborough describes what happened: 'I went up to the house and remember very well the three of us [Attenborough, Hopkins and Jenni] walking around while I tried to convince him he could do it. Then he took himself to a health farm and went on a very strict diet, but when he came back he'd decided he simply couldn't do it. I was quite bowled over actually because I was fully intending to go through all the possible make-up tests that might have evolved. At the end of the day Tony *and* John Hurt, another actor I'd just seen for Gandhi, were both absolutely right. They just wouldn't have been convincing.'

Dick Hopkins had remarked to Hopkins, on hearing that his son was up for the title role in *Gandhi*: 'It's going to be a comedy, is it then?'

Hopkins admits that 'What he [Attenborough] got to, for me even to consider it, was my ego. Had I done it, it would have been an act of terrible vanity and really only proving I could cosmetically change myself, lose ten stone and end up in a coffin. For I would have died, I know that! I looked at myself in a mirror and thought: He's crazy! I can't do Gandhi. I can't go through a year of macrobiotic junk. I enjoy my food too much and I'm impossible to live with without it. I mean, I'd die. Attenborough was wonderful; he understood. I wished him luck and hoped it would work out eventually for him.'

7. MONSTERS

After finishing *Magic*, Hopkins took Jenni off for a holiday to the Grand Canyon. When they returned he found a cable from England waiting for him. It was from James Cellan Jones, head of plays at the BBC, asking if he would like to play Edmund Kean in Sartre's barnstorming, romantic comedy about the flamboyant nineteenth-century actor. The cable suggested that Hopkins was the only actor 'capable' of playing the role.

'When they appeal to your vanity, it's almost irresistible,' says Hopkins. 'But I knew the play. It's a damned good role and requires almost a virtuoso performance. I rang up Jones and said that if it were still open, I'd do it.'

Cellan Jones had first broached the idea when they met briefly while he was working in the States: 'I remember that Tony was high on abstinence at the time. He was brimming with energy and looked terrifically fit and well. We met and chatted and I told him about *Kean*. I said that I'd wanted to do it for ten years and since I had it in my contract that I could also direct two plays a year, I was determined to do the Sartre. I eventually got on to his agent and was told the usual thing that "He doesn't want to mess with a little TV thing." So I contacted Tony direct who said I shouldn't take any notice of agents.'

Kean marked Hopkins' return to Britain after three years away and was his first work at the BBC for almost five years. For a multiplicity of reasons, art and life coincided with a terrible vengeance during the making of the drama. It was, to put it mildly, a volatile, often harried production; Hopkins stormed out at least twice.

All sorts of theories can be put forward for why that

short production period should have been so explosive and, for some, so unpleasant.

One of the more intriguing ones is that it poignantly provoked the sort of memories that had earlier contributed to his hasty exit from the establishment – a revival of the dreaded 'Gang' mentality.

The actor–writer Julian Fellowes, who first met Hopkins on *Kean* and subsequently became a close friend, explains: 'I don't necessarily offer this as an absolute truth, but on it is predicated both our friendship and quite a lot of Tony's activity in the business. In English show-business for the past two decades there has evolved a kind of self-regarding, self-promoting clique at the centre. "Clique" is perhaps an inappropriate word: it's as much an attitude as a selection of personalities. Tony and I have always called this particular band The Gang, and the domination of the Gang has created a kind of out-of-date centre in the English business; it's actually very sixties. A lot of it emanates from the Royal Court of that period and, subsequently, the National.

'As you know, Tony hadn't got on too well at school. When he eventually arrived in London to go to RADA and then on into the theatre, he was, I suspect, quite inarticulate and inclined to sort of . . . burst with talent. This didn't mean, as some directors presumed, that he wasn't intelligent. They started to patronise him and some want to patronise him still. That's why in the early years you often come across these incidents of great rage and explosion, of screaming and breaking things. He was frustrated that they couldn't recognise that he wasn't a fool.

'This became further complicated when they had to start listening to his opinion instead of simply admiring his talented biceps. And that then also contrived to build up tremendous inner rages. One of the results of his inarticulacy in early life was that if he disagreed with someone he needed to work himself up into a rage before he could do anything. He was so browbeaten intellectually that he needed to stir himself up – needed to get himself up to about

70 mph before he could go into the attack; so one would watch directors who thought everything was going well then – boom! Vesuvius! A combination of the Gang and the patronising had helped him decide to leave England.

'At the time of *Kean* Tony and Jenni had taken a flat in Earl's Court, and since I was living near there too I'd often give him a lift home after rehearsals. I remember saying to him not long after we first met, "You're living in America now, aren't you?" He said he was and I then said that he was so "wise to have got out of all this nonsense" and was he having a marvellous time? This surprised Tony, because he automatically assumed that anyone he'd be working with was bound to suggest he'd sold out and that he should really be doing *'Tis Pity She's a Tart* for threepence at Wolverhampton. This is the moment we became friends.

'*Kean* was his first job back for a while and he was feeling tremendously threatened and very defensive about whether or not the play would be successful. This was a very Gangy show; you know, "How's Glenda, darling?" much of the time. That, and Cellan Jones going on about "we, the Welsh boyos, two lads from the Valleys", absolutely triggered all his phobias.'

Hopkins blames many of the production problems on what he perceived as the director's lack of preparation, in particular with the blocking (the actors' specific moves in the various scenes): 'Within a few days I could see it was chaos. You can't work if you don't know where you're going. I had gone into the production *not* wanting to be regarded as the bloody nuisance I'd been thought of in the past; I was going to be Mr Nice Guy. So I made a terrible misjudgement and delayed in making any move. It was a big play and a big part and I should have gone to Jim straight away with my worries, but instead I let it all build up for about a week. When we did have our confrontation there wasn't any shouting or screaming. I basically told him that if things weren't sorted out I refused to carry the can for him or the BBC. James felt let down and expressed his disappointment, so I walked.'

Cellan admits it was 'a very turbulent time. It seemed to start off well and then went funny. I remember that Diana Rigg was rehearsing in the next-door studio and, with perhaps memories still of *Macbeth*, that didn't exactly calm Tony. I like to think that I have a strong affinity with actors but in this case I was shaken and hurt. I had, I felt, done a tremendous amount of preparation – possibly too much – and in fact it may have been too blocked. Perhaps I didn't handle him right. There's also a lot in the thought that Tony had become almost like Kean himself; I know that had happened a bit to Alan Badel when he played the role.'

Some indication of this comes in an interview with Rosalie Horner of the *Daily Express*, who wrote that the making of *Kean* had 'produced more traumas and dramas than any other production for Tony. He has stormed and shrieked, been weak with despair at himself, yet he gives a performance which indicates all his spent emotion.'

During taping at the Regency Theatre Royal in Bury St Edmunds, Hopkins told her: 'Acting drives me mad. It drives me up the wall. I just feel crazy with this part. It's such bloody hard work. It's the most emotionally demanding thing I've done. The difficulty I had to learn the lines – I wonder sometimes if the end justifies the agony. I don't know how some actors do it. I enjoy acting – the process of rehearsing and finding out if the part suits – but I wish there was a more peaceful way of doing it. Kean can't see the difference between reality and what is on stage. I suppose I am like him in parts. He is one of the greatest actors of his day, but a chronic drunk who died at 43 a shattered man. I usually get to play this kind of crazy wild character. But it is immensely disturbing playing it.'

Later he told Cecil Smith of the *Los Angeles Times* about a curious case of BBC austerity: 'On the final night of recording, people kept watching the clock. I was told that if we didn't finish by ten, they'd pull the plug on us. There was one scene we had to do over and time was running out. People were in an absolute panic. You could feel it. We did the scene and we finished just two minutes before ten. Then I was told that if we hadn't finished by that time, we'd have had to wait three months to get the studio again to do the scene – productions were that backed up.'

So where did the fault, if any, really lie?

'At the time,' recalls Fellowes, 'I was entirely on Tony's side, but remember I had just met him and Tony's a sort of magic man – very charismatic and exciting – so I was very much caught in the romance of it all and wasn't inclined to see Jimmy's [Cellan Jones'] side at all. Looking back, it was much more six of one and half a dozen of the other.

'Jimmy is fairly instinctive and hadn't done much preparation – I know he denies that, but it certainly seemed that way. That didn't mean, though, he hadn't thought about it and didn't mean he didn't know what he wanted it to be. At some point Tony decided Jimmy didn't know what he was doing. Then we're all like Tinkerbell: if people don't believe in us, we don't exist. The more that Tony thought he was with what he regarded as this ludicrously inefficient director, the more the whole thing became chaotic.

'Even the producer David Jones [who would later direct Hopkins in 84 Charing Cross Road], a more methodical man, was flailing around at one point. Was he going to take over? We were all in huddles, and for me it was really quite a thrill after months of boredom in the West End in a long stage run. I thought I'd suddenly turned up in a Lana Turner movie.

'This will give you some idea of how the office had got it all wrong. When Tony stormed off in a great rage and had gone back to the flat, I said to someone, "Well, I'm going back that way. Do you want me to go round and see if he's all right?" They said, "No, no, Robert [Stephens] and Sara [Kestelman] are going round," the implication being that I was playing a small part and of course they were playing the leading parts and therefore would somehow be much better for the job. Of course, they were the very worst people to be sent round because they were absolutely the two Gang members of the cast. Not that he didn't like them – he was particularly fond of Bob – but it was just that they were thinking to comfort him with manifestations of Gang thinking; what they didn't understand was that Gang thinking makes him sick.

'So he'd walked into the middle of that with an instinctive rather than methodical director. I think that, in a sense, Jimmy was suggesting to Tony that somehow he should "do his magic" as if he were something to be let out of a stable to do its tricks. Now there are a hundred ways to skin a cat and there is no particular reason why, if everyone had entered into that spirit at rehearsal, it might not have had as many results as if we'd all been given dance steps. It was, maybe, a question of timing – in this case, bad timing on Jimmy's part.'

For all the problems, Cellan Jones professes himself happy with much of the finished result (of which Stanley Reynolds, in *The Times*, wrote of Hopkins' 'virtuoso performance. Looking thinner, younger and exceptionally fit, he flew away with the part. At times it seemed like a one-man show.'): 'The climax of the play is Kean playing Othello, which he does wearing black tights, blacked-up face and eyes, and with blubbery red lips. That was the style of the time. The way Tony did that was absolutely electrifying and a lot of his performance is wonderful. It also stimulated Robert Stephens [who was playing the Prince Regent] into regaining much of his former authority. I remember seeing Tony play Othello later in Jonathan Miller's television version and thinking it was a disaster. I blame Miller for that. And I thought at the time, "If only Tony had had the same electricity he generated in doing that bit in *Kean*." In spite of everything, I admire him enormously. I've had real problems with just three actors in my time; Tony is the only one I would want to work with again.'

Just ten days before shooting was due to start on *The Elephant Man*, its young American director, David Lynch, excitedly revealed his intricate blueprint for John

Merrick's horrific make-up. His colleagues were indeed horrified – but not quite in the way Lynch had anticipated. Recalls Terry Clegg, who was the film's production supervisor: 'It wouldn't even have passed muster at a children's concert. It was rather like someone wearing a pair of long-johns covered in rubber latex – an utter disaster.'

Consequently the design was handed over to the expert Christopher Tucker, who went away to re-think and re-design a head that must be so horrifying as to explain why the unfortunate Merrick should have been star exhibit in a foul Victorian freak show before becoming the darling of a curious, prurient society. While Tucker tinkered with his prosthetics, filming had to forge ahead, with this unforeseen hitch already responsible for a 25 per cent increase in production costs.

Whether the expensive (and somewhat humiliating) setback was responsible or whether Lynch – making his first major film following only the low-budget cult success of his experimental *Eraserhead* – was just naturally reticent, Hopkins found the director a tricky proposition from the day he arrived on the set. Hopkins was to play surgeon Frederick Treves (from whose poignant reminiscences the screenplay is partly derived), who discovered Merrick in sideshow squalor and helped, temporarily, to rehabilitate him. Shooting was to begin in the London Docks area.

Hopkins had taken it upon himself to grow a beard for the role, which he felt would be in keeping with his Victorian character. 'I want the beard off' Lynch told him at their first encounter on a wet Monday morning. Hopkins refused. Lynch asked him again, but Hopkins was adamant.

The pressure on Lynch increased as the scenes in which John Hurt (as Merrick) could be filmed with a sack over his head began to run out (there was still no usable mask); accordingly, Hopkins' relationship with the director became ever more tense.

Hopkins was worried: 'He [Lynch] wore this big

brown trilby, a long black cloak and tennis shoes and I had the feeling most of his performance as director was going into his hat. I said to the producer, Jonathan Sanger, why the hell doesn't he get rid of the hat and communicate with us instead of just standing there and playing director? I remember Mel Brooks [whose company Brooksfilms was behind the film] saying, "The guy's a genius. Even *I* don't know what he's talking about." The fact was, he was a perfectly pleasant fellow and I was the one who was unpleasant because I became increasingly irritated with what I felt was his rather arrogant lack of communication. We were somehow supposed to understand his thoughts.'

In the absence of what he perceived as any suitable guidance, Hopkins devised his own method of tackling the role: 'I thought, "This guy's not going to help me in any way and he keeps poking the viewfinder up my nose, so I'm going to play it very muted as if the camera wasn't there at all." As a result the film became a rather fascinating experience for me, like a very private trip.'

Armed with this confidence, Hopkins came to the scene where he first lays eyes on Merrick. John Hurt was absent because the mask was still not ready and so they used a stand-in. Lynch wanted this time to talk through the scene but Hopkins declared firmly, 'Just let me do it. I see the Elephant Man and I'm horrified. Let me use my imagination.' They did the crucial scene in one take.

Hopkins' approach to the role, and to film acting in general (bearing in mind perhaps his armed neutrality with Lynch), can be gauged from an intriguing interview he gave during filming to Tony Crawley of *Films Illustrated*: 'I've found out how to be as simple – sparing – as possible, so that one barely acts at all. Just speak the lines, play the situation as honestly as one can, and get the balance right. There is not much more you can do with Treves, which, to say the least, is a loaded subject where one could go overboard, tread perilously near to sentiment. I'm playing a doctor who picks up this grotesque freak, puts him in hospital and looks after him. That's simply it. That amounts to the plot. Oh, he also overcomes a little opposition from the hospital authorities.

'The temptation would be, and I've been keeping an eye on it myself, to play a caring person all the way through the film. I could do that – the loving doctor, the hero. But he has put this man on display again, and for his own egotism, until he realises what he is doing. I mustn't be soft-eyed and warm-acting all the time. Not necessarily. Life's not like that. I think there are moments when he actually hates Merrick. Treves is a victim, too.

'I remember, when we were doing *War and Peace*, the scene where the old peasant Platon Karatayev is dying on the retreat from Moscow. I went back to Tolstoy and he described Pierre's disgust and anger because the old man is dying. Pierre is pushing the cart and hears a dog's howl echoing out – and Platon is dead.

'When you read it, you want to cry. But Tolstoy is brilliant. He wrote how all Pierre could think of was how many miles to the next town and he wished the dog would stop howling. And I think – I hope – there may be moments like that in *The Elephant Man* where Treves would think "Urgh! . . ."'

Crawley then suggested, 'Actor, direct thyself?'

Hopkins agreed: 'Look, if a man suddenly comes in here and shoots up the entire bar with a machine-gun and kills the barman, I don't have to act *horror*. Put that on film and I don't have to do anything. The audience does the rest. Take a scene we've been doing today, just a short scene – well, it's a dramatic turning point. They've found Merrick [he has been spirited away from the hospital back to the freak show], a problem is resolved . . . There's a big reaction shot of my face, while I'm sitting at a desk. Somebody comes in. "It's all right. They've found him." Blank face. I don't have to do any more than that . . . But the director always wants you to show it. To *act* the scene. "Gee, I dunno, Tony . . . Can you give me a little more?"

No! There's nothing to show. Once you show them more, what you show them, in fact, is bad acting.'

Cinematographer Freddie Francis – who happily worked again with Lynch, most recently on *The Straight Story* – stoutly defended the then 32-year-old who was clearly operating in an atmosphere of some animosity: 'Tony seemed to be rather bad-tempered much of the time and a lot of the unit were muttering endlessly about "this young American who doesn't know what he's doing". When it was all over, I remember David suddenly turning up on my doorstep one night and he was distraught. He had a letter from the front office saying they had seen a "rough cut" and didn't think much of it. "Should I re-edit it?" he asked me. "It's a wonderful picture," I assured him. So he ignored them.'

Executive producer Mel Brooks, who also championed Lynch through thick and thin, separately offered a more colourful response when confronted over the telephone by the Paramount bosses with: 'Gee, it's a great film, but we think you should get rid of the elephant at the beginning and the mother at the end.' Brooks apparently replied, furiously: 'We are involved in a business venture. We screened the film for you to bring you up to date as to the status of that venture. Do not misconstrue this as our soliciting the input of raging primitives,' before slamming down the phone on the studio executives.

Surrounded by some of Britain's finest technicians – including, along with Francis, the editor Anne Coates and the designer Stuart Craig – Lynch, communicative or not (but unsure of himself, and certainly inexperienced, according to Terry Clegg), still managed to oversee what resulted in a remarkable, haunting movie perfectly complemented by monochrome. 'If there's a wrong note in this unique movie – in performance, production design, cinematography or anywhere else – I must have missed it,' wrote Paul Taylor in *Time Out*.

Hopkins – who admires the film immensely but resolutely recalls Lynch as 'obtuse, obscure and very puzzling' – had his thoughts during filming underscored when Margaret Hinxman in the *Daily Mail*, praising the piece as 'not a peepshow for horror addicts, but as a moving and uplifting tribute to the tenacity of the human spirit,' also noted: 'Treves (played with troubled restraint by Anthony Hopkins) is forced to wonder whether he hasn't unwittingly imposed another kind of sideshow bondage, albeit more comfortable, on Merrick.' Also on his wavelength was Pauline Kael: 'John Hurt and Anthony Hopkins – both specialists in masochism – might have leaked so much emotion that the film would slip its sprocket. But Hopkins comes through with an unexpectedly crisp, highly varied performance – the kind you respect an actor for.'

Freddie Francis said that even twenty years after making the film he is still moved by that 'one take' scene when Hopkins first sees Merrick at a private viewing: 'It was a long, long tracking shot with the camera moving in very, very slowly on Tony's face. At the end of it, a tear drops from his eye. It couldn't have been controlled, it must have been real. It's one of the most wonderful moments I have ever seen in cinema.'

The Elephant Man received no less than eight Hollywood Oscar nominations but, in the year of *Ordinary People, Raging Bull* and *The Coalminer's Daughter*, not a single statuette. As some sort of compensation there were three awards from the British Film Academy, for best film, design and, for emoting beneath Chris Tucker's heavyweight make-up (38 inches in diameter, it took five hours to fit), John Hurt. Hopkins was ignored on both sides of the Atlantic.

All anyone remembers about *A Change of Seasons* – if they can remember anything at all about what was after all an eminently forgettable romantic comedy – is Bo Derek frolicking about naked in a hot tub with Hopkins. He plays a menopausal English professor at Harvard having an affair with one of his students (Bo). When he tells his wife about the fling, she (Shirley MacLaine) decides to take a younger lover herself (an amiable furniture-maker, played by Michael Brandon). It all becomes quite absurd when the quartet end up holidaying together in a ski lodge in Vermont. But it was that hot tub scene which clearly taxed journalists' minds, and headline writers' invention, when Hopkins spent the early part of 1980 shooting the film in Vermont and at studios in Hollywood.

The tub was, apparently, the idea of Bo's husband John. The original script contained a steamy bed scene between Bo and Hopkins, because after the success of her previous film, *10*, the producer was anxious that the audience should again get a good look at the shapely young actress. So, explains Hopkins, 'They'd written in the usual heavy-breathing bit where I'd be in bed with her. It wasn't nice at all – this great hunk on top of that lovely girl. John made the alternative suggestion of the tub, which I think was rather charming. Jenni waved me off to work the morning we shot it, saying, "Have fun, but don't get too wrinkled." '

Hot tub or no, the caption to a photograph of Hopkins in the *Los Angeles Times* stating 'Anthony Hopkins ... happy on the set' could hardly have been further from the truth. The problem was not Bo, but Shirley MacLaine.

Filming had got off to a bad start when the original director, Noel Black, was fired because, it seems, no one appeared too happy with the way the processed material was looking. There had, incidentally, been reports of interference on the set by John Derek which prompted the Dereks to call a press conference to deny they had anything to do with Black's exit.

It was now late on a Friday afternoon and Hopkins was in bed with his co-star rehearsing the scene in which she finds out about his infidelity. Black's replacement, Richard Lang, came over to them and said: 'Right, when we're ready, let's go and shoot.' MacLaine said, 'Give me some feedback.'

Lang: 'What do you want to know?'

MacLaine: 'Come over here and tell me what's the scene about.'

Lang: 'We've just been rehearsing it.'

MacLaine: 'Can he [Hopkins] speak faster than he's doing?'

Hopkins (sitting up in bed beside her and trying to smile sweetly): 'You want me to speak faster?'

MacLaine: 'Yeah!'

Hopkins: 'OK, I'll speak faster if you want.'

There was no filming that weekend and Hopkins also had the Monday off. When he came into the studios on the Tuesday, he could sense an 'atmosphere'. The scene they were shooting was where the professor returns home to find his wife *in flagrante* with the younger man.

All Hopkins says, 'The scene didn't call for much. I just come in and say, "What's going on here?" Shirley turned to the director and said, "Is this supposed to be comedy? Is he going to play it like this?" I knew that a bad time was brewing and I was feeling myself becoming so angry that I just walked off the set.'

Lang sought him out and asked: 'Are you OK?'

Hopkins: ' "No, I'm not OK. This cow's getting cross with me. She thinks she can push me around. She thinks I'm just some English faggot." I walked into my dressing room just as a friend was trying to get though to me on the phone. He asked me how everything was going and I told him. He told me to phone a producer friend of mine, Renee Valente, who'd just made a film with Shirley and James Coburn. So I called her – it was about 9.30 in the morning – and said, "Am I going crazy, or is Shirley MacLaine totally impossible?" Renee said, "She's difficult. Just get her off your back, don't lose your temper but tell her you're not going to put up with it." Then she came out with that very American thing, "Tony, the thing about Shirley is she needs a lot of love."

'I said to Renee, "Bullshit. *I* need a lot of love. Don't tell me she's insecure; I'm terrified." I sat down and wrote out a couple of lines of a speech I was going to make to her. I knew I had such an awful temper I thought it better to learn something. I took a couple of deep breaths then went to see her . . .'

MacLaine (pre-empting the speech): 'Do you know anything about timing?'

Hopkins: 'No, I don't know anything about timing. I don't care about timing. I just wanted to tell you that I've always respected you as an actress . . .'

MacLaine (with mock-English accent): 'Oh, thank you, sir!'

Hopkins: '. . . but if you think I'm going to be paralysed by my respect for you then you've got another think coming. If you want to get Dick Van Dyke, Jerry Lewis or Jack Lemmon to do that kind of mayhem comedy, then be my guest – I don't give a fuck. Just get off my back, don't mix it with me. If you don't want me, get me fired. I don't give a shit.'

MacLaine threw away her cigarette and said, 'I'm not talking to you.'

Minutes later Hopkins bumped into the director and told him, 'I've just told her to piss off.' Lang replied, 'God!', then 'Thank you – you've saved me a bit of time. I didn't know how to deal with her.' Hopkins said: 'I'm quite willing to go if you want me to. What I don't need is this bitch telling me what to do. It's up to you.'

Hopkins stayed, MacLaine stayed, but they never talked off-camera again. He now bridles at the very mention of the actress: 'I found her the most obnoxious woman I've ever worked with. She's a very experienced, accomplished actress, a rich woman too. I was no competition to her, she wasn't being upstaged by me. She just decided to make life miserable. It was madness.'

According to Bo Derek: 'No one had a good time as far as the filming was concerned. Once a film starts the way it did, it can't really be saved. I think Tony and I got on very well together [Hopkins found her 'sweet and lovely']. He never sat me down and said, "Here are my words of wisdom", but being with him and seeing him fight for what he believed in – and I saw him go through a lot – was very helpful to me. He'd pat me on the back and say, "Go get 'em!" I think they really wanted Tony to be someone else, a sort of Cary Grant. OK, Cary Grant is wonderful. But if you want him you should get him.'

Hopkins' unease seemed to communicate itself to the critics, who delivered some devastating judgements on both the film and his performance.

'The worst performance by a major actor since Richard Burton roared his way through *Bluebeard* ... Hopkins' way of playing an adulterous intellectual is to fiddle with his glasses and to hem and haw and clear his throat, thereby stretching every banal line of dialogue out to twice its normal length' (David Denby).

'Hopkins looks harassed and ill at ease most of the time' (Ian Christie). 'Ironically it is Mr Hopkins who gives the film the lie by taking it too seriously. He peers into the script's cupboard and his horror at finding it bare is undisguisable' (David Castell).

Nigel Andrews, in the *Financial Times*, condemned with faint praise: 'Anthony Hopkins is an odd actor. His head with its mannered bobbings and weavings is so loose on his body that it often seems in danger of falling off, and his voice is all sudden clotted consonants and sibilants, as if he'd had his vowels stolen on the way to the studio. In *Magic* he played a ventriloquist "possessed" by his dummy and the role still seems to be with him in *A Change of Seasons*. Here he plays as if operated by a hand up the vertebrae ... it [the film] echoes to rent-a-bromide dialogue with which only the eccentric Mr Hopkins, head bobbing and consonants colliding, has any winning way at all . . .'

In view of all the tensions that haunted the set of *A Change of Seasons*, there is a delicious irony in the fact that the project's original working title was *Consenting Adults*.

The story goes that while Hopkins was already working on *A Bridge Too Far* Olivier arrived in Holland to start his role in the film. It had been some time since they had seen each other and after Olivier had taken one look at

Hopkins, with his severe hair parting and small moustache, he blurted out: 'My God, dear boy, you look exactly like Hitler.'

A little over four years later, at a French TV-production studio in Joinville outside Paris, Hopkins sat in his dressing room watching intently in the mirror as make-up artist 'Lon' Bentley put the finishing touches to carefully-glued bags under the eyes and a toothbrush moustache. A picture book of Adolf Hitler lay open on Hopkins' lap and round the edges of the mirror were snapshots of Hopkins in Hitler poses – 'my rogues' gallery', he would tell visitors.

Hopkins was starring as the Führer in a CBS telemovie called *The Bunker*, based on a book by James O'Donnell. O'Donnell was an American army officer and foreign correspondent who had visited Hitler's underground hide-out in Berlin in July 1945, was fascinated by the events that had so recently transpired as the Third Reich drew to its claustrophobically horrific close, and so recreated the last 90 days of Hitler and his entourage in a bestselling book.

There were no photos and no written records of that period so O'Donnell, having discovered that a number of the people down in the bunker at the time were still alive, pulled together, through exhaustive research, a unique memoir. He could not, he wrote, 'guarantee the historical truth, but rather a psychological truth' of the events that culminated in mass suicide.

An important adviser to the production was to be one of those survivors, Hitler's armaments minister Albert Speer, who made available photographs from his private scrapbook and showed the film-makers drawings of the bunker made at the time.

The executive producer, David Susskind, had already talked Hopkins into playing Hitler when he approached producer-director George Schaefer with John Gay's script of *The Bunker*. It was a fortunate contact because Hopkins and Schaefer had wanted to work with each other again ever since making another telemovie – about the early seventeenth-century voyage of the *Mayflower*, Pilgrim Fathers and all – off the coast of Maryland during a steamy summer a year earlier. Hopkins had played the gruff ship's captain, Christopher Jones, opposite a cast that included Richard Crenna, Jenny Agutter, David Dukes and Trish van Devere.

Recalls Schaefer: 'When you read the script of *The Mayflower*, you'd have thought it was going to be one of those multi-million-dollar epics with sea voyages, storms and so on. In fact, we had a very, very tight budget and things were mightily chaotic. We did, though, have a first-rate cast. Tony, for instance, had an attack on his role which lifted it right off the page. He offered this fierce, dedicated love of the sea and hatred of all things religious, which made him a wonderful foil for Dick Crenna, playing the leader of the flock. The scenes between the two of them were particularly well-written. Despite the various problems – among them mosquitoes, almost unbearable humidity and jellyfish – we ended up with a fairly exciting, and quite successful, show.'

The location for *The Bunker* was altogether more civilised than that of the tiny, heat-encrusted stand-in for an ancient craft that had to be rocked manually at its moorings during that East Coast summer. It offered Paris hotels, restaurants and an eminently sensible continental filming regimen that prescribed rushes at 11 o'clock each morning, a decent lunch, eight hours of steady shooting, home, a nap and, finally, a nice, large French dinner.

Hopkins spent six weeks preparing for the role. He studied Hitler's face in picture books, watched hours and hours of documentary film to try to get his gestures right – for example, an open-handed way of talking that was almost feminine – and listened to speeches to pick up cadences of the voice. The research was meticulous, the internal preparation obsessive to the point that, as shooting progressed, he was Hitler on and off set, even to the point of a thunderous row with Jenni back at their hotel. His face, she recalls, was twisted and distorted, like that of someone she had never seen before. Each morning in the hotel room Hopkins would stand naked in front of the mirror, listening to Hitler tapes and then going through it himself, working himself up to the character, to get the right rhythms and mannerisms.

Schaefer was aware of the effect the role was having on Hopkins: 'Jenni told me she couldn't have stood much more shooting on *Hitler* [*The Bunker*]. By the end, you could see the effect it was having on him. He'd come in on those days we were doing some of the really big scenes all coiled and tense. Nevertheless I found him very dependent on the director – more so than many actors I've worked with. On *The Bunker*, in a particularly emotional scene, Tony would say, "In my mind's eye, I know just about where I can go with this and I'm going to be almost insane at that moment. Make me hold back just when you do the technical stuff. Don't let me blow my stack until we're ready to shoot it because I'm not sure that I can do it more than once or twice."

'The result is, there are two or three scenes in *The Bunker* that we have on film that are absolutely extraordinary. He was as mad as a hatter; he'd got that insane look behind his eyes that Hitler must have had.'

It is a full ten minutes into the film when the audience gets its first view of Hitler, sitting impassively in conference playing with a pen: 'Thank you, Speer. We've heard enough.' Then down comes the clenched fist as he outlines his Scorched Earth policy – 'The German people left don't deserve to live.' As the rest of the two-and-a-half-hour drama unfolds, Hitler degenerates into a dangerous lunatic – 'I will destroy Bolshevism. I will wipe out the scourge of Jewish Marxism,' he screams.

Schaefer is right. It is an extraordinary performance, chilling, even faintly Pythonesque, yet utterly compelling. By the end, the trembling hands and feet have finally given way to a pathetic, shambling wreck with just enough strength to give poison to his belated bride, Eva Braun, then to bite into the cyanide and shoot himself.

It is probably just as well that Hopkins was so eye-catching in the central role for there were other elements in the film that could have contrived to sink it without trace, notably a New York-Jewish actor (Cliff Gorman) as a kind of Bronx Goebbels, another American (Richard Jordan) as a faintly-heroic Speer – both obvious casting concessions to the American network – and a Frenchman (Michel Lonsdale) as Martin Bormann.

Julian Fellowes, one of a group of fine low-profile English actors (Andrew Ray, Martin Jarvis, Michael Kitchen among them) in the production, recalled his favourite story of the shooting: 'One day we were doing a scene where one of the Nazis has to look up and, as Michel Lonsdale comes through the door, say to him, "What's up, Martin?"

'At this point, Tony went over to George Schaefer – normally he'd never interfere in this kind of thing because he thinks actors should sort out their own scripts – and said, "Honestly, George, this is simply beyond the limit. We can't have someone saying, "What's up, Martin?" George said to Tony, "Oh, you think it won't work?", and made us all take five while he went into huddle with the writer. Five minutes later we were ready to shoot and ran through the scene again. This time, the actor looked up and said, "What's up, Bormann?"

'It's at those moments you realise you're quite simply shouting down a well and that the only thing to do is to get the money as quickly as possible into your bank account. "What's up, Bormann?" went round the unit for about the next month.'

Part of Hopkins' obsessiveness with the role seemed to consist of wanting to dine out every night at a restaurant called Au Vieux Berlin and eat *Wiener Schnitzel* because, said Fellowes, 'in his head he was in Germany'. Fellowes, who knew Paris well and loved French history, was determined to try to broaden his friend's mind: 'I once dragged him round the Louvre in a high sulk and held his head at the *Mona Lisa*, but that was about it. I kept going on about wanting to show him Versailles but Tony was totally uninterested. All he wanted to do was to get back to the *Wiener Schnitzel*. Then, one day, we were sitting in the hotel having breakfast; Jenni was there too and it was a beautiful morning and most of the film was finished. Tony suddenly looked up and said, "Would you like to go to Versailles?"

'I was so surprised I nearly dropped my fork. I replied, "Yes, yes, how lovely." And he said, "All right, we'll go if we can go *now*!" Whereupon Jenni and I jumped up, raced to get a taxi before he could change his mind, and we did actually get him to the Trianon. But that was because all the stars were in the right position. For once we could do it; we could have *my* day.'

David Swift was in the film too (like that of Fellowes, his casting had been at Hopkins' bidding) and Paula joined him in Paris. When it came to dining at Au Vieux Berlin, she put her foot down: 'I didn't like the food and the whole ambience. I simply couldn't stand the place. So I said no. We would go instead to Chez André where you could sit outside, which we liked doing. Tony didn't like it because of passing dogs peeing on the chairs. When we managed to get him to sit outside a couple of times, he always insisted being on an inside chair, out of the way of the dogs.'

Though the subject matter was exceedingly grim and Hopkins, for the most part, was intensely preoccupied with his portrayal, there were lighter moments during shooting, such as the time they were filming a Christmas party given by Hitler. His officers lined up to receive festive greetings from their Führer and as Hopkins came to Swift there was a twinkle in his eye. Knowing his chum to be Jewish, and this, remember, was on a 'take', Hitler offered his 'Aryan' underling a mischievous 'Happy Chanukah!'

The Bunker turned out to be a very-much-argued-over telemovie. The neo-Nazi element in America hated it because it seemed like just another Zionist-inspired anti-Hitler film. More curiously, Schaefer recalls, 'a much larger Jewish element came out saying it hated the film too because it felt we were showing a sympathetic portrait of the man which, God knows, was the last thing in anyone's mind.'

Less committed critics were unanimous about one element, at least – Hopkins' searing performance: 'Anthony Hopkins' Hitler is the genuine article, from make-up to mannerisms, and the ranting seems a natural extension of the man's ego; when he describes Goering as "brutal", there's a nice irony that Hopkins, Gay and director George Schaefer use effectively. Hopkins is absolutely first-rate, dead-eyed and deteriorating; it's a terrifying realisation' (*Daily Variety*). 'Hopkins' portrayal of Hitler is riveting in its complexity – he invokes insights into the strange vicissitudes of the man's drug-addicted personality without inspiring any unwarranted sympathy, distracted introspection credibly gives way to uncontrollable fits of temper, and nervous mannerisms are invested with an organic naturalness that once again attest to Hopkins' excellence as an actor' (*Hollywood Reporter*).

When they handed out the Emmys the following year, it came as no great surprise when Hopkins was named 'best actor in a limited series' (to add to his other Emmy award four years earlier). Rather more controversy surrounded his 'best actress' counterpart, Vanessa Redgrave, for her role as Auschwitz survivor Fania Fenelon in Arthur Miller's *Playing for Time* (which Schaefer had been asked to direct, but turned down, after *The Mayflower*).

After their two telemovies together, Schaefer says he would love to have worked again with Hopkins. They talked about a theatre play – specifically Shaw's *Man and Superman*, in which the director thinks Hopkins would have made a fine Tanner. Schaefer, who was at that time represented by the same agents as the actor, got the feeling Hopkins was feeling restless and also upset that he was not being offered more romantic or leading parts rather than just character roles. So he sent him one of three one-act plays written by a then unknown playwright, Ernest Thompson (before his later acclaim for *On Golden Pond*).

'In it,' says Schaefer, 'he would have been playing this very romantic, handsome soap-opera star who is terribly vain and gets his kicks by pursuing ladies who have written him fan letters. It was a very funny role. He read it, thought it delightful and that it would be great fun to do, but then thought better of it. It was, admittedly, all going to be done for peanuts, for public television where everyone works virtually for nothing. I was sort of disappointed because it would have been another entirely different facet of him. But at the time he seemed to be going through a lot of . . . you know, "Where do I go with my career?" '

Earlier, during a Yule break in filming *The Elephant Man*, Hopkins was in Wales with Dick and Muriel for the first Christmas at his parents' home since he and Jenni had moved to Los Angeles. On Christmas Day Dick had fallen asleep while watching *Goldfinger* on television and when he woke up he could feel severe pains in his arms. Hopkins told Muriel to call the doctor straight away: 'I'm glad I was there because I knew he was having a heart attack. A producer friend of mine in Los Angeles, much younger than my father, had had the same symptoms. The doctor gave him an injection and put him to bed. He said, "It's touch and go the next 24 hours. He mustn't be moved. He's a very tense man and I don't know if it's a big heart attack." '

In fact it was not fatal, but the next time Hopkins saw Dick, while shooting *The Bunker* in Paris, his father was still looking far from well and had aged distinctly. Hopkins tried to keep in touch as much as possible when he moved on to Greece for another mini-series, *Peter and Paul*, an interminably dour biblical saga loosely derived from the *Acts of the Apostles*. Hopkins was playing Paul (Peter was portrayed by an unexciting actor named Robert Foxworth) and many of the 2000 actors and extras wore costumes previously used in *Ben-Hur*,

Spartacus and *Cleopatra*. Some of the filming was done at a studio outside Athens in which the roar of the city and, in particular, the clucking of nearby chickens could be heard because soundproofing was basic. There were extensive locations on Rhodes, too. Hopkins' Road to Damascus was, however, more bizarrely located – in California's Painted Desert, with a wind machine to blow the sand around and a strong arc lamp to provide the light from Heaven.

The sequence was the last to be filmed in the show and after it, in January 1981, Hopkins returned to Wales. Dick's health was beginning to deteriorate rapidly: 'He was very sick and I thought he looked awful. However, he had a few surges back and we even managed some short walks but eventually, in March, he was taken into St Woolos hospital in Newport. I asked the doctor how long he might have and he told us that he could go at any moment. He thought it would be better if we went home and he'd call us if there was a crisis. My mother was so worried and couldn't sleep; then, about 1.00 in the morning, the phone went and we drove to the hospital. A nurse told us to wait, then Dr Jones came in and said, "Your father has just died. I'm sorry." It was about five minutes before we arrived. He'd been in a coma for two days so the doctor said it had been very easy.

'I remember saying that I hadn't ever seen a dead body before when the doctor asked if I would like to see my father and I said, "Yes". I felt his legs and they were still warm; it was extraordinary. It was also, I suppose, quite devastating but I'm glad I was able to cope despite having been off the booze for some years. He'd been very puzzled by all my personalities when I did drink because I went through Jekyll and Hyde moods. I didn't know what I was doing and they'd both been frightened for me. I was glad I'd been able to put all that behind me before I saw him go. Seeing him then put things in a sort of perspective; it was like some great double-bass in my head thundering, "God, I'm not exclusive, none of us is exclusive." '

After the endless anxieties during Hopkins' childhood,

Dick (and, of course, Muriel continuingly) had been delighted with his son's success.

Paula Swift remembers Dick warmly: 'He was a wonderful, warm man with this loudish – though not over-loud – Welsh voice. Very jolly, and he loved his drink as well. There he was in Paris, a bit red in the face, slightly balding but with tufts of hair sticking out, displaying undisguised joy that Tony had made it. As we walked about in the city you got a sense he was saying: "Look at us, this is my boy." '

Dick was dying when Hopkins started playing Othello (all those auditions had finally come home to roost) in Jonathan Miller's production forming part of the BBC's Bardathon.

'It was awkward,' recalls Hopkins. 'I couldn't really concentrate. Jonathan and I weren't getting on too well and I don't think I knew what the hell I was doing; I was all over the place.'

Another sort of confusion had been apparent from this production's very outset. Under the headline 'To be or not be black', the *Standard* revealed, on the eve of taping: 'a clashing of swords will soon be heard over the BBC's casting of exiled National Theatre actor Anthony Hopkins as Othello. Equity [the actors' union] and increasingly militant members of our black thespian community are furious that the role hasn't gone to a black British actor. . .' Hopkins had been cast after Equity had actually blocked a great black actor, James Earl Jones, an American, for the part. So there was something a little belated, and feeble, about Equity whingeing 'We think the BBC has unnecessarily mucked it up. We're not so much confused as angry. Our own black actors of ability should be given the chance to play the major parts when they come along. This is a vicious circle that must be broken.'

Suggesting that in *Othello* the issue of race has always been too greatly emphasised and tends to overshadow the more important issues of envy and jealousy, Dr Miller had originally considered setting his production on Cyprus in 1954, with Othello as a Sandhurst-trained Indian officer who had been put in charge of the security forces at the time of the EOKA unrest, with Iago as an army sergeant.

'The person I had in mind as the model for this Othello,' wrote Dr Miller in *Subsequent Performances*, 'was King Hussein of Jordan, who is Sandhurst-educated and rather well-spoken with tightly cropped hair and a moustache – a Hashemite warrior, drilled in British Army manners, who married a white woman. Othello forgets his racial difference and this point is reinforced and made much more interesting if instead of stressing the extent to which he is exotically different the production reflects his yielding to the temptation to try and assimilate. The differences should be eclipsed by a large central area of similarity so that their visibility in performance is reduced to a thin line or tiny crack. This came through in Anthony Hopkins' performance, although I think we probably allowed the make-up people to do too much to him. In casting him as the Moor, I found someone who could embody the exotic magnificence of a foreign warrior, a Mediterranean magnifico who comes from elsewhere. But since the issue of race has now become as inescapable in the theatre as it is in real life, I got into terrible trouble for asking a white actor to play the one part which is now judged to be the crowning privilege of a black performer.'

Dr Miller does not say why he decided to abandon his fifties motif. Hopkins' Othello turned out to be not so much Hashemite or even Moor, rather Berber: quite light-skinned, with some darkening around the eyes, exotic certainly, hair in ringlets, a trimmed beard, swarthy and Arabic. The dress seemed pure Elizabethan – doublets, starched ruffs – the high-voltage drama distinctly Jacobean. But just when it seemed that this might be a reversion to pure classical came Bob Hoskins' rasping Cockney Iago to inject some serious unorthodoxy.

According to Hopkins, the way Miller visualised Iago and the way Hoskins played him was as 'a kind of bullet-headed, tough street killer. He's the original anarchist. He hates everything that is beautiful, everything that is civilised, everything that is harmonious. Most of all he hates rank and power as typified by Othello. But he's very cunning. And the Moor is gullible. He doesn't understand people like that.'

He and Miller felt that Othello was well aware that he was capable of senseless volcanic rages through jealousy, and that he was a man who kept his emotions carefully in check. But then he had never known anyone like Iago. Some critics appeared to find difficulty in reconciling the two principal performances when at the outset, suggested one, it is 'mind-boggling that so superior a creature as Othello would fly off the handle through the slanders of a little pipsqueak gossipmonger like Iago.'

Dennis Hackett said in *The Times*: 'Physically, Hopkins is not cut out to be the towering Moor and here, it might have been thought, Hoskins' diminutive stature would help, but somehow he closed the gap by sheer energy.

'I found it difficult to believe that anyone could ever have been deceived by him – certainly not the quiet-voiced, under control Othello we saw in the early part of the play. Iago here was not the cunning dog of war but the con man with a card around his neck.'

Hopkins' portrayal certainly divided American reviewers. For James Wolcott in the *Voice*: '[Hopkins] portrayed Othello not as a warrior brought low by self-deceit but as a mad dog in the full heat of froth. As Hopkins spat out curses and accusations, his teeth flecked with foam, he looked like a rabid cod-pieced Little Richard searching for a piano on which to pound out his rage. . .

'Watching him pop his cork and spray foam across the room wasn't a thrilling treat, but it wasn't a chore, either. Seeing a drably repressed actor like Hopkins loosen his bolts isn't without its weird fascinations.' On the other hand *Los Angeles Times* TV critic Cecil Smith praised the production unreservedly and declared: 'Hopkins, one of the most gifted actors of our age, is a brilliant Othello, a bit dusky, darkened around the eyes, rather exotic and Arabic in appearance, not negroid. But it's the performance, not the make-up, that counts; he begins quietly, a precise, aloof military professional. We watch his jealousy slowly rise like bile within him until it explodes in terrible rage.'

Some time later, back in the States, Bob Palmer remembers sitting with Hopkins and Jenni in a viewing theatre watching a private screening of the play: 'It was long, very long; it just seemed to go on and on. At the end Jenni said, "It's a bit slow, isn't it?" and I said something like, "Well, it's not *The Dukes of Hazzard*." We all just broke up.'

In the early spring of 1982 Hopkins, Jenni and Julian Fellowes (who was then living in California too) drove out to Lynn Redgrave and her husband John Clark's house in Topanga Canyon for a Sunday afternoon party. If you drive due west out to the beach, go north for about ten miles on the Pacific Coast Highway then turn right into the Santa Monica mountains, you eventually climb up high into wind-swept Topanga. It is 50–60 minutes' drive from Beverly Hills. John and Lynn remember Hopkins gazing out over the Canyon – the views are breathtaking – and saying, 'God, I'd love to live here.' Trying quickly to seek Jenni's approval for what seemed a spur-of-the-moment notion, Hopkins started to go on about how peaceful and calm the place seemed, how one could live a really normal life here. Jenni made it perfectly clear that she was not at all keen, even when Hopkins suggested that it might be pleasant to have somewhere to go at weekends: 'I really wasn't enthusiastic,' she recalls. 'Apart from anything else I liked being about five minutes from Beverly Hills city and all our friends. I knew Tony, and I knew this was dreamsville. If you're the sort of people who have a cottage and have got used to going off on a Friday night and returning on Monday morning then that is a kind of rhythm you get into. We'd never been like that and I just couldn't imagine us – particularly with the cats and everything – utilising a place like that. So I guess I just shrugged the whole thing off.'

Hopkins had, however, got the bit between the teeth

and the next day he and Julian drove back to Topanga to visit estate agents. They were taken up to a wooden, three-level house which was about to be vacated by a young couple who were selling up so they could take off around the world.

To Hopkins, it was like something out of *Easy Rider*, a sort of throwback to an easy-going sixties, hippy time. The house was on the opposite side of the Canyon from Lynn and John but the view was just as spectacular. Hopkins told Jenni he had found a place and wanted her to give it the once-over. The viewing was arranged, 'So I went and looked at it but I have to say it wasn't the sort of house I'd have chosen. It was a wooden ranch, with a huge open-plan living area and a sort of terrace-cum-verandah outside. It seemed very much a left-over from the sixties, people into organic food and all that. Rather passé, I thought. If, like John and Lynn, you had a young family, then it might be lovely but, in this case, I simply couldn't see it. But Tony was enthralled with the whole idea and the couple, about to go off on their travels, were only too happy to leave virtually everything behind that made the place work. That was it. We bought it though we didn't really have any idea how we were going to use it.'

A couple of weeks after buying the house, Hopkins suddenly announced to Jenni one day: 'I think I want to take off on my own for a bit. I think I'll just get in the car and drive. I *need* to be on my own for a while.' Jenni asked him where he thought he might go. Tony seemed undecided. 'For God's sake,' said Jenni, 'we've got the Topanga place. Why not go there? It won't take long to make it habitable for you. Surely you don't want to go charging off in a car, staying in hotels? That would be too boring.'

So they piled the car with essentials like sheets and towels – a telephone, hi-fi and basic furniture were already there – and set off for the mountains.

'I don't know what I'm going to do,' Hopkins told Jenni. 'I'll probably do some work in the garden, go for jogs on the beach, just be on my own. I need to think over a few things. I'll check in but I probably won't phone every day. You don't mind, do you?' Jenni, a little bemused by this turn of events, drove back to Beverly Hills.

It was ten days before Hopkins first made contact. 'How's it going?' Jenni asked. He was having a wonderful time, he said: 'I get up early in the morning, go for a jog on the beach, have a nice breakfast, listen to music, go to my alcoholics' meetings, work in the garden . . .' Work in the garden?, thought Jenni. *Tony* working in the garden? All he ever did at Clearview Drive was sit in it. 'He said he'd got a lot of equipment and was having a fine old time getting the garden straight. I remember thinking suddenly, "Who is this man?"'

After this call there was silence again. Another couple of weeks went by before Jenni decided to phone: 'He was still having a wonderful time and all the rest of it. He then said to me that he didn't know whether he wanted to be married any more. There was absolutely nobody else, but he wanted to stay out on his own. He was taking a good look at his life, doing a lot of meditating, pondering on life, love, death, religion and all that. He didn't seem prepared to say more than that. It was more or less "Leave me alone and let me work something out."'

Jenni put the phone down in a sort of daze. She felt hurt, confused and impotent. What am I meant to do now? she wondered.

The only indication of Hopkins' frustration with her seemed to be in veiled suggestions that maybe she wasn't taking the implications of his alcoholism and recovery seriously enough – enough, for example, to join one of the family support groups attached to Alcoholics Anonymous.

Jenni reflects: 'What he seemed to be saying was I didn't really understand what he was going through, what his life now had to be like, how difficult it often was. Whether this was just an excuse because he felt guilty and therefore had to find some justification for

what he was doing, I couldn't say. I was so astounded by
what was going on I thought, "Come on, girl, you better
get yourself along to a support group pretty sharpish." I
felt at that time that probably *I* could use a support
system because 90 per cent of what was going on
probably had to do with the fact he was a recovering
alcoholic. The obsessiveness, the quirkiness. It was
typical. So I started going to meetings and indeed got
quite a lot out of it though I must admit that I went into
it thinking it wasn't something I really wanted to do on a
regular basis. Perhaps that was arrogant of me, but I
didn't feel I needed it. I already had good, understanding
friends – like Nancy – to talk to. I didn't feel I wanted to
go and talk about my life and Tony's life in a room full of
people. Anyhow I did, and perhaps another ten days to
two weeks went by before Tony rang and this time he
suggested we meet for dinner at a Chinese restaurant we
used to go to regularly in Beverly Hills. It was like going
out on a date again.'

Hopkins seemed pleased she was attending, and
getting value out of, the support group and after they
dined he returned to Topanga. A week later he called
again for another dinner date.

This time Jenni asked him gently about his plans:
'Don't know. Just taking a day at a time. I'm in touch with
my agent. It's not as though I'm cutting myself off
completely,' was the reply.

Jenni: 'My instinct was to give him space, give him
time. I knew there was no one else involved – I knew that
absolutely. I wasn't going to push him or get neurotic,
certainly not grind on at him about when he was planning
to come home. I think I knew him well enough to know
that this wouldn't be the way to go about it.'

At the end of five months Hopkins phoned to say:
'Could I come home this weekend?' Jenni said: 'Of course
you can, it's your home, you can come home whenever
you like.' Hopkins asked again: 'Are you sure it'll be all
right if I come home this weekend?' Jenni said: 'Yes. To
stay for the weekend? Or are you saying that's it, you're

coming home properly?' Hopkins hesitated: 'Umm, I don't know. It'll probably be just for the weekend. I'll see.'

That weekend he returned to Clearview Drive and never spent another night in the Topanga house. It was rented out to a series of troublesome tenants and eventually sold at a vast loss.

It had been a long, strange episode that, according to Hopkins, had been initially precipitated by a feeling of desperation and restlessness fuelled by a rare bout of unemployment. 'I think I'm going mad,' he told Bob Palmer. 'I feel I'm on a treadmill. I get these black, bloody moods. I know I'm not nice to be around but I can't explain it.' When he saw Topanga and the house he thought that here could be an answer: 'It was where all the drop-outs live and I suppose I had some idea about becoming a sort of hippy. At the time it seemed fantastic.

'I wouldn't listen to any cautions, I just wanted to get the hell away, so I bought it. I thought I wanted to study astronomy so I got a telescope to look at the stars. I used to go running up the side of the mountain, would walk for hours on the beach. I couldn't work out *what* I was looking for. I'd listen to country-and-western music all the time. It was like I was tripping out and yet I wasn't taking anything.'

In a small, gossipy town like Hollywood, there were inevitably the odd rumblings during these months. Jenni recalls a journalist ringing her to ask something along the lines of, 'I understand your husband's gone off – do you want to say anything about it?' 'I was very angry about that,' she remembers, 'and thought if anybody's got to answer those sorts of questions, let it be him. I didn't see why I, on top of everything else, should have to do that. So I quashed it completely by just replying, "We've got another house and he's gone to do some things up there because he's got no work on at the moment" and left it at that.'

To this day, Jenni says she still doesn't really know what was at the root of it all: 'But in retrospect I think I may have got more out of it than even he did. It made me realise that I had to construct a life for myself alongside him. I'm not saying that I couldn't now rely on him – I rely on him absolutely – but what he couldn't be any more was the 101 per cent of everything for me. I realised I had to have my own life too. I had to be more resilient. Tony's a great believer in the fact that nobody should live through another person; everyone should try and get on as much as possible with their own lives. I've always believed that too, but the Topanga episode made it really come home to me. It helped take away all the smugness from our relationship.'

With perfect timing, and a nice sense of irony, an intriguing job offer virtually coincided with his return from Topanga – a six-hour mini-series of Piers Paul Read's novel *A Married Man*. The acclaimed book had been out for a couple of years when Julian Fellowes first read it while he was in Los Angeles: 'I'd been toying for a while with the idea of forming a production company. Getting a production off the ground would naturally be that much easier if one could put together an attractive package. When I read the book, I realised straight away that there was a wonderful part for Tony. Anyway I came back to England and set up a company called Lionhead Productions. We got the rights to the book and then discovered that London Weekend Television were quite interested in doing it with John Davies, who had directed Tony in *War and Peace*. They rang me, or I rang them – I can't remember which way round – and said they'd like to make it their submission to Channel 4 that year.

'Separately, Tony's American agent had booked him into a job on Benedict Arnold – one of those historical figures, another CBS yawn. Our director Charles Jarrott wanted Tony but didn't really mind too much either way. The powers-that-be at LWT – though not John Davies – wanted Paul Freeman to do it because he was quite hot at the time. When the news came through that Tony was busy, things seemed all set for Paul. However, I knew that Tony didn't want to do the Arnold thing and wasn't quite as hooked into it as his agent was saying. With

John Davies backing me, I rang Tony in America and he told me he'd like to do our series but we'd have to get the scripts out to him right away. There was mad panic; the scripts were stuck together with Sellotape and whizzed off to the States. Then Tony rang again and confirmed he'd do it.'

In *A Married Man* Hopkins played John Strickland, a successful barrister whose escape route from a long, sterile, upper-middle-class marriage (to Ciaran Madden) and painful male menopause was to take a smart mistress (Lise Hilboldt) and become a Labour politician. There was a messy murder (of Strickland's wife), social satire and a lot of sex. Rather too much sex, it struck Hopkins as he read Derek Marlowe's scripts. He could not, for instance, see the point of a particularly steamy session with his wife when their marriage was meant, he understood, to be 'a barren wasteland ... over and dead'.

Hopkins elaborates: 'I told John Davies that I didn't want to do that scene. It wasn't in the book, and it seemed to me it had been put in simply to try and boost the audience ratings. We went through the book again and instead put in a scene where the couple go away to their cottage with the children and they have a family meal which really seemed to sum up this boring, domestic life that was getting them both down. Anyway I don't really enjoy those sorts of sex scenes. They're often rather demeaning and, frankly, just become boring. Maybe it's something to do with my puritan Celtic background. America, for instance, has an adolescent obsession with sex. It seems to be part of a national impotence.'

Julian Fellowes believes Hopkins was quite right to object to that particular scene. At the same time he provides another intriguing insight into an aspect of Hopkins' craft: 'Sex is only any good when you abandon yourself to it and, of course, it's quite hard to do that in front of 50 technicians and a lot of arc lights. Some actors have a kind of exhibitionist side which means they are able to relax and abandon themselves to it in that sort of atmosphere. Quite a lot don't, though.

'Tony, underneath all his instinct and mumbling, knows very well what *he* does well and the kind of vehicle in which he can be most effective. This is a sort of contradiction to the early instinctive animal let loose on a set; he's actually very methodical. When he's inwardly suffering, there's no one to touch him in that sort of role. What he does marvellously is create the impression that he's suppressing his emotion rather than expressing it. It's difficult to impose that screen persona in sex scenes. He's not, I think, an action man as such.'

In its unravelling on, first, Channel 4 then later the ITV network, the leisurely serial achieved a considerable following as audiences warmed to what the *Daily Mail* described as a 'steamy middle-class soap'. In April 1984 *A Married Man* was syndicated on American television. In his preview in *USA Today* Jack Curry wrote that it was 'very, very British; very, very long; very, very talky – and ultimately very, very good ... It's wonderful to see Anthony Hopkins finally get out of the waistcoats and knickers so many of his period-piece roles require. With his pouty little-laddie face and impeccable diction, he brings to the title character a marvellous complexity. It's easy to see the spoiled boy underneath the confused middle-aged man.'

John Davies confirms Hopkins' delight in being able to wear a suit: 'He was especially pleased with the one we had made for him. I also remember him telling me what a joy it was to be back working with scripts like this one and with English actors again. I think *A Married Man* was the beginning of his return to England, of his finding his feet here again. Naturally his eventual return was very welcome to everyone.'

8. CHASING SHADOWS

David Lean said he was first attracted to *The Bounty* for four specific reasons. No one had ever put the true story on film (despite two famous movies – and one rather obscure one – on the subject) or truly reflected the youth of the men involved (Lieutenant Bligh was only 32 and Fletcher Christian 22), the heroism of Bligh's voyage or the power of the sea itself – 'like the desert', said Lean. It was 1976, six years since the failure of *Ryan's Daughter*, when Lean surfaced in French Polynesia, ostensibly with the notion of researching a film about Captain Cook. But after reading Richard Hough's book *Captain Bligh and Mr Christian* he decided to junk *Cook* (a vast undertaking, even by Lean's standards, about, he concluded, a disappointingly straightforward man) in favour of another, altogether more colourful, sea-going saga.

Lean, who had installed himself at the Hotel Bora Bora, 160 miles from Tahiti, sent his friend and agent Phil Kellogg to start negotiations with Warner Brothers, who were keen to make a film with the veteran director. Kellogg explained to Warner's that he and Lean had estimated the project would cost about $17 million, and the studio agreed to back it. The writer Robert Bolt was then summoned out to Bora Bora, where Lean told him that he wanted to make not one but two films – to be called *The Law Breakers* and *The Long Arm* – that would tell the whole story of *The Bounty*, including the voyage, the mutiny and the pursuit of the mutineers.

The scale of the project now began to concern Warner's, in particular the notion of two films *and*, Lean was demanding, the construction of an exact replica of *The Bounty* itself. Including this item, the budget of *The Law Breakers* alone was now being reckoned at about

$37 million. Warner's pulled out of the deal, more in sorrow than in anger.

Meanwhile, at the other end of the Bora Bora beach from where Lean was living, the Italian producer Dino De Laurentiis was ensconced in his own hotel, which he had built to house cast and crew for his current epic remake of *The Hurricane*. Hearing of Lean's problems, De Laurentiis contacted Paramount, with whom he had, as they say in Hollywood, a 'relationship', and soon they all joined forces on the two-film *Bounty* package.

Hopkins was in California when he got a telephone call from Katharine Hepburn asking him if he would ring her old friend David Lean, who had something of interest to discuss with him. Hopkins had not seen Hepburn for a long while and found the roundabout approach odd but irresistible. Lean was in town and invited Hopkins for dinner at his hotel. 'I'm going to make *The Bounty*. Will you play Bligh?' Lean asked. 'I'd love to, of course, but why me?' Hopkins replied. It turned out that while Lean and his wife had been travelling on the *QE2* she had wanted to see a film one evening. Reluctantly, it seems, he had gone with her; the film they were showing was *International Velvet*.

'That,' says Hopkins, 'is what seemed to convince Lean I could play Bligh.' So Hopkins committed himself to the film, or films as they were then, in 1977, but various forces were conspiring to prevent the project being realised for at least another five years.

With delays on reconstructing the *Bounty* and Bolt yet to complete the scripts, De Laurentiis became increasingly impatient. Phil Kellogg had been replaced by a young British producer, Bernard Williams, who, after careful rebudgeting and trying to persuade Lean to be content with just one film, presented a $40-million bottom line to his boss for *The Law Breakers*. When Bolt suffered a massive heart attack in April 1979 that appeared to be the last straw. De Laurentiis and Paramount parted company with Lean. Hopkins heard of all this, thought, 'That's it', washed his hands of the piece and moved on.

With the chance of recreating one famous Charles

Laughton role seemingly down the drain, another quite swiftly presented itself to Hopkins with a fortuitousness virtually bordering on fate. Laughton was 39 when he took on the extraordinary ('appallingly masochistic' in the words of one critic) task of portraying Victor Hugo's hideous hunchback Quasimodo in the 1939 RKO classic *The Hunchback of Notre Dame*. Hopkins was 43 when invited by producer Norman Rosemont to play Quasimodo for a CBS telemovie of the Hugo novel, scripted by John Gay and to be filmed at Pinewood Studios. Rosemont, a large, no-nonsense New Yorker who could be a bit of a bully, regularly raided the classics for his TV remakes – *The Man in the Iron Mask*, *The Count of Monte Cristo*, *Les Misérables*, *All Quiet on the Western Front* and *Little Lord Fauntleroy* among them. It was said that if Rosemont ever lost his library ticket, the British film industry would collapse.

Hopkins inevitably inherited some of Laughton's masochism merely in terms of the logistics of playing the role. For five weeks he had to be up by 3.30 a.m. and into the make-up chair for four painstaking hours every morning. His make-up artist, Nick Maley, explained: 'The pieces went on in a particular order, like building a car. Each piece was sealed to Tony's skin, and the last one in place was the fake eye and eyelash. Then the wig [a carrotty mop] was put on, and the real magic began. I put on the colour, the highlights, shadows, the beardline and the face came alive.' With his cauliflower right ear, nose with a distended right nostril and the addition of false teeth (displaying just one large discoloured fang in the middle of his mouth), a hump and a club foot, Hopkins was ready to face the 12-hour day.

Before they started filming, the director Michael Tuchner arranged a special showing, at Hopkins' request, of the Laughton version. Said Hopkins: 'In those days they didn't have the same make-up techniques we use today. So Laughton's deformity was just sort of stuck on. Even so it was wonderful, and he gave a marvellous performance. After watching it, Michael turned to me and said: "Good luck." I said jokingly: "Maybe we could get all the prints and have it destroyed. How can I hope to follow that?" 'Though understandably concerned about following in the footsteps of the much-admired, and much-spoofed, Laughton portrayal, Hopkins was not afraid to do a spot of borrowing either: 'I couldn't resist the way he hides his face; I thought, "That's too good to leave out." I'm not proud.'

Tuchner remembers how before shooting began some of the actors attended a read-through – people like Derek Jacobi and Nigel Hawthorne as well as Hopkins.

'In his usual rather mild way, Tony said he'd read the Hugo and found some dialogue in translation that wasn't in John Gay's adaptation so he'd changed a few lines. They were very small changes in terms of actual words but, boy, did they improve the rhythm. Gay's version was almost too clipped at times, almost too distilled. By a few simple changes, Tony managed to juice it up a bit and make it play better.'

Under the constant weight of the grotesque prosthetic (which condemned Hopkins to extra isolation for, as he said, 'I couldn't really go into the studio canteen looking like that. It would have put people off their food, so I ate alone in my dressing room, sipping soup through a straw'), it was no surprise that Hopkins' fuse was short and getting shorter by the end of each uncomfortable day.

One particular morning they were shooting the crucial bell-tower scene when Hopkins arrived on the set and immediately detected a tell-tale 'atmosphere'. Girls with rheumy eyes on the edge of tears; other people pale around the gills whispering in corners.

Hopkins: 'Being the paranoid fruitcake I am I thought, "God, here we go." I said, "Morning, Mike." He'd lost his pleasantness and was just rather abrupt in reply. So we started the scene and the place was like a morgue. I thought, "Fuck this", and went over to Mike to find out what was going on.'

Hopkins: 'What's the problem?'

Tuchner: 'Nothing.'

Hopkins: 'Don't bullshit. What's up?'

Tuchner: 'Norman wants me off this particular set by the end of the day.'

Hopkins: 'You mean, we've got to do six set-ups and finish here today? That's impossible. Even with the best intentions in the world, we can't do that.'

Tuchner: 'Don't worry, it's my problem.'

Hopkins: 'It *is* my problem. I'm in the film.'

They shot the first scene, after which Hopkins suggested to everyone they lighten up and take proper time. By five o'clock they had completed one-and-a-half scenes. The stunt man Alf Joint had, quite rightly, also made it clear he was not going to be rushed either, doing what were extremely dangerous scenes up in the rafters. A 'wrap' was called. Before everyone left, they were told: 'OK, tomorrow we're on Stage J.' Hopkins, ready for a fight, exclaimed, 'What does that mean?' He was told: 'We're cutting the rest of the scenes,' to which Hopkins replied, firmly: 'Oh, are we?'

With his make-up still on, Hopkins made a bee-line for the production office and confronted the production manager, Donald Toms.

Hopkins: 'Apparently we're not going to do the rest of the bell-tower scenes?'

Toms: 'Nah, Tony. Norman's pulled the plug on us.'

Hopkins: 'What are we supposed to be doing tomorrow?'

Toms: 'We're going to the other set.'

Hopkins (thinking 'Please God, contain my rage because I want to kill Rosemont'): 'I don't want to go to Norman's office because I'll only drag him out from behind his desk. You go over for me while I take off my make-up and tell him I'm going on strike tomorrow. It's as simple as that. Tell him that I'm not wasting my time sitting for four hours in the bloody make-up chair for this idiot to come and pressurise the director and for me then to be told it's none of my business.

'It *is* my business. I'm going on strike unless he stays away and keeps out of my eye-lines and the director's way.'

▲ As a hard but fair Captain Bligh in the 1983
remake of *The Bounty*.

▲ As Quasimodo off-set in *The Hunchback of Notre Dame*, with wife Jenni.

▼ As the reptilian press baron Lambert Le Roux, with Peter Blythe in the National Theatre's *Pravda*.

▲ 'A bullet-headed welterweight boxer':
Hopkins' King Lear at the National in 1986.

▼ Ready for action as Donald Campbell in the
BBC's *Across the Lake*.

▲ With daughter Abigail at the premiere of *The Dawning*.

▼ Receiving an Hon. D. Litt. from Prince Charles at the University of Wales in 1988.

▲ In his first West End production, as Rene Gallimard in *M. Butterfly*, with G. G. Goei.

◄ As Henry Wilcox in *Howards End*.

Wielding the crucifix as Van Helsing in Francis Ford Coppola's *Dracula*.

As Stevens, with Emma Thompson, in *The Remains of the Day*.

▲ With Richard Attenborough in *Shadowlands*.

▼ As Colonel William Ludlow in *Legends of the Fall*.

▲ Moment of triumph: on Oscar night in Hollywood,
March 1992, with the Best Actor trophy for
his performance in *The Silence of the Lambs*.

Toms: 'Shall I tell him that direct?'

Hopkins: 'The only reason I'm not going to do it is because I won't be able to control myself when I'm in front of him. You be my spokesman.'

Toms: 'Tony, I'll do that word for word.'

Toms went off to see Rosemont and when he returned told Hopkins that the producer's mouth had fallen open and he could not believe the threat.

Hopkins: 'Good. Well, I'm on strike, and I'm not coming back in tomorrow unless I get a phone call.'

The telephone rang just as Hopkins walked into his rented apartment in Arlington House. It was Toms: 'Hello, Tony. It's Don here. The scenes are back in and everything's all right.'

Hopkins finished shooting *The Hunchback of Notre-Dame* in the first week of November 1981. A little over five months later, and more than three years after he had put the whole thing out of his mind, Hopkins got a call from Bernard Williams, now a vice president of the Dino De Laurentiis Corporation, asking him if he were still interested in playing Bligh. Williams, who had recently produced *Ragtime* for Dino, persuaded De Laurentiis to revive *The Bounty* (finally abandoned by Lean since talks with every major studio had broken down and he had switched his interest to *A Passage to India*). Dino, who still owned the now-completed £2 million *Bounty* replica, agreed. The plan, Hopkins was told, was to make a mini-series for television with Bolt's screenplays (he had recovered from his heart attack) adapted into eight one-hour episodes.

That way (both the massive *Thorn Birds* and *Winds of War* were currently in production pointing up a fresh approach) the whole story could be told without drastic dilution. Hopkins confirmed his interest but said: 'I'll believe it when I see it.'

An experienced television director, Alan Bridges, who had made *The Hireling* and *Return of the Soldier* for the cinema, was engaged to make the mini-series. He worked closely with Bolt, travelled to French Polynesia to scout locations and settled on the less-developed island of Moorea – fifteen minutes from Tahiti – as the principal site. Bridges worked on the project for seven months, then was fired for what were described as 'conceptual differences'. Bridges seemed anxious to beef up a homosexual attraction between Bligh and Christian which had been more than hinted at in Hough's book. Others on the production team, particularly the producer, Bernard Williams, disagreed. Christopher Reeve, first sounded out by Lean back in 1980 for the role of Christian, also bowed out when he heard rumours about the homosexual element and that an unknown (to him) director had stepped in for Bridges. The mini-series idea was also dumped because it was felt that this was too masculine a subject for TV's large female audience.

Richard Attenborough, Hugh Hudson (*Chariots of Fire, Greystoke*) and Michael Cimino (*The Deer Hunter, Heaven's Gate*) were all quickly, but unsuccessfully, sounded out for *The Bounty* before a 37-year-old, virtually unknown, Australian named Roger Donaldson, who had moved to live and work in New Zealand, was given the biggest break of his career.

Donaldson's greatest claim to fame at that stage was that he had directed *Sleeping Dogs*, an efficient political thriller (the first Kiwi movie ever to open in the States), and a critically admired domestic drama, *Smash Palace*, which drew endless plaudits on the festival circuit. Dino had seen *Smash Palace* and was discussing a sequel to *Conan the Barbarian* with Donaldson when, early one morning, with shooting scheduled to begin in less than three months, he called Donaldson in for a meeting and told him he was switching him to *The Bounty*.

With Reeve out, the final task was to sign up a suitable Christian. Jeremy Irons, Anthony Andrews and even Sting were considered, then rejected. Eventually, on the suggestion of the Orion Pictures executive Mike Medavoy (Orion was to be one of the film's major backers, investing more than $10 million in the production), it was decided to woo Mel Gibson, who was in the first flush of international success with a couple of *Mad Max* movies, *The Year of Living Dangerously* and *Gallipoli* under his belt. Gibson was flown to England, given a whistle-stop tour of the script, his character's Lake District birthplace and the intricate rocking sets (representing *Bounty's* interior) at Lee International Studios in Wembley. Suitably impressed, he then signed to join with Hopkins – who had turned down Mexico, John Huston and the central role of Firmin, the stupendously drunk ex-Consul in *Under the Volcano*, to stick with Bligh – in forming a tandem previously represented, in 1935, by Clark Gable and Charles Laughton then, in 1962, by Marlon Brando and Trevor Howard.

Hopkins looked at both films but felt no trepidation because *this* script was slanted towards Bligh.

He also knew that however much he admired Laughton – and indeed thought the portrayal magnificent – he had to put that performance out of his mind. In the writing, Bolt's depiction of Bligh had very little in common with the evil tyrant that Laughton created. Here the character was far more compassionate, hard but not unjust, a disciplinarian but not a monster, and blinkered only in the sense that he was determined to get the job done whatever the odds against him. Bligh was a staunch Protestant, trained from the age of thirteen in the Royal Navy, certainly aloof and possibly too isolated, a pedant who, as Hopkins puts it, would write his log meticulously, was a bit *too* ordered and lacked a real capacity to relax. Yet in spite of those flaws, he was a man with whom Hopkins empathised. A Bligh scholar suggested to Hopkins that for authenticity he should adopt a Cornish accent. He tried it, found it did not quite work, so settled for a 'sort of country burr from the west of Bristol'.

On 18 April 1983 the cameras rolled on the third version (not counting an obscure 1933 Australian film with an unknown Tasmanian, Errol Flynn, as Christian) of *The Bounty*.

Some while after the film was completed an American

critic, Stephen Farber, asked Hopkins what kinds of problem were encountered making the movie. Hopkins: 'It was about a sixteen-week shoot – far too long. I think it could have been done far more expediently. But there wasn't enough time for preparation. Working at sea is obviously a problem, both for the director and the cameraman, especially on a big sailing ship. Also Tahiti *is* paradise, but after about two weeks down there the mosquitoes begin to get to you, and you catch something called dang fever, which is too much tropical sun. There's something strange about Tahiti, and maybe that's why the mutiny started.

'It has a spell-like effect on people; after a while you start to go slightly mad and you just want to get back to civilisation ... You begin to go stir crazy because there's nowhere to go.'

Farber also asked Hopkins about Roger Donaldson's contribution to the film. Hopkins replied: 'I think Roger Donaldson has a very unsentimental approach to things. He's very direct. He came in ill-prepared; he was just thrown into the deep end with very little time to get the film ready.'

Unsentimental? Direct? According to Hopkins, with a longer perspective on events than at the time of his Farber interview, the director warned the actor firmly at the outset: 'I'm not interested in your track record, I don't care if you've been in a play with Laurence Olivier, I'm going to come down hard on you, Tony.' The old familiar twitch began twitching again. The day after this little lecture Hopkins rang him and said: 'I want to tell you that I've worked with John Dexter and some other right bastards in my life, so if you come on hard with me, you can get another actor.'

Hopkins found Donaldson a 'rude, arrogant man. It seemed like he had a great Australian chip on his shoulder. He wanted to know nothing about British technical expertise. I had terrible fights with him out in Tahiti, awful stand-up fights and rows. He was shouting and screaming at people so one day I blew up in front of about 200 and called him all kinds of names.'

Williams confirms that there were considerable problems between Hopkins and the director: 'Roger seemed to find it hard to communicate with actors. He would just shout instructions and spend much of the time watching the video playback. That pissed Tony off.

'So there he was one day on a longboat, about eight weeks into shooting, and Tony finally blew up, calling Roger "a fucking idiot" and many other things too. It was a terrible explosion. I told Roger to count to 100 and leave Tony to cool off. To be honest, I don't endorse anyone exploding on the set but you must remember that Tony was very deeply into Bligh's character. He didn't socialise much and indeed isolated himself at the Kiora Hotel on Moorea, just as Bligh kept himself away from the rest of the crew. He was thinking Bligh all the time and putting a thousand times more thought into his performance than Roger.

'About two weeks later we were doing the scenes where Bligh has been cast adrift from the *Bounty* and the action revolved around a series of log-book entries and became a bit bogged down. So we decided to reduce a couple of scenes and Roger did some re-writing. When Tony was presented with the new pages he was outraged and said he wouldn't work with someone else's writing. I had to speak very severely to both of them at that stage. I even threatened to close the picture down and warned that if Dino found out he would use this as a weapon to reduce the balance of shooting and the budget. For the rest of the film, they kept at arm's length.'

Hopkins says he also objected to 'the endless filming. An example: the Tahitians coming out to meet the *Bounty* was filmed day after day after day. We'd finish one lot and think, "That's that", then about a week later there'd be re-shoots, re-takes. People would say, "What, again?" and then we'd start over. My Welsh parsimony, I suppose, but I'd think, "God Almighty, what a shocking waste of cash!" Chaos.

'Overall, though, it wasn't a hateful experience and much

of it was enjoyable; we had, for instance, a nice bunch of actors – Bernard Hill, Daniel Day-Lewis, Phil Davis, all that lot. Also I learned something else from it all. It's a no-win situation having fights with directors. In the first place, there's no need to lie down to abuse – you just say "Stop!" It's pointless losing your temper. It took me so long to learn that; a lot of hard work, patience and diligence. I've learned to calm down and check myself; I don't get angry so much now – anger is just a wasted emotion.'

The story is told in flashback from Bligh's court-martial, in which he is forced to defend himself against charges that he lost his ship through negligence. I wrote in my *Daily Mail* review of the film: 'From the moment Anthony Hopkins removes his wig to scratch his head nervously before embarking on his Admiralty ordeal, he establishes a much more rounded portrait of Bligh than his predecessors. No swaggering sadist, but by turns an ambitious, stubborn, petulant, puritanical and brilliant seaman desperate to get a job (collecting breadfruit for transporting to the West Indies) done. Hopkins dominates the film and his increasingly shrill frustration as the crew, including his friend Fletcher Christian, is seduced by the exotic lifestyle in the South Seas, is chillingly conveyed ... Hopkins in potential Oscar-winning form [he was not even nominated] remains in the memory and just about lays to rest a much-imitated predecessor.'

Variety fully concurred, describing Hopkins' performance as 'sensational, startlingly human'.

It nevertheless raised question-marks over the $20 million film's box-office prospects, particularly as the story had been made 'more complex and shaded than it's traditionally been'.

The trade paper's concern turned out to be fully justified, for at best *The Bounty* probably only broke even. Yet, as Orion's Eric Pleskow confided to Williams before the box-office score became clear, 'We at Orion are very proud to have made the picture.'

Soon after the film was completed Williams was sent an article that had appeared in the *Auckland Times*. In it he read of Donaldson claiming to have made the film single-handedly and, generally, putting everyone else down: 'I was appalled and upset. In fact Roger had been given the most wonderful silver spoon with *The Bounty* – $20 million, great sets, in Hopkins the most supportive actor any producer could have dared hope for, particularly in view of his loyalty to the project over the years, and the ship itself. The piece caused a tremendous row and falling out between Roger and myself that took a long time to heal.'

Hopkins began 1984 in a converted English farmhouse off-Broadway and ended it receiving a five-minute 'welcome back' ovation at the Olivier Awards in London. Between a wintry New York revival of Pinter's *Old Times*, co-starring with Marsha Mason and Jane Alexander, and that end-of-the-year acclaim, Hopkins had decided to end his ten-year American exile and confront his own Room 101 (to invoke Orwell) – the English stage and, by definition, the English theatre establishment.

When Marsha Mason first met Hopkins while filming *Audrey Rose* seven years earlier she became aware that he had just given up drinking after seeing him talk to a strange man outside the studio gates: 'I can't remember exactly how it came up, but we were chatting and he told me he'd started in this programme. He was explaining to me that at the beginning a person is assigned to you, somebody that you can call when you're in trouble. He said that he'd had a rough night and so he'd met this friend of his – who I'd seen – who was in the programme too for a chat before he'd had to show up for work.

'Later, on *Old Times*, we were talking in his dressing room and I was asking him about how I could help and handle this friend of mine who was having the same problem. He said that you just had to let a person go because they had to hit rock bottom before they could turn around and pick themselves up. In other words, you shouldn't try and convince someone to go into the programme. They have to want to go on it. By then it seemed that he was very comfortable with the programme and following it almost religiously. However, by the time we did the play together I did sense that he was struggling – not with alcohol, but with what he wanted to do with his career, what his work meant to him and about how he wanted to spend his time.

'I think that was all part of the evolution of his decision to go back to England.'

Old Times had last been seen in New York in an inventive Peter Hall production with Robert Shaw, Mary Ure and Rosemary Harris way back in 1971. The critical reaction to this limited-engagement (just seven weeks) Pinter revival – a typically enigmatic three-hander of ambiguous relationships, memory tricks and meaningful pauses played out in a converted farmhouse not far from the sea – was distinctly mixed. None, however, was quite as blatantly condemnatory as John Simon in *New York* magazine who, in his very first paragraph, laid down the ground rules for his ensuing onslaught (his 'both Anthony Hopkins and Jane Alexander are convincing' was far too belated for any real comfort): 'In a theater full of phonies, there is, I believe, none phonier than Harold Pinter, whose terminally specious *Old Times* is being revived at the Roundabout, insofar as a corpse can be revived . . .'

New York's two other Broadway butchers, Frank Rich (*Times*) and Clive Barnes (*Post*), left their cleavers at home this time round and were particularly struck by Hopkins, as the film writer-director Deeley. Rich: 'Mr Hopkins, seedy in his leather car-coat, slowly transforms Deeley from a snappy terrier into an aroused bulldog – and eventually a howling one.' Barnes: 'Hopkins, with his sudden mirthless Cheshire-cat grin, his combative bustling and windy aggressiveness, gives a wonderfully devious impression of a man broken by his life and times.'

Marsha Mason enjoyed the experience of *Old Times*: 'I remember we talked a great deal about creativity and anxiety. We had both read a book of which the premise was that anxiety is actually where a lot of creativity comes from.

'I know that from the *Audrey Rose* time I had found Tony charming and funny. I remember him doing an imitation of Cary Grant, and you felt he wanted to be the man. Cary Grant was dapper and elegant; I don't think Tony would ever define himself as dapper and elegant, although he is in his approach to friendships, relationships and work. But it's a different kind of elegance, not the superficial kind of well-dressed men. He was also very intense, not exactly a happy-go-lucky guy. Insecure? I don't think I've met an actor who isn't in some way. That's partly what can make them good actors. From the start I found Tony very available, with not a lot of cover, and that continued to be borne out on *Old Times*.'

Lesley-Anne Down found it altogether easier to communicate with her co-star on *Arch of Triumph* than she had a couple of years earlier on *The Hunchback of Notre-Dame*: 'Doing *Hunchback* I never really got to know him at all in any way because of his Quasimodo make-up. By the time I strolled into the studios at around 7 a.m., he already had one eye on the top of his forehead, a nice hump and could barely speak, poor thing. When we did *Arch of Triumph* it was like working with him for the first time. *Him* and not that horrendous thing.'

Arch of Triumph, filmed in Paris by CBS and Harlech TV, was an elegant if fairly pointless remake of a soppy 1948 tearjerker with Charles Boyer and Ingrid Bergman based on the novel by Erich Maria Remarque. Hopkins played Dr Ravic, a once distinguished Munich surgeon, now a caring, scarred refugee from Hitler's Germany reduced to examining nightclub whores to earn a crust.

When one night he spots aspiring chanteuse Lesley-Anne Down looking suicidal on a bridge over the Seine they begin, haltingly, one of those inevitably doomed wartime affairs which end in death and soft focus.

Down recalls their working relationship with pleasure: 'After we first meet in the film, we have to go back to my hotel room, where my lover has died of natural causes. It's quite a tense little scene and I remember that just before they called "Action" we were standing outside in the hallway absolutely piddling ourselves with laughter. Luckily for me the tears were fine because I was supposed to be very unhappy and we managed to go in and do the scene with total concentration. Some actors have to really work at acting – I'm sure Tony does, too – but by the time he's on the set, he's done all his homework. He doesn't need all that other stuff about perfection, like not being spoken to all day in order to make it work. And that makes him extremely pleasant to work with.'

Considering the dreadful dialogue they had to spout – 'If there's a bottle of Calvados within three blocks, it just comes to me', 'Human beings can stand a great deal' – it is surprising they didn't howl with laughter on camera as well as off.

During a break in filming Hopkins flew down to Cannes where *The Bounty* was showing at the Festival. There he told journalists that he could hardly wait to finish his various filming commitments so that he could get back to Benedict Canyon 'to read about the Russian revolution and play the piano'. Would he now be putting in a swimming-pool – the earnings from his non-stop work must surely be stacking up?

'I don't want the trouble one goes through with the cleaning of swimming-pools. But if *The Bounty* does well and I get lots of offers I might take the plunge and buy one. But it will be just for me and the wife. The hangers-on in Tinsel Town can use their own.'

The Grand Tour continued with yet another reunion, this time during a Roman summer for another long mini-series, *Mussolini: The Decline and Fall of Il Duce* (also known as *Mussolini and I*), in which Hopkins and Bob Hoskins reversed the pecking order of their *Othello* roles. Hoskins, bald and brash, was the Fascist dictator while Hopkins played his scheming son-in-law and foreign minister, Count Galeazzo Ciano. An American-Italian-French co-production for cable television transmission in the States, the cast reflected this cosmopolitan set-up: Kurt Raab from Germany, Annie Girardot (France), Susan Sarandon, from Hollywood, playing Mussolini's daughter, Edda; there were even some real Italians, such as Fabio

Testi and Barbara de Rossi. Hopkins, who had the opportunity to wear some smart Italian suits and pretty uniforms, said the film was 'engrossing, a complicated story. We had interpreters on the set so we could communicate. I never learned languages when I was at school, so I don't speak Italian or German, but we got along fine.' Shooting almost simultaneously (in Yugoslavia) with this piece was yet another Ducefest, *Mussolini – The Untold Story*, with George C. Scott, Lee Grant and Raul Julia. 'If,' said Steven Scheuer's *Movies on TV* guide, 'you had to choose between these mini-series, you might be better off settling for Jack Oakie's lampoon of Mussolini in *The Great Dictator* ... ' About the best thing to come out of it, apart from a reputed $450,000 fee, was a covetable testimonial for Hopkins from the rival Duce.

George C. Scott told an interviewer: 'I think Hopkins is the best English-speaking actor today. The mantle of Olivier will rest on him if he doesn't get too commercial.'

Well, if Olivier can be forgiven the occasional 'commercial' lapse, such as Harold Robbins' *The Betsy* (in which the 70-year-old peer sliced off some vintage ham), then surely Hopkins should be allowed the occasional *Hollywood Wives*. Hopkins remains refreshingly unapologetic about his foray into the deepest suds of network soap – 'it was great fun, definitely better than doing Shakespeare' – though $300,000 must have helped and he was able to use the time in California (one of his rare returns in almost two years of predominantly European assignments) to start clearing the decks for a full-time move home to Britain, in particular, selling the Clearview Drive property.

'I don't know if you're interested, I don't even know if I should tell you,' Hopkins' agent said when he rang to inform him that Bob McCullough's script of Jackie Collins' bestseller had arrived at the William Morris office. Hopkins read it and thought, since there was nothing overtly pornographic about it, 'Why not?' According to Collins, as soon as Hopkins signed 'everyone fell into position and we ended up with twelve stars. The moment he agreed to do it, he added a great deal of respectability to the project. Everyone wanted to be in it, which I think is a great compliment to him. He later told me that he had a great Shakespearean actor friend who called him up and said, "Now tell me, my boy, what are you up to?" Apparently, Tony sort of mumbled a reply under his breath because he was a little bit embarrassed: "Well, I'm just doing this television thing, *Hollywood Wives*."

'The other actor boomed, "Oh my God, that's absolutely wonderful. What role will you be playing in it?" And he named all the characters in the book. Tony thought that very funny and felt vindicated in a way because the guy was somehow giving it his seal of approval. But he never told me who the actor was.'

In five hours full of extravagant names (Sadie La Salle, Gina Germaine, Montana Gray, Ross Conti and so on), deathless dialogue – 'In Hollywood, there is no art, only control' – and convoluted plot, Hopkins' contribution, like his English director character's name, Neil Gray ('big talent, small keester'), was comparatively restrained, apart, that is, from his deliverance: a massive heart attack while indulging in an energetic bout of infidelity with a sexy blonde, played by Suzanne Somers. Collins giggles as she recalls his performance: 'I think he brought a lot more to the character than I'd written. He gave a lot of shade and light to it and he was wonderful in all scenes except I think he got a little bit camp in the heart attack scene. Mind you, it can't be easy to act making love then keeling over like that.'

Stefanie Powers, who was playing Hopkins' new wife and co-screenwriter Montana, confirms Hopkins' glee with the whole deliciously absurd enterprise: 'He was having the ball of his life. He just couldn't believe his good luck. For him, the absolute frothiness and silliness of the part and the project represented to him all the things he'd never been able to do. Here he was doing stuff that theatre, or so-called serious, actors would normally consider to be beneath their dignity. He was in the hotbed of Hollywooditis with everybody being as ridiculous as possible with an equally ridiculous story, which had not one shred of real truth, fact or emotion that one could conjure.

' "It's so nice," he told me, "to put on such lovely clothes and to walk round seeing all these pretty ladies." He was really enjoying it. I don't think the piece taxed him very hard. By just walking on the set he immediately rose above the material. There wasn't much you could do with it apart from know your lines, hit your marks and go home and be happy.'

But where was 'home'? 'How the hell do you live out here?' Jonathan Miller once said to Hopkins. 'It's like living on the moon.' Later, when Hopkins was making *The Bounty*, a number of his fellow actors, including Daniel Day-Lewis, said, 'Why don't you go back to the theatre?' Then, while Hopkins was wrapping up *Hollywood Wives*, he was asked if he would be interested in doing a new play in London called *Pravda* by David Hare and Howard Brenton. There was no script as yet but it sounded intriguing.

Hopkins describes how he reached a decision: 'I thought maybe I should do it, if only to prove to myself I had the nerve. Jenni wanted to go back too. So we sold everything. Made sure the cats went to good homes. If I was going to do theatre in England, I couldn't just work there because of the tax situation so I thought I'd better sell everything and move back properly. Yet right up to the last moment, the moment I remember I was standing outside the house locking up for the last time – you could hear the humming birds – I thought, "What am I doing? Why am I giving up this life? Because I *love* it." Common sense dictated I was doing the right thing. I could, after all, end up like some British actors who go out to Hollywood and sit around the pool until their teeth fall out. They then get capped teeth and face jobs and end up in comedy series.'

9. NATIONAL HERO

With *Pravda* in the pipeline, Hopkins also decided to commit himself to another piece of theatre to ease himself, as it were, back into stagecraft. He and Christopher Fettes, who had taught Hopkins at RADA (and been something of a guru ever since) and was both a founder member of the English Stage Company and originator of the Drama Centre in London, had talked for at least five years about working together. Fettes sent Hopkins a number of plays to consider – 'some of them very heavy German things which I didn't think I could do' – until Hopkins eventually settled on Schnitzler's *The Lonely Road*, a comparatively unknown turn-of-the-century work from an author best known for *La Ronde* and *Undiscovered Country* (which Tom Stoppard had adapted for the National in 1979). *The Lonely Road*, which had been described as 'more a *fin-de-siècle* melodrama than a searching work of art', was, nevertheless, an ideal vehicle for Hopkins, in the role of Julian Fichtner, a dissolute, globe-trotting painter who returns, after years of exile, to his native Vienna to confront the past, notably a 23-year-old son who is not aware of his father's identity.

Hopkins and Jenni arrived back in England on 29 November. Two days later rehearsals started for the Schnitzler. With a cast that included another exile, Samantha Eggar, as well as Alan Dobie, Rupert Frazer and Colin Firth, *The Lonely Road* opened a month and a half later at the Yvonne Arnaud Theatre, Guildford, for a fortnight's run before coming into, irony of ironies, the Old Vic, now under the commercial management of the irrepressible Canadian entrepreneur 'Honest' Ed Mirvish.

Michael Billington enthusiastically welcomed this

'first-rate revival of a buried masterpiece ... but perhaps the greatest pleasure lies in watching Hopkins back on the stage.

'He plays the painter like a man aching for human commitment: in one unforgettable scene he stands downstage, eyes slowly moistening, as his son (Firth) gazes at a portrait of his mother and begins to understand his origins. Hopkins, playing with mature quietness, has the naked-souled quality of the real actor.'

By the time *The Lonely Road* had moved off for a final week-long stint at the Theatre Royal, Bath, Hopkins was already deep into rehearsals for *Pravda*. He and Jenni were living in Draycott Avenue, Chelsea, their last temporary home before moving into a charming new terraced house they had purchased elsewhere in Chelsea, when *Pravda* arrived, hot off the typewriter. Hopkins, whose mind was on things Viennese, read it, felt he could not make sense of it and immediately thought that perhaps he did not want to do it after all. So he gave it to Julian Fellowes to read, who insisted, 'It's marvellous! A wonderful part.' 'Is it?' Hopkins said. 'I can't tell.' Jenni read it too: 'You must do it,' she said. Says Fellowes: 'Tony was so submerged in what he was doing at the time that had he been offered Rhett Butler, I think he would have hesitated. He also may have thought that his comeback to the National would be more in the classical mould. Reading the play and the extraordinary part of Lambert Le Roux must have fazed him a bit.'

Pravda was Hare and Brenton's first script together since their fulminating black comedy *Brassneck*, about civic corruption, in 1973 for the Nottingham Playhouse (later memorably adapted for the BBC).

Brenton had had the idea of using Fleet Street for the new project, but once he got together with Hare it became less and less specifically about Fleet Street and more about the place as a metaphor for power and corruption, as well as outrageous comedy. The central joke is, of course, the title itself. The word '*pravda*', less-than-coincidentally also the title of an official Soviet newspaper, ironically means 'truth'.

Lambert Le Roux does not make his first entrance until the third scene of the first act. In the preceding scenes, he has been referred to, tantalisingly, by others. To one he is 'a South African, of impeccable liberal credentials', to another he is merely 'a racist'. From the various exchanges, alternately guarded and raucous, it is clear that Le Roux is both mighty powerful and predatory. Then he appears, walking on to an empty stage. The script describes him thus: 'He is in his early forties, heavily built, muscular and dark. He is wearing a dark suit. It is plain, anonymous, of the greatest quality.' His first, memorable, speech spoken directly to us concludes: 'What I do is the natural thing. There is nothing unnatural about making money. When you are born where I was born, you do have a feeling for nature. What I admire about nature is ... animals, birds, plants; they fucking get on with it and don't stand about complaining all the time.'

Le Roux is a double-dyed monster. On second reading, things became clearer to Hopkins: 'Le Roux is like the bogeyman. He comes out of the darkness of everyone's fears and he stands there and just lambasts everyone and he has no feelings; he doesn't care what anyone thinks of him. He ploughs on like Jaws, like some predator.'

Hopkins had very effectively imitated monsters before – Hitler included – using copycat techniques. Now he had to create one from scratch.

His memorable portrayal of Le Roux is perhaps best remembered, apart from the explosive use of Hare and Brenton's language, for a remarkably sustained rasping South African accent, an aggressive physical stance, back bent into a pronounced lean and bull-neck thrust forward, and the darting tongue of some monstrous reptile. The accent came from tapes provided by playwright-actor Athol Fugard, the stance from an American producer, David Susskind, with whom Hopkins had worked on both *All Creatures Great and Small* and *The Bunker*, and a mobile tongue exaggerated from his mimicry of Olivier.

Hopkins remembered being invited once to a restaurant in New York by Susskind: 'He said "Waiter!" and the waiter came over. "What do you want to drink?" he asked me. I said, "Perrier." He said to the waiter, "Give him Perrier water." Everything was very efficient. I remember these soft, feminine hands of his and these cold, hooded eyes and I thought, "There's a man I could use." Now, David wasn't a fiend or anything, but he ran a large corporation and was a Le Roux sort of figure.' David Hare was in New York about a year after *Pravda* had opened and was in a restaurant one day, 'and by the most extraordinary coincidence I heard this man, who I was told was David Susskind, talking about me. He didn't know I was there so I looked at him and saw his back was bent in the same position as Tony's had been. Later, I asked Tony if he'd got that lean from Susskind and he said, "Absolutely." '

Hare, who was also directing *Pravda*, had originally wanted Hopkins for his film of *Wetherby* but as he was unavailable the role went to Ian Holm (much later Holm also stepped into another plum part when Hopkins decided to pass on Len Deighton's spy saga *Game, Set and Match*).

What particularly impressed Hare about Hopkins was his 'maniacal energy. For this part you had to have that pulsing out of you. My view of Tony is that he's a character actor and once the mask goes on of the character, or the voice, then he is extraordinarily liberated as an actor. In fact, he can be quite pale and wan when he hasn't got a face, a look or a gesture. To begin with, we were all terribly nervous of the part. There was a general feeling of "Is he really going to speak in this incredibly tortured accent for the next two hours?" It meant, though, he could find the freedom to do what he wanted. It is the deepest mystery of acting.'

Howard Brenton, writing in the quarterly theatre review *Drama*, explained his feelings as the play moved from the page to performance: 'I sat in the middle of the packed Olivier Theatre watching the first preview of

ANTHONY HOPKINS

Pravda. David Hare and I had driven each other on to make the play a comedy, committed to laughter or dreadful failure. We had never before attempted, as dramatists, either together or singly, to "go over the top", in the First World War phrase the theatre uses for outright commitment to one thing in a show.

'Because collaborative writing means that you speak, often shout, each line out, or scribble then try it out on your fellow writer, who at once grins or grimaces, and because we wanted to go on the attack against the sort of writing Fleet Street passes off on its readers, we decided from the start to make the play, if we could, a monstrously funny monument, set up on the most prominent stage in the country . . . A few seconds before the lights went down on the first preview, I had a nightmarish thought: "Oh my God, this lasts three hours. What if only David and I find these scenes, lines and foibles of human behaviour funny? And if there is not a single laugh between now and curtain call?" '

Recalls Hare: 'When Tony walked on stage in the preview there was a great ovation, which moved him. He went on to give a sublime performance. It came to the first night and he was ludicrously confident. I realised that the only thing that could destroy it was over-confidence, so half an hour before the opening curtain I asked him if he would like to play Lear. He gave a wonderful performance that night and said to me afterwards he hadn't really been able to think about the part because of what I'd asked him. Anyway, about ten minutes after he'd come offstage, he said he would do Lear.'

In *Plays*, Alan Brien wrote: 'Reading the text in advance, I thought half a dozen of our leading actors could have embodied this part, with Nicol Williamson as perhaps my number one choice. Now, having seen Hopkins, I cannot imagine an equal to his performance. He becomes at once a quite engaging, humorous, endearingly anti-Establishment adventurer and what can only be described as a force of nature, some kind of wood demon come to town, a Christmas tree, festooned with evil wishes, that starts to walk shaking off its hangers-on, leaving them broken and unmendable. It is rather like meeting Stalin in the Garrick Club.'

The late Emlyn Williams described Hopkins' performance as the greatest in post-war theatre. Most critics, many with distinct reservations about the play itself (from 'dreadfully crude and shallow comedy' to 'bilious burlesque'), were unreservedly ecstatic about Hopkins.

Unspeakable monster as he undoubtedly is (and as he was surely intended), Le Roux somehow manages to emerge as some kind of maverick hero for, as Lyn Gardner noted, perceptively, in *City Limits*, 'They've created a character of such comic stature that the others dwindle into insignificance when he appears. In the presence of such ineffectual opposition, his blunt right-wing views begin to sound all too dangerously plausible.' It is the fundamental weakness of an otherwise rip-roaring piece of theatre.

Hare remains in awe of Hopkins' achievement through a run of 160 performances: 'He could barely put a foot wrong as Le Roux, certainly not with the spirit of the piece. But there was a stage when I felt he was becoming rather stiff and jerky. So one night I said to him, "Try making him a fluid, fluent reptile rather than a stiff reptile." And he went on and re-interpreted every single move and gesture in the entire play. It was a most wonderful performance. I asked him afterwards how he had done it and he said, "You told me to relax more and I did." But really, it was like the hand of God had lifted him up. He wasn't like an actor, he was like God's puppet. *Pravda* was, I think, an extraordinary coincidence of a role and an actor and he gave something that English audiences were starved of at the time. He was a great leading man who was sexy. A lot of it, which was never referred to, came from that. He was dangerously sexy and attractive in a role which was revolting. The performance had sexual virility. The other thing which almost nobody commented on was of a great rush of sexual need which came to the stage from the audience. It was wonderful to see that on an English stage.'

Exactly a year after he received that thunderous ovation at the Olivier Awards – 'I thought Mick Jagger must have walked on behind me' – when participating merely as a presenter, Hopkins was back to pick up a trophy in his own right: the Kenneth Tynan Observer Award for 'outstanding achievement in the theatre'. The Best Actor award had gone to Anthony Sher for his roles in *Richard III* and *Torch Song Trilogy*. Hopkins also won awards from the British Theatre Association, *Drama Magazine* and the Royal Variety Club for *Pravda*. Towards the end of 1985 he was combining stage at night with filming in South London by day. *The Good Father*, an adaptation of Peter Prince's novel by Christopher Hampton, reunited Hopkins with the director Mike Newell, with whom he had last worked on a BBC Play for Today, *The Childhood Friend*, a decade earlier.

Newell recalled him as having been at that time, just after walking out of the National, 'vulnerable and jumpy. Now he seemed much more settled, definite and clear about what he thought and wanted and the direction in which he wanted to go. It was some time after *Pravda* had opened. It had been decided to offer him the role of Bill Hooper in *The Good Father* but I didn't talk to him about the part until he'd read the script. Because it was a tight schedule, just five weeks, and a wordy piece, and there were some high-quality actors assembled in the cast, I wanted to rehearse it, and we'd allowed for a week to ten days' rehearsal period before shooting. Tony phoned up very late in the day, about 36 hours before we were due to rehearse, and said he didn't want to. I had to persuade him into it, which I did with no little tact. He consented to try it for a bit and so we worked on a day-by-day basis. Eventually he did it right through and I think he quite enjoyed himself.'

According to Hopkins: 'At the beginning, I thought Mike was making it a bit complicated. I phoned him up and said, "With due respect, I think I know what you mean about this character. But I'll tell you now: I know this character. He's me. I can play it standing on my head. We'll rehearse it if you want, but it's an easy part." And it was, really. I must say I had a lovely time doing the film and Mike was very good.'

Why should he have not wanted to rehearse? Newell says: 'Tony makes a god of his intuition. He is intuition-led and intuition-driven and if it doesn't meet his intuition right then I think he can't work with it. There was one occasion, and I stress it was one occasion out of about 500 possible occasions, when I couldn't see why he was playing a scene a particular way. It was difficult to perceive what he was doing. So I had to ask. I said: "If you tell me what you're aiming for, I can help ..." And he couldn't quite explain it. I learnt a lesson there: that one had to try to look at him not from a logical point of view, but from the point of view of what his feelings or intuition were prompting him to do. He doesn't like making his feelings public property, having them chewed over. He doesn't like them being accessible for others to try and adjust. He doesn't like people getting sticky-fingered with his work. So, it's partly intuition and, I think, partly defensive.'

In *The Good Father* (which eventually went on to win the Prix Italia) Hooper is a middle-aged bike boy, separated from his wife and allowed only limited access to his little son. He is toweringly bitter and vindictive.

His meeting with a mild-mannered schoolteacher who is going through an even more exaggerated domestic crisis – involving a lesbian wife and a young, adored child – gives Hooper the excuse for a sort of vicarious revenge, which, ironically, goes further than either husband had wanted.

Pauline Kael wrote in the *New Yorker* that the film 'has the festering gloom and dissatisfied-with-itself hatefulness that seem to be the current English badge of integrity. Anthony Hopkins appears in the starring role, and the whole movie is summed up by his face. He has taken over the Peter Finch crown of middle-class suffering. Quoting various critics, the ads say that Anthony Hopkins is spectacular, brilliant, stellar, riveting, high-voltage, terrific, a smouldering fury. Those are all the things he isn't. Hopkins is Hopkins – thoughtful, masochistic, a man whose emotions are convincing within a small, dark range. Hopkins never dazzles you; he never dazzles himself.'

Hopkins recalls: 'There was a moment when I was filming with Harriet Walter [playing his estranged wife] in the child's bedroom and I suddenly broke down and started crying. My own situation with my first marriage, not seeing my daughter any more and so on, suddenly all came back to me. I had buried it at the time along the lines of "I don't need all this in my life any more" – family commitments, etc. Being there with the child's bed and the toys made it all come back as if out of nowhere. When I cleared off from my first marriage my daughter Abigail was in her cot. Doing the scene – they shot it again – all seemed very real.'

The explosive, resentful Hooper could not have been further away from Hopkins' next film persona, that of the gentle bookstore manager Frank Doel in *84 Charing Cross Road*, again fitted in between *Pravda* performances.

King Lear rehearsals were still months away and further down the line still was now yet another National commitment, to play opposite Judi Dench in Peter Hall's production of *Antony and Cleopatra*. Meanwhile they were teamed as husband and wife for a handful of short scenes in this clever 'opening out' by Hugh Whitemore of a transatlantic literary love affair. Whitemore had already adapted the original book, by Helene Hanff, for television. A successful London stage production (which later ran for a while in New York) was the award-winning work of adapter-director James Roose-Evans.

Hall, incidentally, had mentioned to Dench the idea of doing the Shakespeare quite some time before this. 'When I hadn't heard from him for a long time about it,' she recalls, 'I just thought that maybe it had been something that he'd said over an evening; so I didn't take it very seriously. In fact, I took it so unseriously that I told the Royal Shakespeare Company I'd do it for them. Then I met Peter again and said, "You wouldn't be offended if I did it for the RSC?" He said, "I'd be very offended indeed." Then he told me he'd asked Tony to do it and I was delighted, so much so I followed it up with a letter – not knowing him – to Tony saying, "Look, I'm prepared to make a fool of myself. Please do it as well. Let's both throw ourselves in at the very deepest end." We were both quite worried about doing the play.'

Meanwhile there was work to do back at Charing Cross Road. The film-of-the-play-of-the-book, *Q's Legacy*, is a slice of autobiography detailing a twenty-year correspondence between a feisty New Yorker, Miss Hanff, and the staff, principally Doel, of Marks & Co., an antiquarian booksellers of the eponymous address in London, who find and send out-of-print classics across the ocean to her.

Hanff, played in the film by Anne Bancroft (her husband Mel Brooks' company Brooksfilms was making the movie), and Doel never actually meet. But a touching sort of relationship flowers despite their being an ocean apart, against a background of changing American and British cultures between 1949 and 1969. When she does finally make it to England, it is too late: Doel has died of peritonitis. It was an unlikely subject for development beyond the printed page, yet one that seems to have worked triumphantly in all media. The stage play had perpetrated a 'white lie' by never mentioning Doel's wife. By going back to the original letters, Whitemore in his script managed to turn the story almost into a subliminal love triangle. At the end of the film Nora Doel writes movingly to Hanff: 'I must tell you that I've been very jealous of you for many years because you appealed to something in my husband that I could never reach.'

When Whitemore finished the first draft of his adaptation, David Jones, an experienced stage director who had made only one previous cinema film, Harold Pinter's

Betrayal, with Jeremy Irons, Patricia Hodge and Ben Kingsley, sent it to Hopkins, the actor he most wanted to play Doel. 'Will you pass my thanks on to Hugh Whitemore?' Hopkins wrote back smartly. 'This is the most intelligent, literate script I've been offered in ten years. When do we start working?'

Hopkins and his 'co-star' Bancroft met just twice, before production began and at an end-of-shooting party. Otherwise, it was a ships-in-the-night business, much as it had been on two previous assignments in which they had both been involved, *Young Winston* and *The Elephant Man*.

The morning Hopkins went off to start shooting at Shepperton Studios (where Eileen Diss had designed a remarkable series of sets), he phoned David Swift, who had played Doel on stage: 'He didn't make a great thing about it but it was a lovely thing to do and it meant a lot to me. I'm realistic enough to know I wasn't right for the film,' said Swift.

Dench, who with her husband Michael Williams had actually turned down the stage version ('We wrote back saying it was marvellous but "it's a recital evening". That's the story of my life'), was much helped by Hopkins on set: 'I'm a very uneasy film actress indeed and Tony is simply marvellous at putting you at your ease. The very first shot I had to do was in bed and just before it he said: "Isn't this fun, off we go, all working together!" It was kind and reassuring. I tend to get embarrassed acting in front of someone I don't know but we seemed to get on straight away. We talked a great deal too. There was a shot to do in Richmond Park and we had a long, long time just talking in the caravan about everything – fears, expectations. We had a lot of nostalgic fun dancing in Embankment Gardens. But apart from that I didn't really get to know him then except in fairly jokey terms.'

For Hopkins, playing Doel was a delight: 'He is the kind of man who went about his job, got on with his life in a very undemonstrative way. Of course he was a widely read man, a man of good education, but he didn't just brag about it, just quietly read and observed and probably in his own way became a philosopher. There's a part of me that loves that stillness, and the other great thing about playing him was that I didn't have to shout.'

David Jones, who had experienced Hopkins in more tempestuous vein eight years earlier when he produced *Kean* for the BBC, found an altogether more relaxed actor this time round: 'Tony loves to appear very casual about the whole thing and he will crack jokes up to the last minute. He'd keep saying, "What's my next line?" This gave a half-impression that he hadn't learned them. What he in fact wanted to do was to give the impression of finding words out of nowhere. We recorded all the letters before the main shooting began. When it came to doing those scenes where the letters are being voiced over, I offered Anne and Tony a minute earpiece so they could actually hear the letter to which they were meant to be reacting. I would have bet that Tony would have accepted and Anne turn my offer down. In fact it was quite the other way round. I don't know whether Tony managed to memorise all the letters, but the way he reacted without actually knowing what was coming next made me think he had some sort of ESP. It was brilliant and quite uncanny.'

Jones also describes the time when, more recently, he was due to work on a new film with Robert De Niro and the American actor carried out his usual exhaustive research, which included checking up on the director. He ran *84 Charing Cross Road* and was absolutely riveted by Hopkins' performance. 'So truthful,' he told Jones.

Hopkins' performance (for which he won Best Actor award at the Moscow Film Festival) and the peerless ensemble playing of other British actors in the cast, among them Maurice Denham, Ian McNeice, Wendy Morgan and Eleanor David, prevent the film's charm from becoming too cloying or its resolute sweetness turning to pure schmaltz.

For Mel Brooks, Hopkins' timing was 'the most exquisite I've ever seen. There's a scene where he's eating a meal with his wife. He tastes the food, he digests it, he looks at her before he speaks. It takes a full minute on the screen. Then he says, "Very nice, very tasty." Hugh Whitemore wanted a moment of a sort of gentle, dull civility, the worn fabric of life, and he got it in that one sentence. Tony is so powerful in his understating: his muted colours are better than everybody's primary colours. For me, he's the Beethoven of acting – profoundly creative and brilliantly orchestrated.' That same little scene also struck Patrick Garland: 'It's quite comical really. He gives more resonance to it than it deserves. His strange inflections make it full of import and somehow invest it with a special significance, although it's only an ordinary conversation. And it works.'

There is also a gem of a sequence when Doel visits the elderly Denham character who is dying in hospital and rather distractedly reads him the latest letter from New York. 'This was one scene when he didn't joke around,' remembers David Jones. It was, in fact, a poignant, and quite painful, reminder for Hopkins of visiting his father during Dick's final illness at St Woolos.

Previously, in the spring, while he was still filming *84 Charing Cross Road*, a journalist had asked Hopkins about *Lear*, and he had told him: 'I did glance at the play the other day, panicked and threw it into the corner. It can stay there for a bit longer yet.' At the end of the summer of 1986, after he had also finished *Blunt* for the BBC (in which he played, with outrageous camp charm, a curly-haired Guy Burgess opposite Ian Richardson as Anthony Blunt and Michael Williams as Goronwy Rees), he and Jenni took the Orient Express to Venice, where they joined the Swifts for a week's holiday. As the Hopkinses had never been to the city before David and Paula gave them a Cook's tour, which included an unscheduled stop at a theatrical costumiers. This, Paula recalls, was more like 'Aladdin's Cave, full of clothes and wonderful Edith Sitwell-like hats which they let us try on, much to everyone's amusement'. This

European foray would be Hopkins' last chance to relax for several months.

On 29 September Hopkins began rehearsals for *King Lear*. It was the first-ever production (rather surprisingly) of the play by the National since the company was founded 23 years earlier, director Hare's Shakespeare début and Hopkins' first Shakespeare role on a London stage since the traumas of 1972–3. Peter Brook's production in 1962, with Paul Scofield, made Hare (and others of his generation, he is sure) 'decide they wanted to work in the theatre ... What he [Shakespeare] wants to show is what life is like when people have no way of knowing whether their faith might or might not be well placed. That's where the terror comes from. This doesn't, as some critics have argued, make it an "absurdist" play. Not at all. In fact what I most remember of Brook's supposedly "cruel" production is its exceptional sweetness.'

'Lear?' said Michael Gambon when Hopkins asked him how he had approached the role when he played it for the RSC in 1982. 'Piece of piss. Stand centre stage, shake a bit, shout your words and don't take your eyes off the bloody Fool for a moment. It also helps if the Fool isn't too funny.' Hopkins also had a letter from Olivier telling him not to worry, that the role wasn't as demanding as its reputation suggested.

From the outset Hopkins and Hare agreed about certain aspects of the play. Hare describes the approach: 'It was not a drama of senility. He wasn't going to shake or quaver; even some of the greatest Lears have achieved their effect by wobbling about. We made it totally unsentimental about old age and that was a great achievement. The second thing we agreed was that the second half of the play would be the climax, whereas it usually climaxes in the storm. We had the meeting with Gloucester [Michael Bryant] as the most moving scene and we shifted the weight of the play on to the fourth and fifth acts.'

So where were they at odds? 'I always saw it as a progress towards death,' explains Hare. 'I wanted a Lear who knew what he was doing. He knows he must soon die and therefore he conducts this great experiment to find out the meaning of life. Traditionally, he doesn't know what he is doing, or else does it for impetuous or petty motives. To me, the motives are not petty. Intellectually Tony agreed with me, but he didn't want to play it that way, not in his deepest being, and I couldn't make him. He also found playing the part incredibly disturbing. Basically, he lost his marbles in the middle of it. I told him he was playing the most difficult part ever written in the most difficult theatre in England, that he was planning to play it one hundred times in rep, so he shouldn't have been surprised.

'I think it had been a dream for him in *Pravda* and he found it very hard to return to the unsatisfactoriness of a regular theatre production. I think he didn't want to go the whole way you have to go with that part. Le Roux was a great virtuoso role but it was about blasting out psychic energy, about the great destroyers, nihilism and destruction, and Tony has this limitless energy to give out. Lear is an introspective role; the energy is directed inside yourself to introspective areas, and Tony wasn't up to that in his soul, at that time and for various personal reasons.

'I remember we had a rough series of previews where the performance would be in and out of focus, and before the first night I said to Tony, "I think you should just forget about the character of Lear and bring your own pain, your own personal suffering, on to the stage." And he gave a wonderful first night. But afterwards he said, "I know what to do on the nights when I'm juiced up but now I need to know what to do on the second performance when I fake it. I need the technical performance" – meaning for the times when he wasn't so emotional. I don't think he ever found that in Lear and it caused him terrible grief.'

For Hare the play was a watershed because, he says, 'it raised that question of just *how* do you make every theatrical performance fresh. I used to go and see the production and it would break my heart to find it wasn't what we had had in the rehearsal room. Or else, I'd see it and be moved by the fresh, spontaneous things which had been brought to it by Tony. But it was the beast out of control. It was also a watershed in that it posed for me problems of theatre directing which were insoluble, and so I gave it up; it was a very bruising experience for me.

'But having said that, it played for a record number of performances [with 100, Hopkins was the first actor ever to give this number of performances of the role on the London stage] to full houses, and often to standing ovations. But neither Tony nor I were very happy about it. Possibly it was *Lear* itself, or maybe I was the wrong director for him. He made it quite plain about how he was feeling; he wanted to run away from the stage.'

When the critics had their say they were not quite so unanimous in their praise for Hopkins as they had been for his performance in *Pravda* and, indeed, were of distinctly mixed opinion about the production itself, generally considering it too cold and austere. At this point Hopkins felt something akin to panic setting in: 'One smell of failure, one questionable review, unnerves me, shakes the foundation, makes me feel I'm on quicksand. When I actually feel I have failed, as I did with Lear (both David and I were out of our depth), I have always equated it with some moral defect in myself. That it's *me*, somehow, that I'm worthless. Absolute bollocks, of course. David Swift said to me: "Tony, you have had some terrific reviews. One or two of them didn't much like the play, but most of them liked you. One or two of them said it was a good attempt ..." And I told David, "Yes, but what about the bad ones ... ?" Anyway, I went over to the London Library and read all the reviews I could find of other *Lears*. I discovered that Olivier had had an appalling one from Ken Tynan and I must admit that made me feel better. Even Scofield had a few bad ones.'

The fact remains that Hopkins' gruff-voiced, bullet-headed, sparsely bearded and, in one critic's phrase, 'superannuated welterweight boxer' of a king, actually pleased far more than it pained.

Paranoia about the odd carping review was however only a symptom of a greater insecurity that had begun to bubble up as early as halfway through *Pravda*.

Hopkins reflects: 'It became painfully clear that, for me, working in the theatre was an exercise in futility. Perhaps it had something to do with not drinking any more. I used to wake up in the mornings and absolutely dread going into the National. Every day I would try and pump myself up with positive thoughts but I'd always be defeated by it. I would think back to when I walked out in 1973 and remember how exhilarated I was. Now I'd gone back a second time and put myself through the mill again. I stayed the course, which I suppose was something, but I stayed there with gritted teeth and with no enjoyment at all. I think you have to have a special temperament and a rigorous dedication. I have to improvise all the time; it would drive me mad to become a talking record-box. So I busk it every night within the structure of the verse, trying to make it always as if it were the first time. Some regard that as a lack of discipline, or unprofessional.

'Part of the temperament is to be able to fit into an ensemble and one of the things I so dislike about the theatre is the so-called "family atmosphere". This is probably a hangover from my school days. Somehow the actors are the naughty children and there is a matriarchal frown from the casting department or a tyrannical paternalistic presence, like the director. The point is, I've never been able to live comfortably in groups of actors, particularly with a parentalistic director. Some can; I simply can't. I don't have a plain-sailing personality; acting certainly doesn't come easy to me.

'I have to patch together a pretty flimsy technique to make it on to the stage and I know I'm not easy for actors and directors to work with because I'm all over the place. I often don't know what I'm doing. In *Lear* I'd resort to throwing people round the stage. Michael Bryant used to say, "Oh, it's your sex-and-violence night tonight, is it?" I'd go out there with a bulldozing technique and it sort of got me through. To do a hundred performances of *Lear* and then a hundred performances of *Antony and Cleopatra* is an act of madness, I think. Shakespeare's so bloody difficult and I don't like failure. I don't mind failing in private. You can fail on film, but there's nobody actually there in the flesh to watch you failing.

'In the theatre, there's this sense we should all be brave and stiff-upper-lip and take our punishment, particularly from the critics. I don't believe that; I don't see why it's necessary to stand up there and have somebody throw mud at you. All I understand about myself is that I have a prodigious memory and enough balls and muscle to get up and do it. God knows I admire people like Ian McKellen, Judi Dench, Maggie Smith, Gielgud and Olivier, who, when you look at them on the stage, seem to be at home there. They're a special sort of animal.

'So, anyway, when I opened in *Lear* and realised, in my own terms, that it was a total disaster, to have to go out there night after night to resurrect what I saw as a complete washout was my version of Hell. At the end of it all, all I was really able to say was, "I've had a go at it – I've climbed a bit of the way up the mountain." But it was still Hell.'

The snow lay quite thick in London when, in early January 1987, the cast of *Antony and Cleopatra* got together for their first meeting, in Conference Room 3 at the top of the National.

Before that Judi Dench had rung Hopkins up and told him she had not yet read the play: 'He was frightfully pleased about that because he hadn't either. That first morning I got there fearfully early because I was very, very frightened. I just remember seeing Tony and noticing he was extremely jumpy. I put that down to the same kind of fright as I had. But I think it was more than that. In fact, I know it was . . . now.'

According to John Dexter, 'He should have known about Antony. Apart from Romeo, it's the worst romantic Shakespeare role because you're missing at all the key points. You work your knickers off in the first half of the play, then you disappear and she takes over. Later on you spend your time with your back half to the audience and get a crick in the neck. You must take to the part supreme self-confidence – in the verse, in everything. If Tony had had a word with Olivier, Larry would have said "No"; he did it himself and it's bloody difficult.'

Hopkins says: 'I didn't know a single line. I was so overwhelmed by *Lear* that I felt just washed out. I said to Peter Hall: "I can't do this, I'm sorry." He turned on his charm and said, "You've got to do it." '

About three weeks into the twelve-week rehearsal period, Dench bumped into Hopkins one morning by the stage door.

'He dragged me outside and said, "I'm not going to do this." I could see this coming. I said, "Well, that's all right, if that's how you feel. What you must do though is catch Peter before we go back to rehearsal. Don't wait until he comes in and we're all there. Catch him now."

'That's what he did. Peter sent him home – I think it was a Thursday – then came and asked me what I thought about it. I said, "Well, he's so tailor-made for the part I think he could do it in three weeks" – there were still about eight weeks of rehearsal to go – "so now he should rest and take some time off." But my heart was in my boots. Peter said, "Yes, I quite agree." We girded our loins and battled on. In fact Tony was back on the Monday having been told he must take a week off. Those kinds of insecurities beset him to the most amazing extent throughout the play. Some days he was very up and strong, on many others . . . on his way to the theatre he'd suddenly want to rush off and hide in one of those blue movie places in Soho because nobody would think of looking for him there. That became a kind of password between us.

'In fact the rehearsal period was thrilling. Peter was on the most perfect form for those weeks. The first scene is very formal and at first we couldn't crack it at all. Then Tony said why didn't he and I come in early, get everyone out of the way and we'd work on it – which we did, and we ended up being all over each other on the ground. There was this passion. There's a great sense of expectation about this particular play and, in a way, everything was loaded against us at the beginning. For example, every time I did an interview they'd ask me if I was surprised to get the part, and I'd reply, "What you want me to say is how can a 54-year-old, five-foot-tall woman be anyone's idea of Cleopatra." All the way through I felt that Tony had made up his mind that this was something he had to conquer, though there was never, for a second, the impression his heart wasn't in it.'

Hall asked them whether they wanted the piece 'set', that is, the moves all worked out. They both said no. Dench explains: 'That way, you keep it very much alive and more spontaneous. Curious, though, that when one is so fearful already one should want to add more fear to it. I suppose the fear turns to adrenalin. Mind you, there were nights when I didn't ever know quite what was going to happen. I could see Tony coming towards me with what I'd call cash-register eyes. And I'd think, "This is it. This is when I go flying out into Row Six." In fact, it helped enormously. These were such complex characters that to have a bit of not knowing where the other person was going to jump next seemed very much to do with their lives.'

On one occasion just before the play opened, in front of a preview audience, they went through a technical crisis. Hopkins describes the effect this had: 'Something didn't work, something went wrong. And we all went into a deep depression.

'I spent the Sunday feeling very miserable. I was reading a book by Ken Tynan of his reviews and there were some of Richard Burton back in the 1950s, and Tynan said something about Burton and the Welsh people being rather sombre and not an extrovert race of people; that part of Burton's quality was [that] he wasn't a ready smiler or laugher. As I read it, something choked up in me and I phoned Peter Hall and said, "I've got it. I know this technical thing is another question, but I've just been reading this piece and I think I can do what you want. But with all due respect, you wanted me to create some kind of charmer and I'm not that. I'm not an extrovert, romantic actor. I'm an anti-romantic. That's what the Welsh are like." Peter said: "Whatever you have to do to get it, do it." I settled into this and Hall said: "That's exactly what I want. It's that peculiar, dark, sombre side we once talked about. If you can sustain that, then fine." That's his great magnanimity and humility as a director; he likes actors to get on with it.'

Antony and Cleopatra opened in April. Whatever doubts may have lingered about Dench's physical equipment for the Nile queen were triumphantly dispelled, as a series of remarkable notices (and subsequent awards) demonstrated.

And Hopkins' own endless self-doubts should surely have been quashed by some similarly ecstatic reviews. In the *Guardian*, Michael Billington wrote: 'It is not only the most intelligently-spoken Shakespeare I have heard in years but it also contains two performances from Judi Dench and Anthony Hopkins that, in their comprehensive humanity, rank with Ashcroft and Redgrave at Stratford many moons ago ... Hopkins' magnificent Antony [is] a real old campaigner – you can believe he ate "strange flesh" in the Alps – for whom Alexandria represents escape and fantasy. Mr Hopkins, like many heavyweights, is extraordinarily light on his feet, externalises the conflict in Antony between the soldier and the lover; when recalled to Rome he prowls the stage hungrily like a lion waiting to get back into the arena. But what I shall remember most is Mr Hopkins' false gaiety – and overpowering inward grief – in the short scene where he bids farewell to his servants. From that point on, the knowledge of death sits on Antony; and when Mr Hopkins says he will contend even with his pestilent scythe it is with a swashbuckling bravura that moves one to tears.'

After completing two weeks of performances – *Lear* and *Antony and Cleopatra* were going to overlap for a full five months – Hopkins and Jenni took off to Lucerne in Switzerland for a fortnight's holiday.

The trip did not refresh him: 'I was utterly miserable there. I couldn't enjoy it because of the dread of going back to those two mammoth pieces. There seemed no way out of this tunnel ahead. Of course, it was my own fault for doing them both. Peter Hall had charmed me into doing the second play and I thought at the time, "In for a penny, in for a pound." Funnily enough, as it went on, I didn't mind Lear so much, but with Antony I was getting really despondent.' Not even his inclusion in the Queen's Birthday Honours List that summer, when he was awarded a CBE, seemed to bring him much cheer.

'I began to think, "What's the point? I've never been able to get to grips with the part." One or two of the papers said I was hopeless and I took that to heart. I found myself more and more just playing it in anger. And then on the 78th performance, shortly before Christmas, I finally found out how to play it.

'It came about like this. I had a really bad cold and on the Friday I went out on stage feeling really rotten. My throat was raw, I was deaf in one ear because I had some sinus [trouble] and I didn't know where the hell I was. I even tried to cut out half a speech. On the Saturday I went in to do the matinée and actually felt a bit better, even though the throat was still pretty raw. That evening it was better still and I thought it sounded rather good too.

'On the Monday afternoon I had to go to a little studio in Audley Square to do some looping on *The Dawning*, a film I'd made in Ireland that autumn. On the screen was this fellow with a beard about the same length I had to have it for Antony and I thought, "I don't look too bad; that's quite a nice-looking fellow up there." I'd taken off some weight, looked a bit of a rough diamond and that was the way, I suddenly thought, I should have been playing Antony.'

When Hopkins went to the theatre that night his voice was still fairly hoarse. Judi Dench asked him how he was feeling. Hopkins said, 'My voice is a bit better. You know,

I'm really looking forward to tonight.' She said, 'You know, I am too.'

Hopkins recalls: 'I went on, opened my mouth and this voice – it was still rough and a bit gravelly – came out. I suddenly thought – actually I hardly dared think it in case it went away – *this* is how I want to play the part. Now I could see this character clearly at last. This besotted, dissipated, battle-scarred old general, like a battered old tomcat; scarred, bruised, raucous, drunken, but a great spirit. It was sheer chance that my voice had played itself into my subconscious that way. And why, I thought typically, had it taken so bloody long to get it right?'

10. WORKAHOLIC: PART II

'**B**ut what of the man beneath so many masks? "Upon what meat doth this our Antony [Anthony] feed, that he is grown so great?" A friend once presented him with a teddy-bear toting a gun – which illustrates him well: delightful, cuddly even, but steely hard and deadly when necessary. Nowhere more so than in his well-publicised conquest of alcohol addiction. He fought his way to freedom and has been a tireless worker for Alcoholics Anonymous. He has spent so many hours helping and counselling others that many people, famous and unknown, owe their freedom to his love and care. Apart from that, I am in a position to inform you, Chancellor, that he loves cats, hates sport, doesn't cook, loathes housework and detests gardening. I have it, however, on the highest authority that he does have one secret habit. When he needs to unwind or prepare for a great event he reverts to his army days and "spits-and-polishes" a pair of shoes, which is why, Sir, we on this stage have been dazzled by their brilliance this morning . . .'

Professor Brian Morris was delivering the encomium at the University of Wales where, before its Chancellor, the Prince of Wales, Hopkins received the honorary degree of Doctor of Letters on 16 July 1988. For the self-styled graduate of 'the University of W.H. Smith', who had managed to muster only one O-level during his more formal education, it was a singular honour, particularly in his native Wales. He had, coincidentally, just completed his second uniquely 'Welsh' role on the trot, though a rather different kettle of Celt from Ayckbourn's knockabout Daffyd ap Llewellyn.

In *Heartland*, filmed for BBC Wales in the Preseli

mountains, Hopkins was playing Jack Phillips, a hard-pressed dairy farmer who falls foul of EEC bureaucracy after tangles over complicated agricultural subsidies. With his already precarious living terminally threatened, Jack resorts to more drastic measures, such as kidnapping a pair of European commissioners. 'I always seem to be cast as the fiery, independent character ... like Jack Phillips,' Hopkins told local journalists, 'but the difference between me and the hero is that for me going into a milking shed was worse than the inquisition. Cows look all right in the field, but when you get up close to them you realise what big animals they are ... When it came to milking the cows and fitting those things on their teats I was a bit nervous. And the farmer whose dairy we used referred to me more than once as "Tony Perkins". Not that I minded. I was among people who have their lives to lead doing the job they know best and I felt a great deal of sympathy for them ... I just approached it as a professional actor. I have to get on with the job of acting and, besides, I was with a farmer who had been through all this business about the milk quotas. I don't know that much about it. He does.' A Surrey correspondent to the *Radio Times*, Miss E. Waterson, was speaking for many critics when she described Hopkins' performance in this uneven, over-long film as 'outstanding, stirring, heartfelt'.

Another day, another role. In August Hopkins was outside Paris, near Versailles, reunited with his old sparring partner from *The Hunchback of Notre Dame*, the producer Norman Rosemont, for a telemovie of Graham Greene's novella *The Tenth Man*. Greene had had a wartime deal with MGM – 'a slave contract' is how he actually described it – during which time he wrote what he later remembered as being merely a two-page idea for a novel set in France immediately after liberation in 1944. Forty years on, that 'idea', in fact some 60,000 words, was discovered in a Hollywood vault by MGM archivists and published in book form in 1985.

Hopkins played Chavel, who, sentenced to die in Nazi-occupied Paris in 1941, swaps his money and estate with another, poor, prisoner who is happy to forfeit his life instead so that his mother and sister can be wealthy. After his eventual release Chavel goes to work anonymously for the women at their country home, but it all becomes even more confusing when a phony Chavel suddenly announces himself. Filmed in just 24 days, *The Tenth Man* was ready for transmission on American network television by 4 December.

Meanwhile, after months of indecision, a succession of scripts and much self-doubt about his singing ability – not to mention the less-than-enticing prospect of at least two cold, damp months in Budapest – Hopkins finally turned down what would have been one of his biggest-ever paydays playing Peachum in a lavish, star-studded version of Brecht-Weill's *The Threepenny Opera*, from the mercurial Cannon team of Golan and Globus. So Peachum joined a number of other intriguing might-have-been roles in the Hopkins portfolio. Back in 1971 he had been offered the Del Henney part of the marginally sympathetic rustic rampager in Peckinpah's *Straw Dogs*. Nauseated by the script's apparent preoccupation with blood, Hopkins wrote back to the director, 'I think you've got a menstruation complex.'

Ten years on he was to have played a 'tormented, syphilitic and ultimately deaf German composer', who, the press release continued extravagantly, 'brought the symphony to its peak as a form of musical expression', in Ken Russell's *The Beethoven Secret*.

But just as Hopkins, Glenda Jackson, Charlotte Rampling and Jodie Foster were about to plunge into Russell-induced mayhem, the plug was pulled at the eleventh hour by a Berlin-based tax 'shelter' group which was to have financed the multi-million-dollar movie. And on the subject of megalomaniacs, there was protracted speculation that Hopkins would portray Napoleon in a film by Stanley Kubrick. During 1988 he turned down, among other things, a play about Bomber Harris and a film about Auschwitz.

With no autumn *Opera*, something fast resembling a work void began to open up. Suddenly, in September, Hopkins decided he *had* to get away, 'or else I'll go mad. If I don't I will be ringing my agent every day.' He took himself off alone for a fortnight in the States. On his return he walked straight into a new mini-series version of *Great Expectations*, being filmed in Kent and at Pinewood Studios by Disney in conjunction with Harlech Television. Sporting, at different stages of the shoot, a hair-cut *en brosse* and a long, straggly grey wig – not to mention a fearsome facial scar – Hopkins was playing the convict Magwitch; in fact, he was a late replacement for the American actor Stacy Keach, who, because of his notorious British drugs conviction, was refused entry to work on the production in England.

As his 51st year – perhaps his busiest and most varied ever – came to a close, Hopkins finally had time to reflect more fully on one of the more intriguing turns in what has been to date a career full of coincidence and no little irony. In March he confided: 'When I came back from the States I had this deep sense of discomfort. I can't really describe it and, honestly, it's taken me three years to try and work it out of my system to see if it's in *me*.

'It is some kind of personality problem and it has got worse and worse, the feeling of alienation, unable to fit in emotionally. Doing these long runs has been an exercise in futility. It has been so bad that I've decided I can't work in the theatre again. In a more positive way I'm glad I did the National Theatre things, because in doing them something went out of me and that left me feeling much better. What had been beaten out of me – or what I've managed to get rid of myself – is the final illusion that the theatre is of importance to me. After all, I only came into the theatre in the first place to do films.' We had already talked at length about John Dexter, a Mephistophelean figure in Hopkins' memory bank, a summation of the best and worst in the actor's assessment of his theatrical past, 'a marvellous director ... a bastard ... brutal ... very influential'.

Three months later, I was lunching with John Dexter, who had just returned from New York after winning a Tony award for his direction of an extraordinary new drama, M. *Butterfly*, which was also named Best Play of the Year. Written by David Henry Hwang, M. *Butterfly* takes place in a contemporary Paris prison and, in recall, the years 1960–86 in Beijing and Paris. The events of the play were suggested by newspaper accounts of a recent international spy scandal, tracing the story of a clandestine love between a French diplomat and a beautiful Chinese star of the Peking Opera.

I told Dexter about both Hopkins' ambivalent feelings for the director and of his 'never again' vow about the theatre. Dexter told me: 'If he's not going back to the stage that would be a great pity. I certainly intend offering him *Butterfly* when we stage it here, but whether he'll take it is another matter.

'But if he does, he'll have to realise he'll be in the same situation he was in *Equus*, of going into a production that's physically worked out. So none of that "Can I sit here ... can I do that?" or he loses the part, which is probably the best male leading part in any play recently. The great thing with Tony is never to push; he must never feel he is being talked into something. It depends entirely on his reading of the script though, obviously, [this play] arrives with certain recommendations, such as huge success on Broadway, awards and so on. If he's at all nervous about going back to the stage, that should do much to allay those feelings. The other thing is that he *should* be doing new plays. You're too easy a target in classical revival because you're being weighed up against everybody who ever played it. In a new play you have the chance of people looking at what *you* have done, which would help him with the security aspect, since Tony's number one problem is acting security. He's a wonderful technician but I think he somehow despises technique or else doesn't quite trust his judgement.

'Our relationship? Well, we've never had a row. He's removed himself from me – but then actors do that. That's part of the process. When you get them to a certain point, and they don't remove themselves, you then have to give them a thump and push them away and make them do it on their own. The actor must do it; the director can't stand up and do the performance. As for my reputation, I'm aware of it. It's useful though: it does a lot of work for me, like keeping people quiet at rehearsals. You do know that Tony invents stories, don't you? He's not mendacious, but also he is not a strict observer of life's truths, because if the truth is going to be unpalatable or unpleasant he will avoid it both in himself and in other people.

'I have a suspicion that from the few conversations that we've had more recently, a lot of that has gone now. He's much more secure. I think he is the best modern actor we have; there's plenty of time for him yet to lay claim to the classics. In the case of *Butterfly*, I'm making him the offer of the best fucking part there is around this year: that should tell you how I really feel about him.'

That Dexter should even have been considering Hopkins had come about as the result of overtures on behalf of the actor by his London agent, Jeremy Conway: 'I hadn't seen it but various people from New York rang me up and said it was a wonderful play and I ought to get my hands on it. I read the reviews and thought the part sounded terribly right for Tony. I rang John and said, "Are you going to do *M. Butterfly* over here?" and he said he wanted to. I said, "What about Tony doing it?" He said, "I've been thinking of [Michael] Gambon." I don't think after all that had been said in the past Dexter ever thought Tony would work with him again. I said, "I do think it's a wonderful part for Tony." Then he suddenly said, "Well, we'll get him to read it."'

Conway rang Hopkins while he was still filming *Heartland* in West Wales to confess what he had done. 'What did John say?' asked Hopkins. 'He said he'd love you to do it,' Conway replied. Hopkins took a weekend off from the production and travelled back up to London to meet Dexter. 'It's about time we got together again,' said Dexter. Later, he asked: 'Why did you walk out of

Misanthrope and what was that all about in New York?'
Hopkins replied: 'Because I couldn't work under those
sorts of conditions. If I feel I'm being hassled, I just take
the exit.' Dexter asked: 'Did you find me difficult to work
with?' 'Yes, I did,' said Hopkins, 'but you're still the best
director I've ever worked with.' These mixed feelings
remained with Hopkins as he went back to Wales to finish
Heartland, but while certain misgivings continued to nag,
'a cunning, even machiavellian, little thought' also began
to take root: 'this would,' thought Hopkins, 'be a perfect
way of getting an old mess out of the system; a chance, as
it were, to sort out some unfinished business. I would
tackle it almost as an exercise. Part of my *raison d'être* is
to keep proving to myself that I can overcome anything in
my life. I kept remembering how John [who died in 1990]
would shout at actors, "Why can't you learn your fucking
lines?" He'd caught me short on *Equus*. This time, I'd
have them all off pat and beat him at his own game. Beat
the devil, you see.'

Before starting rehearsals for *M. Butterfly*, Hopkins
had flown to New York to see Dexter's production where
he watched David Dukes (who'd taken over from the
award-winning John Lithgow) in the role of the self-
deluding diplomat, René Gallimard. It was, he thought to
himself, 'a pretty showy-looking piece' as Gallimard leaps
in and out of character, one moment narrating the story,
the next playing out scenes from the Frenchman's complicated private life, all climaxing with an extraordinary, and
thrilling, *coup de théâtre*.

'No read-throughs,' barked Dexter at the actors
(including Lynn Farleigh, who'd just worked with
Hopkins in *Heartland*) when they all turned up at
Leicester for the pre-London tryout. Most of the actors
were, according to Hopkins, 'shit scared' at first because
of Dexter's reputation but, in the event, he was 'a pussycat
with me and the others too'.

He can only recall one day when the director 'played
Genghis Khan', otherwise Dexter cheerfully camped up his
combative banter, telling Hopkins, 'She knows her lines

then, dear. We're all *very* impressed.' Hopkins felt confident enough these days to tell him to 'Fuck off!' The game went on all the time, but on this occasion Dexter was generally far less economical with his compliments and the star was delighted at Dexter's obvious approval of his performance. 'It was a tremendous breakthrough for me,' said Hopkins. 'I could face him again.' A ghost was laid.

That pleasure soon evaporated when the play opened at the Shaftesbury Theatre (marking Hopkins' one and only West End stage appearance to date). According to him, 'the critics savaged the play'. Of course, that wasn't quite the whole story. The reviews were mixed; some very good; a few awful. Hopkins inevitably focused on the few and began wondering whether his six-month contract was more in the nature now of a short, sharp prison sentence. The despair was happily short-lived as the audiences poured into the theatre. 'To hell with the critics, I'll just get on with it,' thought Hopkins. It was a very pleasant company of actors; after matinées, they'd all have fish and chips together.

As spring turned into summer, Hopkins began to count the days. The show, requiring some spectacular cross-dressing and a big death scene, was physically very demanding and though, he claims, the role didn't dig too deep into his own personal reserves, it all too quickly became 'a bit of a bloody effort'. One non-matinée afternoon in late August, Hopkins took himself off to see *Mississippi Burning* and, as he walked back to the theatre to get ready for the evening performance, pondered how nice it would be to do 'a big Hollywood movie'.

At the same time, as part-consolation, part-excuse, he reasoned, 'Well, that part of my life's over; it's a chapter closed. I suppose I'll just have to settle for being a respectable actor poncing around the West End and doing respectable BBC work for the rest of my life.' It was quite early when he got back to the Shaftesbury and there was still time for a nap before he needed to start thinking about Gallimard again. A call from his agent woke him. There were, suddenly, not just one but two new movies in the offing, Conway told him. A remake of the old Bogart–Fredric March hostage thriller, *Desperate Hours*, with Mickey Rourke in the Bogie role, to be directed by Michael Cimino. And also, added Conway, 'a film called *The Silence of the Lambs*'. Hopkins, who hadn't heard of the second project, fastened swiftly on to the first, telling his agent he wanted to work with Cimino. Conway told him 'not to jump in too quick' and that he should think equally about *Silence*, which 'was a wonderful script'. 'Is it a proper offer?' Hopkins asked. Conway didn't know. In which case, Hopkins said, he didn't want to read it. Conway insisted. The script was sent round and Hopkins began reading, became scared of it and, because he didn't want ultimately to be disappointed if things didn't work out, slammed it shut.

On edge that night, he poured his feelings into the performance and the audience got a generous money's worth, with change to spare. The next morning, he spoke again to Conway who told him that the director, Jonathan Demme, was planning to come over to see him. By the time Demme came over from the States for their meeting, Hopkins had skimmed through the script again, still not wanting to be completely ensnared by it.

Jenni had read it. Or at least had begun to read it, but simply couldn't continue past the first few pages because she was so appalled by the horrific content. Thomas Harris' original novel, a sequel to the earlier *Red Dragon* (which had been turned into the admired though not especially successful film *Manhunter* in the mid-eighties) was first published in 1988 and had shot to the top of the best-seller charts. Re-introducing the character of Dr Hannibal 'The Cannibal' Lecter (who had been played by the Scots actor Brian Cox in Michael Mann's movie), *The Silence of the Lambs* greatly consolidated what had been a very shadowy character in the first book. This time he became an integral part of an even more compelling plot in which, from behind prison bars, the man-eating psychiatrist tortuously helps a young FBI trainee, Clarice Starling, trap a serial killer almost as dreadful as himself. Though maximum security comes between Lecter and Starling, they still manage to develop a remarkable, almost erotic, relationship as the courageous young woman starts to unravel a horrific mystery via Lecter's convoluted prompting.

The film rights were first snapped up by Gene Hackman seeking, rather belatedly, a project on which he could make his debut as director. The idea was that Michelle Pfeiffer would play Starling, with John Hurt as Lecter and Hackman himself as the FBI boss, Jack Crawford. Hackman, fresh from his Oscar-nominated performance in *Mississippi Burning*, then apparently went cold on the idea, perhaps fearing another subject as bleak as that of Alan Parker's fine film. The rights passed to the then still moderately rampant Orion Pictures (who had backed *Mississippi Burning*), and they handed the assignment over to Demme, who'd directed the company's droll *Married to the Mob* that year.

Demme cheerfully admits to believing that he always considered himself a most unlikely choice for such a film, even taking into account an almost uncategorisable *curriculum vitae*, ranging wildly from Corman's *Caged Heat* to the Talking Heads' concert movie, *Stop Making Sense*. The idea, though, of a strong female protagonist was a key factor for him. Who better to play her than Pfeiffer, who'd served him so well in *Married to the Mob*? Except that she, like Hackman earlier, had now completely cooled on the piece. Meanwhile Jodie Foster had begun strongly lobbying Demme for the role. Mike Medavoy, Orion's head of production (and now head of Tri Star Pictures), called Demme up and asked him to consider Robert Duvall for Lecter. The director rang him back to say that he didn't think Duvall could play the role – surely he was more the Crawford type? – and said he'd rather go with Tony Hopkins.

Medavoy was flabbergasted. 'My God, an Englishman [sic] playing that part? But it's not written that way,' he told Demme. The executive added that he knew Hopkins – from the actor's previous incarnation in Hollywood when, Medavoy recalls, Hopkins always looked 'frightened, alone' – and that, 'yes, he could be terrific.' But, continued Medavoy, 'how about you take Jodie Foster and I'll then go along with Hopkins?' Demme agreed.

Demme's championing of Hopkins had its roots in his performance, nearly a decade earlier, as Dr Treves in *The Elephant Man*. For Demme, the combination of 'intense humanity and intense intelligence' which Hopkins displayed then would be perfect for Lecter. Even so, when Hopkins had his first meeting with Demme in London, he had to confess he was 'amazed' that the director actually wanted *him* for the part.

There was still another month or so to run of his stage contract, but in those weeks Hopkins began to pore over the script and started to hear a voice and conjure an image very powerfully in his head. 'I could sense Lecter. I just knew how to do it. I somehow knew everything about this man. I'd see him in this half-light, in his oakwood office in Baltimore, dark hair slicked back, white shirt, black suit, beautifully-manicured hands, black shiny shoes. A man with luminous eyes. Like a machine.'

The day after his theatre run finished, Hopkins was on his way to New York to attend a Monday-morning script reading at Orion's offices. The night before, he met up for dinner with Demme and the producers at Des Artistes and found himself sitting next to the screenwriter, Ted Tally. Though drained by the play, he felt on a 'high', thrilled to have overcome what he considered a 'savage beating' by critics and still gone on 'working my balls off night after night', and now to be in New York was 'a tremendous release'. Between courses, Tally gently asked him how he was going to play Lecter. Munching away on the restaurant's delicious bread, Hopkins said: 'Hard to describe, but I think his voice is like HAL the computer in Kubrick's *2001*. You know, like the disembodied voice at the end of a long dream. That's how I see him.'

Hopkins was staying at the Plaza and, next morning, before going off to Orion on Fifth Avenue, he went for a run in Central Park. Suitably limbered up, he arrived at the film company offices, where he met Jodie Foster for the first time and also some of the company's top executives, who'd be at the reading too.

His first scene. In for a penny, in for a pound, Hopkins thought. 'I was going to try some cockamammy American accent which I knew I couldn't identify. I knew I had got them all because there was this amazing silence at the end of my first speech, and Demme then let out a "My God, yehhhh ..." When the reading was finally over, they all gave me a big hug and said, "yes, that's it."'

But before Hannibal Lecter in Pittsburgh, there was to be the small matter of tackling a Vietnam war hero and lawyer called Tim Cornell in Utah. Salt Lake City was the setting for Cimino's *Desperate Hours*, a reworking – suitably desperate, one might say – of Joseph Hayes' family-in-jeopardy thriller. (This was originally a successful stage play, which then became the William Wyler film in 1955, when the March character was called 'Dan Hilliard'.) All kinds of emotional complications and violent twists had been rather unnecessarily added to the original potboiler to give it, one must suppose, some contemporary relevance. When Hopkins arrived in Salt Lake City after travelling via Los Angeles, the film company was out of town shooting some scenes.

As soon as they returned, Cimino assembled the actors for a reading and Hopkins' immediate feeling was that he didn't think he was going to enjoy making the film. Hopkins said: 'Mickey Rourke [playing the psychotic armed robber, Michael Bosworth, who takes Cornell's family captive in their own home] was such a remote character, monosyllabic, like some latterday James Dean. He acted very strange and wouldn't speak to anyone, certainly not to me. I later thought that this was probably understandable because I was, as it were, his opposite number in the film and he was trying to keep a sense of alienation.

'My first scene was to come out of the house, get into my car then drive to the bank to get some money. While I'm doing this, he punches me on the shoulder. All I can remember was that this made me so angry, I punched the side of the car in genuine rage. In fact, I punched it so hard, I knocked a dent in it. Cimino was very pleased about that and said they'd use it in the film.'

After this explosive beginning, Hopkins was given five days of freedom before his next 'call'. So he climbed into a hire car and set off on a twelve-hundred mile driveabout through Wyoming, Montana, Idaho and Washington state, staying in motels, getting up early, just pointing the Pontiac. Apart from an unexpected rendezvous in, of all places, Boise, with an old acquaintance from the National and the odd ex-drinkers' meeting, his odyssey was deliberately solo and all exceedingly tranquil, affording Hopkins a great feeling of contentment and peace, before the onset of more Rourke-essness back in Salt Lake City.

'Strange actor, Mickey,' said Hopkins. 'He got very violent on the set, would like to break things to get himself going and fire guns too. "This is a very interesting experiment," I remember thinking to myself, "but I don't know what the hell it's all about." We had one bust-up on the set. He was pushing me around once – which he had to do in the film – and I suddenly thought, "I've had enough of this shit" and walked off the set – then straight back on again. At the end, he wrote me a sweet note saying that he doesn't like actors much but had enjoyed working with me. I was black-and-blue at the end of it all, and certainly a great deal stronger physically. As for Cimino, he was tough on the crew, a dictator, but didn't give me any trouble at all.'

Hopkins had two firm dates in his diary when he finished filming *Desperate Hours* at the beginning of December. He was meeting Jenni, Muriel, and David and Paula Swift (who were coming over to see their daughter Julia in the National Theatre production of *The Merchant of Venice*, with Dustin Hoffman) for Christmas in New York, and was then due to join Demme's unit in Pittsburgh to begin shooting *The Silence of the Lambs* early in January. Before Christmas, he also needed to fit in an initial trip to Pennsylvania for make-up tests, so he got back into a hire car and drove four thousand miles to

Pittsburgh. By the first afternoon, he was at the Colorado border, then it was on to Durango, across to Oklahoma City and next down into Texas. Mile after mile of relentless freeway, with Philip Glass or Handel blazing out on the tapedeck. Hopkins recalls, for instance, the occasion of a 'burning yellow afternoon coming in to Dallas. I was negotiating the camber of the giant road and suddenly the city, with its great Ayn Rand-like buildings, loomed up out of the smog. At that moment, "Unto Us a Child Is Born" from the *Messiah* began to swell on the cassette. It was like something out of *Close Encounters* or a Kubrick movie.' Then it was on to Houston, Baton Rouge, New Orleans, through Georgia, up to Charleston (where he stayed with friends) and finally into Pittsburgh.

He returned to the city in the New Year, having heeded the make-up department's instructions to keep out of the sun (so he'd remain suitably pale) and maintain his hair in a slicked-back style. Lecter's cell was re-created in a disused Westinghouse factory in Turtle Creek, outside Pittsburgh. Before his first meeting with Clarice, Demme asked Hopkins how he felt his character should be initially encountered.

Flattered to be consulted, Hopkins told Demme that perhaps they could have the camera shooting down the corridor, from Foster's point-of-view, 'to build tension. The characters have already been talking about Lecter so I think I should be first seen standing in the middle of the cell, as if I'm waiting for her. There would then be direct eye contact straight away. "How would he know she was coming?" Demme asked me. I said, "He's omnipotent; he can smell her coming."

That kind of give-and-take appeared to characterise the whole filming which, despite the less-than-cheerful subject matter, seems to have been the best fun Hopkins ever had on a set: 'Demme's a great director because he never makes problems. He works extremely hard, is demanding and very precise, but he never imposes unless he feels it can improve. Perhaps it's too easy to say in retrospect but, even at the time, I got a sense that it was going to be a big hit. I saw all the "dailies" and really wanted to because I was enjoying it so much. I could sense something from the people around the place that I'd really got it right. The actor's mask fitted.'

Hopkins was also impressed by the way Demme dealt with the sort of violence and horrors that might have been unwatchable in lesser hands. He told *Empire*: 'Jonathan made it a point to cut away from the really horrible scenes. He didn't focus on a scene where my character slices off somebody's face but he did show, in detail, an autopsy because that was an important reality. But, for the most part, he just showed you glimpses of violence. He liked to deal much more with the psychological terror. Now this I find truly frightening.'

Demme, who once intriguingly described *The Silence of the Lambs* as 'a woman's picture', said that he felt 'violence wasn't that necessary an element within the film. Terror is represented through characterisation. Here's a character, Lecter, who we *know* has committed horrific crimes, but Tony gives him this humanity, this compassion. And Lecter cares, he *cares*. It makes his character very complicated and somewhat unpredictable.' Demme claimed he was just trying to be as 'loyal' as he could to the spirit of Lecter as he understood it from the books and the script. Luckily, added Demme, Hopkins also 'got the joke'.

On another occasion, in *Interview*, Demme tried to analyse what made the film tick and the reasoning behind the sequel-paving ending: 'If we didn't fuck the book up, and I don't think we did, you've got to give the lion's share of the credit to Ted Tally because he wrote a blueprint for the best possible movie version of it. I think it's a great book, and a very singular book – it's not "some sort" of book. It's a book with a big heart which isn't that easy to perceive when you're reading it but the impact is there.

'The ending defies all the rules of morality which are unspoken yet operate in a very powerful way in how movies get resolved. Certain people who read the script took umbrage at the end: "Surely you're not going to let it end like that," admitting Lecter's tremendously likeable, "but ..." I'd always reply, "It's not because he's so likeable that it ends like that. It's beyond my ability to describe why this great character, born of literature, is the way he is, or why it concludes like this." Maybe, we're just too smart about how immoral this world is. And finally, with all the heartbreaking injustices going on in every direction we look, just how upset are you gonna get about this fictional cannibal not meeting his usual fictional fate?'

It was to be almost a full year between the end of the filming and the American première on, of all dates, St Valentine's Day. That twelve months was another almost unstoppable grind in the progress of a workaholic actor who could still be less than choosy. After joining Jodie Foster on stage at the 1991 Oscars to hand out a Best Screenplay award, Hopkins flew down to Mexico for *One Man's War*, a promising-sounding project telling the true story of a Paraguayan doctor investigating the torture and mysterious death of his son. It seems to have proved an unhappy experience on all sides, and currently the completed film – which did extremely well on television – remains unreleased in the cinema.

Then across the world to Melbourne for *Spotswood*, to play a time-and-motion expert in a gentle, Ealing-style comedy; just another name-in-the-frame for a glossy mini-series, *To Be the Best*, off the relentless Barbara Taylor Bradford treadmill; revoicing his late mentor Laurence Olivier for the restored 'bathing' scene in a reconstructed version of *Spartacus*; and *Freejack*, alongside Mick Jagger (making his first film for 20 years), as a villainous power-broker in the futuristic world of mind-body swaps. Said Hopkins: '*Silence* was taking a long time to come out, and people would say to me that I must have a lot of work on. Well, I hadn't any work at all. As I hadn't ever done a sci-fi film before, I thoroughly enjoyed doing *Freejack*, playing a sort of Lambert Le Roux character in the part of the movie where they had all the special effects. I haven't seen the film yet.' Perhaps he shouldn't.

The Silence of the Lambs didn't so much open as erupt. The best of all possible worlds, a critical hit *and* a box-office blockbuster, it also became the most talked-about film of 1991 and lines like 'I ate his liver with some fava beans and a nice chianti' passed into instant mythology. As for the Lecter character itself, the skill of the script and Hopkins' careful characterisation probably helped to make him the most diabolically likeable movie villain since Norman Bates. Harris had described Lecter as 'small and sleek'. Hopkins, squeezed into a tight prison uniform, perfectly suggested that description. While Harris' book is relentlessly scary, Demme's film – in which Foster's intelligent, gutsy performance mustn't be underestimated – craftily adds a blackly comic edge which makes such grim material just about visually bearable. The film, like the book, remained neatly open-ended, simply begging a sequel.

A more immediate, though inevitably drawn-out, sequel would be the film's involvement in the subsequent trawl for the year's awards to climax, or possibly anti-climax, a full year later at the next Hollywood Oscars. The timing of its release could have meant that, come the end-of-the-year resumés, Demme's film might have slipped out of sight and, more significantly, out of mind. As far as the Academy Awards themselves were specifically concerned, history also seemed to be against the film. Though scare-the-shit-out-of-you thrillers like *The Exorcist* and *Fatal Attraction* (not *Psycho*, though) had been in the frame, they were never realistic contenders, so what chance for *The Silence of the Lambs* that could, with some justification, be dismissed as a glossy slasher-movie?

Hopkins' role accounted for some 30 minutes of screen time: did this mean too much for Best Supporting, too little for Best, or no chance at all because Brits (Daniel Day-Lewis for *My Left Foot* and Jeremy Irons for *Reversal of Fortune*) had won the top actor award in the two preceding prize-givings? Also, it had only been a couple of years since Foster, still only in her twenties, had last won an Oscar, for *The Accused*. And was the film, applying the Spielberg factor, just too popular?

In fact, by the time the Oscar nominations were actually announced, almost a year to the week after the film had first been launched on an unsuspecting American public, Hopkins might have been forgiven for triumphantly thinking – which he didn't – that it was all over bar the shouting. He had already been named Best Actor by the New York, Boston and Chicago critics, won the Paul Muni Award for Best Villain, and earned the supporting actor title from the prestigious National Board of Review. Hedging its bets, *Premiere* magazine revealed that Hopkins had been declared Best Actor *and* Best Supporting Actor in a readers' poll.

He had, however, been beaten to the Golden Globe – often regarded as a signpost for the Oscars – by Nick Nolte for *The Prince of Tides*. When the nominations for Best Actor were announced, and Hopkins' name appeared (for the first time in an Oscar list) alongside Nolte's, as well as those of Robert De Niro (for *Cape Fear*, which also contained distinguished work by Nolte), Warren Beatty (*Bugsy*) and Robin Williams (*The Fisher King*), Hopkins mentally logged off. (There were also six other nominations for *Silence*, which also included Foster as Best Actress, Best Film, Best Director, and Best Adapted Screenplay.)

Hopkins' working year since the film's massive box-office achievements had been no less frenetic than before, but this time it included – along with the ubiquitous voiceovers, a BBC radio production of *Pravda* and an appointment to the presidency of the National Trust's Snowdonia appeal – an assignment with two of the industry's more maverick talents, Merchant Ivory and Francis Ford Coppola, from either end of the film-making spectrum: Merchant Ivory, cool and miniaturist; Coppola, massive and colourfully operatic.

Howards End was back to *A Room with a View* territory, exploring in exquisitely re-created Edwardian tones E.M. Forster's story of the clash between two very different families, the bohemian Schlegels and the stuffy

Wilcoxes, led by the decent, if straitlaced, Henry Wilcox, the sort of chap who says things like 'The poor are poor. One is sorry for them, but there it is . . .' Hopkins had read the book some years earlier after making *The Bounty* and when he was approached wasn't quite sure why anyone should want to make a film of it. He skimmed through the script, checked to see if he was still on the last page – 'a very cavalier way of doing things, I realise' – and prepared to meet Ismail Merchant and James Ivory, whose productive partnership was entering its 30th year.

Convinced by them, though slightly taken aback at what seemed to be director Ivory's almost studiedly laid-back attitude to film-making, Hopkins dived back into the script. 'I have to say I was a bit worried at that point and I suddenly wondered if I could actually play this character who isn't very warm. My agent said I couldn't get out of it and I simply had no idea of what I was going to do. Then I went for hair and make-up tests and first I was given this ghastly Edwardian cut. Chrissie Beveridge, who was in charge of make-up, said that James was wondering if I'd wear a moustache. Would I grow one? No, I replied, I don't want one. She persisted, "I've got a false one here, let's try it on." And that was it. It totally focused the character for me, and even dominated the clipped way I spoke.'

The subject of facial hair also came up in discussion of Hopkins' characterisation of vampire hunter Professor Van Helsing for Coppola's version of Bram Stoker's Victorian Gothic novel, *Dracula*. Unlike a number of previous versions, which were based on a twenties stage adaptation, Coppola was determined to get back to the original source material, emphasising the horror, eroticism and even the principal character's psychological motivation. As for Van Helsing, the Count's constant Nemesis, Coppola would describe him as 'part priest, part wizard', but that was before the long process of rehearsal and refinement.

Coppola admitted at the outset that while trying to remain generally faithful to the original, this Van Helsing was somewhat different than Stoker's creation: 'In the book, Van Helsing really is a kind of bumbling guy. He just talks and talks and there are pages and pages where he's saying things like, "Ah, you have the good heart of a woman," all the stuff that women in the audience would all hiss at if they heard it . . . also I felt I had an extraordinary actor who was capable of bringing much more vitality and more interesting thematic development to the role.

'Dracula is a metaphysical character, being that he is alive for all these hundreds of years, who I portray as being fascinated by science. Van Helsing, on the other hand, is a scientist who ultimately becomes fascinated by metaphysics. I wanted audiences to feel upon his entry, "yeh, this guy is really going to get to the bottom of all this," whereas I always felt that the Van Helsing in the book, and in some of the earlier movies, was just a rather kindly old man who really didn't know what he was doing.'

Hopkins was fairly nerve-racked at the prospect of collaborating with Coppola, especially after watching, more than once, *Hearts of Darkness*, the warts-and-all documentary about the making of *Apocalypse Now*. 'My God, is this really the man I'm going to be working with?' he pondered, as a great hairy bear of a man was portrayed riding roughshod over all and sundry throughout a rainy season in the Philippines.

'Of course,' said Hopkins, 'it turned out that he was a quite amazing director. Maybe the best. Jonathan [Demme] was wonderful in his own way – sharp, disciplined, ebullient. Coppola was the other side of the coin. Much darker, very moody, a man who'd had a lot of tragedy in his life. When he did flare up once during rehearsals and stormed off, I remember repeating to myself, "This is the way he is; he's a great director. I'm just going to learn the lines and show up. Just don't argue." Everything changes all the time, which certainly keeps you on edge. There's lots of improvisation, which I hadn't done for years. He was fond of saying how he's able to count from one to twenty, but doesn't necessarily do it in chronological order.

▲ As Chianti-loving cannibal Dr Lecter in *The Silence of the Lambs*.

▲ With Jenni outside Buckingham Palace after collecting his Knighthood in the 1993 New Year's Honours List.

▲ As Dr John Harvey Kellogg in *The Road to Wellville*.

▼ As President Nixon in *Nixon* with James Woods.

As Pablo Picasso in *Surviving Picasso*.

Hopkins versus Bart the Bear in *The Edge*.

▲ In action as a sword-wielding masked avenger in
The Mask of Zorro.

▼ As John Quincy Adams In *Amistad*, with director
Steven Spielberg.

▲ Reprising his role as Dr Lecter in *Hannibal*, with Julianne Moore.

▼ As Dr Lecter once again in the *Lambs* prequel, *Red Dragon*, with Edward Norton.

▲ As a psychic on the run in the Stephen King short story, *Hearts of Atlantis*, with Mika Boorem.

▼ As Coleman Silk in *The Human Stain*, with Nicole Kidman.

▲ As trusted confidant Ptolemy in *Alexander*

▼ With Jodie Foster receiving his star on the Hollywood Walk of Fame.

▼ With new wife, Stella, at their St David's Day wedding.

'He seems to thrive on chaos and during rehearsals – which he shot as if it was the film – created pandemonium, endlessly rewriting pages of script which were then all fed into a sort of computer memory bank. During the rehearsal period, we had got to a fairly skeletal scene of Van Helsing lecturing when Coppola suddenly announced, "Let's have you lecturing everyone here and now." It started, people all around the set, his crew too, firing questions at me – "Are you a Faustian figure?", stuff like that. It all began to give me clues. This man had been down to the murkiest depths, had done *everything*. He'd have been an absinthe drinker, probably a drug taker, met Modigliani – and come out the other side rather like burnished steel.'

One day, Coppola came on set. 'Morning, Van Helsing' – he liked to address the actors by their characters' names. Then he inquired whether he'd recently been in touch with Mesmer. This gave Hopkins a thought: 'I asked him whether I could go off to make-up and try a few things. I wanted them to give me a great duelling scar on the left side of the face. When I returned, he asked me where I'd got it. "Vienna, in 1876." That satisfied him.'

Hopkins' other thought was to grow a rough beard and play Van Helsing a little like Walter Huston in *The Treasure of the Sierra Madre*, 'as a prospector, a mad old coot who can, nevertheless, still smell gold.' The stubble went on. Coppola wasn't really convinced, so it came off. Then, another message: 'Grow it.' This time, it stayed. According to Hopkins, Van Helsing is now 'like a Messenger of Light that comes to a family in peril. He must get their attention because there's an evil that will destroy them. "Come on, wake up," he cries. He's powerful, frightening, even scary, but, essentially a good man.'

Hopkins, who also appeared as a heavily bearded priest in the brief but bloody fifteenth-century preface and provided a narration for the film, saw something of himself in turbulent young British actor Gary Oldman, who had beaten off competitors like Antonio Banderas and Gabriel Byrne, to play the title role: 'I remember we were doing a very intense scene, right at the beginning. He was so concentrated, and he got impatient with himself. And I set him off. I said to him, "You know what you remind me of? You remind me of *me* twenty years ago." I could see what he was going through, all those same kinds of energy and intensity. I also used to get very angry and upset about things. But now it just gets dull.'

Just before the final countdown to Oscar night itself, *Howards End*, with exquisite timing, opened in the States to the sort of reviews that most film-makers can only dream about. Who can tell what the effect of such a reception may have been when the Academy voters finally made their selection? When Hopkins, who had just won the BAFTA award, flew into Los Angeles four days before the Monday ceremony on 30 March, he was only aware of two distinct schools of thought about the eventual outcome. Friends and acquaintances were convinced he was going to win, and that the film might even achieve some sort of clean sweep. Well, they would, wouldn't they? The weekend press, on the other hand, saw it as a much more open race, with Nolte as clear favourite for Best Actor.

That Monday morning, Hopkins felt physically sick, and when it got to midday he was quite certain he didn't want to go through the protracted torture ahead. It was lovely to be nominated, the others were all terrific actors, but what the hell! By now, he'd convinced himself he couldn't possibly win. It was, he reckoned, Nolte's prize.

Hopkins recalls: 'At three o'clock, the car arrived. I felt very calm now, as if I'd swallowed a glass full of Mogadon. We [he, Jenni, and Bob and Nancy Palmer] were driving very slowly down Wilshire Boulevard and then came to the big protests [by gay and lesbian activists, protesting against, among other things, the alleged homophobia in *The Silence of the Lambs*] and got stuck in a traffic jam. I said to Bob this was wonderful and perhaps they wouldn't let anyone else through, and why didn't we go straight on to Rex's Restaurant and watch it on TV like everybody else? Then, despondency as the car got through the police cordon and finally drew up at the Dorothy Chandler Pavilion. People were screaming and shouting as I had to stand on a podium and talk to Army Archerd. Inside the building, it was rather peaceful, almost banal. Before the show started, I shook hands with Warren Beatty and said to Jenni, "Let's just enjoy ourselves." '

Anyone who watched the Oscars as they happened (on satellite television, outside the States) must have sensed the tide turning towards Hopkins the moment host Billy Crystal was wheeled on to the stage by white-coated attendants and wearing that grotesque Lecter restraint-mask. Crystal even came down off the stage and into the celebrity audience to shake Hopkins' hand. 'They're just giving me a nice send-off, letting me down gently,' Hopkins reasoned. When Jack Palance got Best Supporting Actor for *City Slickers*, as he had in the Golden Globes, Hopkins was sure the rest would now all go the way of the Globes.

'Then,' said Hopkins, 'it came to the Adaptation Screenplay. The Oscar goes to ... Ted Tally. Jodie looked across at me and mouthed, "Yehhhh". As he went off, down centre stage came Kathy Bates to present Best Actor and, at that moment, I *knew* I'd got it. It was like *déjà vu*.

'I had put some toothpaste on one of my shoes – they were an old pair I'd got for the stage run of *Pravda* and the ones I had also worn the year before when presenting an award – so that I could focus on a white mark and relax myself. Now, though I'd somehow seen it all before, I still couldn't really grasp it – yet felt quite cool as I went up on stage.' As he received one of the evening's few standing ovations, all Hopkins' notions of a premeditated speech evaporated. 'My God,' he told the audience, 'I can't believe it. This really is unexpected. It's a great honour to be here, especially with such great actors like Nick Nolte, Warren Beatty, Robin Williams and Robert De Niro [who was not actually present]. First of all I want to say hello to my mother. She's in Wales watching this on television. My father died eleven years ago tonight, so maybe he had something to do with this as well . . .'

Seconds later he was being whisked backstage by Kathy Bates to the huge pressroom for photographs and some instant reaction. Then he heard about Foster's and Demme's awards, climaxing with Best Film, announced by Elizabeth Taylor. It was not only the first clean sweep of the top awards since *One Flew Over the Cuckoo's Nest* in 1975, but, along with the 1934 Capra comedy, *It Happened One Night*, one of only three in Oscar history. Everyone from the film was ushered back on to the stage at the end and Hopkins found himself standing next to Taylor. 'Hello,' he said to her, 'we once worked together.' 'Yeh,' she replied, 'on *Victory at Entebbe*. By the way, I hear you just phoned your mother.' 'Yes, in Wales,' said Hopkins, in his best Burton. 'Don't do that,' she giggled.

When Hopkins eventually rejoined Jenni and the Palmers – Bob had just about recovered from a crying 'jag' – she told him about *her* premonition much earlier that same day in which she'd been flashed an image of him holding up the Oscar. The rest of the evening passed as if in a daze. The traditional Governor's Ball, where Hopkins got a chance finally to exchange hugs with Nolte; Rex's Restaurant, where Jeremy Conway and other friends had assembled and, finally, back to the Miramar Hotel on Santa Monica where their room had been stacked with flowers. As a kind of 'thank-you', Hopkins took his statuette down to the desk to show the late-night staff. Around four o'clock in the morning, he woke with a start. The full impact of his triumph was just beginning really to dawn on him.

'It's somewhat difficult to comprehend what's happened. In one way, I feel it is right not to try too hard to grasp it; it is better to accept what has happened with gratitude. I feel as though I am no longer thinking my own thoughts, feeling my own feelings or planning my own life. It's as though someone has been living for me.'

About a fortnight after the Oscars, Hopkins was in Prague to play a cameo role in Harold Pinter's adaptation of Kafka's *The Trial* when he jotted these thoughts in his diary. A General Election had come and gone too. Not content with invoking Hopkins/Lecter's name whenever a severe case of mass murder now hit the headlines, the press also delightedly seized on Tory candidate (and now ex-Minister of 'Fun') David Mellor's catchpenny condemnation of the ex-Labour leader when he said, during the campaign, 'only one Welshman can be a big winner in frightening millions of people and it's Anthony Hopkins. Hannibal Kinnock is the greatest serial spender in history – his policies would eat you alive.' Whatever anonymity Hopkins had once enjoyed has now been all but blown because of one extraordinary role.

If the Prague datelined entry in his journal written in the afterglow of the 1992 Oscar success seemed to have hinted at some kind of serendipity at work in mapping out his career, then it could almost be said to have come full circle when Richard Attenborough asked Hopkins to do a three-day stint in *Chaplin*, his star-studded biopic of the great comic actor.

It was of course *Limelight* and especially Claire Bloom which had eventually convinced the teenager, after he'd seen the film fifteen times at the Regent in Port Talbot, that becoming an actor might be a good wheeze. At the time, he wrote a fan letter to Chaplin and received a good-natured reply. Forty years on, Hopkins was to be found at Chaplin's beautiful family home, Manoir de Ban in Vevey, on the shores of Lake Geneva, sitting at the master's very own piano, tapping out the First Movement of Rachmaninov's Second which he was beginning to tame. As if this wasn't serendipity enough, Hopkins was then told by one of his co-stars, Chaplin's own daughter, Geraldine, that he had apparently been her late mother Oona's favourite actor and that there was a copy of *The Dawning* in the video recorder when Oona died.

Chaplin, in which Hopkins, as part of the film's rather contrived linking technique, played the invented character of a publisher jogging the memory of the now elderly Charlie as they go through the manuscript of his autobiography, was to prove just a short-lived Swiss idyll before the onset of perhaps his most relentless schedule of work yet. Five films in less than eighteen months punctuated by the award – much to his professed surprise – of a Knighthood (following his 1987 CBE) in the 1993 New Year's Honours List for 'services to the performing arts'. There was, very disappointingly, not much art, and even less sense, in John Schlesinger's misguided version of Ian McEwan's *The Innocent*, adapted by the author from his chillingly good novel about espionage, love and graphically violent death in coldest war fifties Berlin.

Whether or not it was to appease the various strands of financing, some bizarre international casting certainly conspired fatally to flaw the film from the outset. Campbell Scott, an American, was playing a virginal Englishman; Isabella Rossellini, the forty-something Italian, was meant to be a mature – but not *that* mature – German *femme fatale*, while Hopkins ('I can't play a full-blooded Midwesterner') was simply wrong as the devious American CIA man, Glass: 'I really don't know what John was playing at though I think he had a lot of problems getting the money. He was fighting big battles all the time and it wasn't a happy film.'

Hopkins' next two assignments had fifties settings too and also shared with Schlesinger's film the distinction of being adaptations of already-acclaimed contemporary writing. But after that, any resemblance between *The Innocent, The Remains of the Day* and *Shadowlands* has to be purely coincidental. And if the suspicion still lurked that the success of *The Silence of the Lambs* and to a lesser extent *Howards End* might prove just sporadic highs in Hopkins' film fortunes, then it was firmly dispelled by, in quick succession, his triumphant return to the bosom of Merchant-Ivory followed by a fifth, and arguably his most successful, collaboration yet with Richard Attenborough.

If Stevens the butler and C. S. 'Jack' Lewis, an Oxford don, tend to suggest at first glance merely different sides of the same coin of repressed and class-ridden British manhood, then that is perhaps rather an oversimplification which doesn't begin to do justice either to a pair of altogether more complex types or to the skill which lifts them from the realm of potential caricature into fully fleshed-out characters. Mind you, flesh and blood seems hardly applicable to Stevens, the icily efficient major domo of Darlington Hall whose 'unquestioning faith and dedication to duty were', as the screenplay spells out, 'misplaced and cost him dearly in his own private life'. What private life? A romantic novel, the odd cigar, Gigli on the gramophone enjoyed in the peace and quiet of his own quarters? But this wasn't just simply Hudson and *Upstairs Downstairs* all over again (although this aspect undoubtedly helped to make the film almost irresistible to some American audiences).

In flashback from the days of post-war austerity, when the Hall has been bought by a retired American diplomat and Stevens is seeking to entice the former housekeeper Miss Kenton back into service, we now observe the machinery of a great country house in its thirties pomp; not just any house but, as presided over by the well-meaning yet naive Lord Darlington, one at the centre of crucial events like the shadowy politics of appeasement. At the hub of this constant *va et vient* is the rock-like Stevens, whose dealings with his own father, the ageing and increasingly inept under-butler Stevens Sr, His Lordship's silly-ass godson to whom he's deputed to explain the birds-and-bees, or even the politicking bigwigs, are studiedly unemotional and uninvolved.

Yet the film is so much more than just a series of beautifully reconstructed tableaux and carefully-observed minutiae. There is, at its core, the poignant, ultimately painful and tragically unspoken love story which haunts the film from the amusingly spiky first meeting between Stevens and Miss Kenton to the final, agonisingly sad shot of the butler trapped forever by the denial of his feelings for the housekeeper. Hopkins and Emma Thompson, inspirationally reunited following their extremely effective work together in *Howards End*, bring a marvellous sense of playfulness and pathos to their scenes. There is perhaps no better nor achingly sadder moment in the film than when Miss Kenton, in flirtatious mood, corners Stevens in his room as he's reading one of his pot-boilers. They are now face to face, guards apparently down, but just when it seems they might finally embrace, Stevens steps back, a protecting hand thrust up in front of his face as he rasps, with desperate finality, 'This is my private time; you're invading it.'

According to Thompson, 'The fact that we'd done *Howards End* helped in a sense because it was like we were in a continuation of something. That scene with the book is so erotic because eroticism is about hiding, not revealing; so the more you hide the more erotic it is. Playing that scene actually made me kind of breathless because there was this incredible attraction and yet he was so utterly repressed. Then Tony's hand comes down and you think he might touch her head which to me is much more sexual and interesting than any fully-fledged hump.'

The correct tone of the film was set, Hopkins believes, by filming first – 'back to front', as it were – the fifties reunion scenes between Stevens and Miss Kenton on the North Somerset coast: 'I remember sitting on the pier at Weston with Emma and it was all a bit like Chekhov. There was this depressing out-of-season light, the dance hall in the background and the sound of "Blue Moon". I said to her, "You know, this really is heartbreaking." I don't know how James Ivory directs; he just does it without fuss. He's not the jolliest chap in the world but he manages to create just the right atmosphere. And that atmosphere we got at Weston then seemed to permeate everything we did from that moment on.'

Though, visually at least, appearing to have something in common with a sort of latent Lecter, Hopkins actually used a much older memory for inspiration. In the post-war days of the family bakery, one of its irregular visitors was a Mr Yeats, 'known as Yeats the Traveller', Hopkins recalled. 'He used to travel from Cardiff as a rep for United Yeast. He looked a bit like Sir Malcolm Sargent, was rather handsome, wore a gaberdine coat and a brown trilby hat over slicked-back hair, and was a perfect gentleman. When Emma and I did the scene early on about how she and her future husband, Mr Benn, used to laugh at me, I suddenly thought of Mr Yeats and worked backwards from there.' Hopkins, Peter Vaughan (a master stroke of casting as Stevens Sr even though there was actually only fifteen years between the actors) and other below-stairs staff also got a few handy hints from an old boy who'd been head steward at Buckingham Palace starting out in the days of King George VI.

The soul of discretion, he never passed on any juicy Palace secrets, restricting himself instead to tips like, 'The thing about being a butler, you just have to be quiet. When you're in a room, you have to be invisible. Be discreet and keep your distance with the youngsters.' Hopkins also recalled the useful comment of his chum Julian Fellowes: 'When a butler's in the room, it's even emptier.' His Stevens is a towering performance ('one of the greatest in the history of the British cinema' glowed the *Daily Mail* with abandon) but it is intriguing to reflect on it again in the light of David Thomson's comments made in the 1994 revise of his masterly *A Biographical Dictionary of Film*: '*The Remains of the Day* . . . depends on repressed emotion and a level of morality that is indistinguishable from etiquette or good service. The film is built around the astonishing performance of Anthony Hopkins who is so very clever, so lyrically hidden, so minutely detailed and expressive in the rendering of a man who cannot show his feelings that I felt tortured. I do not blame Hopkins. Actors can do very little but be, or try to be, intelligent, brilliant and revealing. Stevens, the butler, is unactable in truth. The concept of the character breaks apart once we see an actor trying . . .'

Long before Hopkins and Emma Thompson were cast, an earlier incarnation of the project (when Mike Nichols was all but set to direct a Harold Pinter version of Kazuo Ishiguro's novel) had thrown up the fascinating, not to say bizarre, possibility of Jeremy Irons and Meryl Streep as Stevens and Miss Kenton. Irons was also in

Attenborough's mind's eye when he first tried to visualise C. S. Lewis, theologian and author of *The Screwtape Letters* and the *Narnia Chronicles*.

'But of course,' explained Attenborough, 'he's a second-row rugby forward. He's a butcher with great huge shoulders, a thick neck and not ascetic-looking at all. I just knew then that Tony was just potentially the most wonderful casting.'

Attenborough had invited him to Abbey Road Studios to listen to some of the music recording on *Chaplin* and just before Hopkins left, he thrust a copy of the *Shadowlands* script into Hopkins' not altogether willing arms. That same evening, Attenborough's phone rang. First a disconcerting pause then, 'You bloody devil . . . you knew exactly what you were doing, didn't you? I had to put that script down three times in order to get through it and the last time I had to go out and walk up and down outside the house. It's the most emotionally disturbing piece of writing I think I have ever read . . . I'll kill any actor who came between me and his part.' With Hopkins' enthusiastic involvement, Attenborough was able to put the project together quicker than any of his previous eight films as director.

Shadowlands, about the doomed love story between the middle-aged Lewis and feisty New York poet-and-mother Joy Gresham, was originally written by William Nicholson as a BBC TV play in 1985, with Joss Ackland and Claire Bloom. Four years after that it became an award-winning stage play in both London and New York (starring Nigel Hawthorne on both sides of the Atlantic). When Nicholson came to work on the screenplay, he was given invaluable help by not only Attenborough but also another interested observer, director Sydney Pollack. A little nervous that the playwright was also penning the screenplay, Attenborough lost all reservations when he observed a universally positive response to the writing.

'The only thing I asked of Dickie,' said Hopkins, 'was that when we did the film, we mustn't be sentimental. "No, no, you're absolutely right," he said and then he got to play

Joy the most unsentimental actress in the world. Debra Winger. She's a killer but she's terrific. Has a reputation, pretty spiky but keeps you on your toes, challenges you all the time with things like, "What do you mean by that?" The one thing I was dreading about her was that I'd heard she'd worked at the Actors' Studio for some years and I thought, "Oh God, we won't all have to go to hospital for weeks on end looking at cancer patients?" '

He needn't have worried although, from the outset, it was clear her preparation was somewhat different than his. As Attenborough explained it, 'Debra will research to the point where she knows more about Joy than anyone else alive and it all goes into her head and she then uses it as required, but it tends to support her performance rather than dominate it. Tony will read a biography, perhaps two, and nothing else because he believes that what he has to convey is in the screenplay and anything which doesn't illuminate that screenplay is baggage ... by the time he comes on to the floor he knows it absolutely backwards and he improvises ... Tony has this extraordinary ability to make you believe when you hear him that it is the very first time he has ever said that line. It's an incredible gift.'

As far as Winger's concerned, *Shadowlands* 'is Tony's best work, ever ... ever. You've not seen this before from grown men on the screen. It was my experience that he just learns his lines and shows up. What he doesn't mention is the life he has lived.

'He has led a wild life and he has been pushing it down and suppressing it for years. It only comes out when he acts. I watched him very carefully and I'd think maybe he might run out of those experiences and have to start preparing all over again.'

Attenborough told David Robinson: 'Tony doesn't like rehearsal at all. He has convinced himself that too much rehearsal robs the dialogue of its spontaneity, and that it only really works if you can get it very quickly. When you are working with him, although he doesn't put off the other actors, he will say all sorts of things in rehearsal which are wholly appropriate but which are not what is written in the script. That doesn't mean that when he comes to the take his words are not perfect. But he almost always prefers to shoot straight away, once you've done the technical rehearsal.

'Now Miss Winger is the antithesis. She likes to rehearse and rehearse and rehearse – but it doesn't seem to damage her performance or in any way take away her freshness. But for the director, working with this duo was something of a problem. I very often used to walk through Tony's part with Debra so that she would have a lot of time rehearsing in advance; and only at the last moment would I put in Tony for one rehearsal with her; and it worked, and brought out the best in both of them. Tony is so unchallengeable in his reality. Debra just melted in front of him – and vice versa. Tony does a wonderful characterisation in *The Remains of the Day*, but for me his performance in *Shadowlands* is infinitely superior. You see the real processes of that person, not the acting.'

Despite all its best intentions, the film inevitably suffers just the occasional lapse into sentimentality but it would have taken an altogether cooler and more detached director than Attenborough – a James Ivory, perhaps – to have side-stepped this true story's often painfully high emotions. The story is – and the set was, if the stories are to be believed – a vale of tears. Little Joey Mazzello, who played Joy's son Douglas, just had to 'think of something sad' to make himself cry and Hopkins admits that 'it was difficult *not* to cry in some scenes'. He also told this story of his director: 'Dickie's a very emotional man, as we all know, but it's a very genuine emotion and when we're doing the death scenes we would laugh in between takes [Hopkins had a nice line in Bogart imitations just before Winger renewed the fraught business of terminal cancer] otherwise it would just become darker and darker. The only problem was that we'd do the scene only for our sound man Simon Kaye to say, "That's a great take but we can hear the director crying!"'

At awards time, Hopkins found that he was often having to compete against himself for Best Actor but while the Los Angeles critics gave him their prize for his work in both *The Remains of the Day* and *Shadowlands*, critics in London as well as the National Board of Review and BAFTA all honoured him for his performance in the Merchant-Ivory movie alone.

Three days after he finished filming on *Shadowlands*, Hopkins had swapped Oxford's dreaming spires for the wide open spaces of the Canadian Rockies about an hour outside Calgary. 'Want to play in a Western?' his American agent, Ed Limato of ICM, had asked. Hopkins, who as a young film fan had revelled in the frontier antics of John Wayne, Gary Cooper and James Stewart, needed no further bidding to fulfil what had long been a 'dream fantasy'. In *Legends of the Fall*, based on Jim Harrison's novella, he was to play Colonel William Ludlow, a veteran army officer who, fed up with the brutality of cavalry life, decides to make a fresh start for his family in the relative calm of the new West in Montana. When his wife then quits the ranch for less harsh winters in the East, Ludlow, with the help of his Native American hands, is left to bring up his three young sons, played by Brad Pitt, Aidan Quinn and Henry Thomas. The story, which begins before the turn of the century, spans more than 60 years and includes some extremely vivid Great War scenes (shot, remarkably, in yet another corner of Calgary).

Western or not, Hopkins' first encounter on the set with his director Ed Zwick, co-creator of TV's *thirtysome-thing* and the man behind that magnificent Civil War drama *Glory*, did not bode too well, recalling as it did memories of some of Hopkins' less favourite film-makers: 'It was my first day there and I wasn't actually involved with the shooting when I saw him hurl a cellular phone across the set, frightening all the horses. So I asked people what he was like and they said "a nightmare".

'I went quietly to his assistant Jed and said, "Look, do me a favour. Tell Ed that I have a very violent temper, have even been known to draw blood. If he throws a fucking act like that again, I'll walk off the set and stay in my trailer four or five hours; I may even stay in my hotel.

We're not discovering a cure for cancer, we're just making a stupid film. He'd just better behave himself when I come on set tomorrow. Please tell him all this word for word. No hard feelings."'

The next day, Hopkins started filming and Zwick was a pussy-cat.

'Thank God you're on set,' Brad Pitt told him, 'because he's now on his best behaviour.'

'I just don't like shouting,' Hopkins explained to his young co-star.

Before they started filming, Hopkins had confessed to Zwick, 'I've done Shakespeare, Ibsen and Chekhov but I've been rehearsing to be a cowboy all my life. I'm just getting paid to play out all my childhood fantasies.' Despite the 'atmosphere', Hopkins grew rather to like his director who was known by all and sundry as 'The Terrorist'. Black hair, black beard, 'quite mad', said Hopkins. 'He just didn't know when or how to stop working. One day we were doing a shot and a plane flew over at about 47,000 feet and just as he was about to start up he quickly checked himself, looked at me and we both laughed. I don't know whether it's an American thing but he was rather like Coppola and Cimino, feeling as if he had to prove himself all the time. Perhaps it's a power and prestige thing. He was under pressure from the producers and he passed a lot of that on to poor Brad. In fact, we did end up having a bit of a set-to when he called one of his guys an arsehole. I walked off and didn't come back – but I'd finished filming anyway!'

Legends of the Fall, which went through an agonisingly slow period of post-production during which it was rumoured to have been recut to play up Pitt's role, actually turned out to be a handsome, sprawling epic complemented by some quite stunning cinematography.

Hopkins, boasting a Bligh-like Cornish lilt (in the script), plays very much the supporting role in this long drawn-out tale of sibling rivalry between wild Pitt and stuffy Quinn after the third brother is killed at Ypres. However, he did get to suffer a stroke, enjoy numerous changes of hairpiece and kill a couple of men, so Western honour was completely satisfied.

Just as there had been certain period similarities between the two earlier British-based productions, so Hopkins was to continue an American, and even hairier, historical theme with his next assignment *The Road to Wellville*, as Dr John Harvey Kellogg, turn-of-the-century guru of Battle Creek, Michigan, and, according to writer-director Alan Parker, 'surgeon, inventor, author and crusader for biological living', not to mention the man who gave the world corn flakes. However, this wasn't to be the respectful biopic of an eccentric genius but, as adapted from the as-yet unpublished galley proofs of a new book by T. C. Boyle, a broad, scatological and sexy farce in which no bodily function was left undiscussed and no fundamental orifice remained unexplored. When Hopkins first received Parker's screenplay from Ed Limato, he read it and thought, 'This is disgusting, how can we do it?' He was, though, keen to work with Parker who, in some ten films since the mid-seventies had become perhaps the most accomplished of all the British film-makers from a commercials background. Hopkins was certainly Parker's first and only choice for the role of Kellogg and even put back his start date when he knew the actor was already committed to doing both *Shadowlands* and *Legends of the Fall*. For quite a long while, he couldn't get even close to a 'yes' from Hopkins.

Hopkins' reservations began to be eased after he and Parker met for breakfast in Oxford during *Shadowlands*. There were, he told Parker, two things he simply wouldn't do in the script; the first was where he had to give a lecture wearing a pink corset and the second was a sequence showing Kellogg administering his own enema. Was Parker adamant about retaining these scenes? Not at all, explained the director whose only concern was to snare an actor who for him, with performances like *Pravda*, had proved he could tackle just this sort of 'out there' role. And no, an American accent wasn't crucial either. Parker's attempted seduction continued some months later on the West Coast.

'As he tells it,' said Parker, 'we had dinner in Los Angeles and to stop me pathetically begging him to do the part, he said yes so that we could enjoy the rest of our dinner. Great mimic that he is, I feel his impersonation of me in tears on my knees is closer to the National Theatre than the reality of the Italian restaurant we were eating in at the time. I would also add that directors have to be good actors, at times.' Hopkins admitted that when it finally came to signing up with Parker – 'it was a good script and a big, bold character' – he was 'an easy lay'.

While shooting *Legends of the Fall* in Canada, Hopkins began to work on the Kellogg role: 'I thought I may as well go for an American accent as this character's so outrageous. I kept seeing Teddy Roosevelt and John Huston and then just as I was dozing off to sleep one night – I must have been somewhere in the twilight zone – I was in a car and I suddenly saw Bugs Bunny at the side of the road hitchhiking.

'Then I went to sleep properly and when I woke the next morning, I thought, "That's it! This man is a vegetarian nut and he's turning into a big rabbit." Later on, I went to a dental mechanic in London and asked if he'd make me some teeth. He put them in a mould and when I returned for a fitting I asked if he could make them even longer. And that was it, that was the character; it even changed me vocally.'

The day Hopkins arrived on set at a hotel in the foothills of the Catskill Mountains, which the production was using for the exterior of Kellogg's famous sanitarium, the word went out that he was going to 'surprise' Parker. 'Tony wants you,' the director was finally told and when he turned round there was this vision in a white suit, with a moustache and goatee beard, buck teeth and shaved head.

'I didn't recognise him at first,' recalled Parker. 'He was an extraordinary sight. Although I had given him as much research as I could, all of that "look" came entirely from him.'

In a film full of Keystone slapstick, Hopkins offers an uninhibited *tour de farce* entirely in keeping with his mentor, Bugs Bunny, getting those teeth round great Kelloggisms like, 'The tongue is the billboard of the bowels', 'We are but lifeguards on the shores of the alimentary canal' and 'An erection is a flagpole on your grave'. Parker remembered saying to Hopkins, 'I shouldn't be allowing you to get away with this.' Yet the director decided to take his cue for the rest of the film from him. 'Jumping without a parachute,' Parker called it.

On a late afternoon towards the end of Autumn 1994, the talk around the North Wales market town of Mold was of *August*. For *August* happened to be the title of a new play which was breaking new box-office records at the prestigious Theatr Clwyd, which hadn't been especially short of success ever since being opened by the Queen in 1976.

A full hour before curtain-up and the foyers and bars were buzzing, even in mid-week, with atmosphere and anticipation. A large board was covered with photographs of the cast – Leslie Phillips, Gawn Grainger, Hugh Lloyd, Rhian Morgan and, in the middle, Hopkins. 'He's so cool,' purred one teenager – the feature of this growing, excited throng was its wide range of age – probably thinking more about svelte Dr Lecter than in contemplation of the bearded, shaggy-haired old drunk in a crumpled white suit and straw hat whose character Hopkins would inhabit on stage for two enthralling hours later that evening.

Elsewhere around the foyer were other 'on sale' reminders of the actor and local hero who, now less than two months away from his 57th birthday, had chosen Theatr Clwyd for his first theatre role in five years and, much more apropos in view of the location, for his first stint on a Welsh stage in more than 30 years (since the curiously-titled *Have a Cigarette?*): the *Cambridge Illustrated History of the British Theatre* boasted an inset photo of Hopkins and Michael Bryant tussling in Shakespeare, while *Anthony Hopkins' Snowdonia* featured a cover shot of the National Trust's appeal president in natty flatcap framed in the foreground of the mountain.

Some minutes after the scheduled start of the performance the doors to the main theatre were finally closed with a capacity audience having been shoe-horned into a handsome auditorium, already boosted by the addition of several extra rows of seats to cope with the demand. 'The action,' explained the programme, 'takes place outside and inside the very large house at the centre of the Davies' estate, in the 1890s.' But despite the play's Welsh setting and characters called Mair and Prosser, there was a distinct whiff of Russian about the whole enterprise, for *August* turned out to be nothing less than a fairly faithful reworking of Chekhov's *Uncle Vanya*. Though Vanya had become Ieuan, Yelena Helena, Sonya Sian, Astrov Lloyd and Serebryakov Blathwaite, the sense of melancholy, repression, disillusion and downright gloom, not to mention occasional (and welcome) outbursts of sunny farce, were downright familiar and, as etched by playwright Julian Mitchell working from a translation by Tania Alexander, seemed entirely appropriate to this claustrophobically Celtic setting.

'The object,' wrote Mitchell, in an explanatory note, 'is not, however, to find modern or Welsh equivalents for everything in the original but to liberate the play from its false British "Russianness" and allow it to speak to us directly.' It certainly seemed to speak directly to Hopkins, who after first being approached by Theatr Clwyd and its artistic director, Helena Kaut-Howson, at the beginning of the year 'to do something with us', was initially sifting thoughts of anything but Chekhov. *The Entertainer, The Dresser*, a Rattigan, even *The Dance of Death* passed through his mind before he agreed to commit instead to a one-off Masterclass on a February evening. Julian Mitchell, who 18 months earlier had been commissioned to write an adaptation of *Vanya* aimed principally for Theatr Clwyd's second, and smaller auditorium, the Emlyn Williams Theatre, was invited to compère the occasion. He rang Hopkins up to discuss a format for the evening, told him about his play and sent him the script, then called *Scenes from a Country Life* (Chekhov's original subtitle for *Uncle Vanya*).

The Masterclass – dealing with the subject of film and stage acting and 'the differences, similarities, pitfalls and challenges' – was followed by a screening of *The Remains of the Day*, but while a full house stayed on for the second part of the show, Hopkins, Jenni, Mitchell and some of the Theatr's management team adjourned instead for a late supper in another part of the building. Kaut-Howson renewed her longer-term invitation and Hopkins continued to mutter about 'doing something when I'm free'. But almost no sooner had he uttered this polite vacillation than he suddenly announced, with a slight warning look from Jenni, 'I'd like to do Julian's version of *Uncle Vanya*,' adding that he not only wanted to be in it but *direct* it, too.

As if that wasn't enough surprise for one evening, Hopkins ('bit of pause then make my stance now') then delivered another and, if possible, even more intriguing bombshell to the small gathering – 'I'd also like to do a film of it!' This second proclamation, though fairly stunning to most of the supper party, was not quite so out-of-the-blue as it first appears and actually had its origins at dinner a month before at the home of Edward Hardwicke, who played Hopkins' brother in *Shadowlands*. The two men, also old National Theatre colleagues, were saying how they would love to make their own film when another guest, June Wyndham Davies, a formidable producer for Granada, picked up on the notion and suggested, among other things, that Hopkins might like to direct Hardwicke in a Charles Wood-scripted film adaptation of Rattigan's *The Winslow Boy*.

The day after the Masterclass, Hopkins rang his agent to get him to offer Mitchell's script to Wyndham Davies and Granada. Before he had a chance to backtrack and claim it was all some sort of enthusiastic aberration, Hopkins heard, with a haste not often associated with film financing, that the project had been given a firm go-ahead. Now, as if to compound an already exceptional arrangement, Hopkins had one more important suggestion: to make the film first in order to solve the problem of the summer location in the garden, because the stifling summer heat and the omnipresent threat of seasonal storms are almost like tangible characters in *Vanya*. Granada and Wyndham Davies ('who has no fear' recalls an admiring Hopkins) went along with this too.

Hopkins was lying in the bath one morning when it suddenly dawned on him: 'I'm going to direct this film.' In his mind's eye he visualised a big tree in North Wales, that under the tree was a hammock and near the tree was just the sort of house they needed for the film. With these cryptic instructions, a location manager was despatched to find the house in question. Several photographs and videos later, there was still no fitting location. Then, one day, Hopkins got a message that the latest recce might have struck lucky. He flew up to Granada's studios in Manchester and got into a helicopter for the next leg to Caernarvonshire where it landed in the garden of a private home, set in 6000 acres. 'It was on the Llyn peninsular just past Abersoch and almost straightaway I knew that it all just fitted perfectly – the trees, garden, everything,' he remembers.

Now it was just the small matter of getting the script right, casting and, most annoyingly, finding a new title because the producers had just learned about an Australian film called *Scenes from a Country Life*, directed by Hopkins' old NT sparring partner, Michael Blakemore. Blakemore once told me, with exquisite extra irony in view of this new circumstance, how the man who had walked out of his production of *Macbeth* was, despite any other shortcomings, 'a marvellous Chekhovian actor, where the words and text are an outward expression of concealed feelings.' *Vanya* was obviously not on nor, for that matter, *Uncle Ieuan*. Hopkins and Jenni had been to a one-man show in Hammersmith about Truman Capote and were on their way home when, after emerging from

South Ken tube station, Hopkins blurted out 'August', with all its connotations of late summer and roses. And so, with the imminent prospect of a short PR trip to Cannes, *August* it became.

When it came to casting, Hopkins remembered seeing Leslie Phillips in Lindsay Anderson's production of *The Cherry Orchard* and thought he would be perfect as Blathwaite/Serebryakov, the pompous city academic who, in this version, is a self-pitying old Englishman who exploits the Welsh relatives condemned to looking after his country estate. 'Wales!' rails the testy professor. 'It's like living in exile. I feel as if I've fallen off the earth onto some undiscovered planet' (the regular cue for much audience amusement). He'd prefer to settle in Cheltenham. Around the veteran Phillips, Hopkins would gather a predominantly Welsh cast – Rhian Morgan, Mena Trussler, Rhoda Lewis and Hugh Lloyd (born just over the border in Chester). But what about Dr Lloyd/Astrov (a role Hopkins himself had played in Cedric Messina's BBC TV production 24 years earlier), a character as hard-drinking, frustrated and love-starved as Vanya/Ieuan, the role which Hopkins had reserved for himself?

'I needed,' said Hopkins, 'someone to play a man who was deeply sad in his life, on the edge of ruin, who had been drunk a lot. But I didn't have a clue who could play it and I didn't know many Welsh actors. Then I suddenly thought of Gawn Grainger, who's actually Scots-Irish. I phoned him and he said he'd think about it. He was doing *A Month in the Country* at the time and his co-stars John Hurt and Helen Mirren both told him to do it, and finally he agreed as long as he didn't have to "do Welsh". I told him he could be Anglo-Welsh which was fine.' Hopkins and Grainger had, of course, been great drinking mates in old, subsidised, theatre days but now they enjoyed a 'looser' friendship, having met extremely rarely in the past few years.

'In the old days,' said Grainger, a recent widower who was to marry Zoe Wanamaker during the theatre run of

August, 'our drunk scene would probably have been for real and then gone on several days. Although I have stopped from time to time, I now drink which is nice for me. But Tony says, "It's not fair. You're an amiable drunk and I was an explosive drunk." He still has, though, an addictive streak and we've both been getting a bit worried about smoking too many cigars.'

The final, and perhaps keypiece of casting was for Helen, Blathwaite's second, and much younger, wife who becomes the less than obscure object of desire for both Lloyd and Ieuan.

Hopkins was in Los Angeles at the end of March for the 66th Academy Awards where not even his lucky shoes could help prevent Tom Hanks (for *Philadelphia*) from pipping him (for *The Remains of the Day*) and fellow nominees Daniel Day-Lewis (*In the Name of the Father*), Liam Neeson (*Schindler's List*) and Laurence Fishburne (*What's Love Got To Do With It*) for the Best Actor Oscar. At Roddy McDowall's traditional party, Hopkins bumped into Richard Burton's Americanised daughter Kate who said she had heard he was going to do *Uncle Vanya*. She asked if he had cast it yet and, if he hadn't, said she would love a chance to play Serebryakov's long-suffering daughter, Sonya, who's secretly in love with Astrov. Though he had known her since her teens, Hopkins knew her mother Sybil better. Whether it was because he 'saw the same sadness in her eyes that I saw in her father's' or it was part of some sentimental desire for a sort of South Wales symmetry is not quite clear, but there and then, without consulting anyone, he offered her the role of Helen, American accent and all.

By July, the production was fully cast, crewed up and ready to roll. Robin Vidgeon, who had been a young focus puller (that's third in the lighting team behind director of photography and camera operator) on Hopkins' first film, *The Lion in Winter*, was DOP this time round and impressed by the amount of preparation undertaken by the débutant director: 'He had worked out many shots and sequences for the film and in the many meetings we had before filming started, ideas continued to pour out of him like a waterfall. One of the problems, though, was that he seemed to be *seeing* it from the other side of the camera so in order to make complete sense of it, I had to learn quickly too. I also discovered that he hates close-ups of himself and would also tend to cut away from himself a little too quickly at times. "Just let it run on a bit," I would occasionally suggest.' For his part, Hopkins told Vidgeon, 'I don't really know what to do but I know what I want to see on screen,' to which the cinematographer replied, helpfully, 'Well, whatever you want to see, I'll put it there.'

If Hopkins had any 'first night nerves' about directing, not to mention acting too, they were soon dispelled by an epic first day's filming which saw no less than 26 set-ups in the morning alone. That pace, helped by a settled major location which meant wet weather cover instantly at hand, all contributed to what seems to have been, by all accounts, a blissfully happy shoot and completion of filming some four days ahead of schedule. According to Grainger, 'The one thing I knew going in was that Tony knows all about movies so I had enormous confidence in him. When he wanted to give you notes – and there were plenty of notes – he would come up quietly and walk round with you. It was done with encouragement.

'He had an expression – "less is too much" – which I think he learned from Attenborough and he also benefited greatly from terrific back-up.'

Admitting he found filming 'surprisingly easy', Hopkins also claims he worked people '... hard. I liked repeating things. I would say, "Let's do it just once more ... no, let's do it three more times ..." I was especially concerned about diction. I told the cast to "skewer the kebab". Pauses wouldn't work, audiences would only get bored. To Rhian, for example, I made the point about not playing it sentimentally. There was a lot of emotion but she should push it down. That way, I told her, "it will be much more moving. You're the survivor in this family." She's very strong, especially at the end.'

The various journalists who visited the set in North Wales were to find an almost indecently relaxed film-maker given to utterances like, 'I was thinking there must be something else I could do with my life but act and now I've found a whole new career. They [the producers] seem to be very pleased and everyone is very happy on set. I don't see what the hell is the point of creating mayhem and horror around people. So I've found my new career and I wouldn't really care if I never acted again.'

Hopkins was combining theatre rehearsals for *August* with cutting his film when he was suddenly confronted with a major problem: 'We'd all been working hard, long hours and very fast too. Towards the end of shooting we were doing a scene with the two girls when I noticed Kate Burton hobbling about. The next day she obviously wasn't well when we had to do a big scene with a chase round the drawing-room. It turned out she had a recurrence of an old thing which was a form of rheumatoid arthritis. Then, when she turned up for the first play rehearsals in September, she was still hobbling about, trying to be brave. I knew then we couldn't go on like this and that I'd have to replace her. There was no acrimony; it was just all very sad.'

So out went Burton, 'with a wonderful cold quality', and in, at extremely short notice, came the younger, breathtakingly beautiful Lisa Orgolini, authentically American-accented (Julian Mitchell had already, to accommodate Burton, written in a line of dialogue about 'being from Philadelphia'), who after a slow start began to warm to her stage role of the desirable Helen. Grainger commented, 'In some ways, it changed the balance of the play. While Kate had sophistication, this girl had youth and so, in a way, Tony and I became a bit like a couple of dirty old men.'

Even though Hopkins was tucked well away in Wales (for just under a month at Theatr Clwyd, followed by three days at the New Theatre in Cardiff), this return of the native was inevitably the source of much greater national interest (and international, if you count the night Raquel Welch was in the audience), especially as he'd added the directorial string to his bow.

Despite the odd demur, the response was not just respectful but in some cases downright adulatory, especially when it came to noting some of the director touches: 'He uses this large stage with unobtrusive skill. Watch his characters moving across the stage, handling objects, walking off abruptly and then coming back to finish what they were going to say and you will find that everything is dictated simultaneously by the needs of staging and by the pressures of the quiet psychological earthquakes that take place within ...' (John Peter, *Sunday Times*). It was, though, some of his film director techniques that were beginning to preoccupy Hopkins as he and his editor Eddie Mansell assembled an early 'rough cut' of *August*. As he watched the ungraded footage, it all seemed to be 'so slow; the garden scene especially really sagged and I hated my close-ups'.

Reassuring him that nothing he'd shot was ever really wasted, Mansell told Hopkins to leave the film with him and 'come back in a week'. Back again at Granada's viewing theatre, the editor now told his small audience, 'Hold on to your seats, you may be a bit surprised; I've changed some bits and pieces.' According to Hopkins, 'He'd changed focuses, rhythms, put things back in that I'd shot but then discarded and even cut three whole minutes of a dialogue scene. The film now ran just 91 minutes and felt fast. I was delighted.'

Hopkins' euphoria was, like the film's subsequent box-office performance, short-lived. Julian Fellowes summed it up like this: 'What *August* taught Tony was he didn't want to direct. He got so bored of it, especially the editing and the post-production. He suddenly thought to himself, "Why am I doing this when what I really like to do is turn up on the set, do my part and go?" *August* eventually became this kind of huge anvil around his neck.'

Hopkins said: 'I don't have it in my nature to be a director. The strain wasn't even being in it as well as directing; it was the editing afterwards that drove me totally nuts. I just couldn't be bothered with it. I suppose I respect directors more now because of the experience and it's no wonder there are times when actors want to shoot you.'

As that wasn't already bad enough, the critical reaction to the film, for which he'd also composed musical themes, ran, with the odd exception, from apathetic to plain dire. 'The critics slaughtered it,' he admitted long after, adding with huge oversimplification, 'that's why I live over here [in Los Angeles] now.'

11. GONE HOLLYWOOD

On the wall hangs a picture of Abraham Lincoln and, alongside it, there's a touching verse which begins 'Lives of great men oft' remind us ...' from Longfellow's *Psalm Of Life*. After he'd stood for a while in the boyhood room at Yorba Linda, California of the future thirty-seventh US President, Hopkins claimed he began to feel he 'knew' Richard Milhous Nixon just a bit better. The small room on the lemon ranch his father once owned near Whittier is now part of a shrine to Nixon and Hopkins admitted that during his brief visit he got 'all choked up, what with this little house where Mr Nixon heard the train whistles, and dreamed of his future'.

Hopkins didn't think he'd be recognised during his incognito stopover but, he later told John Dean, Nixon's sometime Counsel, 'this woman, who I guess is the curator, spotted me. She said, "I understand you are playing Mr Nixon." I told her, yes, I was. She said, "Well, I certainly hope you're not going to do a hatchet job on the President." Oh, no, no, no, I assured her.' Then, according to Dean, Hopkins turned to him and asked, 'I'm not doing a hatchet job, am I?' Dean, who was being employed as one of four 'technical consultants' on the film, assured him he wasn't.

Director Oliver Stone who had been particularly attracted to what he regarded as the 'inherent drama and contradictions' of Nixon's life had first commissioned a screenplay on the subject more than six months before the ex-President died in 1994. For Stone, who would get his massive film rolling less than a year later: 'Nixon remains one of the most fascinating and frustrating figures of twentieth-century history. He's, in fact, a man of the century – he lived through the promise of the California pioneers, the

Depression, the Second World War, the Cold War, Vietnam, the war at home during those years, the end of the Cold War and world Communism. It's almost as if he embodies everything that's right or wrong about America in general and American politicians in particular. There's no question that he was brilliant but he used it for less than noble ends. His potential was limitless, but ultimately was limited by powers that even he couldn't control.

'To some degree,' said Stone, 'the film I wanted to make was about the *illusion* of power. Nixon himself said that he had been to the highest peaks and the lowest valleys. He is a giant of a tragic figure in the classical tradition. Humble origins, rising to the top, then crashing down in a heap of hubris.' If *JFK*, Stone's fascinating 1991 epic about the aftermath of President Kennedy's assassination, was, in the director's words, a 'murder mystery' then this unofficial sequel was, according to Stone, 'a character mystery'.

But who would portray Richard M. Nixon? It was no easy issue, for unlike long dead heroes or villains, Nixon, just twelve months on from a triumphant funeral which had belied his earlier disgrace, was still very much alive in the public mind and imagination. Stone wanted to find an actor who could breathe life into his subject without falling into caricature and someone with the physical and artistic stamina to handle a tremendously demanding role that would require 55 days of intense work in a schedule that was limited by budget (around $42 million) considerations to 61 days. The script alone was a thick 170 pages.

When Hopkins was told by his agent that Stone was sending him a script about Nixon, his first reaction was, 'Well, I can't think of any English characters who were involved in all that.' 'No,' came the reply, 'he wants *you* to play Nixon!' Though no stranger to biopics – he had after all played everything from C.S. Lewis to Hitler – a three-hour probe into the life and psyche of a uniquely American icon seemed an impersonation too far. Hopkins thought Stone crazy even for considering him and told him he didn't think he could possibly play Nixon. 'The next thing I knew, Oliver turned up in London and on my way to meet him for breakfast, I already began to sense that this wasn't just an opportunity to play a great part. I felt it would be a challenge to me not just as an actor but to me personally. A chance to see if I had the guts to do something truly ambitious and risky. I suddenly realised that it would be insane to turn it down. So 24 hours after we met for breakfast, I phoned him up when he returned to Los Angeles and told him that I wanted to do it. Oliver said "You're sure?" I said "Absolutely sure." And he said "You can't turn back now."'

Stone might like to call his project a 'character mystery' but, at the outset, the real mystery seemed to be why he had settled on Hopkins as his first choice for this particular character. He explained: 'I obviously thought of American actors first because that was the natural inclination and the financing from the studios was more available to American box-office stars. It was a tough battle to get him but I do think he was in my first short list of names because something in Tony reminded me of Nixon. I can't quite put my finger on it but when I saw him in *The Remains of the Day* he had that sense of depression and isolation which I felt about Nixon. And here I disagree with many other people. I think he does have a physical resemblance to Nixon. He has a big head, a naturally large nose and there's a bowl-like flatness to his face. But aside from everything, he's just a great actor who can, I believe, play anything he sets his mind to.

'Tony was certainly concerned, and scared at times, about the size of the role, and a couple of times he was, I think, quite close to backing out. He would vary between boldness and fear, between running off to do a smaller project somewhere else and taking a proper shot at playing this gigantic American figure. What especially worried him, I think, was the vast amount of dialogue in an American accent with American mannerisms of a well-known figure. He thought that he possibly could be mocked by the American public and so he was worried about being an embarrassment.

'Tony certainly brooded long on it. Out of all the great actors he has a strong element of doubt in his make-up and that doubt is what gives him some of his margin of greatness. He's played every kind of part – very bold roles, bad men and kings – and I thought that if anyone had the courage to do Nixon it would be him. I had a cogent vision about the film that I think he shared with me. I can't say what was in his mind – and there was no one magic word I said to him – but I think some instinct told him to go and do it.'

Hopkins was still undecided when he met Julian Fellowes for a curry at The Red Fort in Soho. He told his friend that he was exhausted and simply didn't see how he could manage a huge role like Nixon and that his workload was already heavy enough. Fellowes said to him, 'You just have to imagine that you're driving down the Strip and suddenly you see this enormous poster saying, "Nick Nolte Is Nixon". How would you feel about that?' Hopkins thought for a second then replied, 'I'm going to play it.'

Once firmly committed to what has been, to date, perhaps the most testing role of his career, Hopkins immersed himself in an ocean of books, films and video-tapes, studying Nixon's mannerisms and voice, seeking subtleties of interpretation in addition to the most obviously recognisable. In his research, Hopkins found himself seeking what he called a 'place of empathy' which he felt would allow him to portray Nixon with something approaching three dimensions. 'I don't have any judge-ments, political or apolitical. I was just trying to play the human being that he was. I think the mechanism that got Nixon into the White House was also the mechanism that ended him. Whenever I watch his final walk to the helicopter after resigning the Presidency [in the wake of Watergate], I find that so moving and tragic. My interpre-tation of that look on his face was, "What the hell happened? Why have I blown it?" I think he blew it because he was tormented by the demons inside he couldn't reconcile. Some people can overcome their inner demons and monsters. Nixon was one who couldn't. That was his tragedy ... and his pain.'

Not for the first time Hopkins drew on memories of his father as he prepared to play the role: 'Maybe it's something in my background,' he told journalist Martyn Palmer, 'but I do feel compassion for the loser. Nixon was a loser and my father who had a great personality felt like he failed. He reminded me of Willy Loman in *Death of a Salesman*. He would say things like "just my luck to buy the wrong brand" or "just my luck it started raining today". He worked hard and died of heart disease. And he always had great dreams – like Nixon's father. While Oliver was filming some of the early years of Nixon's life, he put pictures of his own father in the scenes and I found that very poignant. I saw my father struggle and I have a sympathy for people who struggle. I remember my father looking really exhausted, he was a tough guy and my grandfather was the same – a tough old monster and a bit of a dictator.' Stone, whose father died before seeing any of his son's major films, would eventually dedicate *Nixon* to his memory.

Stone gathered an extraordinary cast round Hopkins, including Joan Allen as his wife Pat Nixon, James Woods as H.R. Haldeman, Powers Boothe as Alexander Haig and, in a particularly juicy cameo, Bob Hoskins – one time Iago to Hopkins' Othello – as a campily malevolent J. Edgar Hoover. But even as the cast gathered together for the first read-through of the script – co-written by Stone, Stephen Rivele and Christopher Wilkinson – Hopkins still harboured considerable reservations about his suitability ... and especially his accent. It was a daunting moment. After three hours, Stone broke it up and suggested lunch at which point Woods went up to Hopkins and smiled, 'That's a great German accent you've got there ...' That, according to Hopkins, 'broke the ice'.

Filming *Nixon* began on 1 May 1995 inside the Oval Office set at Sony Studios, an Oval Office dressed exactly as Nixon's with its imperial golds and blues, bird statues on the shelves. For Hopkins, the lifelong Amerophile, this rather strange new incarnation as a real-life US President was a sort of day of destiny. Stone had already decided in the pre-production phase to eschew 'mask' make-up for this Nixon, choosing instead to allow the actor to try and recreate the role from the inside out, as it were, with some subtle physical alterations.

Stone said: 'What I didn't want was the audience to sit there and say, "Wow, what a fantastic make-up job! He looks exactly like Nixon," instead of concentrating on the character and story. We wanted to *suggest* Nixon rather than a nightclub impressionist's act which we felt would only distract the audience. In fact, we did experiment for several tests and at great expense with Nixonian prosthetics – the jowls and the prominent nose – but you always risk the Madame Tussauds pitfall.'

And so, working with a hairpiece, Nixon-esque upper teeth, brown contact lenses and more prominent eyebrows, the make-up artists turned Hopkins on a daily basis into Nixon. But unlike, say, Paul Sorvino whose normal Italianate visage underwent a scarily accurate, prosthetic-heavy transformation into Kissingerland, Hopkins, despite some surface trickery, remained always recognisably Hopkins as he settled sensibly for an impression of the soiled statesman rather than a slavish impersonation.

It certainly managed to convince another of the film's 'technical consultants', Alexander Butterfield, who had served as Nixon's Deputy Assistant and Secretary to the Cabinet from 1969 to 1973, the year the President resigned in disgrace. Butterfield felt that Hopkins had 'very definitely captured the essence, or aura, of Nixon. First of all, his years of voice training gave him the ability to nail down the precise pitch and tone of Nixon's voice … this in addition to mastering the American accent. Secondly, he had the posture of Nixon, the gestures and mannerisms, down pat.'

As one critic would note later it was an 'embodiment so extraordinary' that a shot of his back 'is not only recognisable as Nixon but communicates something of his complexity'. Full frontally, those windmill hands and elbows often in frantic overdrive, there were just occasionally moments of quite spooky authenticity especially when the camera sought him out in often painful close-up underlining the alternately shifty, sweaty, uneasily smiling, five o'clock shadowy style of most infamous recall.

After nearly three months, cast and crew moved finally from Los Angeles to, rather appropriately, a torridly hot Washington D.C. in high summer for key capital scenes that had required some complex permissions in high places. There was an important night-time meeting between John Dean (David Hyde Pierce) and Watergate conspirator E. Howard Hunt (Ed Harris), shot on the Inlet Bridge with the illuminated Jefferson and Washington Memorials looming dramatically in the background. Then, in the wee small hours of 27 July, a shot of Hopkins ascending the steps of the real Lincoln Memorial (to tie in with sequences previously shot on Sony's Stage 30 in Burbank), provided a fitting finale for such an ambitious production.

For Hopkins, making *Nixon* was, and still remains, 'a remarkable experience', one which, it may be seen later, was possibly a life-changing one too, that would eventually affect not just the geography of his life but also its physical and emotional well-being. Hopkins had thought Stone 'completely raving mad' when he was offered the role and his first instinct was to turn it down. 'I asked him why he wanted me to play it and he said, as you'd expect, because he thought I could play it. So I asked him again and he said he'd read somewhere that I always felt like an outsider. I suppose most people do, this feeling that you don't belong anywhere. However, I didn't know whether that was enough to go on for *Nixon*.

'Then I thought, here's one of the great directors of the day, someone who pushes you right to the edge and drives actors really hard. I could play it safe and go on with some of the nice boring parts I usually do or else take a chance and run the risk of falling flat on my face. In the event I'm really glad I did it, and I'm also glad I survived Oliver Stone. Gary Oldman [who'd played Lee Harvey Oswald in *JFK*] told me I'd either love him or hate him. He's a little crazy, certainly obsessed but I liked him very much. He was relentless, the pace was forced and he worked fifteen hours a day – it was like a furnace. For me the biggest problem was that it was such a massive part to learn. At the end of ten weeks' shooting, I was on my knees.'

The finished film, stylistically a cross between *JFK* and Stone's provocative *Natural Born Killers*, utilising black and white, colour, archive material – real and simulated – hand-cranked footage and even the odd bit of crafty computer-generated morphing (as Hopkins' Nixon slips into frame with the likes of De Gaulle and Churchill) proves an exhausting and only patchily enjoyable mixture of history and sheer speculation which might test even the most dedicated Watergate watcher.

But in between all the ultra-complicated conspiratorial stuff – which becomes just a little clearer, but shouldn't have to, after reading a 560-page book of the film, complete with annotated screenplay – not to mention a re-run of Stone's JFK assassination theories, there are some magnificently human moments. These range from flash-backs to Nixon's dirt-poor background growing up in the shadow of a formidable Quaker mother and the deaths of two brothers from tuberculosis, to his strange relationship with long-suffering wife Pat whom he called 'Buddy', arguably the film's conscience.

I remember Stone anxiously asking me, after I'd chaired a press conference for *Nixon*, whether I believed my colleagues had 'got' the film. At the time I recall flannelling furiously. What I had wanted to say was: if 'getting it' was to better understand the man behind the tarnished Presidential seal who, to paraphrase his own words, scaled life's greatest heights and plunged into its deepest valleys, then Stone had probably succeeded in some measure. But then again, and despite a monumental performance by Hopkins as a boozing, lying and exple-tives-undeleted Commander in Chief, was it really audience-friendly entertainment in the way, say, *JFK* had so intelligently and successfully sustained its often inspired paranoia across more than three hours?

There's a wonderful moment in *Nixon* shortly before his final exit from the White House when the crushed, self-pitying President shuffles to a stop in front of a full-length oil portrait of Kennedy. He looks up at the painting and confides: 'When they look at you, they see what they want to be. When they look at me, they see what they are . . .' It was perhaps the final irony that President Kennedy, who'd cast a constant shadow over Nixon in real life – a spectre that's brilliantly evoked throughout the film – would also prove to be a fatal phantasm when it came to a comparison between Stone's two longest and boldest movies to date.

The sheer logistics of *Nixon* dictated that it was always likely to prove a hugely stressful enterprise, one that not even Hopkins' dismissive mantra about 'better than working for a living', less disarming than self-deluding, could really hope to disguise or simply help evaporate this time round. Notwithstanding Oliver Stone's own 'marquee value' and the actual subject matter, this was, set in the strictest career context, quite simply Hopkins' most important and challenging role to date. He was, for the very first time in two Hollywood incarnations, carrying a megadollar movie. By comparison, Hannibal Lecter was merely a walk-on. Carrying that kind of weight on his own back, metaphorically and, indeed, literally, would eventually prove just too much. Later he admitted, frankly: '*Nixon* was the one that sent me off my head'.

Yet just three weeks after being 'on his knees' in California Hopkins was in France allegedly fitter than ever, fifteen pounds lighter than his Presidential fighting weight following a crash course of diet and exercise, preparing to tackle another biopic, this time about the painter Picasso. 'Not the wisest thing to do,' he'd concede after the event. Set between 1943 and 1953 – beginning when the artist was 62 – *Surviving Picasso* was more specifically the account of his turbulent relationship with sometime art student Francoise Gilot who, after mothering two of his children, Claude and Paloma, finally walked out on him after ten years of use and abuse.

Promisingly, the role meant Hopkins' return to the Merchant Ivory fold for the third time in as many years, and with memories of *Howards End* and *The Remains of the Day* still fresh in the mind. Rather less encouraging was that this – only the second ever biographical film from the prolific duo – was following so soon in the wake of another Gallic excursion, their worthy-but-dull *Jefferson In Paris*.

For director James Ivory, 'Tony seemed the natural choice for Picasso. Physically he was absolutely right. Beyond that, I felt he was one of those actors – and they are rare – who can convincingly portray a man of genius.' Al Pacino, who had apparently signalled his considerable interest in playing the artist, was also briefly in the frame. But after Hopkins was given a dark tan, close-shaven haircut and dark contact lenses, Ivory further enthused, 'He looks tremendously like Picasso and even has the same build.'

Two months earlier it wasn't so much a question of their star's physical authenticity as whether Merchant Ivory, along with their producing partners Warner Brothers and David Wolper (with whom Hopkins made *Victory at Entebbe!* in 1976) even had a film to make. Claude Picasso and his mother, Gilot, whom the filmmakers hoped would co-operate, suddenly withdrew their approval, claiming breach of copyright and privacy laws. It was, Ismail Merchant explained, 'a serious setback.

'Although the Picasso heirs had never encouraged filmmakers in the past, nothing had prepared us for such a dramatic standoff. We knew that others – most recently Anthony Quinn – who had tried to make films about Picasso had always met with opposition from the artist's estate. But Gilot had initially been very enthusiastic about our idea for this film, and we had been delighted to have her blessing bestowed on us over a lunch in the Russian Tea Room in New York. Although we were under no obligation to do so, we had sent Gilot a copy of the script as a gesture of good faith.

'However in the meantime Warner Brothers, who had initiated the project – which had originally included Gilot in a writing partnership with Arianna Stassinopoulos Huffington [upon whose book *Picasso, Creator and Destroyer* Ruth Prawer Jhabvala would eventually base her screenplay] – became cautious about committing the initial sum of $250,000, which was the amount we had agreed to pay Picasso's estate representative, The Artists' Rights Society, for the rights to use the artist's original work in the film.'

Now, maybe something to do with the rumour that Picasso *fils* was planning his own film 22 years after his father's death, Gilot suddenly objected to Merchant-Ivory's script, claiming that Picasso had been portrayed as – surprise, surprise – a 'very flawed character'. Since Gilot's own account of her years with Picasso, published in her autobiography *Life With Picasso*, was itself highly critical of the artist's 'tyrannical, even sadistic, nature and is, ultimately, far more damning of him than our script is,' her combative new stance clearly fazed the film-makers. The net result of all this *va-et-vient* was that Claude refused the film-makers access to Picasso's work and even challenged Warner Brothers' right to make the film at all. For his part, Merchant refused to be bowed and told him that the film would still be made, 'with or without his permission, and with or without his father's art'. Warner Brothers, who'd already invested considerable money in the project, supportively took exactly the same position.

With the threat of legal action permanently pending, filming finally got underway on *Surviving Picasso* – code-named, for cloak-and-dagger purposes, 'Number Nineteen' (it was Ivory's nineteenth film as director), to divert any obvious attention – with scenes shot on a private beach near Le Lavandou on the Cote d'Azur. These were recreations of tender moments and the odd romp between the painter and twentysomething Gilot, played by newcomer Nastascha McElhone, as captured once in famous photos by their friend Robert Capa towards the end of the Second World War.

Meanwhile, the real-life Gilot, 73 and ensconced in her New York home, was telling anyone who'd listen about her furious stance. According to the *Daily Mail*: 'It reminds me of a film I saw about Michelangelo [*The Agony And The Ecstasy*] in which he was played by Charlton Heston. It was obscene – and so is this. Anthony Hopkins is a good actor. But selecting him to play Picasso is outrageous when you consider the calibre of the person they claim the film is about. Merchant Ivory have turned my life into a soap opera. The script is so below grade it is ridiculous. It would make me laugh if it wasn't such outrageous fiction.' But, she added, magnanimously, 'I'm a reasonable person. I've told them I will abandon my efforts to stop the film if they take my name and Picasso's out of it. They might even want to set the story in 1914. That way Merchant Ivory could have the nice costumes they like in their films and not have to worry about understanding great art.'

Naturally Merchant Ivory weren't about to abandon anything and decided the best way forward was to simply to ignore all the threats and proceed as planned even though it meant, by French law, they would never be able to reproduce Picasso's canvasses in the film. Their way round this knotty little problem was outlined by co-producer Wolper who explained, 'Obviously paintings will have to be done in the film. We are showing how Picasso's art changed with the women in his life. The law is tricky but if you show a preliminary phase you are not showing Picasso's paintings.'

Said Merchant: 'We read in the newspapers of threats made by Claude Picasso that, if we were to shoot even a single frame of any Picasso art, he would send in the gendarmes to confiscate our film.' The idea was then to have alternate locations arranged in advance so that in the event of any trouble the unit could be swiftly shifted to another place with minimal loss of time. Merchant Ivory naturally wanted as far as possible to shoot on as many authentic locations as possible but contingency plans were also drawn up to film just over the border on the Italian coast, out of the jurisdiction of the French authorities.

All the Paris interiors would be filmed at Pinewood Studios except for those at the Brasserie Lipp and Café de Flore, Picasso's two most favoured Left Bank watering holes. In a kind of guerrilla raid, the production grabbed scenes in both places. 'We decided to take that risk because,' said Merchant, 'those scenes could be shot briskly and discreetly – by the time Claude Picasso alerted the authorities we would have completed the job and moved on.'

There was, however, no 'discreet' way that the film-makers could, with the same degree of authenticity, easily get round shooting key scenes involving the Occupation of Paris by the Nazis and the subsequent liberation of the city by the Allies. The intention was to film in the Place de la Concorde and the Place Dauphine, the heart of the matter, as it were. The solution turned out to be truly ingenious. It just so happened that Merchant Ivory also needed an Occupation scene for *The Proprietor*, the production being completed before starting *Picasso*.

Merchant explained: 'At six o'clock on a Sunday morning in late August 1995 – the last day we could shoot this scene in the relatively deserted capital before the Parisians returned from their summer vacations – we marched into Place de la Concorde with three cameras, a huge crew, hundreds of extras and a fleet of period cars and tanks. The slates for both films that day had *The Proprietor* written on them which was the truth – though not the whole truth. The battalion of Nazi troops goose-stepping across the Place in time to a marching band were the most ambitious crowd scenes we had ever done outside India. What a sight it would have been if they had been stopped by a process server waving a paper!'

Though *Surviving Picasso* was never going to be anything like, as Hopkins put it, 'the wearing, grinding schedule' of Stone's film, it posed its own particular problems, not least: how do you portray genius, especially if circumstances dictated you couldn't even show the proper fruits of that genius?

The first task, as Hopkins saw it, was at least to try and look like the man as much as possible. He viewed a couple of documentaries, including Clouzot's invaluable *The Mystery of Picasso* (1956) which entertainingly portrayed the artist at work: 'In a film you only have a very limited area in which to work so it's always a sketch. You can never reproduce the work or personality of a man like that, or anyone really because it's such a narrow keyhole through which to look. But that's what you must deal with and that's what you try to cope with. I suppose it's a minimalist thing; you just have to paint a few strokes here and there and hope it conveys itself.'

Aware of, but perhaps deliberately keeping a distance from, the controversy surrounding the film, Hopkins also tried to read as much as possible about Picasso: 'I can't sit in judgement on the man. He was obviously complex, a selfish man and probably a generous one too ... a complete paradox. It's their tunnel vision, an obsession, that makes great artists. Such artists don't have much time for people outside that and it makes them abominably selfish.' He might have been describing himself and Hopkins agreed that he could personally relate to aspects of Picasso: 'As an actor one has to be pretty ruthless, very tough, very strong. And perhaps I've got tougher and stronger over the years. I probably don't waste much time now [on people?].'

Costing $17 million, making it Merchant Ivory's most expensive ever production, *Surviving Picasso* proved to be one of the company's rare failures. However the makers might protest to the contrary – and they did – the official Picasso 'ban' didn't help.

According to cinematographer Tony Pierce-Roberts, 'Because we had no co-operation from the Picasso people I had to make it quite dark because we simply couldn't show too much. I think that probably worked rather well in the sculpture scenes where you were aware of them but not too aware. In the case of the canvasses, we either had to show someone else's painting or else be behind them so you couldn't actually see the pictures. It's only when you saw a much talked-about scene with Matisse's work that you realised how much you missed by not seeing Picasso's art properly.' As a colourful sketch of an elderly egotistical roister-doisterer, the film was adequate. If it was an attempt to try and nail down painterly genius – after all, the source material was subtitled 'Creator And Destroyer' – the canvas was botched.

Hopkins had said: 'With Picasso I can understand his obsession, single-mindedness and treatment of people. Any extreme, extraordinary, remarkable human being like Picasso is not going to be comfortable to live with.' Those final thoughts would, in the event, prove chillingly close to home for as 1996 dawned, and with *Nixon* and *Surviving Picasso* completed, Hopkins and Jenni were effectively, if not officially, living apart. The difference between this particular separation and the usual countless months of marital rupture down the years due to Hopkins' enthusiastically nomadic lifestyle now appeared to be summed up in a series of lurid newspaper headlines like 'Hannibal's Tortured Love Life' and 'The Actress Who Helped Tony Live Again'.

What had happened – Hopkins doesn't talk about it now but neither does he deny it – was he'd met Joyce Ingalls, a mother of two and sometime actress-model, at an AA meeting in Los Angeles. Their friendship had burgeoned to the point that on New Year's Eve, 1995, Hopkins' fifty-eighth birthday, he had apparently stood up in front of the group and declared that he was making changes in his life which would include 'this beautiful lady'. Naturally, not even the eponymous anonymity of the organisation could prevent this tantalising tidbit from hitting the fan. The press soon fastened on to the fact that Ingalls, who'd once co-starred with Sylvester Stallone in a wrestling drama, was a very tabloid commodity juiced up by the fact that not only was she still unhappily married to a Hollywood screenwriter but she also seemed to have a colourful emotional history. They dug up, for example, a former 'fondness' for the Welsh singer Tom Jones which inevitably, indeed irresistibly, led to the epithet, 'a 45-year-old boyo-loving blonde'.

In the furore that followed nothing that was said or done dampened down the story as Hopkins was reported further fuelling the romantic fire with florid quotes like 'I have all these feelings I've put on hold for years. I think now is the time to really start living, really embrace the unknown. I want to do that with Joyce. She has given me back a passion and vigour that has been dormant for years. Sometimes my feelings for her frighten me, but she gives me the confidence to explore them ... her smile alone brightens my day.' Their liaison – if that ever really was the right word – even earned 'Relationship Of The Week' in the *Sunday Times*, with the in-house aunt agonising, 'Both Joyce and Hopkins bring a loaded past to their friendship. If you're both carrying the emotional baggage of failed relationships and disappointment in yourself, it can often seem as if you are living in the same suitcase – that you have merged.'

Then, almost as quickly and a lot less spectacularly, it was all over. Jenni, who back in London had steadfastly refused to comment publicly throughout the brief palaver despite a doorstep packed with press, explained to me much later: 'Joyce Ingalls? I think she was around for a few months and I found out subsequently she had been with Tony in Paris. Was it a serious affair? It's something we've never really ever talked about. By the middle of February, by which time the Oscar nominations had come out, he phoned me and said things like, "It's all over ... don't know quite what that was all about ... here I am again ... wonder if you'd like to come out and go to the Oscars with me ... we can go back to normal." All I know is that she was a woman he met in AA and it was "just one of those things", a brief fling, I suppose. Something about which he said, when we met up again, "It's finished, it's over and I don't want to talk about it." I don't think he ever specifically apologised for it. His attitude was "that was then, this is now, cancel and pass on".' Jenni, loyal to a fault, settled for that.

Who ended the affair? Jenni says she doesn't know but according to one brief if tacky sequel which reared up shortly before Oscar night, Ingalls was colourfully reported as wanting to make it very clear, 'Hopkins didn't dump me. I dumped him. The man *begged* me to marry him. Can't you see that Hopkins and his people are practising damage control because of the Oscars? It makes my blood boil.' The more likely explanation was that when it began to appear that things were beginning to get too serious, he felt cornered yet again and simply backed away.

The fall-out from this rather tawdry episode would echo on, notably in some corners of the press to which Hopkins had previously managed, on the whole, to remain immune. Invoking the old spectre, the *Sunday Telegraph*, with a mean-spirited profile catchily headlined 'Burton Lite' ripped in with, 'For years he was dismissed as a bargain-basement Burton. Today at 58, he's a sort of Burton Lite: he has a smaller accumulation of ex-wives (just the one, though according to which gossip columnists you believe, his second marriage is headed the same way), and he's more of a heckraiser than a hellraiser . . . in the half-dozen pictures preceding Nixon his bewildering array of voices and wigs makes Meryl Streep look typecast . . .

'Hopkins never seems to have anything at stake in his films. Jodie Foster was the money name on *The Silence of the Lambs*. On *Nixon*, Stone was the star, and he took the rap when it flopped at the US box office. But *Nixon* has brought Hopkins another Oscar nomination and, even when he's not up for an award these days, the Academy seats him in the front row of the ceremony. After his Oscar for Hannibal Lecter, Her Majesty's Government rushed to confirm Hollywood's verdict with official recognition – in essence, knighting him for a role in which he sliced a man's face off.'

Hopkins seemed to have gone from national treasure to gossipy column item to over-rated star in just a flash.

Not even their brief rapprochement at the Academy Awards (where his *Nixon* lost out to Nicolas Cage for *Leaving Las Vegas*) could disguise the fact that their marital *modus operandi* was not just unconventional but – from Jenni's standpoint surely – profoundly unsatisfactory. She hadn't even gone out to join him at Christmas, 'because I hadn't been invited. Muriel went out but he said he didn't want me there'. Was divorce ever mentioned? 'We never discussed it,' says Jenni.

There was, of course, the Topanga episode back in the eighties when Hopkins had headed solo for the hills for five months before returning to their home in Los Angeles. His bolt-hole this time round was not quite as obviously remote but potentially, in both logistical and emotional terms, much, much more distancing. While Hopkins was preparing to film *Nixon* he had decided to buy a house in Pacific Palisades. It was a two-bedroom, very typical one-storey Californian home, set on a hill and facing the ocean with, from the deck, great views of the sea and, in the distance, airplanes taking off from Los Angeles airport. Bright, light, quite pretty, it had a small garden too.

It was reported later that he'd bought the house 'against Jenni's wishes'. Not true, she says, although it was, to all intents and purposes, a *fait accompli*. 'At the time, he said to me, "I know that you don't like California, but I'm going to buy the house because I do like it here." It was more like he was saying, "I'm going to do it, and I don't care what you say." ' They had both just got their Green Cards again having given them up when they returned to England ten years earlier. Jittery as ever about work, Hopkins felt it was crucial for the future with US-based films like *Nixon* perhaps pointing the way ahead. 'I think,' says Jenni, 'it was a question of his just having a place he could call home because it was obvious he would spend more time over there.'

However Jenni rationalises it, this was the first clear sign of Hopkins attempting to put down some new

American roots, if not deliberately starting to try and erect some sort of continental wall between himself and his British 'commitments', which included Jenni. If Jenni made a mistake, and it was an honourable one, it was that as keeper of the flame looking after his London office and Charitable Foundation, she had allowed him to become something of an 'institution'.

There are certain great actors like Olivier who have been content to become institutions. There are others like, say, Steve McQueen for whom a febrile and elusive quality is necessary to survive. It's as if they have to keep checking that not all the doors are shut, otherwise they feel trapped. That's the way with Hopkins too. In the end, it seems, he doesn't like being with people who think, rightly or wrongly, they are important to him; that creates its own kind of angst. For Hopkins, it is said, combines absolute ruthlessness with tremendous guilt. And the moment he began to feel guilty towards Jenni, it then became necessary to leave her – or, at the very least, put a continent between them. As friends have noted, somewhat plaintively, 'Tony is a bank account where one must make payments – but must remember not to write a cheque'.

Towards the end of that year, by which time Hopkins had, echoing his own words, 'gone off his head' – according to others, 'really bonkers' – with a mixture of overwork and some hospital scare-worthy bouts of physical pain, he had not just geographically but also mentally relocated to California. From that moment on, Jenni would, more than ever before in their 23-year marriage, be marginalised.

According to director Lee Tamahori, the warning signs began flashing from the first day of shooting in Canada. For reasons then unknown to the film-makers, Hopkins was unceremoniously popping painkillers. 'He seemed to be just knocking them back unsupervised, and they were clearly having an adverse effect,' recalled Tamahori, a nuggety little New Zealander. 'Even on that first day, Tony kind of started out being in some kind of hallucinatory state and we had to check him into hospital for an overnight stay.' Six weeks later, still just halfway through a three-month shoot on his latest thirty million dollar film, Hopkins, no longer able to stoically endure increasingly agonising back pain, quietly checked himself into Calgary's Foothills Hospital on a Thanksgiving weekend and underwent surgery for a herniated, or ruptured, disc.

Three days later he was back on the set and, laughed Tamahori, 'I was now having to suppress him, stop him becoming like Superman and try and get him back to the way he should be.' The legacy of *Nixon* and that stressfully stooping posture as well as, Tamahori ventured, Hopkins' working out to extremes 'without proper training' had finally manifested itself in, as Jenni would put it, some 'floating garbage around the third vertebra'. The operation perilously required his voice box to be pushed to one side as the Canadian surgeon 'went in' via a crease in his patient's neck to deal microsurgically with the back problem. 'He was,' says Jenni, 'very, very lucky.'

Just to add yet more spice to this already rather intriguingly fraught real-life scenario, the production in question was not some cosy drawing room comedy but a sprawling great action adventure for which that expression The Great American Outdoors might have been invented. Back from the brink, as it were, Hopkins would now be required to fight a monstrous bear, run through dense wilderness and endure immersion in freezing water. Not quite the kind of rest-and-recuperation as possibly envisaged by his good doctors at Foothills.

Scripted by David Mamet, *The Edge*, as it became befuddlingly titled after being called *Bookworm* (for more obvious reasons) during filming, was basically about how two men try to survive against all odds after their plane crashes in the remote Alaskan backwoods. Married to a supermodel, Charles Morse (Hopkins) is an intellectual billionaire who only knows about real life from books; the younger man, Bob Green (Alec Baldwin), is a macho photographer who, to tickle up this often gloriously preposterous tale, has been screwing Morse's wife.

Naturally it comes as no real surprise to discover that *in extremis* it's Morse and not Green who turns authentic action hero gaining, as perhaps the title intended it, the edge in the ensuing struggle merely to stay alive.

Tamahori said the studio would have been originally happy for him to make the film like an extended episode of Grizzly Adams. 'Let's shoot at Lake Arrowhead just out of Los Angeles,' he claims they pleaded, 'that way we can keep costs down – and no one will know the difference.' The director would have none of it. 'Look,' he explained carefully to the powers-that-be, 'this is about two guys lost in Alaska after a plane crashes. It may not be on the page but the audience *must* get a sense of what this landscape is really like.' They relented, but since Alaska was deemed too expensive, Canada – more specifically the Rocky Mountains in Alberta – was the compromise location. Baldwin was always first choice for Green but Hopkins couldn't have been further from the film-makers' thoughts when they began trying to cast Mamet's script.

Said Tamahori: 'We had never for a moment considered anyone like Tony. It was written for an American, a sort of East Coast establishment figure, someone with inherited wealth, or perhaps even a remittance man, which would make Alec's character despise him even more. He was also written as the same age as Alec. We looked at everyone from Hoffman to De Niro and I went through six months of casting hell. People seem to take about a month to say "no" and it just begins to wear you down. De Niro was still shooting *The Fan* when we got a "yes ... perhaps". It was after that Tony then threw his hat into the ring and our immediate reaction was, "My God, why didn't we think of that?" Here was Tony telling us: "I'm well-read, a bit of a bookworm, kind of insular, and don't mix very well with people. This character is me."

'It proved such a happy accident at first and we reconfigured it straightaway to make him older. We only altered a few words and I didn't even want Tony to be an American. "Just be a Welsh billionaire," I told him. "No one's going to ask any questions. You're just rich." Suddenly we had RADA versus The Method and it helps exacerbate what was going on in the film.' As for that corner of Canada in the early fall – with its blinding blizzards, icy rainstorms and some sites so steep and perilous to reach that helicopters had to be summoned up on occasion to sling in equipment – it was, as Tamahori seemed to require, a location to die for. Well, up to a point anyway.

'I wanted that extreme ruggedness – the almost overwhelming sense that this was a big dangerous country. The actors had no idea what they were in for ... otherwise they might have backed off. I did say it wouldn't be a picnic but the truth is, the only way for this to have credibility was to take it to a place that was really incredible and make it look like Tony and Alec were at the end of the earth. I remember them sitting out there at one stage in the middle of the wilderness when Alec turned to Tony and said, "The script didn't read like this when we were going through it in that apartment in New York." Anyway, I felt it would be not only uplifting for them but for the picture too.'

But Tamahori's best-laid plans looked to have come rather unstuck when, after that first day scare, the truth came out about Hopkins' back condition. 'I think,' said Tamahori, 'Tony must have thought he could probably get away with it and was, of course, determined not to let us down. As filming went on, the big worry for me was that his back problem was making him hunch his shoulders and it made him look like a tired old man when in fact he should have been in pretty good shape. After we staged the plane crash he tried to use that as a mechanism to explain why he should look like that. I was forever monitoring him with, "Tony, don't slump your shoulders!" I was getting just one take out of him and sometimes he couldn't do stuff at all. He was clearly in extreme agony but when the cameras rolled, he tried to drop it all away. It was horrible.

'Then, after fully thirty days in what must have been agony, he didn't turn up for work at all. Without telling anyone he booked himself into hospital and had elective surgery which also horrified everyone because we didn't have insurance for that. We shut down for three days and he came back to us a new man.' Tamahori called it, 'an extraordinary act of bravery'. Hopkins was back at work the following Wednesday, having missed only one day of filming.

Months on, he seemed to rationalise it like this: 'It was like a rite of passage for me as well as my character. For those first weeks of shooting, as the pain became progressively worse, I was somehow able to put all my energy into the action, braving the elements and cold as I tried to forget the pain. But as soon as I let go and went back home at night, the pain became worse and worse.' Jenni, who had spent a couple of weeks in Canada with him at the beginning of the shoot, now flew back out again and arranged for him to be moved 'from a rather big cold house' to a smaller, cosier digs as she attempted to supervise, domestically at least, his proper recovery.

When Hopkins' career is recalled by others, one suspects *The Edge* may merit little more than a footnote which does scant justice to a thoroughly entertaining and often quite literally ripping yarn. Beautifully photographed (by Donald McAlpine) and rousingly scored (by Jerry Goldsmith), it's an often engrossing piece of highly suspenseful cat-and-mouse ... except in this case, the cat's a Kodiak bear and the mouse is Man until, yet further mangling the metaphors, the bookworm turns.

This epic duel required Hopkins to renew his acquaintance with one-time co-star Bart the bear who had previously made the fur fly on *Legends of the Fall*. Nineteen years old, fourteen hundred pounds in weight and a card-carrying member of the American Screen Actors' Guild (with all the usual benefits and residuals), Bart is, according to Tamahori, the 'John Wayne of bears'. An 'incredible creature', Hopkins confirmed. The centrepiece of the film is a thrillingly staged series of encounters as the bear, after mauling to death a third survivor of the crash, begins to stalk and then finally confronts Morse and

Green. The bear's contribution to the action was to have been a mixture of Bart, animatronics and a man inside an eight hundred pound bear suit. In the end, said Tamahori, the animatronics proved 'hopeless' and the efforts of the furry stand-in were 'letting us down'. So – and this adds an extra frisson when the film is viewed now – the end result was, purred Tamahori, 'ninety per cent real bear'.

A rather droll sequel to this state of affairs, which began to unfold long after Hopkins had returned to Los Angeles before flying back to England for Christmas, unreeled itself as the producers were tying up all the film's loose ends in post-production and especially finalising the credits. The lawyers for Bart's trainer, the redoubtable Doug Seus, were demanding that Bart's name should figure right up front just after his human co-stars, Hopkins and Baldwin. The film-makers were horrified and pointed out that this might give the game away about a bear in the unfolding adventure. A compromise was eventually reached that Bart's name – and just that – had to be the first title at the end of the film.

Tamahori was furious claiming this would make it 'look like a stupid Disney film'. After more than a month of legal wrangling, the solution was to surround the credit with words to distract from the name. Between 'Casting by . . .' and 'Production Manager' unfolded the following: 'Twentieth Century Fox and the producers wish to thank Bart the bear and his trainer, Doug Seus, for their contribution to this film.' Said Tamahori, 'I can tell you they fought tooth and nail over every word.'

Hopkins had a catchphrase throughout the filming of *The Mask of Zorro*. It was: 'I want to do two hours of popcorn.' Co-producer David Foster had never met Hopkins before volunteering to meet him at the airport in Mexico and admitted he was a little nervous about greeting '*Sir* Anthony Hopkins . . . don't screw up, I kept telling myself. Then in the middle of all these people coming through I spotted the guy wearing a T-shirt, western boots, Levis and an L.A. Dodgers baseball cap.

After we got into the car I said something like, "it's amazing you're doing this picture". And he replied, pleasantly, "I want to do two hours of popcorn".' The catch-phrase was born.

For someone who had spent much of his youth gazing adoringly at Hollywood movies in the Regent Cinema just across the road from home in South Wales, this assignment must have been like some kind of dream, the apotheosis of his lifelong love affair with America. His childhood heroes had been Bogart and Cagney and here he was at last getting the chance, unlikely as it might seem, to be a latterday Flynn or Fairbanks. Not even, as it happens, fulfilling the usual British requirement of playing the hissable Hollywood villain (that was fellow Brit, Stuart Wilson) but actually embodying the shamelessly heroic persona of the eponymous swashbuckler. Naturally Hollywood still wanted to have its cake and eat it too, which meant that there would actually be *two* brave Zorros; the first, alias Don Diego de la Vega, who twenty years on would then, Obi-Wan-like, hand over the avenger's mantle to a younger, cuter, protégé called Alejandro Murieta.

For such a simple, indeed delightfully old-fashioned, concept, the project had lingered oddly long in development hell ever since Steven Spielberg, who'd grown up on a steady diet of Saturday morning twelve-chapter cinema serials, including 1937's *Zorro Rides Again*, at his neighbourhood theatre in Scottsdale, had persuaded TriStar Pictures to buy him and his company Amblin the rights to Zorro in the early nineties. Ten years before, for one particular horse-train-truck chase scene in *Raiders of the Lost Ark*, Spielberg had apparently lifted not just a similar sequence but also the camera angle from that Zorro serial of such happy memory.

Zorro (Spanish for 'fox') began life in 1919 on the pages of a serialised novel called *The Curse of the Capistrano* by police reporter Johnston McCulley who wrote pulp fiction on the side. A year on, in *The Mark of Zorro*, Douglas Fairbanks Sr first gave silent screen life to the black-masked avenger. Two decades later Tyrone

Power starred in a succesful remake. Since then, apart from a television series, some forgettable B-movies and a campy George Hamilton version wittily subtitled *The Gay Blade*, Hollywood had effectively given up on one of cinema's most popular characters.

The fact it would take Spielberg nearly six years to get his new model off the ground suggested that, in the studio's eyes at least, the world wasn't perhaps ready for yet more colourful cut and thrust in old California. With Spanish actor Antonio Banderas always pencilled in to play the younger incarnation of Zorro, Spielberg, who never actually planned to direct the piece, first worked on the project with former cinematographer Mikael Salomon before they had a parting of the ways due to 'creative differences'. Then there was a deal with Robert Rodriguez, best known for down, dirty film-making like *El Mariachi* and *Desperado* (with Banderas) on budgets which enabled him to retain maximum control not just as director but also usually as cameraman and editor too. Spielberg's Zorro was always going to be much, much bigger potatoes and so Rodriguez, whose vision was clearly somewhat different, also bowed out.

David Foster, a Hollywood producing veteran who'd started as a publicist on *The Graduate* in the sixties, was developing a lavish western with *Goldeneye* director Martin Campbell when Spielberg called up to ask if Campbell would be interested in *The Mask of Zorro*. Campbell, a New Zealander, told him he couldn't quit Foster, to which Spielberg simply replied, 'Bring him along with you.' Although derived from McCulley's creation, the idea this time round was rather different from previous interpretations of the story. Campbell explained: 'Ours was not the traditional story of Zorro being a nobleman's son. It had much more to do with a Merlin/King Arthur type of relationship where an older Zorro trains a younger man to become his successor.'

Campbell said he was particularly attracted to the character because he was such an anachronism in a more cynical action genre as defined in the nineties: 'He's the perfect hero. From a moral point of view, he doesn't go out to kill as many bad guys as he can. He cleverly disables them, embarrasses them and makes fools of them.' The producers' buzzword for the production was 'operatic'.

If Banderas was tailor-made for Zorro then the same couldn't really be said at the outset for Hopkins whose rather improbable casting would in the event prove quite inspirational. In fact it's difficult to discover why he even came to be in the frame at all for such an atypical role. Maybe a transatlantic clue could be gleaned from the knowledge that McCulley had based his Hispanic character on the Scarlet Pimpernel, arguably the archetypal two-faced British hero.

What we do know is that at the same time he was handed the Zorro role, Hopkins was also tempted with an offer to play the villain in the eighteenth 'official' Bond film, *Tomorrow Never Dies*, but reluctantly passed because the media mogul baddie, though very well written (in Hopkins' estimation), seemed somehow just a re-run of his barnstorming stint in *Pravda*. Quite coincidentally Campbell had also decided, after making such a success of *Goldeneye*, to resist overtures to stay on 007 duty for the follow-up.

Another of McCulley's inspirations was the real-life California outlaw Joaquin Murieta who fought land-grabbing gold-rushers, which at least helps explain the name of Banderas' character. Then, as if to compound the deliciously perverse nature of Hopkins' initial involvement, Campbell settled on Catherine Zeta-Jones, another South Wales native, to play the older man's feisty daughter, Elena. It would prove a career-making role for the 27-year-old actress. She and Hopkins had worked together before in 1992 when he directed her in a one-night-only musical version of *Under Milk Wood* in aid of the Prince's Trust. After this latest reunion, he commented: 'She's wonderful. I'm only sorry they didn't need her to sing in *Zorro* because she has a beautiful voice.'

After first looking at locations in present-day California and even Spain where any nineteenth-century views tended to be perennially blighted by everything from high-voltage power lines to satellite dishes, the filmmakers moved south of the border, first to Mexico City's Churubusco Studios and then, principally, to a series of picturesque sites near Pachuca and Tlaxcala, both some four hours from the capital. Not even a severe epidemic of Montezuma's Revenge which once necessitated closing down the production for four days could dim Hopkins' pleasure with the place: 'The weather was beautiful, the local people were friendly, the extras were warm-hearted and the crew was great,' he recalled.

In some ways he was still having to pinch himself that here he was in the unaccustomed role of the kind of old-fashioned Hollywood action man for which not even *The Edge* had quite prepared him: 'When I was young, I remember seeing both the Fairbanks Sr and Power versions of Zorro. But when I became an actor I never thought I'd ever get to play that kind of role.' Apart from the recurring popcorn motif, Hopkins had also told the producers when they offered him the part, 'Now I'm in my autumn years, I may as well have some fun.' He'd admit later – long before the film would become that best-of-all-possible-worlds, a critical and box-office hit – that he was also aware *The Mask of Zorro* could be his 'last shot at a commercial movie'.

As a classically-trained actor, Hopkins had, of course, duelled before but his stylised swordplay at the National didn't quite ready him for what they had in mind for this $65 million brand of swashbuckler. Swordfights require a great deal of space to accommodate actors whose arms are extended with three and a half feet of sword. 'Swordfights are far, far more difficult than people imagine,' said Campbell. 'Staging them is complicated and intense.' In charge of that crucial aspect was Bob Anderson, a one-time Olympic fencer whose subsequent film work across more than 45 years had spanned everything from choreographing swordfights and stunt doubling the likes of Sean Connery to donning a Darth Vader suit for the light saber duels in the *Star Wars* trilogy.

What swordmaster Anderson particularly liked about the specialist action in this story was that the confrontations were pure swordfights and not just the customary landing of one or two blows before one person scrambles away. He choreographed each fight with distinguishing broad moves (such as a fall down a staircase or parrying against multiple opponents) with added flourishes like swishing, missing and sweeping while also taking into account each actor's personal style. He commended Hopkins as an 'amazingly quick student who took pleasure in perfecting his swordplay,' while Banderas was, in his opinion, the most 'natural' sword-wielding actor since Errol Flynn, with whom Anderson had worked in the fifties.

As if a sword wasn't enough, Hopkins also got to play with another potentially lethal weapon, but it was only the actor's single-mindedness that managed to turn his whip from an incidental prop into one of the film's key accessories. While he was making *The Edge*, his stunt double was Alex Green who during his down time on the set would, Hopkins remembered, be in some corner or other cracking a whip: 'He even gave me a whip as a present when the film wrapped. Little did I know what was in store for us.' On *The Mask of Zorro*, the versatile Green was now the official 'whip coach'.

'Originally,' said Campbell, 'I didn't have the whip in the film apart from the opening scene. When we started shooting I would keep hearing cracking noises offstage. It was bloody Hopkins forever practising with this whip. One day he came up to me and presented this idea about how we could work the whip into the crucial cave scene where he's instructing Antonio in the art of swordplay. The idea was he would use the whip to strip Banderas both physically and psychologically, as it were.' Much to Hopkins' obvious delight Campbell proved extremely receptive and ended up shooting the scene pretty much as he had choreographed it. 'I think it turned out to be one of the best scenes in the film,' the director conceded.

Disguised in a monk's cowl and mask but employing the cheesiest of grins, Hopkins' Zorro is in action from the off as he spectacularly foils a public execution and then cuts a sword-swishing, whip-wielding swathe through the plaza before exiting on his faithful steed Tornado. He even has time to offer encouraging words to a couple of adoring young peasant brothers (one of whom we just know will grow into Zorro's successor). As one critic would later write, admiringly, of the film, 'It's the full cliché, with every flourish successfully realised. In fact, one of the reasons the film is so enjoyable is the obvious craft with which the film-makers maintain the overall action-adventure structure while shifting fluidly between comedy, romance and melodrama, deploying clichés refreshed with irony.'

Then, in the twinkling of an eye and still much *Zorro*-bound, Hopkins suddenly turned from inspirational choreographer to, groaned Campbell, 'a scheduling nightmare'. Spielberg, who was just three weeks away from starting his next feature as a director, telephoned Hopkins from his office at Universal Studios to ask if he'd be prepared to play ex-President John Quincy Adams in *Amistad*, a searing real-life nineteenth-century drama set in America and Africa against the background of slavery. 'What about *Zorro*?' Hopkins queried. Oh, replied Spielberg, they could arrange to fly him from Mexico up to Universal, then back to *Zorro* and finally back up again for some East Coast location scenes. It would all work out fine, Hopkins was assured. 'Can you let him off?' Campbell was asked by Spielberg. Naturally, the question was rhetorical.

As far as Hopkins was concerned, such a summons from arguably the most powerful figure in contemporary Hollywood, just as naturally needed no second asking. But he also insisted that he be allowed to retain his personal make-up/hair designer Chrissie Beveridge for the *Amistad* odyssey. Said Beveridge: 'When they realised that Tony wanted to take me with him, I spoke to the producer

Colin Wilson because I think they expected me just to do the make-up, but I told them that I did both. I have an excellent wig maker in London and I realised I could fax her information about the character. She also went to the library and looked out good references about Quincy Adams. The wig was made very quickly, with beautiful white hair, then sent out to us. Tony agreed to shave his head which was so helpful because we were then able to get a perfect look for the character at that time in his life. About two weeks before we were due to arrive in Los Angeles, we finished work one day on *Zorro*, took the make-up off and then did him up as Quincy Adams. We videoed the test and sent it off to Spielberg. He told us he liked it very much but requested we make his lips look "older".'

Unlike *Nixon*, John Quincy Adams, the sixth US President, was, Hopkins would quickly be relieved to discover, merely a crucial bit-player in the unfolding drama following a slave mutiny on the Spanish ship *La Amistad* off the coast of Cuba in the summer of 1839. Led by the redoubtable Cinque (played by Benin-born Djimon Hounsou), they armed themselves, took control of the ship and reclaimed their freedom with the intention of returning to Africa. But their joy and liberty proved short-lived. Relying on a couple of surviving crew members to navigate them home, they were tricked and instead fetched up on the Eastern seaboard of America where they were captured by an American naval ship and eventually put on trial, charged with murder and piracy.

Their plight became even more poignant when it was clear that their fate had less to do with natural justice and much more to do with political expediency. Pro-slavery President Martin Van Buren (Nigel Hawthorne) seeking re-election, was willing to sacrifice the Africans to appease the South – this was, of course, twenty years before the Civil War – as well as Queen Isabella of Spain. It was finally left to a 74-year-old Adams, more than a decade after his one-term Presidency and long-retired as a distinguished lawyer, to be persuaded back into the legal fray and triumphantly fight the Africans' cause in the US Supreme Court.

Zorro's mere six years in development was positive lightning compared with *Amistad*'s thirteen, which had begun in 1984 when a black producer Debbie Allen, better known as an actress, dancer and choreographer, first came across two volumes of essays and articles on this fascinating if widely unknown piece of history penned by African-American writers, historians and philosophers.

But all efforts to push the project forward in Hollywood were stonewalled. It was after seeing Spielberg's *Schindler's List*, that Allen claimed her hopes were renewed: 'I realised that here was a film-maker who could understand and embrace this project and help me get it done.' Fortunately Spielberg, buoyed by his Oscars for *Schindler's List* and possibly seeing this as some kind of logical, if unofficial, companion piece to his ambitious-but-flawed *The Colour Purple* in the eighties, climbed on board having, he said, been 'inspired' by Allen's pure passion for this remarkable story.

For all the film's sheer decency and right-mindedness and some scenes of breathtaking power, notably the mutiny itself and heartbreaking flashbacks to the African origins of Cinque's predicament, *Amistad* proved an unwieldy epic. At times it became almost bogged down in the film-makers' honourable desire for complete period authenticity, ranging from distracting acres of facial hair to masses of Mende speech, native to Sierra Leone. This urge for realism – perhaps political correctness is more apt – only served instead to dilute the drama across its massive length.

Beyond any reproach was 33-year-old Hounsou whose introduction to the cinema had been as a child in West Africa trading detergent box tops in exchange for a ticket to see a John Wayne or Gary Cooper western dubbed into French. The story of the slave rebellion was new to him and sometimes, he said, reduced him to tears on set: 'There was no experience I could draw on to play the part. I had never been chained or put in prison and treated like an animal. I had to make it believable for myself so that the audience could look at me and understand a little of the pain that Cinque must have endured.' Hopkins would comfort him with hugs between takes and also, said Hounsou, passed on 'the greatest piece of advice. He said to me, "You know all those things you learn at drama school . . .? Drop them in the garbage bin at the front of the stage and then just come and *be* the part." '

Hopkins' more overt contribution to this occasionally indigestible 155-minute feast was barely a quarter of an hour of which no less than eleven minutes were consumed by his barnstorming climactic oration before the Supreme Court.

Unable to secure permission to film in the actual Supreme Court in the Capitol Building in Washington D.C., production designer Rick Carter instead crafted an exact replica on a soundstage in Waterford, Connecticut. Transformed by his favourite make-up artist Chrissie Beveridge from a walnut-stained Zorro into an elderly, bald, mutton-chop-whiskered US President, Hopkins predictably stole the show. Said Spielberg, 'Tony brought the same august tenor to the speech that Adams must have had. He put in the kind of performance that for me, as the director, just listening to it made me feel I was actually there . . . back in time.'

As predictably, Hopkins earned one of only three Oscar nominations for *Amistad* (he was pipped by Robin Williams for *Good Will Hunting*) in the year *Titanic* sank almost all opposition.

12. TOO GOOD TO WASTE

'You know he was out of his mind when he did the film?' said Julie Taymor, the director of *Titus*. 'He did tell you he went mad on the shoot? Tony did some things and said some things which had us all literally terrified, like when he was wielding this knife with the boys hanging naked upside down in the kitchen by meat hooks. At the time he was, I believe, a little angry with one of the actors. It was scary. *He* was scary. Sometimes he'd have very grotesque ideas like, "Oh, I'll just get up and piss on them." I said that I didn't think that was such a great idea. Yet Tony was also inspired on the film in a way that only a mad man could be. I don't think any other actor would have dared to go as far as he did. It's *out there*. And, of course, he did think it was his last role.'

Long before Hopkins gave his Rome press conference during *Titus*, declaring 'It's all over', the omens were ominous not least given the context of his famously turbulent history in the shadow of Shakespeare. He'd walked out of *Macbeth* (those directorial words, 'hostile to guidance', would come echoing through time) in the seventies and barely endured that back-to-back 'Alcatraz of words', *Antony and Cleopatra* and *King Lear* in the eighties.

Yet now, at a time when he was fond of telling everyone that he just wanted to have fun or 'make popcorn', here he was locked into a comparatively low-budget film version in ever-chaotic Rome of perhaps Shakespeare's most explicitly lunatic play, *Titus Andronicus*, with a 'visionary' first-time feature film director who despite her admitted inexperience behind the camera still had a very, very clear idea of what she wanted, indeed expected, from her carefully hand-picked actors.

The blocks were firmly in place for close encounters of a potentially explosive kind.

You can't, of course, blame it all on the Bard, just as it's also very easy to understand why Hopkins so readily – at first – decided to latch on to Taymor's extraordinarily fresh approach to Shakespeare's rarely-performed play, first etched in her acclaimed off-Broadway stage production which ran briefly in 1994. Two years later, and after long being one of America's best-kept secrets in the world of theatre, opera and dance, Taymor had her first truly mainstream success as director of Disney's *The Lion King* stage show (a triumph she'd repeat later with the London production). Taymor, a multi-talented fortysomething who also designed the costumes, co-designed the masks and puppets and even wrote some additional music and lyrics, was the first woman ever to win a Tony award for the direction of a musical.

Hopkins hadn't experienced her *Titus Andronicus* but had most certainly seen *The Lion King* in New York when, while still down in Florida shooting *Instinct*, he received a letter from Taymor passed on to him by his agent, Rick Nicita. After outlining her movie ideas, the note concluded with something like: 'This is *your* part and I need to meet you. I know you don't want to do Shakespeare but this is why I think *you're* the person who should play this.' 'Okay, let's meet,' came the reply.

'So,' recalled Taymor, 'we got together for what was meant to be an hour but eventually ended up as three hours. Incidentally, I didn't know beforehand he'd seen *The Lion King* but it seems he was suitably impressed and although it was nothing like *Titus*, it was clear to him that it also had a "director's hand", a "vision", if you like. I was also told he loved the screenplay which I'd made extremely visual; all the ideas in the Shakespeare became visual metaphors. Titus' Achilles' heel is his rigidity and you begin to see him start literally to break down. I think Tony responded to the fact that I had very specific ideas about where to shoot those scenes; more particularly, how to make it a *movie*, rather than just a theatre happening on screen – because I definitely didn't want to do *that*.

'Anyway, there and then, he said he wanted to do it. I'd been told he was very polite, was a nice man and he might say "yes" but that I should take it a bit tongue-in-cheek. I told him, "You don't have to commit now . . . think about it." But, no, he was adamant he wanted to do it and when was I going to start? I said in the spring but he replied he would still be busy with *Instinct*, so what about the fall? He then said he wanted to see everything I'd done. I had a video tape with about five of my things on it, including about five minutes of the *Titus* play.

'I began to get rather self-conscious but he said I didn't have to be, adding, "You don't have to sell me on you any more. I just want to see some of your stuff." I left him with it as well as a copy of *Playing With Fire*, a book about my career. I was very moved by our meeting and we really seemed to click. He had said, touchingly, "You know, you're going to have to help me," and was very honest, particularly how he felt he'd overacted in the past and was abominable as *King Lear*. When I got home, which was about twenty minutes after I left him, his voice was on my machine, and he seemed totally ecstatic.'

But before this budding match made-in-heaven there was *Instinct* to complete, a 'popcorn' film par excellence and one that should have been plain-sailing if it hadn't been for the fact that, nearly three months into the Florida filming, Hopkins snapped an Achilles' tendon in his left ankle during one of the more rigorous bouts of action. Chrissie Beveridge remembered the moment well: 'There was a fairly violent scene between Tony and Cuba Gooding Jr. He had to grab Cuba round the neck from behind and then come down on his knees. Cuba had his stunt double do the scene but Tony wanted to do his own stuff. He hadn't, I think, properly limbered up first or had any massage and probably bent down far too quickly. At first he didn't think he'd done anything to himself.'

'The strangest thing of all,' director Jon Turteltaub recalled, 'was that Tony refused to admit he was hurt for about five days. He finally went to a doctor who told him he had to have immediate surgery and he said, "No, I'd rather just finish the movie and limp the rest of my life." We had to convince him that he was a rather important movie star and that the world would wait and we'd rather he not limp.' Said Beveridge: 'Tony was terrified of the consequences and really didn't want to stop the filming. There was a nurse there but that didn't do any good because she didn't know what was wrong and was massaging his calf when it was his ankle tendon that had gone. It was frightening to realise he'd actually done so much damage.'

In the event, Turteltaub added, 'We changed the whole schedule around to shoot round him. After he'd had surgery in Florida we shot him from the waist up for about two weeks while he was sitting down. Actually it was fun, a challenge even.' However, it soon became obvious that a sedentary star wouldn't fully suffice so that in April the producers called a halt to shooting for three months. It was summer when, after proper recuperation followed by a publicity jaunt for The Mask of Zorro, Hopkins and Beveridge rejoined the cast and crew for a final month's filming back at the studio in Los Angeles.

'Suggested', as the credits cryptically billed it, by Daniel Quinn's novel Ishmael, which, according to Turteltaub, was effectively 'a dialogue held telepathically between a man and a gorilla in a room', Instinct, a sort of eco mystery-thriller, proved merely a distant and ultimately overblown bastard relation of this rather intriguing original concept.

After being accused of mass murder in Rwanda, Hopkins, as reclusive primatologist Ethan Powell, has been transferred back from Africa to the States to serve his sentence in Florida's inappropriately-named Harmony Bay Correctional Facility. But what drove this civilised boffin, found standing over the corpses of several natives, to commit such a terrible act? It sounds like the perfect case for ambitious young shrink Theo Caulder (Gooding Jr) from the University of Miami's Department of Psychology who knows that if he can get the defiantly mute headline-grabbing monkey man to speak then his career will be made and a bestseller assured. So begins an awkward, and at first entirely one-sided, dialogue as Caulder attempts to ingratiate himself with the troubled Powell.

Set alongside this pair's often fascinating and sometimes violently confrontational 'journey' back into the recent past, as Powell finally – actually some forty minutes into the movie – begins slowly to speak about his extraordinary life with the gorillas, is the altogether clunkier tale of day-to-day existence inside Harmony Bay where a sadistic chief screw (John Ashton) rules like some urban king of the jungle over terrified inmates.

Because we can guess pretty much from the beginning just what did cause Powell to go ape then it's as if the film-makers can't quite fully trust the anthropological material, which is perhaps why the movie veers so eccentrically between *Gorillas in the Mist* and *One Flew Over the Cuckoo's Nest*, with a bit of *The Shawshank Redemption* on the side. But at least it wasn't *Congo*, thanks to some of special effects wizard Stan Winston's best-ever counterfeit primates who gambolled with Hopkins in the Rwandan jungle (actually Jamaica).

Gooding, fresh from his Oscar-winning performance as a ballplayer in *Jerry Maguire*, claimed it was a 'little intimidating' working at first with Hopkins because soon after meeting each other their opening scenes together were those initial, intense cross-table confrontations. 'At that point,' said Gooding, 'I didn't quite yet know what he was like to work with but the process helped the whole chemistry between us because he and I had, like in the movie, to build a friendship. The trouble was that after every take, he'd say, "Show me the money," and laugh wildly; and I would have to try and smile, "Oh, great . . . great." I'd also heard him say in an interview, and I know this because I was with him, the stuff about how he just likes to turn up and say the lines. That's a huge lie; he's the most prepared actor I've ever met.'

Added Turteltaub, already behind a string of hit films including *Cool Runnings*, *While You Were Sleeping* and

Phenomenon: 'In terms of, does he just show up on time and hit his marks having learned his lines ... ? Yes, he does all that. I think what he's implying is "Don't worry about things that don't matter ... don't overthink the part." He is very clear on what he wants to do and does an enormous amount of work on the role. It's just that he tries to take the day of work itself very simply.

'Before I started this movie,' said Turteltaub, 'everyone said, "Oh, it's so exciting that you're working with Anthony Hopkins." My response was that as a director, the idea of "working" with someone is very odd; you're not acting with them, you're just watching them act. Hopkins did the working. I did the watching. What I worry about is, "Are they *fun* to work with, are they *nice*, are they *funny*, are they easy to get along with?" Tony was all of the above. This was the only time that I've ever been on a film where I've stepped outside of myself and been aware that I'm actually directing somebody of that calibre. He seems to enjoy being on the set, but I'm not actually sure he likes acting as much as he likes being an actor.'

As for those times when Hopkins would run through his range of funny voices from Sir Ralph to Tommy Cooper, the expected reaction was admittedly more out of politeness than hilarious recognition because, smiled Turteltaub, 'most of us didn't actually know the guys he was doing!' Back in character, and with a powerfully intense and often extremely physical performance – which drew some unlikely comparisons with Dr Lecter – Hopkins helped turn the hokum that was *Instinct* into a small harvest at the box-office.

But not even another thoroughly decent turn could do much for *Meet Joe Black* which, like *Instinct*, had also been 'suggested'; in this case, by a soufflé light thirties film fantasy called *Death Takes a Holiday*, itself adapted from a popular Broadway play. The Grim Reaper assumes human form to see what makes us all tick but then, to complicate matters of life and death, he falls in love. The result, first time round, was seventy-eight minutes of delightfully mindless froth.

Boasting the kind of track record (*Beverly Hills Cop*, *Midnight Run*, *Scent of a Woman*) which unsoundly licenses complete creative freedom in Hollywood, director Martin Brest, who claimed he had been 'haunted' for years by the original material, first began thinking seriously about re-doing it – 'not a remake' he insisted – as early as 1982. But unlike the 1934 film which principally revolved around Death's three-day stay on a ducal estate in some unnamed foreign land, the equal focus for Brest was to be Death's host in a firmly New York-set story that centred on a wealthy, powerful and universally respected businessman, Bill Parrish (Hopkins), and his family. The impetus of the story would be the man's assessment of his life as well as the effect on his household by the otherworldly presence (Brad Pitt) in his home, following spectacular intimations of mortality on the eve of Parrish's 65th birthday.

Enjoying perhaps his best-ever payday, Hopkins also rightly relished the opportunity to do a sort of Spencer Tracy in Tracy's own backyard in the kind of film which, in another year, might reasonably have been expected to clean up at the box-office and earn a hatful of awards. Hopkins' public relations tapdance at the time would come back to haunt him: 'As soon as I read this script I knew I had to do it,' he said. 'It's very good, very fine, a very romantic film. I think audiences are going to be entranced by it. It's a real uplifter. It's going to leave you with a wonderful feeling, and it's a gorgeous, sumptuous production. I'm a big movie fan and this is a real movie-movie.'

What Hopkins surely can't have known at the time he offered this enthusiastic testimonial was that Brest's film would end up as a three-hour, self-important treacly marathon when such gossamer-thin material simply cried out to be tearjerking sprint. The implications wouldn't be felt for almost another year, by which time Hopkins was in Rome deeply toga-ed in *Titus*.

In her book *Playing With Fire*, Julie Taymor wrote: 'For centuries, *Titus Andronicus* had been condemned as one of Shakespeare's worst plays, although it was a very successful potboiler in his own day. Many have doubted its authenticity. Its heightened melodrama and obscene and ruthless violence juxtaposed with absurdist comedy seemed distasteful, over-the-top and extremely difficult to stage.'

But it seemed that it was 'precisely those characteristics' which not just fascinated Taymor but also convinced her that the play spoke 'directly to our times'. Taymor had never read the play before being given it as a subject she might consider staging in New York. Even by this time she had already built an enviable reputation fusing all kinds of Eastern and Western influences, ancient and modern, in a series of quite startling theatrical events – everything from operas by Stravinsky and Mozart to a pair of Shakespeares, *The Tempest* and *The Taming of the Shrew*.

'I was shocked when I read it,' she told me. 'The storytelling and the series of events are so overwhelming; I don't think I'd ever seen anything before that kept pushing further and further, which made you really think about the *nature* of violence. I do think it happens to be the greatest treatise on violence ever written. When we show war in things like *Saving Private Ryan* or *Braveheart*, it is always somehow *acceptable* violence; we're meant to accept the ugliness of war and then believe it produces heroes, honour or freedom. *Titus* begins with the glory of war, followed by ritual sacrifice, a father killing his son, rape and mutilation of Titus' daughter Lavinia and an old Roman soldier's final vengeance – all of which have contemporary parallels in a time when audiences feed daily on tabloid sex scandals, teenage gang rape and the private details of a celebrity murder trial; when racism, ethnic cleansing and genocide have almost ceased to shock by being so commonplace and seemingly inevitable.'

But how to stage such a relentless catalogue of dismemberment and death with just the right touch of the blackly comic? According to Taymor, the idea would be to 'play with that tension between what is the poetic stylisation of violence in the theatre and with the gut, *grand guignol* stomach-churning level of violence perceived as real. In a way, to torture the audience and play with their minds. It's what Tony kept talking to me about, and why he was attracted to the material: because it focused on the darker side of what it is to be human.' For the stage production Taymor devised a series of what she called Penny Arcade Nightmares (PANs), a series of striking tableaux to provide visual correlatives for some of the play's states-of-mind and more violent excesses. When she eventually came to plan the film version, many of those PANs would be translated to the screen almost intact, and with an equal degree of effectiveness.

'I felt that what would also help make it a good movie is its directness. There's brilliant poetry but it is less difficult to follow than some of the later, more refined, Shakespeares. The other reason I so like the story is that Titus himself isn't a lowlife. He's a real leader, yet like so many great leaders ends up, through all the mistakes made and after committing terrible acts which he considers justice, a monster. I knew too, from the success of the theatre production that this play, with its contemporary feel, would lend itself easily to film not just a quaint period piece.'

With the right use of locations (from the Colosseum and Hadrian's Villa to Mussolini's E.U.R. Government building), transport (chariots to convertibles), costumes (armour to Armani) and hairstyles (cropped to New Romantic), Taymor planned to turn the play into nothing less than a filmed 'meditation on 2000 years of man's inhumanity to man'. In the event the Roman Colosseum proved unusable because it had no floor required to stage many of the film's set pieces; instead, and creepily appropriate in the wake of recent Balkan horrors, the filmmakers tracked down a perfect replica Roman amphitheatre in Croatia, on the Adriatic coast at Pula. All the interiors would be shot on sets in Rome's Cinecitta Studios.

Financed by a company run by the sister of Microsoft

co-founder Paul Allen, *Titus* gathered together an eclectic cast. Along with Hopkins, there was Jessica Lange as the treacherous Goth Queen, Tamora; Matthew Rhys and Jonathan Rhys Meyers as her barbaric sons, Chiron and Demetrius; Alan Cumming as lascivious Emperor Saturninus; and Laura Fraser, as the horribly abused Lavinia. The only cast member to repeat his stage role was black actor Harry Lennix as the monstrous Moor, Aaron. He gleefully orchestrates the spiralling horrors and enjoys, at his own suitably horrible end, a final line which perfectly sums up the welcome lack of any sentimentality in the piece: '*If one good deed in all my life I did, I do repent it from my very soul.*'

With a budget (of around $17 million) in place – which together with an original schedule would prove painfully inadequate in the unfolding circumstances – Taymor embarked on what she regarded as a crucial period of rehearsal with her cast in Rome. 'As we were going to be mostly shooting out of order, as one does, it was the only way to let them know the "through line", or, if you like, the entire "arc" of the piece. There was also the fact that half of the actors hadn't done any theatre, let alone Shakespeare. It was a wonderful bonding time for the company. The people were doing it for very little money so were, I felt, doing it for the right reasons.'

Taymor had imported Cecily Berry, the '*grande dame* of speech dialect with the Royal Shakespeare Company', to do one-on-ones with all the actors because, 'I desperately wanted this to be extremely good poetry but also extremely realistic; I didn't want to break up the metre, and she's great at making people seem absolutely natural. The actors had to *understand* every single thing they were saying.'

Hopkins may have asked the director to 'help' him when they had first discussed the project but, said Taymor, when now confronted with the venerable Berry, made it clear, at first anyway, that he neither wanted nor needed *her* particular guidance. Following that brief hiccup everything seemed to go smoothly until, after some two-and-a-

half weeks of rehearsal during which time, said Taymor,
'we had got through most of the play, Tony started to
freak out and thought that I was directing too much. He
seemed to feel that I was pushing too much. I don't think
– though I'm not too certain about this – that Tony's been
directed too much in movies; I mean, deeply directed. I
would get into real interpretation, partly because I know
the play so well. At this point, Tony kind of clammed up
and was ready to go home. I said, "You can't ... Don't
worry, I'll back off." In fact he was brilliant in those
rehearsals but this was all, I think, just part of the fear he
had coming into the project.'

Hopkins admitted later there had been 'bust-ups, a
couple of run-ins, because I said "We're not puppets ... if
you want me to be a puppet, get someone else!" She was
certainly a remarkable woman, a force of nature, even
visionary and created great images but she wanted to
impose her will on every line. It was an often nit-picking
intepretation, especially with body movements. I can't
really work like that. I need basically to be given the
freedom to create what *I* want to create – as Stone or
Spielberg would let me – and can't be restricted like that.'
Taymor recalled the 'I'm not a puppet ...' gripe yet,
despite this simmering undertow, it didn't seem to get in
the way of what she described as a 'love fest' between the
two of them ... for the first third of the shoot, at least.

Some logistics of the production were slowly beginning to take their toll. Said Taymor: 'The film was
underbudgeted to begin with; I was aware of that and
obviously not happy. We started in the fall and our
days were short because it would get dark by three
o'clock. Then there was the rain which began to give us
problems. We also had to deal with Alan Cumming
going back and forth to New York because he was
doing *Cabaret*, and there was Jessica Lange never wanting to spend more than three weeks at a time away
from her family in the States.' Hopkins described the
filming as 'chaotic. The production people weren't
tough enough and it probably needed some old guy to

say, "okay, that's time for a wrap," perhaps to crack the whip a bit more.'

It was, admitted Taymor, 'very hard. We didn't have a good assistant director and I had to fire my first director of photography [who was replaced by the incomparable Luciano Tovoli]. This was Italy, for God's sake, and it was very difficult to stop people yapping on the set. From time to time you'd hear Tony yell "*Silenzio!*" in his great booming voice. Yes, it was hard for *all* of us, but I couldn't be screaming at these people; I had to work with them.' The original schedule was clearly blown. Having been set to end before Christmas, it was now obvious that after a seasonal break, cast and crew would now have to return the following January to complete the film. But even before the hiatus, Hopkins' whole demeanour had altered markedly.

The trigger for this conspicuous change was the opening in the States of *Meet Joe Black* for which he'd been given time off in Rome to attend along with its accompanying press 'junket', that traditionally exhausting round of public relations glad-handing. To make matters worse, it quickly became obvious that they were propping up a turkey. Hopkins had remembered the filming itself appearing to 'go on forever; lots of takes, I don't know why; but Marty's a perfectionist.'

Now the critics were lining up to bemoan how the movie appeared 'to go on for days towards' – adding in a typical brickbat – 'a preposterous and unsatisfying conclusion'. If *Nixon* was, despite the Oscar nomination, a genuine disappointment then *Meet Joe Black* was quite simply a disaster, not just at the box-office but also in Hopkins' increasingly troubled mind. *Nixon* could, after all, be rationalised as complex, idiosyncratic even arthouse. *Meet Joe Black* was strictly multiplex meat-and-potatoes and should, he'd be forgiven for anticipating, have been sure-fire.

'He came back to us different,' Taymor confirmed. 'He was so angry, with the press and with a director who'd allowed this three-hour film, jerking off basically; he obviously now felt he was wasting his time with movies but it was still a shock for us when we suddenly read him saying, "I don't want to act any more." ' It seemed all the more shocking to Taymor because after that initial 'I can't do this ... oh yes, I can,' there had been lots of supportive talk between the two of them, even the possibility of another Shakespeare collaboration on *The Tempest*.

More importantly, the rushes were 'spectacular. When you looked at the imagery it was like an eighty million dollar movie. Remember, we'd also been to Croatia [where the Zagreb police academy provided the Roman and Goth Army extras] for ten days where we'd had lots of exteriors with very few clothes on. Tony and Jessica were real solid rocks on those shoots. I think Tony likes to act in adverse circumstances. He seemed to love having his face in the dirt; he loved the rain and the mud, in fact the general discomfort because I think it made him feel he was *there*.'

Despite Taymor's willingness to 'back off', there is no doubt that there remained, if you like, a clash of styles between the director and her star. 'He did get cold feet,' she said, 'but it was probably me directing too much. It was more than just my trying to tell him too many things; that is, after all, normal in the theatre. In film, actors seem to want a certain amount of room for spontaneity; they seem to want a certain amount of chaos in order to be fresh on the set; they don't want it all worked out. In the theatre, it must all be worked out because you repeat it every night.

'Was Tony terrified of repetition? Yes, and also he doesn't like too many takes. Jessica, on the other hand, tends to get better and better with every take. Tony doesn't. If he hits it on the first take, that really *is* the take. What's sad about that is sometimes the camera isn't ready; maybe it's out of focus, and that makes him enormously unhappy. I'm not the kind of director who just shoots everything from every angle. I suddenly have an idea about a camera movement and that might then take a while to set up. It can be a debilitating experience for some actors, but he's used to it and would just go to his trailer and read a book. He always, though, wanted an immediate "That's great!" or "Let's do it again!" But sometimes things can't be like that and you have to have a moment to think about it. He certainly doesn't want you to go back and look at the video monitor again. He just wants to move on.'

Titus was never, even in wildest imaginings, ever likely to be a mainstream audience-pleaser. But after all the real-life nightmares, not to mention the Penny Arcade variety, vividly, if laboriously, hewn during months of post-production, the end result – eventually released in America a little over a year after Hopkins' apocalyptic press conference – happily deserves to be mentioned in the same breath as just a handful of other classic filmed Shakespeare plays.

As with her staging it begins with a modern-day youngster playing frenziedly with his ketchup-stained toy soldiers before being suddenly plunged through a time warp into ancient Rome. Now the warriors are bloodily real and mud-encrusted as they file into the Colosseum after returning from battle, with old Andronicus at the head of the column. The startled boy starts out as a bemused observer of the increasingly horrific tale before becoming an active participant in the guise of Titus' grandson, Lucius.

Set to an amazing classical-thru-jazzy score by composer Elliot Goldenthal, Taymor's closest collaborator, there followed two and a half hours of singular mayhem, climaxing very messily with a vengeful Hopkins, now kitted out in cook's uniform, serving up some very meaty pies to his doomed guests. If you listen carefully, you'll hear Hopkins on a mimicking rampage. He told me, with undisguised delight: 'As I thought this might just be the last thing I ever do, and as it was a great classical play, I did the last scene as Ralph Richardson, Olivier, and Alan Badel with a bit of John Huston thrown in as well.' It's an often outrageously thrilling performance – mad, bad and very dangerous, a suitable case for treatment. But as for Hopkins himself? Depressed? Unstable? A psychotherapist might be better suited to answer those questions.

13. HANNIBAL (RE)CALLING

The last time the cinema audience saw Dr Hannibal 'The Cannibal' Lecter he was in some tropical idyll, positively licking his lips as the camera picked him out preparing to stalk his old Baltimore adversary, Dr Chilton, who misguidedly believed he'd found sanctuary from the man-eating medic. As the pair finally faded from view behind the rolling credits, the words of his last phone message to FBI agent Clarice Starling were still echoing in our ears: 'I do wish we could chat longer but . . .', hissed Lecter across the ether, 'I'm having an old friend for dinner. Bye!'

There had been talk of making a sequel to *The Silence of the Lambs* following the runaway success of the film, which, like the book, was conveniently open-ended. But in 1993 while in Cardiff making *Selected Exits*, a television film for BBC Wales about the writer Gwyn Thomas (who'd been a friend of Hopkins' father), Hopkins was quoted in the local press as saying he didn't think sequels worked as a rule and that, as a subject, he'd 'done it now'. He also made a mild comment expressing his concern that young people had had access, presumably via video, to what was an adult and violent film.

Then, a year later, Hopkins read in one of the national papers that 'he'd turned down eight million dollars for the sequel' and 'regretted' the original film. 'I hadn't turned down anything,' he told me later, 'I hadn't even seen a script. I certainly never regretted making the film and if it was a good script I'd do it like a shot.' At the time, he guessed that it might never get made.

That was 1995. According to Daniel O'Brien's exhaustively researched 'unauthorised' companion to the Lecter trilogy, *The Hannibal Files*, Thomas Harris had signed a lucrative deal for a follow-up novel even before the release of *Lambs* in 1991. Publication was originally expected a couple of years later but with an author for whom the description 'painstaking' might be an understatement, this timescale was clearly far too optimistic.

In fact, another six years would come and go before *Hannibal* was finally published in June 1999 becoming, in the UK at least, the fastest-selling adult fiction title of all time. At the same time Harris delivered his new manuscript to the publisher, he also, O'Brien revealed, sent copies to Hopkins, Jodie Foster and Jonathan Demme. Almost a decade on, he, for one, was obviously still keen on a grand movie reunion. Perhaps even keener to study the long-anticipated new material were veteran producer Dino De Laurentiis and his second wife/film making partner Martha, whom he had married in 1990.

De Laurentiis was still in the last gasp of a forty-year-marriage to his first wife Silvana Mangano when, beginning with *Red Dragon/Manhunter* in the mid-80s, he'd acquired first refusal film rights to all Harris' books. Reportedly so dismayed with *Manhunter*'s box-office performance, he passed on *Lambs* for free without even bothering to read the book. It was a lesson painfully learned so this time round, with forty-something Martha long professionally and now privately by his side, De Laurentiis, at eighty, was firmly back in the Lecter game – or as firmly as you could be with a writer as slow-moving and private as Harris.

Martha De Laurentiis recalled: 'Every six months or so, Dino or I would pick up the phone and call Tom. We'd ask, "How's it going? Do you have any idea when the book is going to be delivered?" We, obviously, knew all along he was writing this sequel. But Tom keeps very much to himself during this process. He's very much a "closed set". So, we'd keep guessing where he was in the process – and where Hannibal was going – from where Tom was in the world. He'd rent an apartment in Paris and we'd wonder, "Hmm, is that where Hannibal is – or did Tom just go there to get a change of scenery to continue his writing?" We were like FBI agents trying to find clues.'

The producers would eventually discover that Lecter had actually fetched up in Florence, one of Harris' favourite cities which, perhaps coincidentally, also happened to be a jewel of De Laurentiis native Italy.

Hopkins also said that in all the intervening years he had continued to think about the character. How could he not when every interviewer on the set of, or at the publicity bash for, the twenty films he'd completed between Lecter duties, would press him for news of a sequel or, at the very least, maybe just a little vocal/visual reprise of the character for his/her viewers/listeners? But, he added, 'I didn't have any expectations of there being a sequel, simply because one had already been made. However, people would keep asking me and I'd say, "Ask Thomas Harris, who wrote the books." I even began to doubt the existence of Tom Harris. I thought maybe he's the figment of someone's imagination because no one ever seems to have seen him. So when the book finally arrived and Dino decided he wanted to make the sequel, he then asked me and I said, "Yes, I'd do it."'

However, any hopes that the entire Oscar-winning team would be reunited were quickly dashed when, first, Jonathan Demme – who post-*Lambs* had made the AIDS-drama *Philadelphia* and Toni Morrison's slave novel *Beloved* – bowed out because, reportedly, he found the source material in Harris' new book simply too graphically violent and gruesome. 'Naturally I was disappointed that Jonathan passed,' said Hopkins, adding, 'I would agree that the book was pretty much over the top and baroque. Jonathan was never specific but I believe felt he just couldn't work with it.'

De Laurentiis had wanted to work with Ridley Scott for twenty years – probably ever since the British director's breakthrough film, *Alien* – and when they found themselves almost alongside each other on Malta – De Laurentiis on the World War Two submarine adventure

U-571, Scott on *Gladiator* – the proximity seemed too good to ignore.

Relieved at the outset that the story had nothing to do with Rome, Carthaginians or elephants, Scott said, 'When Dino and Martha gave me the novel, I was involved in shooting a big movie. I didn't think I'd have time to read a 600-page manuscript. But I read it in three sittings. I just loved the density of the story and characters. I liked the fact that it not only takes place ten years later but it was written ten years later and therefore it feels like something that's totally distinct from its predecessor.'

The fact that it was a sequel didn't particularly faze Scott either although he had turned them down in the past. 'I've never been afraid of doing a sequel. I've just not had that combination of great material and talent that might have compelled me to do one before this.' He admitted that another compelling source of interest to him was the presence of Hopkins. 'I'd wanted to work with him for a long time. I'd always felt there was a lot more to Lecter that couldn't really be got into in *Lambs* because it didn't serve the story. The new novel confirmed that. The opportunity to catch up to him a decade later and explore this unmapped territory was very interesting to me.'

There was, however, the still no small matter of a script which would satisfy all the parties including De Laurentiis' producing partners, Universal and MGM, who struck a deal to share the distribution rights. First crack at a suitable screenplay was taken by David Mamet, equally adept as a writer-for-hire (*The Untouchables*, *The Edge*) and author of his own idiosyncratic writer-director scripts (*House of Games*, *The Spanish Prisoner*). Mamet's script was described to Hopkins as 'the best first draft ever' with, continuing the industry-speak, 'an abundance of riches'. Not enough riches, though, of the reward-variety to persuade the usually tireless Mamet to soldier on with more time-consuming drafts on the traditional script-rewrite treadmill after Universal, at least, felt the screenplay – 'which gave us a terrific start', according to a bright-eyed spokesman for the studio – needed 'much more work'.

Steven Zaillian, who won an Oscar for *Schindler's List* and therefore was no stranger to deft literary adaptation, produced a new *Hannibal* screenplay which, it was hoped, might, among other things, placate Jodie Foster who had all but joined Demme in the exit. She also found the subject matter 'too grisly' and in the end finally decided not to reprise Starling. The reason, depending whom you believe, was either she felt the sequel would 'betray' her character or her salary demands were unfeasibly excessive. It was said that Hopkins was 'furious' with his one-time co-star. 'Nonsense,' he told me, adding that Foster had even taken the trouble to explain her reasons for bowing out in a private letter. As for reports that he was going to be paid $15 million, Hopkins said they were nonsense too and claimed the true figure was a fraction of that sum; probably, though he wouldn't confirm it, around $5 million, plus a very healthy percentage.

In the end, *Hannibal* would actually turn out to be, for Hopkins, a re-union of sorts but with a couple of different actors. After a trawl of other likely Starlings – rumoured to have included Helen Hunt, Cate Blanchett, Gillian Anderson, Gwyneth Paltrow and Ashley Judd, Calista Flockhart and Charlize Theron – they finally settled on Julianne Moore. She was two years older than Foster, but had co-starred rather memorably opposite Hopkins in *Surviving Picasso* as the tragic Dora Maar, one of the artist's legion of discarded lovers. 'I don't have any power in casting,' Hopkins commented, 'but when her name was mentioned, my immediate reaction was, "for my money, I think she's the perfect one for this part." '

And in a kind of reprise of his colourful clash with Hopkins several years earlier in *Bram Stoker's Dracula*, Gary Oldman, eventually unrecognisable under another of make-up wizard Greg Cannom's inspired face-jobs, had signed up to play the equally, not to say graphically, monstrous Mason Verger. He was Lecter's fourth victim, but – and this, as they say, is where the story really starts

– 'the only one that survived'. Oldman is said to have wanted equal billing with Hopkins and Moore. In the event, he cleverly has no credit at all up-front and is 'revealed' only in the final roll-call.

Hannibal is essentially a story of revenge in which the reclusive Verger, a man so rich and influential that he has the ear of government, dangles Starling as bait to bring Lecter out of hiding and, he hopes, to an unspeakably painful end wrought by some specially imported Sardinian wild boars. His pique is understandable for in one of the film's earliest scenes – one that would presage a number of increasingly nauseating gross-out horror sequences – there is a flashback showing how Lecter persuaded a drugged-out Verger to slice off his own face with a piece of broken mirror glass and feed it to his dogs. Hopkins would later be quoted as saying, 'That was one point I said to myself: "Why exactly did you agree to do this film?" '

This seems to have been the mildest of reservations from the actor who, after picking up the threads of an old familiar role, threw himself into what he would describe happily as a 'no-brainer'.

His delight at the presence of Scott behind the camera was compounded from the very first location shooting in Florence, at the exquisite Palazzo Capponi, where Lecter, living under the assumed identity of Dr Fell, is shown playing a grand piano in his apartment. 'It was a wonderful example of how flexible and open to suggestion Ridley was throughout the production,' Hopkins said. 'The first day I had to play the piano and while the cameras were setting up, I was just fooling around playing some of my own music, some music I had composed. Ridley came over and made a comment that he liked it. And when it came time for the cameras to roll, he just got up, said, "Okay, good luck," and that was it. That was the music Hannibal played.'

The climax of the Florence shooting – which, despite much lurid local publicity as to how such a gory film might tarnish the cultural reputation of the venerable city, did film officially in some of its most revered corners –

was the scene where Lecter messily ('What's it to be: bowels in or bowels out?') dispatches nosy and corrupt Florentine lawman Inspector Pazzi (Giancarlo Giannini) from a high balcony at the sumptuous Palazzo Vecchio.

It's a spectacular – and spectacularly unpleasant – scene, and for Hopkins perfectly illustrated just what, with one final darkly amusing reservation, he meant by a 'no-brainer'. He explained: 'I know how to play Lecter, I have a feel for him. You put on the clothes, the funny hat or whatever and in comes this great actor Giannini and he's already in character so very nervous. He's got such a wonderful face, with all that fear in it because he knows who Lecter is and Lecter knows that he knows. It's all about the set up. You don't have to do anything really. You see me putting on the gloves and that's it. I say "okey-dokey" – that was my ad-lib – and wheel him out on to the balcony. It's all about letting the audience do the work, about using the silences and humour. Like when I answer the phone [in mid-kill] and say, "Hello, Clarice." The audience is already anticipating that because it is primed and ready. My job is relatively easy fitting into all that. It's there, you don't have to sweat it.'

However, he added, what was truly 'scary' for him 'was standing on that actual balcony because they had a stuntman to double for Giannini and I had to push that guy over it. When you're pushing someone sixty feet into thin air with a rope around his neck and a harness on [not to mention with his prosthetic bowels hanging out], it's horrible. That really did make me feel queasy . . . because I don't like heights!'

Apart from suffering a slight case of vertigo, it's not difficult to imagine how content Hopkins must have felt to be back albeit so belatedly in Hannibal-mode in a project that was perhaps as much about being a continuing celebration of his own Oscar-winning performance a decade earlier, as with filming a much-anticipated literary sequel from the infrequent pen of a reclusive author. Indeed, you really have to wonder whether Harris would even have bothered with another instalment if Hopkins' iconic portrayal in 1991 hadn't so captured the public imagination.

To make the assignment seem perhaps even sweeter, Hopkins was back in the bosom of Italian culture but without the kind of attendant backstage chaos, not to mention the Shakespearean yoke, which had so traumatically dogged his previous Italian visit to Rome on *Titus* less than two years earlier. Fully rested and revived after twelve months away from a long film schedule not to mention cossetted by an $87 million budget (compare that with *Titus*'s relative penury) – and a nigh critic-proof payday, Hopkins was understandably in high spirits throughout filming. In his commentary for the subsequent DVD release of the film, Scott would close his remarks by paying glowing tribute to the star 'with whom I had always wanted to work', concluding it was 'great fun ... a very easy ride ... I thank him.'

From the title sequence in which, with a brilliantly contrived use of graphics, Lecter/Hopkins' face is ingeniously etched by flapping pigeons in a busy Italian piazza, *Hannibal* seems to be all about perpetuating much of the already familiar iconography of the bad doctor and all his elegantly heinous works. Images of him in photos, cuttings and that particularly harrowing flashback with Verger, punctuate the first part of the film before the audience are finally re-introduced in the flesh, as it were, early in the movie's second act in Florence. In Armani, topped off with a white Panama hat, Lecter looks the essence of upmarket normality as, in the guise of 'Dr Fell', he first meets world-weary Pazzi at the beginning of a short-lived relationship. You somehow sense from the beginning (and even without having first read the book) that it will end very badly for the sad-eyed Florentine copper. Unlike the end of *Lambs,* in which a rumpled-suited, long-haired Lecter is filmed rearview finally disappearing out of shot, the sequel closes on him in almost full-face close-up as the airliner on which he's a first-class passenger transports him to pastures new – and the distinct possibility of yet another profitable sequel.

Despite feisty contributions from Clarice Starling, Mason Verger and even the aforementioned Pazzi, this is unquestionably The Hannibal Lecter Show. For Hopkins it was confirmation that without ever having to resort to the crude prosthetics that decorate the likes of *Elm Street*'s Freddy Krueger, *Friday the 13th*'s Jason Vorhees and *Halloween*'s Michael Myers, he had helped reclaim Hannibal the Cannibal as popular champion in the All-American serial-killer-on-film stakes. And this just months after the actor had become a US citizen.

Ever since he first played Lecter, Hopkins has been constantly asked to explain what he feels is the appeal of such a dubious character, especially one that, considering his repulsive excesses, has been almost elevated perversely to a kind of (anti)heroic status. 'Kids [who shouldn't be watching this film anyway] like to be scared. Grimms' fairy tales, Big Bad Wolf ... all that stuff. Lecter's the bogeyman. When I first read *Lambs* I had a hunch he would be one of those personalities that would catch on, but I had no idea it would take off in this way. I've really no clue to why this guy's caught the imagination. I suppose people are fascinated by the dark side of life ... there's certainly plenty of it around. If this [Lecter] has projected to the realm of movie history, then for what it's worth in the great scheme of things, it's much to my pleasant surprise.'

On another occasion, Hopkins mused: 'I suppose Jungian psychoanalysts would say it's the shadow that we have in all of us. Or maybe it's his certainty, his calmness that we probably envy. Some of the most colourful characters in classical literature – Iago, Richard III, Faust – have those qualities. They're so brilliant. They have no uncertainty. That's what makes them charismatic: they're always in control.'

Reading *Hannibal* before steeling oneself to experience the film version was less about marvelling at author Harris' undoubted literary flair and skill in constructing some dazzlingly cinematic set pieces with and without Lecter, than about wondering just how some of his more stomach-churning plot excesses could possibly translate into acceptable mainstream cinema. Like Hollywood has done before and since, it would all be a question of compromise. That meant an inevitable scaling down of the gore and Grand Guignol. Brain-eating in, eel-induced fratricide out. What, however, was quite unacceptable to the filmmakers was Harris' bizarre ending in which after all their nail-biting cat-and-mouse Lecter and Starling eventually made an unlikely life together in South America.

Zaillian's screenplay duly surmounted this particular challenge with an entirely different denouement – quite literally severing Lecter and Starling's relationship – which, thankfully, displayed an ingenuity and visual restraint which was curiously out of character with much that had gone before. But for many – audiences and critics alike – it was too little too late for them to be able to roundly recommend an at-times unwatchable film with some inexplicable plot contrivances: like how could Lecter wander about in plain sight despite being on the FBI's Most Wanted list?

To be sure, Ridley Scott, re-united with his gifted *Gladiator* cinematographer, John Mathieson, coats – or is it cloaks? – the grisly tale with some scenes of occasionally unsurpassed visual beauty achieving, perhaps unwittingly, a sort of sado-chic. Julianne Moore brings the same chilliness but somehow less humanity than Jodie Foster to a part that was as under-written as in the book. Hopkins, given pretty much full rein by an admiring director, predictably feasts on his juicy role. If his vocal inspiration first time round was HAL the computer, now it seems to have been in not just voice but look too, Truman Capote, elegant and epicene.

Despite some gobbets of dark humour – though none as good as the *Observer* review headline, 'Closely observed brains' – to describe the film as accurately capturing the spirit of the book was surely more a criticism than a commendation. As one American reviewer put it: 'Ultimately, *Hannibal* has nothing to say about the relationship of victim and victimiser or the seductive powers of evil. That's all bluff. The story has only one thing going for it – the ability to make an entire audience go "Euuch". The filmmakers flog that for all it's worth.' By comparison, *Lambs* remains a triumph of subtlety. Compared with the Oscar triumphs of a decade earlier, there would be no recognition at all for Lecter's second helpings. Ridley Scott and his editor Pietro Scalia did both appear in the nominations – not for *Hannibal* but for their impressive work on the otherwise rather tiresomely gung-ho *Black Hawk Down*, about America's bloodily botched intervention in Somalia. Scalia won, Scott didn't. There was, however, by way of a slight consolation, a joint nomination for Hopkins and Moore in the MTV Movie Awards – for Best Kiss.

But perhaps more important, certainly to Mr and Mrs De Laurentiis and their backers, was the fact that despite some reservations about the content, audiences still took massively to the film, apparently posting the biggest ever US box-office opening for an R-rated film before it went on to make millions around the world. Lecter was well and truly back. But how to capitalise quickly on what was clearly shaping up as a megadollar franchise?

Less than eighteen months after the cameras had finished rolling on *Hannibal*, the producers and Hopkins were back on set with another instalment of Thomas Harris' saga ... no, not for a sequel suddenly and miraculously conjured up by the notoriously snail-paced author but with – albeit oddly enough – a re-interpretation of the first Lecter story, *Red Dragon*. This had been filmed memorably but not profitably – as Dino De Laurentiis was ever anxious to point out to anyone who'd listen – as *Manhunter* in 1986.

Set firmly pre-Starling, *Red Dragon* presaged the later pattern of *Lambs* by etching the uneasy relationship between jailed Lecter and brilliant, intuitive FBI agent Will Graham as the world-weary lawman seeks help tracking down an unspeakable killer Francis Dolarhyde, known as The Tooth Fairy, who slays whole families under the full moon. The twist is that it was Graham, with his disturbing and dangerously publicised ability to think like a serial killer, who had actually put Lecter behind bars.

One of the aspects of the cinematic success of *Lambs* in 1991 was the re-release of the *Red Dragon* novel. Harris had written a new prologue for the edition which spelt out the roots of the relationship between Lecter and Graham. Officially, De Laurentiis wanted to get more of the novel on screen and to restore its original ending in a new film adaptation. He was also eager to take advantage of Harris' new prologue and to expand on it. Unofficially, he needed to capitalise as swiftly as possible on the newly-resurrected cash cow of Lecter and all his works. 'For the first time,' De Laurentiis said, in his often impenetrably accented English, 'audiences get to see what Hannibal was doing before he was brought down, who brought him down and how!' Cutting to the nitty-gritty, Martha added: 'Lecter is a character people want to see ... and seeing Anthony Hopkins play Hannibal is irresistible.'

But would Hopkins want to play Lecter a third time, especially with so little breathing space between the two films? Of course he would. A recent poll in *Entertainment Weekly* had voted Lecter, thanks to Hopkins' interpretation, the most popular villain in movie history. It was surely the actor's duty to do what his public wanted. In fact, Hopkins claimed to have some initial doubts about playing the character for a third time – 'I wasn't quite sure,' he said, equivocally – but any mild hesitation he had seemed totally to evaporate when he learned that the experienced Ted Tally was writing the script. Tally had been one of the *Lambs* quintet of Oscar winners who'd also decided he didn't want to be involved with the *Hannibal* film adaptation because he felt the material was 'excessive'. However, he had to admit that he was a bit startled by the intensity of the audience's reaction to Lecter.

'He is a mad man, he is a killer and he is a cannibal,

completely without remorse or response. But people respond to him. They find him seductive. Also, I think there is a part in all of us that likes watching an anti-hero, someone who can get away with doing and saying things we could never get away with.' For Tally, who had scripted films like *Before & After* and *All The Pretty Horses* between his Hannibal Lecter assignments, the idea of adapting *Red Dragon* was both exhilarating and intimidating: 'One of the attractions for me was the thought that here you have a trilogy of books about this striking character. When Dino asked me if I was interested, I thought yes, let's complete the trilogy with this great actor.'

And so he began his adaptation: 'One of the first things we did,' said Tally, 'which Dino and Tom both thought was important, was go back in time to the moment when Will Graham was attacked and create a feeling of a past relationship between him and Lecter. Hannibal is not an easy character to write. He is so smart, so witty and so crazy that it is hard to go there imaginatively as the writer. It's a real challenge to write a character who is smarter than you ... and he is much smarter than I am.'

To fans of *Manhunter*, of which there are many if not enough in De Laurentiis' bought ledgers to have created a profit picture, the idea of reprising much the same subject matter so comparatively soon after Michael Mann's stylish film seemed more than a little odd. Not at all odd, though, to Italian cinematographer Dante Spinotti, who was to be given the rare privilege of returning to the source material he'd photographed sixteen years earlier on his American debut. 'Manet, Monet – I can't remember which one – they painted the same picture eighteen times,' he said. '*Manhunter* was one movie; *Red Dragon* is a very different film. Every movie speaks a different language.'

De Laurentiis who'd mentally wiped the *Manhunter* slate quite clean, described the language of *Red Dragon* another way: 'There was an image that Thomas Harris mentioned to me that I thought was so important. He said, "As I was writing the book, I was walking on the beach one afternoon. I was looking out over this crystal clear ocean, and it was turquoise and beautiful. Then, suddenly, I saw a great agitation in the middle of the ocean – in the distance, but close enough that I could actually see something was eating something else. And that is like this story. Everything is fine on the surface, and underneath it's all this carnage." '

The casting of *Red Dragon* proved an intriguing snapshot of the passing years and changing tastes in Hollywood 'bankability'. Along with Hopkins (for Brian Cox when the character was spelt 'Lecktor') were Edward Norton (for William Petersen, these days another investigative genius in TV's *CSI: Crime Scene Investigation*) as Graham, Mary Louise Parker (Kim Greist), as Will's wife Molly, Philip Seymour Hoffman (Stephen Lang), as fatally interfering tabloid hack Freddie Lounds, Harvey Keitel (Dennis Farina), as FBI chief Jack Crawford and Emily Watson (Joan Allen), as blind would-be victim Reba McClane.

Playing the lunar slayer who is trying to turn himself into a living embodiment of William Blake's great eponymous canvas was Ralph Fiennes (Tom Noonan as Dolarhyde, then with two ls), in some ways Britain's natural heir to Hopkins' one-time stage crown. Back from the cast of *Lambs* were Anthony Heald (with the help of a luxuriant wig to hold back the years) as the slimy Dr Chilton, and Frankie Faison, recreating for the third time the role of trusted warder, Barney. Fascinatingly, Faison had also been in *Manhunter* but playing a cop, Lieutenant Fisk.

Spinotti's previous familiarity with the subject was matched by production designer Kristi Zea, who also worked on *Lambs*. Her original designs for Lecter's cell had been donated to the American Museum of the Moving Image in New York. The filmmakers retrieved the plans to recreate the cell for *Red Dragon*. 'If you're going to bring Anthony Hopkins back as Lecter,' she commented, wryly, 'you better be consistent with the cell.'

The last piece in the jigsaw was the director. De Laurentiis' final selection surprised not just industry commentators but also, it seems, Miami-born Brett

Ratner who actually got the job. 'I don't do dark movies – I do comedy' was his first reaction to the offer, he'd state later, adding, 'I was not an obvious choice.' Unlike Demme and Scott who brought years of experience to the job, Ratner, at 32, had directed just four films prior to *Red Dragon*. However, that slim CV did include the action comedy, *Rush Hour*, and its equally noisy sequel, imaginatively titled *Rush Hour 2*, both co-starring Jackie Chan and Chris Tucker. Their impressive combined box-office bottom line was over half a billion dollars. That opens all doors in Hollywood and, despite Ratner's own reservations about his filmmaking antecedents, he was anxious to tackle a new genre and aggressively pursued *Red Dragon* with the producers after Universal first approached him about the project. Although De Laurentiis wasn't at all persuaded about Ratner's suitability at first, his 'spirit, fresh energy and honest' approach to the material persuaded them he was their man. 'Brett was very convincing,' confirmed Martha.

But even then it wasn't quite a done deal. Ratner explained: 'I thought I was signing up to a Ted Tally script with Anthony Hopkins. But after Dino said, "You got the job, Brett" he then added, "... now go and convince Anthony Hopkins to do the movie." ' Displaying the sort of youthful self-confidence befitting the director of not just box office blockbusters but also more than a hundred music videos – featuring artists like Madonna, Mariah Carey, Public Enemy and P Diddy – Ratner seems to have quickly won over a star more than thirty years his senior. After finishing shooting, Hopkins said of Ratner: 'Brett brings a lot of what Jonathan Demme brought, which is abundant enthusiasm and energy. He does a lot of takes and I'm never happy with that; it took me two or three days to get used to his style of working. He's like a hummingbird, all over the place, but he knows what he wants and he knows what he sees so I trust him. Brett realised we weren't going to reinvent the wheel. Hannibal is who he is, and Brett understood this.'

As well as having Tally's expert script, Ratner believed

he was able to sell the film to what he said was his dream cast by explaining successfully from the very outset what he felt was the tone he wanted to achieve: 'I wanted to make a movie more like *The Silence of the Lambs* [rather than, by implication, *Hannibal*], a movie that scared you more by what you didn't see than what you *did* see. It was not a horror film. I wanted to make a film that was psychological, emotional and smart.'

The only serious concern Hopkins had with the script as written, recalled Ratner, was with the pre-credit sequence when, having been bearded in his own den, as it were, by the dogged Graham, Lecter launches a near-murderous attack on his hunter before being painfully snared himself. Hopkins felt the violence was too graphic so Ratner re-assured him he would be playing most of a startling scene with the camera on their faces rather than on the actual gore.

Apart from the prologue, the rest of Lecter's scenes were confined to that old familiar haunt of the Baltimore State Hospital for the Criminally Insane. Since the building had been mostly torn down since they had filmed there a dozen years earlier, the filmmakers had to borrow a clip from *Lambs* to use as an establishing shot for the location this time round. Ratner, a die-hard fan of *Lambs*, admitted the scariest part of the shoot for him was shooting those jail scenes between Lecter and Graham which would deliberately echo those equally eerie close encounters between Hannibal and Starling. 'I wanted,' he remarked during his audio commentary for the DVD release of the film, 'all the elements to stay true to *The Silence of the Lambs*,' and he had to be most persuasive with Hopkins who was concerned he might just be repeating some of the same unblinkingly snarling *shtick* without the same shock value.

He needn't have worried. The sparring from either side of the bars between the two actors worked beautifully and on a slightly different plane to the Hopkins–Foster two-handers. Norton commented: 'You could say that Will Graham is in the Clarice Starling seat, but he's not the novice she was – he's not out of his league with Lecter. Their mutual hatred co-exists with a great deal of intellectual and professional admiration. Despite the fact that they have become each other's nemesis, they have a bizarre kind of personal affection for each other.' Hopkins, back to the baroque of *The Silence of the Lambs* rather than the pure Gothic of *Hannibal*, obviously relished these encounters describing Norton as 'a quite stunning actor'.

Fiennes' main regret about the film, in which he made a memorably tortured, twisted killer, was not being able to share screen time with Hopkins. Fiennes hadn't even made his own big screen debut when *Lambs* first opened in London. He had, though, been in one of the companies at the National Theatre when Hopkins was still bestriding the English stage. He recalled: 'I saw him playing in both *Antony and Cleopatra* and *King Lear*, and loved him in both those roles. I remember getting goosebumps in his opening scene in *King Lear* as he comes forward, this highly-charged physical presence and that extraordinary voice. There aren't many actors who can carry that on stage. That size – not bigness in terms of going over the top – but the large spirit that an actor has that comes on to the stage. He doesn't have to do anything, he just exists – and I found that thrilling to watch. I think it's sad he won't go back on stage because I think he is a great theatre actor.'

Compared with the stunning and subtle *Lambs* and its sometimes gleefully repellent sequel, *Red Dragon* proved to be an excellently crafted instalment which was back to psychologically-thrilling basics. We first meet Lecter, sporting a rather natty little ponytail, as he's eyeing up – for culinary purposes, principally – the flautist in his local symphony orchestra. Before his pre-credit tussle with Will Graham, we probably also discover whether he actually served up his infamous recipe of liver, fava beans and a nice Chianti. *Red Dragon* has its grim turn-away moments yet it was a brilliantly acted and often authentically scary exploration of some of the darkest corners of the human psyche.

Reviews were decidedly mixed, rewards of the award kind notably sparse. In the *Observer*, Philip French broadly welcomed the film and especially Hopkins who, he noted, played the role with 'the same glee he brought to that other transgressive gourmet' Titus Andronicus. 'Hannibal,' wrote French, 'the gourmet cannibal, serial killer, ultra-snob and unhinged demonic genius makes Professor Moriarty, Dr Mabuse, Harry Lime and exotic Bond villains look like golf-club bores. Audiences love him for his connoisseur's charm, they laugh with him, and join in his contempt for his antagonists. It is as if Satan had become a much-loved member of the *Antiques Road Show* team. Moreover, audiences can pretend, with good reason, that they're going to see police procedural pictures – a respectable genre – rather than Grand Guignol horror flicks.' Hopkins said he tried to play him differently than in the other two films. 'I said this to Brett Ratner straight away that I didn't want to repeat what I did in *Lambs*. In *Red Dragon*, Lecter is so much angrier. He's enraged. And he's furious with Ed Norton's character about being locked away and would destroy him if he could. So it's that anger I wanted to be there. No charm. Just lethal. Brett helped me get there with that.'

In *Sight & Sound*, Mark Kermode, from the ranks of the *Manhunter* buffs, could barely suppress his fury at the sheer cheek of even attempting to go where Michael Mann had gone so memorably before. From 'with almost unerring consistency, *Red Dragon* manages to get wrong everything that was right about *Manhunter*' to 'the self-consciously "first-rate" slate of performers who are to a man (or woman) dismally mis- cast', Kermode roundly berates the film for its 'bottom of the barrel multiplex sensibilities'. As for Hopkins, he was 'now playing Lecter as Fu Manchu on acid, his col- lection of comical facial tics, rolling eyes, flaring nostrils and sing-song vocals now so cosily familiar as to make Brian Cox's electrically edgy Lecktor seem an intruder in his own cell.'

If the filmmakers had even privately thought that the

Oscar lightning which had so brightly illuminated *Lambs* twelve years earlier might strike twice they were quickly disabused of the idea at nomination time. What few awards were going went to Emily Watson, named Best Supporting Actress by the London Film Critics, and to Keii Johnston. Keii who? Johnston was the stuntman doubling for Philip Seymour Hoffman in a spectacular sequence when the nosy hack is kidnapped by Dolarhyde and secured painfully in a wheelchair before being set alight as the chair and victim career down a hill in a grotesquely and terrifying runaway pyre. For his pains Johnston received (joint) Best Fire Stunt in the World Stunt Awards. *Red Dragon*, which cost more to make than *Hannibal*, but grossed – in every sense – considerably less, only proved that, apart from the odd pyrotechnical horror, nothing succeeds like excess.

Relaxing by the hotel pool in Florence between his murderous escapades on *Hannibal*, Hopkins was engrossed in William Goldman's latest non-fiction book, *Which Lie Did I Tell?*, long-awaited sequel to the writer's now legendary Hollywood companion, *Adventures in the Screen Trade* which famously coined the oft-repeated wisdom, 'Nobody knows anything' (of the film business).

Hopkins was reading Goldman's thoughts about Kathy Bates and the film *Misery* – for which she won the Best Actress Oscar – and he thought to himself 'it would be good to do a Stephen King novel'. When he read on another fifty or so pages he came to the bit in the book where Goldman described Hopkins and Morgan Freeman as 'the two greatest actors of the era'. So Hopkins' thoughts would probably have been particularly charitable when three or four days later, his agent came to Italy with a Stephen King book for him to read with a script adaptation by Goldman called *Hearts in Atlantis*. 'It must have been propitious,' Hopkins said, with some understatement.

The original book was a series of interconnected stories in the form of four novellas and a final short story of which Goldman chose to adapt the first and longest,

Low Men in Yellow Coats, and that final brief yarn, *Heavenly Shades of Night Are Falling* for his screenplay about the far-reaching events of a smalltown American summer in 1960 seen mostly through the eyes of some impressionable local children. With much of the darker material excised from King's original – a Vietnam motif and some shape-changing aliens, for example – Goldman's version was much more in King's edgily nostalgic *Stand By Me* mould than the style of, say, the author's stomach-churning *Dreamcatcher* (which the screenwriter more recently adapted for the cinema). 'It's a gentle, small film, not a big story, and I just liked it,' said Hopkins who had, of course, enjoyed juicy roles before in Goldman screenplays like *A Bridge Too Far* and *Magic*.

Hopkins played the mysterious world-weary Ted Brautigan who arrives one day at the home of sweet-natured eleven-year-old Bobby Garfield who lives alone with his bitter, self-absorbed and cash-strapped widowed mother (Hope Davis). Brautigan needs urgent lodging, the Garfields need the cash, and soon, by reading him the newspaper, Bobby's earning pocket money from the old boy to help pay for a new bike. With his love of language and knowledge of the world outside, Ted opens up whole new vistas for the youngster. But his secret life – it seems he's a brilliant psychic on the run from some covert Government agency – threatens danger all round.

'Ted comes out of nowhere,' Hopkins said. 'There's no explanation for him. He's a bit like *Shane* in the western. He has a mystery and a history about him. He's certainly not sinister. He's a good man, a very good man, and a very gentle man. There's nothing spooky about him at all.' The character reminded Hopkins of his maternal grandfather. 'I was very close to him as a child. And he was very close to me. He had a profound influence on my life – a very gentle, but profound influence. He gave me some courage and hope that I wasn't the dummy I thought I was. He was very encouraging in his life and this is what Ted Brautigan is with this boy.' The Atlantis reference comes from one of his lines: 'Sometimes when you're young, you have moments of such happiness, you think you're living in someplace magical like Atlantis must have been ... then we grow up and our hearts break in two.'

With Hopkins attached to the project, the search was now on for the right child actor to play Bobby. Australian director Scott Hicks, who had made the unlikely Oscar-winning blockbuster *Shine*, about the dysfunctional concert pianist David Helfgott, got a promise from the film's producers that they wouldn't go ahead with the film unless they could find 'the right Bobby. Here we were with one of the greatest actors in the world playing Ted. Bobby's role is just as big. There is not a moment that Hopkins is on the screen when he's not accompanied by Bobby. So clearly it was going to need a phenomenal talent to maintain the other half of that duet. It was quite a daunting sort of prospect.'

After the traditional 'nationwide search', a process which involved auditioning hundreds of children, Hicks found his Bobby virtually on the doorstep in the shape of Hollywood-savvy Anton Yelchin. At eleven, he had already appeared in seven films in the past two years working with the likes of Robert De Niro, Morgan Freeman and David Lynch. Born in Russia, he had arrived in the States aged six months with his immigrant parents who were their country's national figure skating champions.

Yelchin insisted on addressing his co-star as 'Sir Anthony' even when invited to call him 'Tony'. Hopkins – who during production began to teach Yelchin to play pieces like *Für Elise* and *Moonlight Sonata* on the piano – called the young actor 'an extraordinary little kid. He made me wonder ... at eleven, I couldn't even speak. I looked at him one day and said, "How can you do all that stuff? How are you so gifted?" But he is. Very interested in everything. I've never been comfortable with kids. But I was with him. I treated him as an adult, with respect.'

The boy returned that respect in a way which rather touched Hicks: 'I think it was a result of his cultural heritage, in a way. His parents were very cultivated, very artistic and they had inculcated in him the privilege of being an artist. So, for him, the idea of being with one of the world's greatest actors was a matter for immense respect. But he never let it intrude into his performance. He would often be rather overawed by Hopkins' presence in the same room, but the moment I said "Action!" it was quite another story.'

Mika Boorem, two years older than Yelchin and equally steeped in screen time including *Along Came a Spider* with Yelchin, played Bobby's childhood sweetheart, Carol Gerber. She described Hopkins as 'really caring. This one time we were doing this really dramatic scene where I was supposed to be crying, and after every take he'd come up and give me a hug.'

For Hicks, working with Hopkins was 'not a problem. He's someone I've long wanted to work with anyway. He was my first choice for this role and it all happened very quickly. There's always something of a process then of getting attuned to how someone else works – what are their parameters, what makes them tick or go off. But that's the same with any actor, really.' Hicks particularly enjoyed Hopkins' amused recollections of working in Australia on *Spotswood* after he'd made *Lambs*. 'The first day he was filming, there was this veteran actor Alwyn Kurts who said to him, just as they were about to start shooting, "Okay, Tony, show us some of that Pommie acting!" Then, at the rushes the next night, a voice piped up from the back of the room, saying, "I don't know; I think he's a bit overrated, don't you?" Very Australian, aggressively egalitarian. Tony really loved all that.'

Hopkins' scenes with young Yelchin work wonderfully well, none more so than when Brautigan reminisces with Bobby about a famous American football player, Bronko 'The Bronk' Nagurski who, it turns out, was watched at an against-the-odds match-winning game for the Chicago Bears by both Brautigan and Garfield senior. The event is a touchstone by which Bobby can remember his father.

Hopkins explained: 'Bill Goldman wrote about this experience having watched Nagurski, a great, great football player back in the 40s. It's a beautiful allegorical little scene which I was very pleased with.' Fans of Goldman's writing might also recall reading Hopkins' touching monologue in the author's novel, *Magic*, written more than twenty years earlier.

Small magical moments like these prove the exception in an otherwise overfamiliar, coming-of-age, reeking-of-period melodrama in which sentimentality too often slides over into schmaltz. 'Nostalgia-porn for undemanding baby boomers,' noted one particularly unkind critic. Said another of Hopkins, who delivers a minimalist, but still effective, performance: 'With his haunted detachment and exquisite diction, Ted could be a stripped-of-evil Hannibal Lecter.' Thomas Harris Meets Stephen King conjures up a suitably striking combination.

Hopkins had no sooner shaken off the rose-tinted glow of *Atlantis* than he seemed to be knee-deep in brash and Bruckheimer for *Bad Company*, one of the energetic producer's trademark shoot-'em-up, rubber-burning action-comedies. Jerry Bruckheimer claimed to have dreamed up the 'concept' – or more likely 'high concept', as in plot-in-less-than-two-lines-on-the-back-of-an-envelope – way back in the 80s. Judging by the eventual result of this wearyingly hand-me-down, unlikely-black-and-white-buddy-buddy picture, he probably should have discarded the lame idea in that same disposable decade.

When 'Sir Hopkins', as the actor laughingly likes to remind journalists of the way some Americans tend to mangle his title, had to say the line, 'Get in the car, bitch', not just once but twice, you know the script and the concept – which had begun life under the title *Black Sheep* – could be struggling. As seasoned CIA field chief Gaylord Oakes, Hopkins was barking at reluctant agency recruit Jake Hayes (Chris Rock), ticket tout and part-time DJ, who had been coerced to take the hazardous place of his dead identical brother, killed in the line of duty. Enough concept. Someone – probably the normally failsafe Bruckheimer who then managed to convince director Joel Schumacher – must have thought it was a terrific wheeze to pair the icily calm Hopkins with Rock, one of a bunch of motormouth black comics all trying – and mostly failing – to be the next Eddie Murphy.

Hopkins, safeguarded by a massive pay day, could not have been more thrilled to be asked to make another inroad on the kind of mainstream big-name Hollywood character-acting normally reserved for home-grown talent, instead of as the foreign villain, perhaps, as essayed in this farrago by ... yes, another Brit actor, Matthew Marsh. 'I'm an action movie buff,' Hopkins declared, before *Bad Company* was released. 'Films with Schwarzenegger or Harrison Ford in the Indiana Jones films. They are all pure entertainment and I like them very much. I'm not good at sitting, watching serious stuff. I get bored. Personally, I'm much looser than the stereotypical image of British uptightness, and so that's how I approached the character.'

And Rock of his co-star? 'Anthony [not, thankfully, 'Sir Hopkins'] and I have nothing in common and everything in common. I had as good a time working with him as I could with any guy, any age, black or white. We're both pretty dedicated to our work and he was really good with comedy. He knows the way for him to be funny is not to act funny and there's an art to being a good straight man,' Rock said.

There was a reunion of sorts for Hopkins when Brooke Smith was cast as a fellow CIA operative. Smith had played Catherine Martin, Buffalo Bill's surviving victim in *Lambs*. Although she hadn't any scenes with him she had sat on the sidelines watching him work as Lecter. 'It was amazing,' she simpered.

In the event, and even taking into account the film's inane dialogue, Hopkins clearly had a whale of a time in *Bad Company,* running about in shades and a baseball cap, firing guns and dangling from fast cars. He easily eclipsed Rock who whined his smart-ass lines in endless chases and shoot-'em-ups spanning locations from New York to Prague. Perhaps confirming the film was indeed twenty years out of date, it flopped.

If the formulaic *Bad Company* with its conspicuously lavish budget characterised all that's thought to be today's norm of safe, predictable studio filmmaking, then the troubled production of *The Devil and Daniel Webster,* despite its title echo from the golden age of Hollywood, could not, in practice, have been more different. By the time Hopkins was on set swapping so-called wisecracks with Chris Rock, his earlier work (between bouts of Hannibal) alongside a cast including Dan Aykroyd, Jennifer Love Hewitt, Kim Cattrall and Alec Baldwin – who was also making his directorial debut – was bogged down in bitter litigation.

First filmed in 1941, *The Devil and Daniel Webster* – also known as *All That Money Can Buy* – is rightly considered one of the very best ever Hollywood fantasy comedy-dramas. Set in the 1840s, it traces the Faustian pact between loan-strapped young farmer and father-to-be Jabez Stone (James Craig) and Satan, alias Mr Scratch (Walter Huston). After granting Jabez seven years of power and prosperity, the Devil comes to collect his soul and the film climaxes with a splendidly surreal court case in which Jabez is defended in his diabolical plight by a great lawyer/politician from those early days of US independence, Daniel Webster (Edward Arnold). Based on a 1937 short story by Stephen Vincent Benet, the subject matter was later turned into an opera before becoming an RKO property which first greatly interested Orson Welles – who wanted to play both Jabez and Webster – before he was consumed by *Citizen Kane*.

Almost sixty years to the month after the first film began shooting, Baldwin's modern-day take on the tale, with himself playing a writer seeking satanic support, went into production, already a week behind schedule after one of many financial crises that would dog the project. According to a number of subsequently fascinating if appetite-whetting accounts of the whole turbulent business – Baldwin himself seemed permanently unavailable for comment – including one by Stephen Holloway in the trade paper, *Hollywood Reporter*, Baldwin had been wanting to make the film for six years. It began its new life as a modest – by Hollywood standards – $13 million project which Baldwin and his producing partner Jon Cornick were developing with Castle Rock Entertainment. When Castle Rock eventually decided to pass on the film, Baldwin made a deal with a company called Cutting Edge, who seemed delighted to be in on the deal – especially when the actor persuaded Hopkins, his co-star from *The Edge*, to come on board at considerably below his usual market price.

The acquisition of Hopkins, even at 'bargain basement' rates, meant, however, a budget escalation to $18 million which then inexorably began to spiral through $20 million when Baldwin decided he wanted to shoot in expensive New York rather than Toronto. With filming due to start on 15 January 2001, the budget was now $28 million – twice its original size – yet still without its full independent financing in place. According to sources, just hours before Hopkins and Love Hewitt – due to play, respectively, Webster and a suitably bedazzling distaff version of the Devil – seemed likely to quit the film because their money wasn't in escrow, Cutting Edge came through with the final wad and the production was able to begin seven days late.

First reports from the set appeared encouraging. Hopkins was reported as saying: 'He's [Baldwin] a wonderful director. Such a nice guy. He's terrific and very focused. I've never worked with a director who works so fast. He's on his feet all day. I don't think he realises how talented he is.' Four months later, *Variety* was reporting that Baldwin was so frustrated with the financiers that he had refused to get involved with the post production of the film (which had finished shooting on time and under budget on 13 March) until he was sure there was money to complete it properly. Baldwin – who was also going through a traumatic separation from his wife Kim Basinger – claimed that he and others hadn't been paid for the final four weeks of filming.

A week after the *Variety* story, the *New York Post* ran a piece revealing that Baldwin had now 'quit *The Devil and Daniel Webster* over unpaid bills'. David Glasser of Cutting Edge was quoted as saying, 'We've been behind him [Baldwin] from the beginning. I don't think I've done one wrong thing.' He admitted that there were some 'vendors' who still owed money but that Baldwin himself had been 'paid in full'. The film would 'definitely be finished, with or without Baldwin's input'.

Galloway's article towards the end of August 2001 described how friction between Baldwin and Cutting Edge had eventually escalated into a 'full-scale battle' with a lawsuit filed by the director 'alleging that the nonpayments had seriously jeopardised Baldwin's reputation and that he had had to give up more than $5 million in other potential earnings to make the film'. However, as Galloway's report concluded, there seemed to be a happy resolution in sight: 'Today, almost three months after the *Devil* legal rift began, Glasser says everyone has been paid, an agreement between Cutting Edge and Baldwin has been reached, and Baldwin's lawsuit has been cancelled.' Baldwin had apparently returned to the cutting room and 'the finished film could be ready by November'. According to Glasser, 'the film looks really good. Alec did a great job.' More than a year later, under the headline DEVIL IS DEAD, Hopkins was allegedly reported on SCI FI Wire as saying the film would never be finished because of a lack of money.

A tantalising glimpse of what might have been – and may yet still be – was offered by Love Hewitt when she came to Britain to promote another film in her then embryonic movie career, which was distinctly on the up following her appearances as a budding scream queen in *I Know What You Did Last Summer* and its equally schlock horror sequel.

After referring guardedly to some of the *Devil*'s production problems, Love Hewitt then gave a fascinatingly fuller account of her work with Hopkins.

'In the movie, Anthony's my greatest enemy. We had to get ready to do our courtroom scene and I had this huge long speech that I present the jury with. Then, of course, he has to get up and present his huge speech. The second I sat down I was like, "Yeah, I've done a good job. Yeah, I'm happy with this" ... and then he got up and did his speech. Unfortunately the camera was on me and I started bawling my eyes out and ran to my trailer because I suddenly realised I couldn't act at all, that I'd been completely lied to, that I'd lied to myself for twelve years convincing myself that I'm an actress. He [Hopkins] threw it all away in one scene. I had no idea what acting was until he did his speech. So I was crying, "I can't act, oh my God ..." and Alec came in and asked what he could do. Then Anthony came in asked, "What's the problem?" in that great voice. And I said, "I can't act!" I then told him the whole story and he said, "You know, I used to feel exactly the same way until I realised it didn't matter ... I think you're doing a great job and I'm very proud of you. So why don't you come back out and we'll do it again, and then maybe we'll do it again and then again after that. After that, you'll feel really good."

'So we did, and it was great. Then when I had to do my close-up, he sat off-camera and said, "Since I'm your biggest fear, you're going to do your entire speech not to the jury but just to me and every time you're going to be scared out of your mind that I'll think you can't act. Maybe sometimes I'll think that, and maybe sometimes I won't. But it doesn't matter because you're going to be strong, you're going to be powerful because you're Satan ... and you're going to be great." At the end he was crying and he told me I did a great job, gave me a hug and it made my life.' At the time of writing, we were still waiting to witness these 'great' performances.

It is difficult to reconcile this almost non-stop post-millennium activity – he also found time to narrate Ron

Howard's Jim Carrey-centric *The Grinch* (note that another ex-pat Brit, Boris Karloff, narrated Chuck Jones' classic 1966 cartoon version of Dr Seuss' fairytale) – with the shock-horror headline which first took flight just before Christmas 1998. HOPKINS: I'M QUITTING ACTING.

According to reports from a press conference in Rome, where he was still filming *Titus*, Hopkins, then sixty, said he found show business 'tiresome, disturbing and deeply distasteful' and was soon going to give it all up. 'I've got to get out,' he explained, 'because I think acting is very bad for one's mental health. I can't take it anymore. This has got to stop. I have wasted my life.'

He ranted on: 'To hell with this stupid show business, this ridiculous showbiz, this futile, wasted life. I look back and see a desert wasteland. All those years spent in a fake environment.' Everything was a 'fake', he said, adding, he had 'been in a deep depression over acting and . . . tried to cover it up . . . I've been in turmoil pretending everything was okay. After 35 years I look back . . . and cringe with embarrassment and say to myself, "How the hell could you have done that?" I've done one or two good films and some bad films . . . it was a complete waste of time.' What of the future, he was asked. "I'm interested in music, I write, I like Los Angeles, and I'm just going to drop out.' Oh yes, he told reporters, he would, of course, complete his current movie before the self-imposed purdah.

When Hopkins and I talked some six months after *Titus*, he told me he had been 'stupidly misquoted' about retiring. 'I just needed a bit of a rest because I felt burned out. No, I was never near a breakdown; I'd just had a bumpy ride for a while. I'm made of stronger stuff . . . I was just working, working, working, and after my herniated disc and Achilles' tendon too, I thought I better stop working for a while.' Misquoted or not, *Titus'* director Julie Taymor for one was convinced, albeit briefly, that *Titus* could have well been his final role. 'Personally, I think it should be,' she told me at the time, 'because how is he going to do Hannibal Lecter again after this? He does it all in *Titus*.' His 'rest' would in fact last for almost a year

give or a take a few 'fun' days Down Under playing a sort
of 'M in an Armani suit' to Tom Cruise's superagent in
Mission: Impossible 2.

Hopkins' post-*Titus* malaise had been further
manifested in the latest of his 'doing a Topanga' bunks
which, this time round, involved the impulse purchase of
a ten-acre Spanish-style home near Ojai, a New Agey
community about eighty miles north of Los Angeles. But
since he had no plans to sell his existing home in Pacific
Palisades where he lived alone anyway, this two-hour flit
into desert country seemed to be merely from himself.

But that wasn't how it sounded when, still ensconced
at Ojai, he first resumed our collaboration on a previous
fourth edition of this biography, 'I love it here,' he told
me. 'I feel so much at peace in California. In England I
always felt *on*. I think it goes back to the fact that I never
felt as such part of the acting profession or that particular
Establishment. I don't feel comfortable around actors or
theatrical people generally. It's not that I have an attitude
about England or Wales, I just don't feel I *belong* there.
Here, I get up in the morning, water the flowers, feed the
cats and the birds and sometimes pop into town for an
English breakfast. It's a very small community and people
leave you alone. About ten years ago I set out to find a
new way of life and I've found it. I can't really explain it
. . . or defend it.'

Of his love life, he said: 'That's all in the past. I'm a
recluse now. I don't go anywhere. That is all over and
done with. It was my mad time. Are Jenni and I separated?
I guess we are. She always said she doesn't like California.
I can't make her like it any more than I can stay put in
England. This is my life here. I like being on my own. I'm
not involved in a relationship. Relationships are usually
disastrous – with women anyway. I don't really have any
close friends. I don't like to get too close to people. This is
the way I've always wanted to live.'

Two weeks after our conversation and less than six
months after he'd purchased the place, Hopkins sold the
house (back to the same people) as quickly as he'd bought

it and in a couple of rapid round trips moved everything back to Los Angeles. Jenni hadn't heard from him for almost two months when there was a message from him on her answerphone in London: 'Tony here, this'll give you a laugh. Thought I'd let you know I've sold Ojai and I'm back in Pacific Palisades.' She phoned him that evening, and he answered straight away. She laughed, 'What now? You never stop surprising me. What brought this on?' According to Jenni, he said: 'You know what I am like. I just woke up one morning and thought: What am I doing rattling round like a pea in a pod? What am I doing behaving like a Hollywood movie star with two houses when I don't want two houses?'

The truth was he nearly went mad at Ojai because however much he'd like to think it, he was neither a country person nor that enamoured with the solitary life. He was more a kind of Garbo-around-town, someone who liked to be in his little eyrie ... as long as that little eyrie was about ten minutes' drive from Sunset Boulevard.

Jenni interpreted the end of the Ojai idyll and his renewed interest in work as 'good news ... a step back into normality, into sanity,' even though their own continental divide still continued in much the same way. There had, since 1996, been odd weeks together but she hadn't actually seen him since Easter 1999. They enjoyed sporadic phone conversations and the latest feeling she got from him was, ' "Now is the time I feel I really want to be on my own, to be left alone on whatever path I'm going, wherever life is taking me." So I left him alone, but as I've told him enough times, as far as I am concerned the door is still open. If he invited me out there, I would certainly go. I think we've established I couldn't live there full-time. I'd be quite happy to go over to California three or four times a year then come back so I can get on with my life and commitments here. Tony was never the sort of person you do things with together. If he was a different sort of person, if we did things together, invited people to the house and lived like a normal married couple, then it might have been all right in California.

'But life with Tony has never been like that. Even within marriage he has always been a loner, has always wanted time on his own. In all the years we've been together, nearly thirty now, I've never taken that as an insult. What if he said he wanted a divorce? I may be wrong, as I've been wrong about many things, but I cannot believe, or at least would be extremely surprised, if Tony wanted to get married again. Its perhaps impertinent of me to put words in his mouth, or even the thought in his head, but I can't see that at 62 there's any point in his marrying again . . .'

As a new millennium dawned, Hopkins proved, as he'd continue to prove regularly on screen, he was indeed capable of a few more life-changing surprises.

14. CHANGE OF LIFE

'So do you believe that every successful person has to have a touch of ruthlessness in them somewhere?' Hopkins was being posed the knotty question by interviewer Martyn Lewis in a fascinating and wide-ranging question-and-answer session for his 1997 book, *Reflections on Success*, in which, the subtitle proclaimed, 'famous achievers talk frankly about their route to the top'.

'Absolutely,' Hopkins replied. 'I don't mean being cruel to other people or taking advantage of somebody else's misfortune or achieving at the cost of someone else's career or life. I mean ruthless with oneself, ruthless enough to make sacrifices.

'One of the negative things that I would say about myself is that although I have a lovely daughter, I haven't been a good father. I don't think I'm the ideal husband because I'm always away. My wife and I talk about it constantly, and she has accepted that I'm very restless. We have a good arrangement in our lives because I am restless and she's not.'

Lewis then asked him: 'How important is it to have another person who is there like a rock?' Hopkins told him: 'It's very, very important. My wife is a rock and a very calming influence in my life. I haven't been a great husband at all. I'm ruthless, arrogant. She says I'm not, but I just want more and more and more. But she can laugh me out of seriousness. She can calm things down by saying, "It's not really necessary to do that, is it?"

'Sometimes I'll talk her around to my way of thinking because I know I have enormous courage, but I won't do anything just to defy Jenni's opinion of what I should or shouldn't do. I'll just say, "I think I can do it, and as long as you don't mind I'm going to go ahead. You may not approve." She'll say, "OK, that's up to you, but don't complain afterwards." I say, "Fine." If you can't take a joke you shouldn't have joined, that is her philosophy.

'Sometimes she'll read the script and say, "I don't think you ought to do that." Then I'll read it and say, "Yes, you're right." Ninety per cent of the time we're in agreement on that. She's a remarkable woman; very patient and very forgiving." '

A month before *Hannibal* was due to start shooting in Florence, it was a damp mid-April day after the turn of a new century when Jenni returned from a quiet lunch with her mother to find journalists camped outside the Kensington house (which was still in a state of some repair after a freak fire some months before). She was apparently the last to know that a little earlier that same day in Los Angeles, Hopkins had officially become an American citizen. 'I was absolutely flabbergasted,' she reflected, three years on. 'It had never been discussed. I didn't even know he'd applied for it.'

At LA's Royal Federal Building, before US District Judge Margaret Morrow, and in the company of his mother, then-girlfriend Francine Kay and a bevy of showbusiness chums including Steven Spielberg, Kate Capshaw (Mrs Spielberg) and John Travolta, Hopkins pledged allegiance to the US. Judge Morrow had apparently ordered the entire seventh floor of the building sealed off to accommodate Hopkins and his well-wishers.

He was reportedly required to observe all the standard protocols for obtaining US citizenship like submitting to an FBI background check, interviewing with immigration officials and passing a test to demonstrate his knowledge of the United States. Hopkins, who had played two American presidents on screen would now, as some wit pointed out, actually be able to vote for one.

After the ceremony, the only official comment came from his spokesperson who said that her client was pleased with his new nationality, adding, 'I know he has been here a long time, and it seems like the right thing to do.' Back in the UK, and particularly in Wales, there was a predictable backlash with headlines like HANNIBAL TRAITOR and HANNIBAL DEFECTOR.

His high-profile presidency of the National Snowdonia Appeal, successfully concluded thanks, in no small part, to a personal donation of £1 million and a £300,000 gift to his old alma mater The Welsh College of Music and Drama, seemed by many to have been conveniently forgotten in the rush to condemn his latest career 'move'. And what about his eponymous Charitable Foundation which had over six years (and with more than a £1million of his own money) significantly helped many financially-strapped students through drama and film schools?

But now his decision to put down more solid roots in the country where he been resident for over four years brought, from Wales at least, charges of 'hypocrite', 'forgetting his roots' and even one call for him to be stripped of the Freedom of Port Talbot.

After keeping his own counsel for a week, Hopkins finally went on the record with: 'America has been very generous to me, really. I thought it would be good to give something back. It was a decision of the heart.' Asked about the anger in Wales, he said: 'I love Wales where I was born. There's been a bit of a stir-up there. I expected it.'

At the time of writing, the last time Jenni saw Hopkins was when he came to England for about 48 hours during a publicity trip on *Hannibal*. 'He was staying at the Dorchester,' Jenni recalled, 'and called me to say that Dino was taking everyone out for dinner and would I like to join them. He said something about how it was easier for him to stay at the hotel than at home. So I did that and after dinner went back with him to the Dorchester, said goodbye and came home in the car. Yes, that was probably the last time I actually saw him.'

Whenever she was in physical contact with him there

was never any hint about finally ending the marriage – 'but that's Tony. He would never be confrontational about anything. How it subsequently happened was, as far as I'm concerned, perfectly within Tony's character and nature. It was eventually by letter that he wrote it might be better for me to get on with my life by getting a divorce. I said that I didn't want to get a divorce. The next thing I heard was that if I didn't divorce him, he'd divorce me. I told him that it wasn't what *I* wanted, "but I wouldn't dream of stopping you" and that I wasn't "going to be difficult about it". Then silence.'

Until that fateful day of 11 September 2001. Jenni said: 'I'd been alerted by a friend to turn the TV on and had been watching for ten minutes or quarter of an hour when the phone rang and, blow me, it was Tony, completely out of the blue. I hadn't heard from him for a long time and of course he was, as we all were, very shocked at what was going on in New York and Washington. I suppose he was acting on the emotion of the whole thing when he suddenly said, "Let's cancel the divorce."

'We then had a long chat and I remember telling him that I was very relieved as I didn't see the need for it anyway. We agreed to talk some more when the event was all over. During the next three or four days he called every day and we chatted. It was like old times, and I thought, "well, this is good."

'Then the calls began to dry up. It got to November and I thought, "that must be that." One day around Christmas I heard from him again and he said it wasn't going to work and that we should go ahead with the divorce. I suppose I always felt it was likely to happen and that 9/11 was just like a sort of temporary reprieve acted on in the emotion of the moment. That really seemed to be that. In the new year I got myself a lawyer.'

In terms of dealing with Hopkins, Jenni now found herself mostly in contact with his business manager David Garelick who seemed to be handling the actual details of the divorce on his client's behalf. Jenni said: 'I dealt with

David, and it seemed silly to make a meal out of it. I knew Tony would be straightforward and generous and I wasn't going to quibble. To cut a long story short, I simply wrote to David with a figure [and here discretion reigns all round despite much publicised multi-million dollar guesstimates]. I certainly didn't take him to the cleaners by any stretch of the imagination. Did we actually communicate at all along the way? I said that I'd like to keep the house, and he said, "Of course, you must keep it." He was completely gentlemanly all the way through. There was no bad feeling at all, absolutely none at all. It was easy-peasy.' After 29 years of this curiously unconventional marriage – the last seven separated by an ocean and a continent – their divorce was eventually finalised in July 2002.

The first Jenni had heard of a significant 'other woman' in Hopkins' life was a few months earlier when their mutual friend Julian Fellowes had been to the Academy Awards to collect his screenwriting Oscar for *Gosford Park*. Hopkins hadn't been to the ceremony himself but invited Fellowes to dinner. When Jenni caught up with him after he returned from Hollywood she asked Fellowes if Hopkins was now with someone else. Fellowes confirmed he was and that she was 'a perfectly nice woman'. Her name was Stella Arroyave.

Hopkins had met Stella a year earlier when he popped into a shop in Los Angeles called Om Asian Antique And Fine Arts to look for some furniture. Stella, petite, dark-haired, South American in origin and nineteen years his junior, seemed to take his eye from the first time he saw her in the store which, in fact, she used to run. Although she hadn't been married before, some rather lurid rumours began circulating in the press as soon as it became known that she and Hopkins were becoming a serious 'item'. It was alleged that Stella, an antiques dealer, had once run up large debts and was declared bankrupt in 1997.

But even headlines like STELLA FINDS HER PRIZE ANTIQUE and his alleged fear of being snared by a golddigger, wouldn't put Hopkins off and it was the worst kept rumour when the news spilled out that 1 March 2003, St David's Day, was designated to be the wedding day for Hopkins and his new bride-to-be. By this time, he'd moved to a cliff-top house in Point Dume, Malibu, from his former home in Pacific Palisades where he'd also just enjoyed a year as the community's honorary mayor. Stella was also a Pacific Palisades resident as was Hopkins' mother, whom he'd moved out to be near him in California from her old home in Wales three years before.

The house was draped with daffodils for the small private ceremony also attended by, among others, Steven Spielberg, Nicole Kidman, Catherine Zeta-Jones, John Cleese, Goldie Hawn and Mickey Rooney. As a continuing sop to Hopkins' native Wales, the bride carried a bouquet of white and yellow daffodils while the groom had a daff' in his buttonhole. US resident, freshly married, Hopkins' West Coast make-over appeared complete.

Hopkins remains on an endless voyage of self-discovery and the old anthem of 'I've never been as happy as I am now' rings out as ever with the odd variation. He really should have a 'save and continue' button, friends continue to suggest. His skill at re-invention in life surely had its most testing recent parallel in art when, to many people's great surprise, he landed the role of Coleman Silk in Robert Benton's film of Philip Roth's coruscating novel, *The Human Stain*.

Set in 1998 during the white heat of the Clinton–Lewinsky scandal, Roth's epic story of political correctness gone mad tells how 71-year-old Silk's life as a respected classics professor at a small American university starts to unravel catastrophically when he's accused of racism. Commenting on the non-appearance of a pair of students at one of his lectures, he refers to them as 'spooks', as in ghosts, not realising that the duo are black and the term he unwittingly used could be deemed derogatory. The bitter fallout from the ensuing row causes the death of his wife and the estrangement of some of his

children. The veteran Jewish intellectual then embarks on
an unwise Viagra-driven affair with his cleaning lady and
part-time milkmaid Faunia (Nicole Kidman), who's half
his age and even more emotionally damaged. And to pile
Peleon on Ossa, it transpires that the light-skinned Silk is
in fact not a Jew at all, but a black man who's been
'passing' for white almost all his adult life to avoid bigotry
and prejudice.

Even for an actor who had successfully impersonated
Hitler, Nixon and a man-eating psychiatrist, this heady
combination of racial deceit and sexual voracity might
have seemed a characterisation too far. Robert Benton,
whose sparse but occasionally glittering filmography
(*Kramer Vs Kramer*, *Places In The Heart*) suggests very
careful choices, had no such reservations when it came to
choosing Hopkins, five years his junior, to inhabit one of
the more vivid characters in contemporary American
fiction.

He explained: 'I was moved by Anthony's humanity
and his tremendous intelligence more than anything else.
He goes beyond acting into something that is more like
life itself, and I felt he alone had the ability to inhabit
Coleman's contradictions, to bring both compassion and
ferocity to the role, and to take both physical and
emotional risks. Coleman is a great character, but he is a
deeply flawed human being. The challenge was to make
him likeable enough so that the audience is right there
with him when he commits his crimes.'

Roth was convinced too: 'You can't pull off Coleman
Silk's kind of self-transformation without tremendous
power, concentration, focus, cunning and toughness – and
Hopkins has these things.' And give or take a few years,
Roth might even have been describing Hopkins when he
wrote of Silk that he was around five foot eight, *'not
heavily muscled'* but with *'a lot of strength in him, and a
lot of the bounce of the high school athlete was still visible,
the quickness, the urge to action that we used to call
pep ...'*

To Hopkins, Silk is a kind of troubled hero: 'He's a

man of great conviction and passion, a man who loathes political correctness and in that sense he is my hero. Throughout his life, he shook the rafters and shocked people, and he just didn't care. On the other hand, everything he does leads to disaster and he is pulled into this relationship with a younger woman which ultimately destroys him.'

Despite their radically different backgrounds, Hopkins said he even found himself relating to Silk's desire to transcend the barriers he felt his racial identity might present: 'I've never thought of myself being any particular nationality,' he said, 'not because I am ashamed of who I am in any way, but because I don't think it really makes any difference. Coleman, on the other hand, wants to escape bigotry, racism and prejudice. But when he says, "I'm a man, an ordinary human being and I want to do what I do", I sympathise deeply with that.'

Hopkins also found compelling Roth's portrait of the seemingly unlikely affair between the old widower academic and a much younger woman: 'It's interesting to me the power that love and sex have to devastate a man's life, especially at Silk's age. I think sex can be at once a very creative and also deeply destructive force. It has destroyed empires and destroyed presidents, and it can just rip people apart. Really, sex is one of the most powerful and frightening parts of our lives, and Coleman gives himself over to that.'

Roth's book deals extensively with Silk as a young man and the casting of a bi-racial actor, Wentworth Miller, could be deemed more apt than Hopkins' casting. Hopkins and Miller both worked to match speech patterns and movement styles with the other. Hopkins even donned green contact lenses to imitate Miller's eyes; he taped Miller's voice so he could practise the younger man's inflections before adding years of experience to it. 'It was,' reflected Miller, 'pretty mind-boggling to me because I mean, he's Anthony Hopkins and he's emulating me!'

On location in Quebec, standing in for Massachusetts

where the fictitious Athena college is situated, Hopkins told *Premiere*'s Johanna Schneller, 'A tragic, doomed love story – I've always wanted to play one before it was too late. Because I'd always played these loners. I thought it would be wonderful to play someone who was caught up, entwined in something doomed. The power of love, the power of sex, can rip you to pieces.'

They were shooting a particularly tense scene between the lovers and Schneller described how tears were running down Kidman's cheeks. Between takes, Hopkins kept his arm around her; he didn't look at her but steadily stroked her neck and her hair. 'We would just chat,' said Kidman, 'he would tell me bits and pieces about his life. He made it easy to walk in and exist as these characters.'

Of the sex scenes, Hopkins said: 'Benton reassures me that it's all working out, but it's a strange area. I've always been rather shy around women. I've worked with women actors and enjoyed it. But I've never been confident. If I looked like Brad Pitt I would be, but I'm not. But now I've come to a point in my life, take it or leave it.'

It's almost too easy to carp at what might seem to be the positively reckless miscasting of Hopkins and Kidman, but their intense, compelling and, above all, remarkably brave performances as unlikely lovers in this almost unrelievedly bleak drama almost (if perhaps not quite) papers over any obvious lack of authenticity. It's certainly Hopkins' most moving and least gimmicky portrayal since *Shadowlands* which – despite the actor's stated espousal of Silk – had its own 'tragic, doomed' dimension as a love story. *Rolling Stone*'s Peter Travers suggested that Hopkins and Kidman were as 'mesmerising' as they were 'miscast' and that 'if you can't accept that Welshman Hopkins is an African-American from New Jersey, there's no doubting his ability to locate the character's grit and wounded grace.'

Variety's David Stratton recalled historical Hollywood precedents of white actors 'passing' for black as he also tried to get his head round the casting of Hopkins – 'a prospect that seems, at first glance, so utterly preposterous as to be dismissed out of hand'. But then, Stratton argued, 'finding an actor from either side of the racial spectrum who could convince in such a role was bound to be problematic'. Conceding that Hopkins gives 'another intelligent powerful portrayal' didn't, Stratton believed, surmount the key problem of ever making you quite believe the transition from young Coleman to old man Silk. The film should, however, do wonders for Viagra sales.

After his endless protestations about his fitness as 'marrying material', Hopkins' third marriage came as much of a surprise to Jenni as the whole new citizenship bit. She now looks back over their own union with a mixture of 'good memories' and still, she admitted, some shell-shock. Could she ever have quite envisaged the various turn of events?

She said: 'In one of our conversations in the last two or three years of sporadic communication, he asked if I had realised how much he had hated coming back to London in the mid-80s, although he knew it was the right thing to do at the time careerwise. "As far as I was concerned, as soon as I came back, it was just a case of waiting my time until I could come back to the US on a different footing," he told me. He was always working towards that. He got scared about not having a green card and was always worried that maybe one day when he went back to America they wouldn't renew his H1 visa. So we had to go through the whole thing of re-getting our green cards. But obviously that wasn't enough for him. I don't think he really felt safe until he actually got his citizenship.'

What she can't understand at all are the reasons for his apparent loathing of the UK and everything it seems to stand for. 'He was given every honour going and very rarely had anything critical or derogatory written about him as either a person or as an actor. The only reason I can come up with is that he wanted some excuse to validate his desire to live a new life,' she said. 'But who knows, maybe things will change one day. I hope so, anyway.' It was as if the past had quite literally become a foreign country.

A year after Hopkins' marriage to Stella, Jenni was still living in their old house in South Kensington, which was brimming with memories of her ex-husband. All his archive material, including press cuttings and annotated scripts, were there along with busts, the odd portrait and most of his film awards, not to mention his Knighthood medal, CBE and Légion d'Honneur. The only piece of his past Hopkins had previously requested to be sent to him in California was his Oscar. Jenni knew it was now 'time to move on', which meant selling up and trying sensitively to dispose of the memorabilia. After consulting Julian Fellowes, Jenni contacted the University of Wales in Cardiff to see if they'd be interested in housing the Hopkins artefacts. They were extremely keen. Jenni wrote to Hopkins saying that if she didn't hear to the contrary soon, his stuff would be sent to the university. Somewhat to her surprise, she received a one-line reply stating, baldly: 'Please ship all memorabilia to me', which, with Fellowes help, she duly did. In due course, she received the briefest of notes from Stella acknowlwdging receipt of the materials. Late in 2003, Jenni finally sold up after fourteen tumultous years in the house and moved close by to a smart flat. She kept just one solid piece of the past – a Gwen Gillen-sculpted bronze bust of Hopkins as he had appeared in *Antony and Cleopatra* at the National Theatre seventeen years earlier.

In 2003, Sybil [Burton] Christopher came to stay with Jenni in Kensington and was shocked when she heard what had happened between her and Hopkins. 'We had,' Jenni said, 'a lot of chit chats over the days she stayed. Her experience was so similar. She told me, "I had Richard's best years." And that's what I feel about Tony. I may be proved wrong, and for his sake I hope I am. But as a person and as an actor, I think I did have his best years. So I have no regrets at all, personally. I would do it all over again. I still have a lot of love and respect for him. I just don't know where he's gone. I can't say he's not the man I remember, because I really don't know what he's like today.'

As for his daughter Abigail, from whom he was estranged for nearly eighteen years until they met up again when she was in her twenties, they no longer seem to be in contact though they did have a period of reconciliation during which Abigail even made brief appearances in *The Remains of the Day*, *Shadowlands* and *Selected Exits*. Hopkins had described as 'earthmoving' the experience of seeing Abigail again. 'It made me open up feelings I had buried for years. I looked at her and it was like looking at me. She wants everything that I wanted and everything I'm in turmoil about.' After Hopkins went to the States, he and Abigail, 35 and currently making her way in the music business, remained regularly in touch by phone. Now, she too seems to be part of a past he has almost completely discarded.

Lord Attenborough, for whom Hopkins made five films – and, hopefully, a sixth if the good lord ever manages to mount the director's film about Tom Paine in which he hopes Hopkins will play Benjamin Franklin – said he keeps in regular touch with the actor. He told me that he has managed to persuade Hopkins to become a patron of a new, still-to-be-built, £180 million studio complex Attenborough is championing outside Cardiff.

Hopkins' fans hope that at 67 he will make good choices with whatever future work beckons. This includes roles in John Madden's film of David Auburn's Tony-winning stage hit, *Proof*, and in Oliver Stone's epic about Alexander the Great, filmed in North Africa with Colin Farrell in the title role. In *Proof*, he's a mathematics genius battling madness whose legacy, in perhaps both mind and matter, he passes on to his depressive twentysomething daughter, played by Gwyneth Paltrow. She also acted the same role to much acclaim when the play was staged by Madden at the Donmar Warehouse in 2002. After shooting scene-setting exteriors in Chicago where the action is set, the production re-located to Elstree Studios marking Hopkins' first film back in the UK for almost ten years.

In *Alexander* Hopkins, re-united with his *Nixon* director, played the venerable Ptolemy, white-haired general and trusted confidant to the youthful Macedonian ruler. He was also the $100 million film's narrator. Elliot Cowan, a 26-year-old, RADA-trained British actor, whose limited experience included regional theatre and odd bits of episodic TV like *Jonathan Creek*, was picked to play Ptolemy as a younger man. In Morocco he was introduced to his older 'self'. Cowan recalled: 'It was hard to meet him at first because his mother had just died. I was aware I'd be bricking myself meeting him but, in fact, he was very easy to get on with and I enjoyed his company. There was one potentially embarrassing moment when, at Oliver Stone's request, I tried to do an impression of a friend of mine. It ended up with Hopkins doing an impression of me doing an impression.' For Cowan, as well as even a seasoned pro like Hopkins, the sheer scale of *Alexander* must have, at times, been almost overwhelming. Cowan said: 'Sometimes we'd be in the middle of the desert with a thousand people round us. There'd be five or six cameras filming and, remember, it would all look even more impressive with CGI [computer generated imagery]. In one scene, there's supposed to be quarter of a million Persian troops. It was bedlam at times on set [with] people getting run over or nearly chopped in half. It was breath-taking . . . and scary.'

'There's nothing safe about Oliver, and there's nothing safe about his films. They are brilliant and outrageous,' Hopkins mused after finishing some very long working days on *Alexander*. Unfortunately, the critical reaction to the three-hour epic veered more to the 'outrageous' – but not in a particularly good way. 'Buttnumbathon' and 'the film's only highlights were in [blond-tressed] Colin Farrell's hair' were two of the less generous comments about a sprawling film, which lost its focus in between some spectacular battles. A mishmash of accents and coyly gay subtext, perhaps the best you could say of it was that it had ambition and sincerity. As for Hopkins' rambling role, interwoven across the film's absurd length, he claimed it was 'the most satisfying time I've had on a set for a long time'.

At the time of writing, Hopkins had just finished his latest film, which had all kinds of strange echoes from his past. Recalling his role as speed king Donald Campbell in BBC's *Across the Lake*, he was playing New Zealander Burt Munro, who, in his late 60s, set a motorcycling land-speed record of over 183mph on Bonneville Salt Flats, Utah. However, unlike Campbell, Munro didn't die in the attempt. *The World's Fastest Indian* – the title referred to Munro's beloved 600cc Indian Scout bike – was another rare star–director reunion, this time with Roger Donaldson which, after their first stormy collaboration twenty years earlier on *The Bounty*, had seemed unlikely to be repeated. Hatchets had clearly been buried.

If Jenni was once, as I have previously noted, the 'keeper of the flame', that task seems now to have passed principally to a multiplicity of Hopkins-devoted websites – notably PlanetHopkins, run by the tireless Tracey Williams – which seem to litter the Internet. Where else could you really hope to learn more about the unofficial 'museum' devoted to Hopkins, which is sited at the YMCA in Port Talbot where some fifty years ago he spoke his first ever lines on stage? Thanks to his own donations, at the 'Y' are his jacket and boots from *The Edge*, a shirt and chair back from *Instinct*, a cap from *Nixon*, an umbrella from *The Remains of the Day*, a clapper board from *August*, and his own leather binder of the *Hannibal* script as well as numerous signed photos and posters.

Julian Fellowes once fascinatingly summed up the conundrum that is Anthony Hopkins.

'What makes him interesting on the screen is that thing that happens with great stars; if you reach up to the celluloid, you feel flesh. With supporting players you know you just hit celluloid. Tony has that element of danger and gives you that feeling he's going to punch you even when you're sitting in Row C. I'm afraid that is indissolubly linked with his inability to arrange a normal life, to have that cosiness around him. The two are connected.

'If he had been a much more rational, ordered being who could make easy connections with his fellow humans, he would probably now be mending bikes in Port Talbot. One way of looking at that is to say, "How sad that a man who seems to have everything, money and success, isn't able to make a contented life." My own view is that the rather discombobulated life he leads is the price he's paid for the success he's achieved.'

Jenni used to say of him: 'For Tony, it's still either black or white, up or down, all or nothing.' Later asked whether there was 'no contented, mellow in-between', Hopkins himself replied, 'No. I'm a little more mellow than I was ten years ago, or maybe twenty years ago perhaps . . . but not much.'

Today, Hopkins is, even in his own 'discombobulated' way, probably as content as he'll ever be. This is a calm period; the years of struggle, which were an essential part of his inner-engine, are over. He has a devoted wife, a beautiful home in the sun, and he makes lots of money. Hopkins has also announced excitedly that an American orchestra is to perform some of his musical compositions in 2005. As his close friends say, 'all that stuff that he's turned his back on his country and insulted his knighthood is absolute rubbish. So he's got dual citizenship. How contentious is that?'

After being told constantly to 'get a life', he has now done exactly that. He doesn't have to worry about anything except by choice; yet because of his early reputation as a hellraiser, critics and commentators still can't quite believe he has somehow quit raging and just settled, for the time being at least, for 'content'. The 21st century Hopkins has surely still to be in the grip of some neurosis, battling against demons, unable to face the bogey of England. Living beyond your anger into the plateau will never be what some people want of you.

THE CREDITS

THEATRE (principal roles in Britain and the United States)

Julius Caesar (1964) The Royal Court. Prod: Lindsay Anderson. Des: Jocelyn Herbert. W: William Shakespeare. Cast: Paul Curran (Julius Caesar), Daniel Massey (Mark Antony), Ian Bannen (Brutus), T. P. McKenna (Cassius), Graham Crowden (Casca), Ronald Pickup (Octavius Caesar), Sheila Allen (Portia), Nan Munro (Calpurnia), A. H. (Metellus Cimber).

A Flea in Her Ear (1966) National/Old Vic. Prod: Jacques Charon. Des: André Levasseur. W: Georges Feydeau (trans: John Mortimer). Cast: Robert Lang (Victor Emmanuel Chandebise/Poche), Edward Hardwicke (Camille Chandebise), Geraldine McEwan (Raymonde Chandebise), Frank Wylie (Carlos Homenides de Histangua), John Stride (Romain Tournet), A. H. (Etienne Plucheux).

Juno and the Paycock (1966) National/Old Vic. Prod: Laurence Olivier. Des: Carmen Dillon. W: Sean O'Casey. Cast: Joyce Redman (Juno Boyle), Colin Blakely (Jack Boyle), Frank Finlay (Joxer), Caroline John (Mary Boyle), Ronald Pickup (Johnny Boyle), Madge Ryan (Maisie Madigan), A. H. (an Irregular Mobilizer).

A Provincial Life (1966) English Stage Company/The Royal Court. Prod: Peter Gill. W: Anton Chekhov (adapted by Gill from his short story 'My Life'). Cast: Geoffrey Whitehead (Mihail Alexander Poloznev), Susan Engel (Anyuta Ivanovna Blagova), Pamela Buchner (Marya Victorovna Dolzhikova), Shivaun O'Casey (Kleopatra Alexandrovna Poloznev), Richard O'Callaghan (Ivan Cheprakov), John Normington (an Old Man), A. H. (Boris Ivanov Blagovo).

The Three Sisters (1967) National/Old Vic. Prod: Laurence Olivier. Des: Josef Svoboda. W: Anton Chekhov (adapted by Moura Budberg). Cast: Jeanne Watts (Olga), Joan Plowright (Masha), Louise Purnell (Irina), Sheila Reid (Natasha), A. H. (Andrei), Robert Stephens (Vershinin), Paul Curran (Chebutikin), Derek Jacobi (Lvovich).

As You Like It (1967) National/Old Vic. Prod: Clifford Williams. Des: Ralph Koltai. W: William Shakespeare. Cast: Ronald Pickup (Rosalind), Charles Kay (Celia), Richard Kay (Phoebe), A. H. (Audrey), Jeremy Brett (Orlando), Robert Stephens (Jaques), Derek Jacobi (Touchstone).

The Architect and the Emperor of Assyria (1971) National/Old Vic. Prod: Victor Garcia. Des: Garcia and Michel Launay. W: Fernando Arrabal (trans. Jean Benedetti). Cast: Jim Dale (the Architect), A. H. (the Emperor).

A Woman Killed with Kindness (1971) National/Old Vic. Prod: John Dexter. Des: Jocelyn Herbert. W: Thomas Heywood. Cast: Joan Plowright (Mistress Anne Frankford), A. H. (Master John Frankford), Frank Barrie (Wendoll), Dai Bradley (Jenkin), Paul Curran (Nicholas), Derek Jacobi (Sir Charles Mountford).

Coriolanus (1971) National/Old Vic. Prod: Manfred Wekwerth, Joachim Tenschert. Des: Karl von Appen. W: William Shakespeare. Cast: A. H. (Coriolanus), Constance Cummings (Volumnia), John Moffatt (Menenius), Michael Turner (Cominius), Denis Quilley (Aufidius), Kenneth Mackintosh (Titus).

The Taming of the Shrew (1972) Chichester Festival Theatre. Prod: Jonathan Miller. Des: Patrick Robertson. W: William Shakespeare. Cast: A. H. (Petruchio), Joan Plowright (Katharina), Susan Tracy (Bianca), Paul Hastings (Lucentio), Richard Cornish (Tranio), William Mervyn (Baptista), Harold Innocent (Grumio).

Macbeth (1972) National/Old Vic. Prod: Michael Blakemore. Des: Michael Annals. W: William Shakespeare. Cast: A. H. (Macbeth), Diana Rigg (Lady Macbeth), Alan MacNaughton (Duncan), Ronald Pickup (Malcolm), Denis Quilley (Banquo), Gawn Grainger (Macduff), Paul Curran (Old Siward), Nicholas Clay (Young Siward).

Equus (1974) National/Plymouth (New York). Prod: John Dexter. Des: John Napier. W: Peter Shaffer. Cast: A. H. (Dr Martin Dysart), Peter Firth (Alan Strang), Frances Sternhagen (Dora Strang), Michael Higgins (Frank Strang), Marian Seldes (Hester Salomon), Roberta Maxwell (Jill Mason), Don Plumley (Harry Dalton).

Equus (1977) Huntington Hartford (Los Angeles). Prod: A. H. Des: John Napier. W: Peter Shaffer. Cast: A. H. (Dr Martin

Dysart), Thomas Hulce (Alan Strang), Joi Staton (Dora Strang), John O'Leary (Frank Strang), Judith Searle (Hester Salomon), Dorothy French (Jill Mason), John Brandon (Harry Dalton).

The Tempest (1979) Center Theatre Group/Mark Taper Forum (Los Angeles). Prod: John Hirsch. Des: Ming Cho Lee. W: William Shakespeare. Cast: A. H. (Prospero), Stephanie Zimbalist (Miranda), Michael Bond (Caliban), Joseph Sicari (Trinculo), Howard Brunner (Antonio), Brent Carver (Ariel), Richard B. Shull (Stephano).

The Arcata Promise (1981) California Center for Performing Arts (Los Angeles). Prod-des: A. H. W: David Mercer (adapted by A. H.). Cast: A. H. (Theo Gunge), Stephanie Hagan (Laura), Ian Abercrombie (Tony).

Old Times (1984) Roundabout Theatre Company (New York). Prod: Kenneth Frankel. Des: Marjorie Bradley Kellogg. W: Harold Pinter. Cast: A. H. (Deeley), Marsha Mason (Kate), Jane Alexander (Anna).

The Lonely Road (1985) Triumph Apollo/Old Vic. Prod: Christopher Fettes. Des: Maria Bjornson. W: Arthur Schnitzler (trans. Ronald Adam, Christopher Fettes). Cast: A. H. (Julian Fichtner), Samantha Eggar (Irene Herms), Alan Dobie (Stephan van Sala), Basil Hoskins (Professor Wegrat), Rupert Frazer (Dr Franz Reumann), Colin Firth (Felix), Ann Lynn (Gabriele).

Pravda (1985) National. Prod: David Hare. Des: Hayden Griffin. W: David Hare, Howard Brenton. Cast: A. H. (Lambert Le Roux), Tim McInnerney (Andrew May), Kate Buffery (Rebecca Foley), Ron Pember (Harry Morrison), Bill Nighy (Eaton Sylvester), Basil Henson (Elliot Fruit-Norton), Peter Blythe (Michael Quince).

King Lear (1986) National. Prod: David Hare. Des: Hayden Griffin. W: William Shakespeare. Cast: A. H. (Lear), Anna Massey (Goneril), Suzanne Bertish (Regan), Miranda Foster (Cordelia), Philip Locke (Kent), Michael Bryant (Gloucester), Bill Nighy (Edgar), Roshan Seth (Fool).

Antony and Cleopatra (1987) National. Prod: Peter Hall. Des: Alison Chitty. W: William Shakespeare. Cast: A. H. (Antony), Judi Dench (Cleopatra), Tim Piggott-Smith (Octavius Caesar), Michael Bryant (Enobarbus), Miranda Foster (Charmian), Sally

Dexter (Octavia), John Bluthal (Lepidus/Clown), David Schofield (Pompey).

M. Butterfly (1989) M. Butterfly Company London Ltd/Shaftesbury. Prod: John Dexter. Des: Eiko Ishioka. W: David Henry Hwang. Cast: A. H. (René Gallimard), G.G. Goei (Song Li Ling), Lynn Farleigh (Helga), Ian Redford (Marc).

August (1994) Theatre Clwyd. Prod. A. H. Des: Eileen Diss. W: Julian Mitchell, from a translation of Chekhov's *Uncle Vanya* by Tania Alexander. Cast: A. H. (Ieuan Davies), Gawn Grainger (Dr Lloyd), Lisa Orgolini (Helen), Leslie Phillips (Prof. Blathwaite), Rhian Morgan (Sian), Hugh Lloyd ('Pocky' Prosser).

TELEVISION (principal roles/year of transmission)

The Three Sisters (1969) BBC. P-dir: Cedric Messina. Scr: Anton Chekhov (adapted by Moura Budberg). Cast: Janet Suzman (Masha), Michele Dotrice (Irina), Eileen Atkins (Olga), A. H. (Andrei), Michael Bryant (Vershinin), Joss Ackland (Chebutikin).

Danton (1970) BBC. P: Mark Shivas. Dir: John Davies. Scr: Arden Winch. Cast: A. H. (Danton), Alan Dobie (Robespierre), Tenniel Evans (General Westermann), Terry Scully (Fabre D'Eglantine), David Andrews (St Just).

The Great Inimitable Mr Dickens (1970) P-Dir: Ned Sherrin. Scr: Ned Sherrin, Caryl Brahms. Cast: A. H. (Dickens), Sybil Thorndike, Freddie Jones, Arthur Lowe, Patrick Cargill, Jenny Agutter.

Uncle Vanya (1970) BBC. P: Cedric Messina. Dir: Christopher Morahan. Scr: Anton Chekhov. Cast: Freddie Jones (Vanya), A. H. (Astrov), Ann Bell (Elena), Roland Culver (Serebriakov).

Hearts and Flowers (1970) BBC. P: Irene Shubik. Dir: Christopher Morahan. Scr: Peter Nichols. Cast: A. H. (Bob), Donald Churchill (Tony), Priscilla Morgan (Jean), Colin Cunningham (Harry), Constance Chapman (Marie).

Decision to Burn (1971) Yorkshire TV. P: Peter Willes. Dir: Marc Miller. Scr: Kevin Laffan. Cast: Helen Cherry, Gerald Sim, A. H., Patricia Brake, John Welsh.

Poet Game (1972) BBC. P: Mark Shivas. Dir: Silvio Narrizzano. Scr: Anthony Terpiloff. Cast: A. H. (Hugh Saunders), Billie

Whitelaw (Jeanne Saunders), Susan Clark (Diana Howard), Cyril Cusack (Dr Saunders), Al Mancini (Elliot Martin).

War and Peace (1972) BBC. P: David Conroy. Dir: John Davies. Scr: Jack Pulman, from Tolstoy's novel. Cast: Morag Hood (Natasha), Alan Dobie (Prince Andrei), A. H. (Pierre Bezukhov), David Swift (Napoleon), Faith Brook (Countess Rostova), Frank Middlemass (Marshal Kutuzov), Rupert Davies (Count Rostov).

The Edwardians (*Lloyd George*) (1972) BBC. P: Mark Shivas. Dir: John Davies. Scr: Keith Dewhurst. Cast: A. H. (Lloyd George), Annette Crosbie (Mrs Lloyd George), Joanna David (Mair), Thorley Walters (Edward VII).

QB VII (1974) Columbia TV. P: Douglas Kramer. Dir: Tom Gries. Scr: Edward Anhalt, from Leon Uris' novel. Cast: Ben Gazzara (Cady), A. H. (Kelno), Juliet Mills (Samantha), Lee Remick (Lady Margaret), Leslie Caron (Lady Kelno), Edith Evans (Dr Parmentier), John Gielgud (Clinton-Meek), Jack Hawkins (Hon. Mr Justice Gilray).

Find Me (1974) BBC. Dir: Don Taylor. Scr: David Mercer. Cast: A. H. (Marek), Sheila Allen (Olivia), David Collings (Stanton), Charlotte Cornwell (Catherine), Stephen Moore (TV Producer).

The Childhood Friend (1974) BBC. P: Graeme Macdonald. Dir: Mike Newell. Scr: Piers Paul Read. Cast: A. H. (Alexander Tashkov), Susan Fleetwood (Janet Morton), George Pravda (Nikolay Tashkov), Alison Key (Alison Tashkov).

Possessions (1974) Granada. Prod: James Brabazon. Dir: John Irvin. Scr: George Ewart Evans (adapted by Elaine Morgan). Cast: A. H. (Dando), Rhoda Lewis (Caffie), Christopher Jones (Tom), Terry Lock (Willie), David Holland (Gomer).

The Arcata Promise (1974) Yorkshire TV. Dir: David Cunliffe. Scr: David Mercer. Cast: A. H. (Theo Gunge), Kate Nelligan (Laura), John Fraser (Tony).

Dark Victory (1976) NBC/Universal. P: Jules Irving. Dir: Robert Butler. Scr: M. Charles Cohen. Cast: Elizabeth Montgomery (Katherine), A. H. (Michael), Michele Lee, Herbert Berghof, Michael Lerner, Vic Tayback.

The Lindbergh Kidnapping Case (1976) NBC/Columbia. P: Leonard Horn. Dir: Buzz Kulik. Scr: J. P. Miller. Cast: Cliff De Young (Lindbergh), A. H. (Bruno Hauptmann), Sian Barbara

Allen (Ann Morrow Lindbergh), Joseph Cotten (Dr John F. Condon), Walter Pidgeon (Judge Trenchard), David Spielberg (David Wilentz).

Victory at Entebbe (1976) ABC/David Wolper. P: Robert Guenette. Dir: Marvin J. Chomsky. Scr: Ernest Kinoy. Cast: A. H. (Rabin), Burt Lancaster (Peres), Julius Harris (Idi Amin), Elizabeth Taylor (Edra Vilnovsky), Richard Dreyfuss (Col. Netanyahu), Kirk Douglas (Hershel Vilnovsky), Helmut Berger (German Hijacker).

Kean (1978) BBC. P: David Jones. Dir: James Cellan-Jones. Scr: Jean-Paul Sartre. Cast: A. H. (Kean), Robert Stephens (Prince of Wales), Sara Kestelman (Elena, Countess of Koefeld), Julian Fellowes (Lord Neville), Cherie Lunghi (Anna Danby).

Mayflower: The Pilgrims' Adventure (1980) CBS. P: Linda Yellen. Dir: George Schaefer. Scr: James Lee Barrett. Cast: A. H. (Capt. Jones), Richard Crenna (Rev. William Brewster), Jenny Agutter (Priscilla), David Dukes (Miles Standish), Michael Beck (John Alden).

The Bunker (1980) CBS/Time-Life/SFP/Antenne 2. P-Dir: George Schaefer. Scr: John Gay. Cast: A. H. (Hitler), Richard Jordan (Speer), Cliff Gorman (Goebbels), Piper Laurie (Magda Goebbels), Susie Blakely (Eva Braun), Michel Lonsdale (Bormann), Martin Jarvis (Hentschel), Michael Kitchen (Misch), Andrew Ray (Guensche).

Peter and Paul (1981) MCA. P: Stan Hough. Dir: Robert Day. Scr: Christopher Knopf. Cast: Robert Foxworth (Peter the Fisherman), A. H. (Paul of Tarsus), Raymond Burr (Herod Agrippa), Eddie Albert (Festus), Jean Peters (Priscilla), Julian Fellowes (Nero), Herbert Lom (Barnabas).

Othello (1981) BBC. P: Cedric Messina. Dir: Jonathan Miller. Scr: Shakespeare. Cast: A. H. (Othello), Bob Hoskins (Iago), Penelope Wilton (Desdemona), Rosemary Leach (Emilia), David Yelland (Cassio), Anthony Pedley (Roderigo), Geoffrey Chater (Brabantio).

Little Eyolf (1982) BBC. P: Louis Marks. Dir: Michael Darlow. Scr: Henrik Ibsen (trans. Michael Meyer). Cast: Diana Rigg (Rita Allmers), A. H. (Alfred Allmers), Peggy Ashcroft (the Rat Wife), Emma Piper (Asta), Charles Dance (Borghejm), Timothy Stark (Eyolf).

The Hunchback of Notre-Dame (1982) CBS/Columbia. P: Norman Rosemont. Dir: Michael Tuchner. Scr: John Gay, from Victor Hugo's novel. Cast: A. H. (Quasimodo), Lesley-Anne Down (Esmeralda), John Gielgud (Charmolue), Robert Powell (Phoebus), David Suchet (Trouillefou), Derek Jacobi (Dom Claude Frollo).

A Married Man (1983) LWT for C4. P: John Davies. Dir: Charles Jarrott. Scr: Derek Marlowe, from Piers Paul Read's novel. Cast: A. H. (John Strickland), Ciaran Madden (Clare), Lise Hilboldt (Paula), Tracey Childs (Jilly Mascall), John Le Mesurier (Eustace Clough), Clive Francis (Henry Mascall).

Strangers and Brothers (1984) BBC. P: Philip Hinchcliffe. Dir: Ronald Wilson. Scr: Julian Bond (from C. P. Snow novels). Cast: A. H. (Roger Quaife), Shaughan Seymour (Lewis Eliot), Cherie Lunghi (Margaret Eliot), Edward Hardwicke (Sir Hector Rose), John Normington (Monty Cave).

Arch of Triumph (1985) CBS/HTV. P: John Newland, Mort Abrahamson, Peter Graham Scott. Dir: Waris Hussein. Scr: Charles Israel. Cast: A. H. (Dr Ravic), Lesley-Anne Down (Joan), Donald Pleasence (Haake), Frank Finlay (Boris), Richard Pasco (Veber), Joyce Blair (Rolande).

Mussolini: The Decline and Fall of Il Duce (a.k.a. *Mussolini and I*) (1985) HBO/RAI/Antenne 2/Beta. P: Mario Gallo. Dir: Alberto Negrin. Scr: Nicola Badalucco. Cast: Susan Sarandon (Edda), A. H. (Count Ciano), Bob Hoskins (Mussolini), Annie Girardot, Barbara De Rossi, Fabio Testi.

Hollywood Wives (1985) ABC/Warner's. P: Aaron Spelling. Dir: Robert Day. Scr: Robert L. McCullough, from Jackie Collins' novel. Cast: Candice Bergen (Elaine Conti), Angie Dickinson (Sadie La Salle), A. H. (Neil Gray), Stefanie Powers (Montana Gray), Joanna Cassidy (Maralee), Rod Steiger (Oliver Easterne), Steve Forrest (Ross Conti), Suzanne Somers (Gina Germaine).

Guilty Conscience (1985) CBS. P: Robert Papazian, Richard Levinson, William Link. Dir: David Greene. Scr: Levinson, Link. Cast: A. H. (Arthur Jamison), Blythe Danner (Louise Jamison), Swoosie Kurtz (Jackie Willis), Wiley Harker (Older Man), Ruth Manning (Older Woman).

Blunt (1985) BBC. P: Martin Thompson. Dir: John Glenister. Scr: Robin Chapman. Cast: A. H. (Guy Burgess), Ian Richardson

(Anthony Blunt), Michael Williams (Goronwy Rees), Rosie Kerslake (Margie Rees), Geoffrey Chater (Guy Liddell).

Across the Lake (1988) BBC/Challenger. P: Innes Lloyd. Dir: Tony Maylam. Scr: Roger Milner. Cast: A. H. (Donald Campbell), Ewan Hooper (Leo Villa), Angela Richards (Tonia Bern), Phyllis Calvert (Lady Campbell), Julia Watson (Sarah Williamson), Rosemary Leach (Connie Robinson), Peter Harlowe (Benson), Dexter Fletcher (Jimmy).

Heartland (1989) BBC Wales. P: Christine Benson. Dir: Kevin Billington. Scr: Steve Gough. Cast: A. H. (Jack), Lynn Farleigh (Rachel), Mark Lewis Jones (Ieuan), Martin Glyn Murray (Glyn), Jane Horrocks (Pam).

The Tenth Man (1989) CBS/Norman Rosemont-William Self. P: David Rosemont, William Hill. Dir: Jack Gold. Scr. Lee Langley, from Graham Greene's novella. Cast: A. H. (Chavel), Kristin Scott Thomas (Therese), Derek Jacobi (the Imposter), Cyril Cusack (the Priest), Brenda Bruce (Therese's Mother), Timothy Watson (the Victim).

Great Expectations (1989) Disney/HTV-Primetime. P: Greg Smith. Dir: Kevin Connor. Scr: John Goldsmith, from Dickens' novel. Cast: Jean Simmons (Miss Havisham), A. H. (Magwitch), Anthony Calf (Pip), Ray McAnally (Jaggers), Kim Thomson (Estella), John Rhys Davies (Joe Gargery).

One Man's War (filmed in 1990, still to be transmitted) HBO–Film Four–TVS/Skreba Films. P: Ann Skinner. Dir: Sergio Toledo. Scr: Mike Carter, Sergio Toledo. Cast: A. H. (Joel), Norma Aleandro (Nidia), Fernanda Torres (Dolly), Leonardo Garcia (Joelito), Mia Michelle (Analy), Reuben Blades (Perrone).

To Be the Best (1991) RPTA–Primetime/Robert Bradford–Gemmy Productions. P: Aida Young. Dir: Tony Wharmby. Scr: Elliot Baker, from Barbara Taylor Bradford's novel. Cast: Lindsay Wagner (Paula O'Neill), A. H. (Jack Figg), Christopher Cazenove (Jonathan Ainsley), Stephanie Beacham (Arabella Sutton), Stuart Wilson (Jack Miller), James Saito (Tony Chiu).

Selected Exits (1993) BBC Wales. P: Geraint Morris. Dir: Tristram Powell. Scr: Alan Plater, based on Gwyn Thomas' autobiography. Cast: A. H. (Gwyn Thomas). Abigail Harrison (Nana), Bernard Lloyd (Walt), Richard Lynch (Walt, as boy), Sue Roderick (Lyn), Robert Pugh (Gwyn's father).

FILMS (year of release in UK)

The Lion in Winter (1968) Dist/Prod Co: Avco Embassy/Haworth. P: Martin Poll. Dir: Anthony Harvey. Scr: James Goldman. Cast: Peter O'Toole (King Henry II), Katharine Hepburn (Eleanor), Jane Merrow (Alais), John Castle (Geoffrey), Nigel Terry (John), A. H. (Richard).

The Looking-Glass War (1969) Dist/Prod Co: Columbia/Frankovich. P: John Box. Dir: Frank R. Pierson. Scr: Frank R. Pierson, from John le Carré's novel. Cast: Christopher Jones (Leiser), Pia Degermark (the Girl), Ralph Richardson (Leclerc), Paul Rogers (Haldane), A. H. (John Avery).

Hamlet (1969) Dist/Prod Co: Columbia/Woodfall. P: Leslie Linder, Martin Ransohoff. Dir: Tony Richardson. Cast: Nicol Williamson (Hamlet), Judy Parfitt (Gertrude), A. H. (Claudius), Marianne Faithfull (Ophelia), Mark Dignam (Polonius), Gordon Jackson (Horatio), Michael Pennington (Laertes).

When Eight Bells Toll (1971) Dist/Prod Co: Rank/Winkast. P: Elliott Kastner. Dir: Etienne Perier. Scr: Alistair MacLean. Cast: A. H. (Calvert), Robert Morley (Uncle Arthur), Nathalie Delon (Charlotte), Jack Hawkins (Skouras), Corin Redgrave (Hunslett).

Young Winston (1972) Dist/Prod Co: Columbia/Open Road. P: Carl Foreman. Dir: Richard Attenborough. Scr: Carl Foreman. Cast: Robert Shaw (Lord Randolph Churchill), Anne Bancroft (Lady Randolph Churchill), Simon Ward (Winston Churchill), Jack Hawkins (Mr Welldon), Ian Holm (George Buckle), A. H. (Lloyd George).

A Doll's House (1973) Dist/Prod Co: MGM-EMI/Elkins. P: Hillard Elkins. Dir: Patrick Garland. Scr: Christopher Hampton, from Ibsen's play. Cast: Claire Bloom (Nora), A. H. (Torvald), Ralph Richardson (Dr Rank), Denholm Elliott (Nils Krogstad), Anna Massey (Kristine).

The Girl from Petrovka (1974) Dist/Prod Co: Universal/Zanuck-Brown. P: Richard D. Zanuck, David Brown. Dir: Robert Ellis Miller. Scr: Allan Scott, Chris Bryant. Cast: Goldie Hawn (Oktyabrina), Hal Holbrook (Joe), A. H. (Kostya), Gregoire Aslan (Minister), Anton Dolin (Ballet Master).

Juggernaut (1974) Dist/Prod Co: United Artists. P: Richard Alan Simmons. Dir: Richard Lester. Scr: Richard De Koker (additional dialogue: Alan Plater). Cast: Richard Harris (Fallon), Omar Sharif (the Captain), David Hemmings (Charlie Braddock), A. H. (Supt. John McCleod), Roy Kinnear (Mr Curtain), Freddie Jones (Sid Buckland).

All Creatures Great and Small (1974) Dist/Prod Co: EMI/Venedon. P: David Susskind, Duane Bogie. Dir: Claude Whatham. Scr: Hugh Whitemore, from the books by James Herriot. Cast: A. H. (Siegfried Farnon), Simon Ward (James Herriot), Lisa Harrow (Helen), Freddie Jones (Cranford), Brian Stirner (Tristan Farnon), T. P. McKenna (Soames), Brenda Bruce (Miss Harbottle).

A Bridge Too Far (1977) Dist/Prod Co: United Artists/Joseph E. Levine. P: Joseph E. Levine, Richard P. Levine. Dir: Richard Attenborough. Scr: William Goldman, from Cornelius Ryan's book. Cast: Dirk Bogarde (Browning), James Caan (Dohun), Michael Caine (Vandeleur), Sean Connery (Urquhart), Edward Fox (Horrocks), Elliot Gould (Stout), Gene Hackman (Sosabowski), A. H. (Frost), Hardy Kruger (Ludwig), Laurence Olivier (Spaader), Ryan O'Neal (Gavin), Robert Redford (Cook), Maximilian Schell (Bittrich), Liv Ullmann (Kate ter Horst).

Audrey Rose (1977) Dist/Prod Co: United Artists. P: Joe Wizan, Frank De Felitta. Dir: Robert Wise. Scr: Frank De Felitta. Cast: Marsha Mason (Janice Templeton), A. H. (Elliot Hoover), John Beck (Bill Templeton), Susan Swift (Ivy/Audrey).

International Velvet (1978) Dist/Prod Co: CIC/MGM. P-Dir-Scr: Bryan Forbes. Cast: Tatum O'Neal (Sarah), Christopher Plummer (John Seaton), A. H. (Captain Johnny Johnson), Nanette Newman (Velvet Brown), Jeffrey Byron (Scott Saunders), Peter Barkworth (Pilot), Dinsdale Landen (Mr Curtis).

Magic (1978) Dist/Prod Co: Twentieth Century-Fox/Joseph E. Levine. P: Joseph E. Levine, Richard P. Levine. Dir: Richard Attenborough. Scr: William Goldman. Cast: A. H. (Corky), Ann-Margret (Peggy Ann Snow), Burgess Meredith (Ben Greene), Ed Lauter (Duke), David Ogden Stiers (Todson).

The Elephant Man (1980) Dist/Prod Co: EMI/Brooksfilms. P: Jonathan Sanger. Dir: David Lynch. Scr: Christopher De Vore, Eric Bergren, David Lynch. Cast: A. H. (Dr Treves), John Hurt

(John Merrick), John Gielgud (Carr Gomm), Anne Bancroft (Mrs Madge Kendal), Freddie Jones (Bytes), Michael Elphick (Night Porter), Wendy Hiller (Mothershead).

A Change of Seasons (1980) Dist/Prod Co: Columbia/American Cinema-Jerry Sherlock. P: Martin Ransohoff. Dir: Richard Lang. Scr: Erich Segal, Ronni Kern, Fred Segal. Cast: Shirley MacLaine (Karen), A. H. (Adam), Bo Derek (Lindsey), Michael Brandon (Pete), Mary Beth Hurt (Kasey).

The Bounty (1984) Dist/Prod Co: Orion-EMI/Dino De Laurentiis. P: Bernard Williams. Dir: Roger Donaldson. Scr: Robert Bolt. Cast: A. H. (Bligh), Mel Gibson (Christian), Laurence Olivier (Hood), Edward Fox (Greetham), Daniel Day-Lewis (Fryer), Bernard Hill (Cole), Liam Neeson (Churchill), Tevaite Vernette (Mauatua), Philip Davis (Young), Philip Martin Brown (Adams).

The Good Father (1986) Dist/Prod Co: Mainline/Greenpoint. P: Ann Scott. Dir: Mike Newell. Scr: Christopher Hampton, from Peter Prince's novel. Cast: A. H. (Bill Hooper), Jim Broadbent (Roger Miles), Harriet Walter (Emmy Hooper), Frances Viner (Cheryl Langford), Simon Callow (Mark Varda), Harry Grubb (Christopher Hooper).

84 Charing Cross Road (1986) Dist/Prod Co: Columbia/Brooksfilms. P: Geoffrey Helman. Dir: David Jones. Scr: Hugh Whitemore. Cast: Anne Bancroft (Helene Hanff), A. H. (Frank Doel), Judi Dench (Nora Doel), Maurice Denham (George Martin), Eleanor David (Cecily Farr), Wendy Morgan (Megan Wells), Ian McNiece (Bill Humphries).

The Dawning (1988) Dist/Prod Co: Enterprise/TVS-Lawson. P: Sarah Lawson. Dir: Robert Knights. Scr: Moira Williams, from Jennifer Johnston's novel *The Old Jest*. Cast: A. H. (Cassius), Rebecca Pidgeon (Nancy), Jean Simmons (Aunt Mary), Trevor Howard (Grandfather), Hugh Grant (Harry).

A Chorus of Disapproval (1989) Dist/Prod Co: Palisades Entertainment Corp-Cinema Seven. P-Dir: Michael Winner. Scr: Michael Winner, Alan Ayckbourn, from Ayckbourn's play. Cast: A. H. (Dafydd Ap Llewellyn), Jeremy Irons (Guy Jones), Prunella Scales (Hannah Ap Llewellyn), Jenny Seagrove (Fay Hubbard), Gareth Hunt (Ian Hubbard), Richard Briers (Ted Washbrook), Barbara Ferris (Enid Washbrook), Patsy Kensit (Linda Washbrook), Lionel Jeffries (Jarvis Huntley-Pike), Sylvia

Sims (Rebecca Huntley-Pike), Alexandra Pigg (Bridget Baines), Pete Lee-Wilson (Crispin Usher).

Desperate Hours (1991) Dist/Prod Co: Twentieth Century-Fox/Dino De Laurentiis Communications. P: Dino De Laurentiis, Michael Cimino. Dir: Michael Cimino. Scr: Lawrence Conner, Mark Rosenthal and Joseph Hayes, from Hayes' novel and play. Cast: Mickey Rourke (Michael Bosworth), A. H. (Tim Cornell), Mimi Rogers (Nora Cornell), Lindsay Crouse (Brenda Chandler), Kelly Lynch (Nancy Breyers), Elias Koteas (Wally Bosworth).

The Silence of the Lambs (1991) Dist/Prod Co: Orion Pictures/A Strong Heart–Demme Production. P: Edward Saxon, Kenneth Utt, Ron Bozman. Dir: Jonathan Demme. Scr: Ted Tally, from Thomas Harris' novel. Cast: Jodie Foster (Clarice Starling), A. H. (Dr Hannibal Lecter), Scott Glenn (Jack Crawford), Ted Levine (Jame Gumb), Anthony Heald (Dr Frederick Chilton), Kasi Lemmons (Ardelia Mapp).

Spotswood (1991) Dist/Prod Co: Meridian Films. P: Timothy White, Richard Brennan. Dir: Mark Joffe. Scr: Max Dann, Andrew Knight. Cast: A. H. (Errol Wallace), Angela Punch-McGregor (Caroline Wallace), Alwyn Kurtz (Ball), Bruno Lawrence (Robert Spencer), Rebecca Riggs (Cheryl), Ben Mendleson (Cary).

Freejack (1992) Dist/Prod Co: Warner Bros/Morgan Creek. P: Ron Shusett. Dir: Geoff Murphy. Scr: Ron Shusett, from Robert Sheckley's short story, 'Immortality Inc'. Cast: Emilio Estevez (Alex Furlong), A. H. (McCandless), Mick Jagger (Vacendak), Rene Russo (Julie), Amanda Plummer (Nun), Jonathan Banks (Michelette), David Johansen (Brad).

Howards End (1992) Dist/Prod Co: Mayfair Entertainment/Merchant-Ivory Productions Ltd. P: Ismail Merchant. Dir: James Ivory. Scr: Ruth Prawer Jhabvala, from E.M. Forster's novel. Cast: A. H. (Henry Wilcox), Vanessa Redgrave (Ruth Wilcox), Helena Bonham-Carter (Helena Schlegel), Emma Thompson (Margaret Schlegel), James Wilby (Charles Wilcox), Sam West (Leonard Bast).

The Trial (1992) Dist/Prod Co: BBC Films/Europanda Entertainment. P: Louis Marks. Dir: David Jones. Scr: Harold Pinter, from Franz Kafka's novel. Cast: Kyle MacLachlan (Josef K), A. H. (the Priest), Jason Robards (Dr Huld), Juliet Stevenson

(Fräulein Bürstner), Polly Walker (Leni), Alfred Molina (Titorelli).

Bram Stoker's Dracula (1993) Dist/Prod Co: Columbia/ American Zoetrope–Osiris Films. P: Francis Ford Coppola, Fred Fuchs, Charles Mulvehill. Dir: Francis Ford Coppola. Scr: Jim Hart, from Bram Stoker's novel. Cast: Gary Oldman (Dracula), A. H. (Van Helsing), Winona Ryder (Mina), Keanu Reeves (Jonathan Harker), Richard E. Grant (Seward), Sadie Frost (Lucy), Cary Elwes (Holmwood), Bill Campbell (Morris), Tom Waits (Renfield).

Chaplin (1993) Dist/Prod Co: Carolco/Lambeth Productions. P: Richard Attenborough, Mario Kassar. Dir: Richard Attenborough. Scr: William Boyd and William Goldman, from Chaplin's *My Autobiography* and David Robinson's *Chaplin: His Life and Art*. Cast: Robert Downey Jr (Chaplin), Geraldine Chapman (Hannah), Paul Rhys (Sydney Chaplin), Dan Aykroyd (Mack Sennett), Marisa Tomei (Mabel Normand), Penelope Ann Miller (Edna Purviance), Kevin Kline (Douglas Fairbanks Sr), Diane Lane (Paulette Goddard), Kevin Dunn (J. Edgar Hoover), Nancy Travis (Joan Barry), Moira Kelly (Oona), John Thaw (Fred Karno), A. H. (George Hayden/narrator).

The Innocent (1993) Dist/Prod Co: World Films/Lakehart Ltd. P: Norma Heyman, Chris Sievernich, Wieland Schulz-Keil. Dir: John Schlesinger. Scr: Ian McEwan, from his own novel. Cast: A. H. (Glass), Isabella Rossellini (Maria), Campbell Scott (Leonard), Hart Bochner (Russell).

The Remains of the Day (1993) Dist/Prod Co: Columbia/ Merchant-Ivory Productions Ltd. P: Mike Nichols, John Calley, Ismail Merchant. Dir: James Ivory. Scr: Ruth Prawer Jhabvala, from Kazuo Ishiguro's novel. Cast: A. H. (Stevens), Emma Thompson (Miss Kenton), James Fox (Lord Darlington), Christopher Reeve (Mr Lewis), Peter Vaughan (Stevens Sr), Hugh Grant (Cardinal).

Shadowlands (1993/4) Dist/Prod Co: Savoy Pictures–Spelling Films/Price Entertainment. P: Brian Eastman, Richard Attenborough. Dir: Richard Attenborough. Scr: William Nicholson. Cast: A. H. (C. S. 'Jack' Lewis), Debra Winger (Joy Gresham), Edward Hardwicke (Warnie Lewis), Joseph Mazzello (Douglas Gresham), John Wood (Christopher Riley).

The Road to Wellville (1995) Dist/Prod Co: Entertainment/ Beacon Pictures. P: Alan Parker, Robert F. Colesberry. Dir: Alan Parker. Scr: Alan Parker, from T. C. Boyle's novel. Cast: A. H. (Dr J. H. Kellogg), Bridget Fonda (Eleanor Lightbody), Matthew Broderick (Will Lightbody), John Cusack (Charles Ossining), Dana Carvey (George Kellogg).

Legends of the Fall (1995) Dist/Prod Co: Columbia TriStar Pictures. P: Edward Zwick, Bill Witliff, Marshall Herskovitz. Dir: Edward Zwick. Scr: Susan Shilliday, Bill Witliff, from Jim Harrison's novella. Cast: Brad Pitt (Tristan), A. H. (Col. William Ludlow), Aidan Quinn (Alfred), Julia Ormond (Susannah), Henry Thomas (Samuel).

August (1995) Dist/Prod Co: Granada/Majestic Films. P: June Wyndham Davies, Pippa Cross. Dir: A. H. Scr: Julian Mitchell. Cast: A. H. (Ieuan), Kate Burton (Helen), Leslie Phillips (Prof. Blathwaite), Gawn Grainger (Dr Lloyd), Rhain Morgan (Sian), Hugh Lloyd (Prosser).

Nixon (1996) Dist/Prod Co: Entertainment/Illusion Entertainment Group-Cinergi. P: Clayton Townsend, Oliver Stone, Andrew G. Vajna. Dir: Oliver Stone. Scr: Stephen J. Rivele, Christopher Wilkinson, Oliver Stone. Cast: A. H. (Nixon), Joan Allen (Pat Nixon), Powers Boothe (Alexander Haig), Ed Harris (E. Howard Hunt), James Woods (H.R. Haldeman).

Surviving Picasso (1996) Dist/Prod Co: Warner Bros/Merchant-Ivory/Wolper. P: Ismail Merchant, David L. Wolper. Dir: James Ivory. Scr: Ruth Prawer Jhabvala from Arianna Stassinopoulos Huffington's book *Picasso, Creator and Destroyer*. Cast: A. H. (Pablo Picasso), Natascha McElhone (Francoise Gilot), Julianne Moore (Dora Maar), Joss Ackland (Matisse), Peter Eyre (Sabartes).

The Edge (1998) Dist/Prod Co: Twentieth Century-Fox. P: Art Linson. Dir: Lee Tamahori. Scr: David Mamet. Cast: A. H. (Charles Morse), Alec Baldwin (Robert Green), Elle Macpherson (Mickey Morse), Harold Perrineau (Stephen), L.Q. Jones (Styles).

Amistad (1998) Dist/Prod Co: UIP/Dreamworks-HBO. P: Steven Spielberg, Debbie Allen, Colin Wilson. Dir: Steven Spielberg. Scr: David Franzoni. Cast: Morgan Freeman (Theodore Joadson), Nigel Hawthorne (Martin Van Buren), Djimon

Hounsou (Cinque), Matthew McConaughey (Roger Baldwin), A. H. (John Quincy Adams).

The Mask of Zorro (1998) Dist/Prod Co: TriStar/Amblin-Zorro. P: Doug Claybourne, David Foster. Dir: Martin Campbell. Scr: John Eskow, Terry Rossio, Randall Johnson. Cast: A. H. (Zorro/Don Diego de la Vega), Antonio Banderas (Zorro/Alejandro Murrieta), Catherine Zeta-Jones (Elena), Stuart Wilson (Don Rafael Montero), Matt Letscher (Captain Harrison Love).

Meet Joe Black (1999) Dist/Prod Co: UIP/City Light Films. P: Martin Brest. Dir: Martin Brest. Scr: Ron Osborn, Jeff Reno, Kevin Wade, Bo Goldman, suggested by the play *Death Takes a Holiday* and the screenplay by Maxwell Anderson and Gladys Lehman. Cast: Brad Pitt (Joe Black), A. H. (William Parrish), Claire Forlani (Susan Parrish), Jake Weber (Drew), Marcia Gay Harden (Allison).

Instinct (1999) Dist/Prod Co: Buena Vista International/Touchstone-Spyglass. P: Michael Taylor, Barbara Boyle. Dir: Jon Turteltaub. Scr: Gerald DiPego, suggested by Daniel Quinn's book *Ishmael*. Cast: A. H. (Ethan Powell), Cuba Gooding Jr (Theo Caulder), Donald Sutherland (Ben Hillard), Maura Tierney (Lyn Powell), George Dzundza (Dr John Murray).

Titus (2000) Dist/Prod Co: Buena Vista International/Clear Blue Sky. P: Conchita Airoldi, Julie Taymor. Dir: Julie Taymor. Scr: Julie Taymor, from William Shakespeare's *Titus Andronicus*. Cast: A. H. (Titus Andronicus), Jessica Lange (Tamora), Alan Cumming (Saturninus), Harry Lennix (Aaron), Laura Fraser (Lavinia), Colm Feore (Marcus).

Mission: Impossible 2 (2000) Dist/Prod Co: UIP/Paramount/Cruise-Wagner Productions. P: Terence Chang, Tom Cruise, Paul Hitchcock, Paula Wagner. Dir: John Woo. Scr: Robert Towne. Cast: Tom Cruise (Ethan Hunt), Ving Rhames (Luther Stickell), Dougray Scott (Sean Ambrose), Thandie Newton (Nyah Nordoff-Hall), A. H. (IMF boss).

The Grinch (2000) Dist/Prod Co: UIP/Imagine Entertainment. P: Ron Howard, Brian Grazer. D: Ron Howard. Scr: Jeffrey Price, Peter S. Seaman, from Dr Seuss' *How The Grinch Stole Christmas*. Cast: Jim Carrey (The Grinch), Jeffrey Tambor (Mayor Who), Christine Baranski (Martha May Whovier), Taylor Momsen (Cindy Lou Who), A. H. (Narrator).

Hannibal (2001) Dist/Prod Co: UIP/Dino De Laurentiis-Scott Free. P: Ridley Scott, Dino De Laurentiis, Martha De Laurentiis. D: Ridley Scott. Scr: David Mamet, Steven Zaillian, from the novel by Thomas Harris. Cast: A. H. (Hannibal Lecter), Julianne Moore (Clarice Starling), Ray Liotta (Paul Krendler), Gary Oldman (Mason Verger), Inspector Pazzi (Giancarlo Giannini).

Hearts in Atlantis (2002) Dist/Prod Co: Warner/Castle Rock-NPV-Village Roadshow. P: Kerry Heysen. D: Scott Hicks. Scr: William Goldman, from Stephen King's short story. Cast: A. H. (Ted Brautigan), Anton Yelchin (Bobby Garfield), Hope Davis (Liz Garfield), Mika Boorem (Carol Gerber), David Morse (older Bobby Garfield).

The Devil and Daniel Webster (2001) Dist/Prod Co: Cutting Edge/El Dorado-Miracle. P: Alec Baldwin, Jonathan Cornick, David Glasser, Adam Stone. D: Alec Baldwin. Scr: Pete Dexter, Bill Condon, Nancy Cassara, from Stephen Vincent Benet's story and the play *Scratch* by Archibald MacLeish. Cast: A. H. (Daniel Webster), Alec Baldwin (Jabez Stone), Jennifer Love Hewitt (The Devil), Dan Aykroyd (Jules Jenson), Kim Cattrall (Constance Hurry). Uncompleted.

Bad Company (2002) Dist/Prod.Co: Buena Vista International/Touchstone-Jerry Bruckheimer Films. P: Jerry Bruckheimer, Mike Stenson. D: Joel Schumacher. Scr: Jason Richman, Michael Browning. Cast: A. H. (Gaylord Oakes), Chris Rock (Jake Hayes/Kevin Pope), Gabriel Macht (Officer Seale), Peter Stormare (Adrik Vas), Matthew Marsh (Dragan Adjanic).

Red Dragon (2002) Dist/Prod Co: UIP/Dino De Laurentiis-MGM-Mikona. P: Dino De Laurentiis, Martha De Laurentiis. D: Brett Ratner. Scr: Ted Tally, from the novel by Thomas Harris. Cast: A. H. (Hannibal Lecter), Edward Norton (Will Graham), Ralph Fiennes (Francis Dolarhyde), Emily Watson (Reba McClane), Harvey Keitel (Jack Crawford).

The Human Stain (2003) Dist/Prod Co: Buena Vista International/Miramax-Lakeshore Entertainment-Stone Village. P: Gary Lucchesi, Tom Rosenberg, Scott Steindorff. D: Robert Benton. Scr: Nicolas Meyer, from the novel by Philip Roth. Cast: A. H. (Coleman Silk), Nicole Kidman (Faunia Farley), Ed Harris (Lester Farley), Gary Sinise (Nathan Zuckerman), Wentworth Miller (young Coleman Silk).

Alexander (2005) Dist/Prod. Co: Warner Bros/Intermedia Films
P: Moritz Borman, Jon Kilik, Thomas Schühly, Iain Smith,
Oliver Stone. D: Oliver Stone. Scr: Oliver Stone, Christopher
Kyle, Laeta Kalogrides. Cast: Colin Farrell (Alexander), A. H.
(Ptolemy), Jared Leto (Hephaestion), Rosario Dawson (Roxane),
Angelina Jolie (Olympias), Val Kilmer (Philip, King of
Macedonia).

Proof (2005) Dist/Prod. Co: Miramax/Hart-Sharp
Entertainment. P: John Hart, Jeff Sharp, Robert Kessel. D: John
Madden. Scr: David Auburn and Rebecca Miller, from Auburn's
play. Cast: Gwyneth Paltrow (Catherine), A. H. (Robert), Hope
Davis (Claire), Jake Gyllenhaal (Hal).

The World's Fastest Indian (2005) Dist/Prod. Co: 3 Dogs And A
Pony. P: Roger Donaldson, Gary Hannam. D: Roger Donaldson.
Scr: Roger Donaldson. Cast A. H. (Burt Munro), Bruce
Greenwood, Diane Ladd, Christopher Lawford, Jessica Caufiel.

INDEX

Across the Lake 4–6, 361
Alcoholics Anonymous 118–19,
    176–7, 283
Alexander 359–60
All Creatures Great and Small 102–3
All in Good Time 31
Allen, Debbie 300
Allen, Sheila 104
Alwood, Dennis 140
Amistad 299–301
Anderson, Bob 296–7
Anderson, Lindsay 32
Ann-Margret 140–2, 145
Antony and Cleopatra 3, 4, 5, 208,
    217–22, 322, 358
Arcata Promise, The 104
Arch of Triumph 195–6
*Architect and the Emperor of Assyria,
    The* 68–72
Armstrong's Last Goodnight 34
Arroyave, Stella (wife) 352–3
Arts Council 17
As You Like It 44–7
Attenborough, Richard 120–3, 138–9,
    141–4, 145–7, 247–9, 265, 359
Audrey Rose 127–9
August 259–68
Aykroyd, Dan 340

Bacall, Lauren 108
Bacchae, The 82
Bad Company 338–40
Bailey, Michael 139–40
Baldwin, Alec 288, 289, 292, 340
Bancroft, Anne 209
Banderas, Antonio 243, 294, 297
Barker, Petronella (wife) 47, 48, 52–3,
    61, 93
Beaux' Stratagem, The 31
Bennett, Hywel 26
Benton, Robert 354
Blakemore, Michael 82–4, 90–1
Blood Wedding 17
Bloom, Claire 87–8, 247
Blunt 212
Bogarde, Dirk 121
Boorem, Mika 337
Bounty, The 182–4, 187–93, 196, 199,
    361

Brahms, Caryl 66
Bram Stoker's Dracula 241–2, 320–1
Brandon, Michael 159
Bridge at Remagen, The 53
Bridge Too Far, A 112, 119, 120–5,
    162–3, 335
Bridges, Alan 187–8
Brooks, Mel 155, 157, 209, 211–12
Bruckheimer, Jerry 338
Bunker, The 163–9
Burton, Kate 264, 266–7
Burton, Richard 2, 219–20

Caan, James 121
Caine, Michael 121
Campbell, Donald 4, 5, 6, 361
Campbell, Martin 294, 295, 296–7,
    298
Cardiff College of Music and Drama
    16–17
Cattrall, Kim 340
Caucasian Chalk Circle, The 31
Cellan Jones, James 148, 150–1, 152,
    153
Central School, Port Talbot 12
Change of Seasons, A 158–62
Changes 34
Chaplin 247–8
Cherry Orchard, The 82
Childhood Friend, The 206
Chips with Everything 28–9
Chorus of Disapproval 6–7
City Limits 205
Collins, Jackie 197
Collins, Leon 60, 61
Connery, Sean 121, 123
Conway, Jeremy 42, 228, 246
Coppola, Francis Ford 240–3
Coriolanus 73–5
Corn is Green, The 30
Cowan, Elliot 360
Cowbridge Grammar School 12–14
Cubitt, Colonel Willoughby 18
Cumming, Alan 311, 312

Daily Express 151
Daily Mail 40, 96, 145, 146, 158, 181,
    192, 280
Daily Telegraph 71, 85

Dale, Jim 68, 69
Dalton, Timothy 47, 48
Dance of Death, The 38–9
Danton 77–8
Dark Victory 112–15, 118
Davies, John 78–9, 87, 179, 180, 181
Davies, Windsor 3
Davies, Phil 192
Dawning, The 221
Day-Lewis, Daniel 192, 199, 264
De Laurentiis, Dino 317, 318, 318, 326, 327, 328–30
Decision to Burn 67
Demme, Jonathan 231, 232, 233–4, 235–7, 239, 317, 318–20
Dench, Judi 4, 208–11, 217–18, 219, 220–1
Derek, Bo 158–9, 161–2
Desperate Hours 231, 234–5
Devil and Daniel Webster, The 340–4
Devil's Disciple, The 35
Dexter, John 72–4, 90, 91, 105, 106, 107, 111, 217–18, 226–30
Dial M for Murder 31
Dobie, Alan 78, 200
Doll's House, A 86–90
Donaldson, Roger 188–9, 190–1, 193, 361
Doolittle, James 130–5
Douglas, Kirk 130
Down, Lesley-Anne 195
Doyle, Mary 110
Drama 203–4
Dukes, David 229

Edge, The 288–92
Edward II 29
Edwardians, The 86–7
Edwards, Dr Raymond 16–17
Eggar, Samantha 200
84 Charing Cross Road 145, 211–14
Elephant Man, The 153–8
Ellis Miller, Robert 97–8, 99–100
Emmanuel 16
Empire 237
Entertainment Weekly 327
Equus 73, 105–9
Essex Gazette 35
Evans, Sir Geraint 3
Evening News 73, 86, 145
Evening Standard 86, 145

Faithfull, Marianne 56

Farrington, Ken 27, 29
Fellowes, Julian 149–50, 152, 166, 167, 174–5, 179, 180–1, 201, 267–8, 272, 352, 358, 361-2
Fettes, Christopher 200
Fiennes, Ralph 329, 332
Films Illustrated 155–6
Financial Times 138, 162
Find Me 104–5
Finlay, Frank 37
Firth, Colin 201
Firth, Peter 106, 108, 109, 111
Five Finger Exercise 25
Flea in Her Ear, A 38
Forbes, Bryan 135–6
Foster, David 292–3, 294
Foster, Jodie 1, 232, 233, 234, 236, 238, 239, 246, 285, 317, 320
Francis, Freddie 157, 158
Freejack 238

Gambon, Michael 213
Garcia, Victor 68–9, 70–1
Garelick, David 351–2
Garland, Patrick 87–8, 212
Gandhi 120, 138, 145–6
Gibson, Mel 189
Gillen, Gwen 358
Girl from Petrovka, The 97–100
Good Father, The 206–8
Gooding Jr, Cuba 304, 305
Grainger, Gawn 83, 86, 91, 111, 263–4, 265
Great Expectations 226
Great Inimitable Mr Dickens, The 66
Green, Alex 297
Grinch, The 344
Guardian 40, 84, 86, 220
Gymerwch chi Sigaret? 20–1

Hackman, Gene 121, 232–3
Hall, Peter 208, 218–20
Hamlet 55–7
Hannan, Patrick 13–14
Hannibal 316–26
Hare, David 201, 202, 203–4, 213–15
Harris, Richard 101
Harvey, Anthony 41–2, 47–8, 51–2
Hawn, Goldie 98, 99, 353
Hawthorne, Nigel 185
Hayek, Salma 2
Heald, Anthony 329
Heartland 223–4, 228–9

Hearts and Flowers 77
Hearts in Atlantis 334–5
Hedda Gabler 29
Henry, Alex (Victor) 23, 24, 28, 83
Hepburn, Katharine 48, 49, 59, 63, 183
Hicks, Scott 336–7
High Society Celebrity Skin 143
Hill, Bernard 192
Hislop, Andrew 5
Holbrook, Hal 98
Hollywood Reporter 118, 168
Hollywood Wives 197–9
Hood, Morag 78, 79
Hopkin, Mary 3
Hopkins, Abigail (daughter) 55, 61, 64, 92, 93
Hopkins, Arthur Richard (grandfather) 9, 10, 14
Hopkins, Jennifer (wife) *see* Lynton, Jennifer (wife)
Hopkins, Muriel (mother) 9–12, 14, 108, 113, 169, 246, 286, 353
Hopkins, Petronella (wife) *see* Barker, Petronella (wife)
Hopkins, Philip Anthony:
  alcohol 2, 39, 49, 78, 86, 92–4, 104–5, 111, 112–18, 122, 176–7
  and Joyce Ingalls 283–4
  at RADA 22–9
  awarded a CBE 221, 248
  awarded a Knighthood 248
  awards, film and TV 109, 119, 168, 206, 211, 238–40, 244–6, 285, 326
  bakery business 9–12, 14, 15, 17
  becomes an American citizen 349
  birth 9–10
  birth of Abigail 55
  Charitable Foundation 350
  childhood 9–15
  death of father 169–70
  directing 252–6
  disillusionment with the stage 6
  divorce
    Jennifer Lynton 350–3
    Petronella Barker 92
  education 12–20
  finances 24, 47, 112, 113, 121
  health 90, 221
    Achilles tendon 304
    back condition 299, 290

    broken arm 51
    phlebitis 109–10
    weight 57
  honorary degree, University of Wales 223
  hypnotism 26
  marriage (see Arroyave, Stella; Barker, Petronella; Lynton, Jennifer)
  music 11–12, 13–14, 24–5, 32, 336
  National Service 17–20
  National Trust's Snowdonia Appeal 240, 260, 350
  Ojai, house in 345–6
  on his father 8, 16
  on his grandfather 9
  on Jenni 348–9
  threatens to retire from acting 344
  websites 361
Hopkins, Richard Arthur (father) 8, 9–12, 14, 15–16, 146, 169–70, 246
Hopkins, Stella (wife) *see* Arroyave, Stella
Horchurch Echo 35
Hornchurch News 36
Hoskins, Bob 196, 273
Hostage, The 28
Howard's End 240–1, 244, 248
Hughes, Nerys 3
Hulce, Tom 134
Human Stain, The 1, 353–7
Hunchback of Notre Dame, The 184–7, 195
Hurt, John 23, 146, 154, 155, 158
Hutchings, Geoffrey 23

Ingalls, Joyce 283–4
Innocent, The 248
Instinct 303–6
International Velvet 131, 135–8, 183
Interview 237
Isaac, Dr Donald 10

Jackson, Gordon 56, 119
Jacobi, Derek 185
Jagger, Mick 238
Jenkins, Cissie 2
Jones, Christopher 54–5
Jones, David 152, 209–10, 211–12
Jones, Freddie 3
Jones, Gemma 3
Juggernaut 101–2
Julius Caesar 32–3

Kay, Charles 46
Kay, Francine 349
Kay, Richard 27, 29
Kean 148–53
Kettle and Moon 31
Key, Janet 83
Kidman, Nicole 353, 354, 356
King Lear 212–17, 332
Knight Hopkins, Shirley 101

Lady 73
Lang, Robert 22, 38
Lange, Jessica 311, 312, 314
Lean, David 182–3
Lee, Michelle 112, 114
Legends of the Fall 255–8
Lennix, Harry 311
Lester, Richard 101
Levine, Joe 120, 138–9
Life Worth Living 27–8
Lindbergh Kidnapping Case 96, 112, 118–19
Lion in Winter, The 41–5, 47–53, 54
Little, Staff Sergeant Ernie 19–20
Liverpool Post 31–2
Lloyd, Hugh 259, 263
Lonely Road, The 200
Look Back in Anger 17
Looking Glass War, The 54–5
Los Angeles Free Press 134
Los Angeles Herald Examiner 127
Los Angeles Times 129, 134, 151–2, 159, 173
Love for Love 36–7
Love Hewitt, Jennifer 340, 341, 343
Lucas, Josh 2
Lynch, David 153–7
Lynton, Jennifer (wife) 60–1, 63–5, 200–1, 365
  and Joyce Ingalls 283–4
  and *The Silence of the Lambs* 231
  at the Oscars 244–5
  divorce 350–3
  in America 105–6, 110–14, 117–19
  marries Anthony 91–5
  on Anthony becoming an American citizen 357–8
  on Anthony's role in *Hitler* 165
  on her relationship with Anthony 362
  on holiday 148, 212, 221
  separation 174–9, 286–7, 350–3

M. Butterfly 227–30
Macbeth 82–6, 88, 89–90
MacLaine, Shirley 158–61
Madoc, Ruth 3
Magic 121, 139–43
Major Barbara 26, 27
Maley, Nick 184–5
Married Man, A 179–81
Marsden, Roy 22
Martin, George 3
Mask of Zorro, The 292–9
Mason, Marsha 128, 129, 193–4
Massey, Daniel 33
Matchmaker, The 27
Matter of Degree, A 30
Mayflower, The 164
Maylam, Tony 4, 6
McElhone, Nastascha 280
McQueen, Steve 121, 287
Meet Joe Black 307–8, 313
Merrow, Jane 47, 48, 51
Miles, Sarah 23
Miller, Jonathan 171–2, 199
Misanthrope, The 82, 111
Mission Impossible 2 345
Mitchell, Julian 260–2, 266
Montgomery, Elizabeth 112
Moore, Julianne 320, 325
Morgan, Rhian 259, 263
Morgan, Wendy 211
Morley, Robert 58–60
Movies on TV 197
Much Ado About Nothing 38
Munro, Burt 361
Mussolini: The Decline and Fall of Il Duce 196

National Theatre 33, 36, 37–9, 40–50, 67–77, 82–6, 90–1, 105–12, 200–6, 332, 358
National Trust Snowdonia Appeal 240, 260, 250
Neil, Hildegard 23
New York Herald Tribune 41
New York magazine 194
New York Post 108, 342
New York Times 41, 108
New Yorker 207–8
Newell, Mike 106–7
Newman, Nanette 137–8
Newsweek 124
Nixon 269–77, 285–6, 360
Norton, Edward 313, 331–2

Observer 46, 95, 138, 325, 333
Old Times 193–5
Oldman, Gary 243, 276
Olivier, Sir Laurence 35–9, 40, 52
    Architect and the Emperor of Assyria 68–72
    As You Like It 45
    Boys from Brazil 144
    Bridge Too Far, A 162–3
    Coriolanus 73–4, 76–7
    King Lear 217
    Macbeth 82, 84
    Sleuth 81–2
    Three Sisters 41
One Man's War 238
O'Neal, Ryan 121
O'Neal, Tatum 135
Orgolini, Lisa 266
Othello 35, 171–4
O'Toole, Peter 41, 42–5, 47–8, 50–1, 64

Page, Richard 42–3, 52–3
Pagett, Nicola 23
Palmer, Bob 116–17, 126, 174, 178, 244, 245
Parfitt, Judy 56
Parker, Alan 257–9
Parkin, Molly 3
Pearce, Jacqueline 34
Peasants's Revolt, The 58
Perkins, Anthony 2
Perry, Clive 26, 27, 29
Peter and Paul 169
Phillips, Leslie 259, 263
Phillips, Sian 3
Phoenix company 26–8
Pickup, Ronald 23, 33, 46, 86
Pitt, Brad 255, 256, 308
PlanetHopkins 361
Playboy of the Western World, The 31
Plays 204
Plowright, Joan 76–7, 81
Plummer, Christopher 73–4, 76, 138
Poet Game 77
Possessions 101
Powers, Stefanie 198–9
Pravda 15, 91, 199, 200–6, 240
Proof 359–60
Pryce, Jonathan 3
Punch 73

QB VIII 95
Quare Fellow, The 21, 31

Quentin, John 29
Quilley, Denis 86

Raab, Kurt 196
Ratner, Brett 329–31
Red Dragon 326–34
Redford, Robert 121, 123
Redgrave, Lynn 174–5
Rees, Angharad 3
Rees, Idwal 12–13
Rees-Williams, Morgan 42–3
Remains of the Day, The 145, 248–52, 271, 359
Reynolds, Adrian 23–5
Rhys, Matthew 311
Rhys Meyers, Jonathan 311
Richard II 29
Richards, Angela 6, 23
Richardson, Ian 212
Richardson, Ralph 53–7, 88
Rigg, Diana 85, 86, 111, 151
Road to Wellville, The 257–9
Roberts, Rachel 108
Robson, Dame Flora 30
Rock, Chris 338–9
Rolling Stone 356
Rosenberg, Marion 57, 62
Rourke, Mickey 234–5
Royal Academy of Dramatic Art (RADA) 22–9
Royal Hunt of the Sun, The 38
Ryall, David 28

San Fernando Valley News 134
Sarandon, Susan 196
Scase, David 21, 30–1, 32, 33
Schaefer, George 163–5, 166–9
Scott, George C. 197
Scott, James 34
Scott, Ridley 318–19, 321, 323, 325, 326
Searle, Judith 131–2, 133, 134–5
Seldes, Marian 106–7, 109–10
Selected Exits 316, 359
Seymour Hoffman, Philip 329
Shadowlands 248, 252–5, 257, 359
Sharif, Omar 101
Shaw, Martin 35
She Stoops to Conquer 17
Sherrin, Ned 66
Sight & Sound 333
Silence of the Lambs, The 1, 145, 231–3, 235–40

Simmonds, Ken 18
Simmons, Bob 57, 63
Sinise, Gary 1
Skin of Our Teeth, The 17
Smith, Ray 3
Somers, Suzanne 198
Sparrows Can't Sing 31
Spartacus 238
Spielberg, Steven 293, 294, 298, 299, 300, 301, 353
Spotswood 238
Stock, Nigel 50–1
Stone, Oliver 269–71, 273, 274, 276, 277, 360
Storm, The 38
Sun 62, 77, 92, 138
Sunday Express 138, 145
Sunday Mirror 61, 62
Sunday Telegraph 96, 285
Sunday Times 45–6, 75–6, 267, 284
Surviving Picasso 278–83, 320
Susskind, David 163, 202–3
Swift, David 27, 28, 29, 47, 79, 91, 167, 212, 215
Swift, Paula 108, 167, 171, 235

Tally, Ted 233–4, 327
Tamahori, Lee 287, 288–92
Taming of the Shrew, The 80–2
Taylor, Elizabeth 130, 246
Taymor, Julie 302–3, 308–10, 311–14, 315, 344–5
Tempest, The 135
Tenth Man, The 224–5
Theatre of Wales 20–1
Thompson, Emma 249–50
Three Sisters, The 24–5, 41
Time 138
Time Out 157
Times, The 5, 40, 66, 73, 81, 85, 153
Titus 302–4, 308–15, 344–5
To Be the Best 238
Toms, Donald 187
Trial, The 247
Tuchner, Michael 184–5
Turteltaub, Jon 304–5, 306–7

Tyler, Bonnie 3
Tynan, Kenneth (Ken) 67–8, 74, 215, 219

Uncle Vanya 77
Under Milk Wood 3–4
University of Wales 223, 358
USA Today 181

Variety 96, 118, 134, 192, 341–2, 356–7
Victory at Antebbe 129–30
Vidgeon, Robin 264–5
Vogel, Anton (Tony) 23
Voice 173

War and Peace 77–80, 156
Ward, Simon 23, 102–3, 111
Warner, David 23
Watson, Emily 329, 334
Weekend Journal 144
When Eight Bells Toll 57–61
White, Jim 'Pinky' 14
White Bus, The 33–4
William Morris Agency 112
Williams, Clifford 45, 46
Williams, Michael 22, 212
Williamson, Nicol 55–6
Winger, Debra 253–4
Winner, Michael 6–7
Winslow Boy, The 22
Winter's Tale, A 35
Wise, Robert 127–8
Witt, Captain Mike 18
Woman Killed with Kindness, A 72–3, 74, 81
Woods, James 273
World's Fastest Indian, The 361

Yates, Marjorie 31
Yelchin, Anton 336–7
YMCA 16

Zaillian, Steven 320, 325
Zanuck, Richard 97
Zeta-Jones, Catherine 295, 353
Zwick, Ed 255–6